Law and the Culture of Israel

LAW AND THE CULTURE OF ISRAEL

Menachem Mautner

OXFORD
UNIVERSITY PRESS

OXFORD
UNIVERSITY PRESS

Great Clarendon Street, Oxford OX2 6DP

Oxford University Press is a department of the University of Oxford.
It furthers the University's objective of excellence in research, scholarship,
and education by publishing worldwide in

Oxford New York

Auckland Cape Town Dar es Salaam Hong Kong Karachi
Kuala Lumpur Madrid Melbourne Mexico City Nairobi
New Delhi Shanghai Taipei Toronto

With offices in

Argentina Austria Brazil Chile Czech Republic France Greece
Guatemala Hungary Italy Japan Poland Portugal Singapore
South Korea Switzerland Thailand Turkey Ukraine Vietnam

Oxford is a registered trade mark of Oxford University Press
in the UK and in certain other countries

Published in the United States
by Oxford University Press Inc., New York

© M. Mautner, 2011

The moral rights of the author have been asserted

Crown Copyright material reproduced with the permission of the
Controller, HMSO (under the terms of the Click Use licence)

Database right Oxford University Press (maker)

First published 2011

All rights reserved. No part of this publication may be reproduced,
stored in a retrieval system, or transmitted, in any form or by any means,
without the prior permission in writing of Oxford University Press,
or as expressly permitted by law, or under terms agreed with the appropriate
reprographics rights organization. Enquiries concerning reproduction
outside the scope of the above should be sent to the Rights Department,
Oxford University Press, at the address above

You must not circulate this book in any other binding or cover
and you must impose the same condition on any acquirer

British Library Cataloguing in Publication Data
Data available

Library of Congress Cataloging in Publication Data
Data available

Typeset by Newgen Imaging Systems (P) Ltd., Chennai, India
Printed in Great Britain
on acid-free paper by
CPI Antony Rowe, Chippenham, Wiltshire

ISBN 978-0-19-960056-4

1 3 5 7 9 10 8 6 4 2

For Betty, Maty, Joseph, Shawn, and Ori

CONTENTS

Preface		ix
Introduction		1
1.	Zionism and the Evolving New Culture	11
	A. The Rise of the Jewish Enlightenment	12
	B. Zionist Thought on the Culture of the Evolving Society in Eretz Israel	14
	C. The Culture that Evolved in Eretz Israel in the First Half of the Twentieth Century	22
	D. Conclusion	29
2.	The Cultural Struggles Over the Shaping of the Law	31
	A. The Attempt to Create a Linkage between Israeli Law and the Halakhah: The Movement for the Revival of Hebrew Law	32
	B. The Anglicization and Liberalization of the Law	35
	C. The Foundations of Law Statute and the Place of 'Israel's Heritage' in Israeli Law	41
	D. The Basic Laws of 1992 and the Definition of Israel as a 'Jewish and Democratic State'	44
	E. Conclusion	52
3.	From Judicial Restraint to Judicial Activism	54
	A. The Concept of Judicial Activism and the Rise of the Court's Activism	54
	B. Doctrines Regulating Petitioning to the High Court of Justice	56
	C. Substantive Law Doctrines	68
4.	The Decline of Formalism and the Rise of Values	75
	A. Legal Formalism	75
	B. Legal Formalism in Israeli Law	78
	C. The 1950s Jurisprudence of the Supreme Court in a Cultural Context	86
	D. The 1980s and the 1990s: The Decline of Formalism and the Rise of Values in Israeli Law	90

	E. Changes in the Perception of the Court's Role in the 1980s and 1990s	96
5.	From Hegemony to War of Cultures	99
	A. Introduction	99
	B. The Decline in the Hegemony of the Labor Movement	103
	C. Anxiety	127
	D. The Jurisprudence of the Supreme Court in the 1980s and 1990s in Light of the Transition to a Post-Hegemonic Situation	143
6.	The Supreme Court and the Future of Liberalism	159
	A. The Court's Two-Front Struggle	160
	B. Rethinking the Court's Judicial Activism	170
7.	Israel as a Multicultural State	181
	A. Israel's Multicultural Condition	181
	B. The Unique Traits of Israel's Multiculturalism	190
	C. The Schism between Jews and Arabs	193
8.	Law and Culture in the Coming Decades	201
	A. Political Liberalism	201
	B. Defining the State's Identity: 'A Jewish State'	208
	C. Defining the State's Identity: Making Room for the Arab Citizens	211
	D. A New Equilibrium between Uniformity and Diversity	214
Conclusion		223
Bibliography		227
Index		261

PREFACE

This book tells the story of the Supreme Court widely regarded as the most activist in the world. The legal culture is premised on step-by-step, cautious, incremental development. But within a short span of time in the course of the 1980s, the Supreme Court of Israel effected far-reaching changes in its legal doctrine and in the way it perceives its role among the state's branches. This book locates those changes in the context of the great historical process that took shape in Israel in the second half of the 1970s: the decline of the political and cultural hegemony of the Labor movement, and the renewal of the struggle over the future orientation of the country's culture.

Two social groups have confronted each other at the heart of this struggle: a secular group that is aiming to strengthen Israel's ties to Western liberalism, and a religious group intent on associating Israel's culture with traditional Jewish heritage and the Halakhah. The Supreme Court, the institution most closely identified with liberalism since the establishment of the state, collaborated with the former group in its struggle against the latter. As might have been expected, the Court lost much of its legitimacy among members of the religious group. The more puzzling fact, however, is that in recent years the Court has lost much legitimacy among the secular group as well, which for many years provided it with unmitigated support.

The story of the Court serves as the axis of another two stories. The first deals with the struggle over the cultural identity of the Jewish people throughout the course of modernity. The second is the story of the struggle over the cultural identity of Israeli law, which took place throughout the twentieth century.

In addition to the divide between secular and religious Jews, there is a national divide in Israel between Jews and Arabs. These two divides are interrelated in complex ways which shape the unique traits of Israel's multicultural condition, first and foremost 'the zero-sum game of Israel's multiculturalism': the more Israel accentuates traditional Jewish elements in its public culture, the more appealing it would be to Jewish religious Israelis, but the more repugnant to Israel's Arab citizens, and vice versa. The book ends with a discussion of this unique condition and with a few suggestions as to how, given this condition, Israel's regime, political culture and law should be constituted in the coming decades. The suggestions borrow from the discourses of liberalism, multiculturalism and republicanism.

The book is aimed at five major audiences of readers. First, law and society scholars interested in the interrelationship between law and society (eg, how a Supreme Court successfully promotes liberal values in the context of a culture governed by a collectivist nation-building ideology, and how various cultural groups engage in an ongoing struggle over the shaping of their country's legal culture). Second, scholars of the modern history of the Jewish people, Zionism, and the State of Israel. Third, comparative constitutional law scholars interested in the ways different constitutional courts function in the context of varying political and cultural conditions. Fourth, legal historians interested in questions such as how 'cultural borrowing' can result from military occupation (the British Mandate over Palestine), radically transform a legal system and determine its character for many decades to come. Fifth, scholars of multiculturalism. Israel's multicultural condition is unique, but it gives rise to the kind of problems that are of concern to many other countries in the world in the current post-nation-state era.

* * *

I am grateful to many friends and colleagues who read earlier versions of the manuscript and discussed them with me: Hadar Aviram, Daphne Barak-Erez, Gad Barzilai, Eyal Benvenisti, Yishai Blank, Jose Brunner, Hanoch Dagan, Meir Dan-Cohen, Yoram Dinstein, Nitza Drori-Peremen, Chaim Gans, Aeyal Gross, Daphna Hacker, Ron Harris, Avner Holtzman, Aaron Kirschenbaum, Aviad Kleinberg, Roy Kreitner, Dan Laor, Shai Lavi, Assaf Likhovski, Guy Mundlak, Ilan Saban, Avi Sagi, Eli Shaltiel, Hila Shamir, Anita Shapira and Merav Shmueli.

Part of the research for this book was done in the course of a sabbatical year at Harvard Law School. I am grateful to HLS and to Tel Aviv University for enabling me to do the research. I wish to thank my friends at Harvard, Lucian A Bebchuk, Morty Horwitz and Pnina Lahav, for their encouragement and support. Special thanks go to Joseph Weiler for many fruitful conversations on the topics of the book and for his lasting friendship.

I also want to thank the Cegla Center for Interdisciplinary Research of the Law at the Faculty of Law, Tel Aviv University, and the Minerva Center for Human Rights at Tel Aviv University and The Hebrew University, for their support.

INTRODUCTION

In this book I take a view of Israeli law as an important arena in which the struggle over the shaping of Jewish culture and identity, which has been part of the life of the Jewish people throughout the modern era, is being waged; as an important arena for tracing the major cultural processes that have taken place in Israel since its establishment; and as a major arena in which Israeli culture and identity in the coming decades will be shaped.

Edmund Burke recommended that 'infinite caution' be exercised before pulling down a functioning edifice and building a new one 'without having models and patterns of approved utility.'[1] Over a short span of time in the course of the 1980s, Israel's Supreme Court introduced a series of far-reaching changes into its jurisprudence: The Court adopted highly activist doctrines enabling it to sweepingly intervene in decisions undertaken by other branches of the state; it substituted its traditional formalistic style of reasoning with a value-laden approach that openly exposes the normative meaning and the distributive implications of the law; and it has adopted, instead of its traditional self-perception as a professional institution whose function is to resolve disputes, a perception of itself as a political institution that, side by side with the Knesset (Israel's parliament), takes part in normative and distributive decisions. These changes are striking, not only because the legal culture is premised on cautious, step by step, incremental development, but also because for almost a decade and a half the changes in the Court's jurisprudence have not encountered any significant opposition or criticism.

The changes in the Court's jurisprudence should be understood in the context of the great historical process that began to take place in Israel in the second half of the 1970s: The decline of the political, social and cultural hegemony of the Labor movement and the renewal of the 'war of cultures' in Israel, ie, the struggle over the country's future cultural orientation. The group I refer to as 'the liberal former hegemons'—identified with Western,

---

[1] Edmund Burke, in J.C.D. Clark (ed), *Reflections on the Revolution in France* (Stanford, Stanford University Press, 2001) 220.

secular, liberal values—lost much power in Israeli politics and culture and found itself facing an alternative cultural option for the country, premised on the Halakhah and traditional Jewish heritage. In these circumstances, the liberal former hegemons shifted much of their political action to the Supreme Court: They submitted many dozens of petitions against the government and the Knesset. The Court, which since the establishment of the State of Israel has been the state institution most closely identified with liberal values, collaborated with the group by devising wholly new legal doctrines, all meant to subordinate the activities of the two other branches to the Court's supervision, and thereby to the values and worldview of the liberal former hegemons.

During the entire decade of the 1980s it was hard to find any serious political conflict anywhere in the world that did not show behind it the not-so-hidden hand of religion.[2]

Israel is one of many countries grappling with the question regarding what place is to be reserved for religion in public life.[3] Even countries premised on the separation of church and state, such as the United States, find the coexistence of religion and state to be far from amiable. The question regarding what place is to be reserved for religion in the life of the individual and in the public sphere has stood at the center of the Jewish people's most divisive disputes in the modern era. Its reappearance in the context of the state of Israel is therefore just one more round in the Jewish people's ongoing contention with modernity.

Israel is one of many countries that have faced the rise of religious fundamentalism in the closing decades of the twentieth century. 'Fundamentalism is generally presented as a response to the crises of modernity rather than as reaction to modernity itself.'[4] In the case of Israel, the 'crises of modernity' are the 'crises of Jewish secularity'.[5] The lack of depth of Jewish secular culture following its transition, within a short span of time, from rejection of the contents of Jewish heritage to their adoption; from a collectivist worldview, which considers the good life to consist of contributing to the national project, to an individualistic worldview that sees life as a project

---

[2] Jose Casanova, *Public Religions in the Modern World* (Chicago, University of Chicago Press, 1994) 3.

[3] Jurgen Habermas, 'Religion in the Public Sphere', (2006) 14 European J Phil 1; Jurgen Habermas, 'Pre-Political Foundations of the Democratic Constitutional State?' in Florian Schuller (ed), *Dialectics of Secularization* (San Francisco, Ignatius Press, 2005) 19; Perry Dane, 'Constitutional Law and Religion', in Dennis Patterson (ed), *A Companion to Philosophy of Law and Legal Theory*, 2nd edn, (Chichester, UK, Wiley-Blackwell, 2010) 119; Ran Hirschl, 'The Theocratic Challenge to Constitution Drafting in Post-Conflict States', (2008) 49 WM & Mary L Rev 1179.

[4] Gideon Aran, 'Jewish Zionist Fundamentalism: The Bloc of the Faithful in Israel (Gush Emunim)', in Martin E. Marty and R. Scott Appleby (eds), *Fundamentalism Observed* (Chicago, University of Chicago Press, 1991) 265, 330.

[5] Id, at 329–30.

of personal self-determination; and from social-democracy to capitalism and neo-liberalism.

Law and religion are two competing cultural systems that constitute individual identities, collective identities and social interaction.[6] As in many other countries in the world,[7] the rise of religious fundamentalism in Israel has threatened well-established constitutional premises. But in Israel we may talk not merely of a clash between religion and state, but also of a clash between *religious* fundamentalism and *legal* fundamentalism.

One of the tenets of religious fundamentalism is that nothing should be left 'outside the boundaries of religion,' '[n]othing remains religiously neutral.'[8] For fundamentalists, religion is 'the exclusive source of authority and guidance in the entire realms of the life of the individual and society.'[9]

If there is one thing that epitomizes the activism of Israel's Supreme Court, it is a saying by Justice Aharon Barak, the Court's Chief Justice for twelve years, and the person most closely identified with the Court's new jurisprudence: 'The whole earth is full of law. Any human conduct is the object of a legal norm.' Barak, an exceptionally creative and innovative jurist with exceptional analytical and argumentative skills, meant by that that every human action is always 'normatively justiciable', and almost always 'institutionally justiciable' in the sense that a court of law should have competence to legally review it. This is nothing short of legal fundamentalism, and hence the clash of two fundamentalisms, one religious, the other legal, in Israel of the closing decades of the twentieth century.

One manifestation of religious fundamentalism in Israel has been the proliferation of the practice of seeking rabbis' rulings in all areas of life (*da'at Torah*). That finds its legal equivalent in the Court's depiction by legal sociologist Ronen Shamir as functioning like 'a council of sages—those that in the name of their wisdom appropriate the authority to determine the criteria of what is normal, appropriate, desirable and acceptable.'[10]

As part of its activism, the Court practically extinguished the doctrine of standing, and dramatically expanded the scope of the doctrine of justiciability. As a result, Israel of the closing decades of the twentieth century turned into a highly legalized country. Submitting petitions to the

---

[6] Clifford Geertz, 'Local Knowledge: Fact and Law in Comparative Perspective' *Local Knowledge* (New York, Basic Books, 1983) 167; Dane, above n 3.

[7] Hirschl, above n 3.   [8] Aran, above n 4, at 296.

[9] Eliezer Don Yehiya, 'The Book and the Sword: Nationalist "Yeshivas" and Political Radicalism in Israel' in Avi Sagi and Dov Schwartz (eds), *A Hundred Years of Religious Zionism* (Bar Ilan University Press, 2003) vol 3, 187, 187 (Hebrew).

[10] Ronen Shamir, 'The Politics of Reasonableness: Reasonableness and Judicial Power at Israel's Supreme Court' (1994) 5 Theory and Criticism 7, 12 (Hebrew).

Supreme Court became part of the routine of political and administrative decision-making: A group dissatisfied with the outcome would petition the Court to overturn it. The Court became the arbiter that has the last word on any important political and administrative decision.

This in turn has had several problematic consequences. Amnon Rubinstein, the author of Israel's leading constitutional law treatise, is renowned for having been the first to identify the new trend when, in June 1987, he wrote: 'Israel is currently amidst a stunning process of profound legalization that has no match in any other country.'[11] In May 2008 Rubinstein said at an academic conference that Israel's public administration has been badly infected with 'the disease of paralysis': Decision-making processes unnecessarily linger on for months and years until legal advisors give them the go-ahead. In a similar vein, Knesset Speaker Ruvi Rivlin said in March 2010:

> Legalization, the disease that has overtaken our public sphere in its entirety, threatens not only the ability to govern, but the sheer existence of a normative space not controlled by legal counsels. The disease has bred a new religion that idolizes the legal

continued Rivlin:

> Once upon a time not everything was justiciable, and people made use of common sense, logic, reasonableness and decency. Nowadays only law's high priests are entitled to determine what is reasonable and appropriate and to apply discretion.[12]

Thus, paradoxically enough, the over-legalization of politics and the public administration has led not only to inefficiencies, but also to corruption: a whole new semi-official industry of intermediaries who 'know' how to expedite decision-making processes has sprung up.[13]

---

[11] Amnon Rubinstein, 'The Legalization of Israel' (June 5 1987) Haaretz.

[12] 'The Legalization that Overtook Our Lives' (March 2010) The Lawyer, 8. The renowned sociologist S.N. Eisenstadt writes that the Court's activism 'weakened—albeit not intentionally—the parliamentary tissue' as well as the 'legitimacy' of 'the democratic order.' S.N. Eisenstadt, *Changes in Israeli Society* (Tel Aviv, Ministry of Defense, 2004) 54 (Hebrew).

[13] As might have been expected, the over-legalization of Israel has also been manifest in the astonishing growth of the legal profession. Gad Barzilai has gathered a data set about lawyers in 39 countries. Here are some of his findings: '[A]mong European and most Western nation-states and most democracies, Israel has the highest number of lawyers per population size. In 2005 the country had one lawyer per 211 citizens, a figure which is significantly higher than in most liberal societies like the US [one lawyer per 434 citizens] United Kingdom [one lawyer per 489 citizens], Germany [one lawyer per 619 citizens], Australia [one lawyer per 672 citizens], Holland [one lawyer per 1251 citizens], and France [one lawyer per 1281 citizens].' Gad Barzilai, 'The Ambivalent Language of Lawyers in Israel: Liberal Politics, Economic Liberalism, Silence and Dissent' in Terence C. Halliday, Lucian Karpik and Malcolm Feeley (eds), *Fighting for Political Freedom* (Oxford, Hart Publishing, 2007) 247.

Also, as might have been expected, expansive legalization has been corrosive of culture. The organizational culture of military units is a case in point. President Theodore Roosevelt famously said that:

[I]t is not the critic who counts; not the man who points out how the strong man stumbles, or where the doer of deeds could have done them better. The credit belongs to the man who is actually in the arena, whose face is marred by dust and sweat and blood; who strives valiantly; who errs, who comes short again and again, because there is no effort without error and shortcoming; but who does actually strive to do the deeds.[14]

Israel's minister of defense, Ehud Barak, said in November 2008 that the fact that a combatant officer needs to take into account, in the midst of military action, possible ex post legal scrutiny of his action may infringe upon his decision-making.[15]

Aharon Barak often celebrates the rise of rights talk in which:

[T]he pupil and the teacher, the patient and the doctor, the employee and the employer, the student and the professor—they all, and many, many others, phrase their arguments one toward the other, and all toward the state branches…in terms of constitutional rights.[16]

Scholars of rights have portrayed a more ambivalent picture of what rights talk entails. They have acknowledged the indispensable contribution of entrenched rights to the assurance of vital human interests, of course, but they have also assailed rights talk for what Mary Ann Glendon famously phrased, in words having their roots in Marx, as

its penchant for absolute, extravagant formulations, its near-aphasia concerning responsibility, its excessive homage to individual independence and self-sufficiency, its habitual concentration on the individual and the state at the expense of the intermediate groups of civil society, and its unapologetic insularity;

for the fact that it 'heightens social conflict, and inhibits dialogue that might lead toward consensus, accommodation, or at least the discovery of common ground'; and for the fact that it promotes 'mere assertion over reason-giving' and 'the short-run over the long-term, sporadic crisis intervention over systemic preventive measures, and particular interests over the common good.'[17]

---

[14] Theodore Roosevelt, *The Man In The Arena*, Speech at the Sorbonne, Paris, France, April 23 1910.
[15] Tomer Zarhin, 'Beinish: "Defense" is not a Magic Word' (November 16 2008) Haaretz .
[16] Aharon Barak, 'The Constitutional Revolution—12th Anniversary' (1994) 1 Law and Business 3, 53.
[17] Mary Ann Glendon, *Rights Talk—The Impoverishment of Political Discourse* (New York, The Free Press, 1991) 15. See also: Michael Paris, 'The Politics of Rights: Then and Now' (2006) 31 Law & Soc Inq 999.

One conclusion to be drawn from Glendon's remarks then is that in conditions of excessive legalization, law, otherwise thought of as the ultimate means for peaceful resolution of disputes, instead intensifies conflict, antagonism, confrontation and rivalry.

Grant Gilmore writes:

The better the society, the less law there will be. In Heaven there will be no law…The worse the society, the more law there will be. In Hell there will be nothing but law, and due process will be meticulously observed.[18]

Gilmore alludes to the famous words of the author of Ecclesiastes, 3, 16: 'I saw under the sun the place of judgment, that wickedness was there; and the place of righteousness, that iniquity was there.' The great Israeli poet Yehuda Amichai gave expression to this same sentiment when he wrote:

From the place where we are right/ flowers will never grow/ in the spring.// The place where we are right/ is hard and trampled/ like a yard.// But doubts and loves/ dig up the world/ like a mole, a plow.[19]

Looked at from this perspective, Israel of the closing decades of the twentieth century was far from Heaven on earth. It was a hard place of wickedness.

The rise of over-legalization in Israel went hand in hand with the ascension of neo-liberal economic ideology. At the core of neo-liberalism is the belief that the logic of the market should be extended to as many spheres of life as possible: The running of schools, hospitals and prisons, the provision of welfare, the comodification of sex and body parts, etc.[20] The rise of over-legalization and neo-liberalism attest to a profound crisis in the status of culture in Israel: the Israelis have very much lost their confidence in their ability to do things together within cultural frameworks. Joint action can take place only if governed either by the logic of the law or by the logic of the market.

There are interesting corollaries between the legal and market worldviews. First, very much like a market exchange, a legal dispute is a competitive zero-sum game. Second, at the core of the legal worldview lies the concept of the (negative) right—a 'defensive wall' that creates for the individual a sphere shielded from external intervention and in which he or she may do whatever they choose to do. That finds its equivalent in the market as a sphere of impersonal, self-regarding action in which individuals work for the materialization of their subjective desires by drawing on the

---

[18] Grant Gilmore, *The Ages of American Law* (New Haven, Yale University Press, 1977) 110–1.
[19] 'The Place Where We Are Right' in *The Selected Poems of Yehuda Amichai* (Chana Bloch and Stephen Mitchell trans, Harmondsworth, Viking, 1986) 34.
[20] David Harvey, *A Brief History of Neoliberalism* (Oxford, Oxford University Press, 2005).

resources at their disposal.²¹ Third, money, the institution that lies at the basis of the operation of the market, serves as the common denominator to which all wishes of market actors are translated and made commensurable. That finds its equivalent in the law's concept of the right into which various interests are translated and through that made commensurable.

What all of this means is that the legal worldview and the market worldview are two specific worldviews of human interaction with quite a few similarities between them. What it also means is that extension of the logic of the law (through over-legalization) and the logic of the market (through neo-liberal ideology) to too many spheres of human interaction entails normative impoverishment: Various spheres of activity, dense with distinct 'internal' values of their own, are being flooded and overwhelmed by the logic of the law and/or the logic of the market.²² This, in turn, may prove to be of far-reaching implications in a setting of rising religious fundamentalism, such as Israel of the early twenty-first century: the greater the number of spheres of human interaction overtaken by the logics of the law and the market, the more the outcome is a sense of normative impoverishment, the more fundamentalist sentiment is nourished, the more liberal law feels threatened, the more it becomes aggressive and expansionist in its struggle with fundamentalism, and so on. A vicious circle is in place.

Israel is not the only country that has witnessed far-reaching legalization of its politics and public administration in the years following World War II. With the enactment of many new constitutions, the adoption of judicial review, and the spread of the human rights discourse, this has been the case in many other countries, as well.²³ But there is a crucial difference between Western countries, such as the United States, and Israel, and not only because according to several assessments Israel of the recent decades has set a world record in legalization. Importantly, the difference also lies in the fact that in Western countries law serves as an expression and bearer of non-contested values that are widely shared in society.²⁴ In Israel, by contrast, with the eruption of the war of cultures between secular and religious Jews, the very existence of liberal law is being contested. Therefore, even if it may be hard to assess the effects of the Court's activism

---

[21] Elizabeth Anderson, *Value in Ethics and Economics* (Cambridge, Harvard University Press, 1993) chapter 7.

[22] Id; Alasdair Macintyre, *After Virtue* (Notre Dame, University of Notre Dame Press, 1981) chapter 14; Pierre Bourdieu, *Firing Back—Against the Tyranny of the Market 2* (London, Loic Wacquant trans, Verso, 2003).

[23] C. Neal Tate and Torbjorn Vallinder (eds), *The Judicialization of Politics* (Oxford, Butterworth-Heinemann, 1995); Kenneth M. Holland (ed), *Judicial Activism in Comparative Perspective*, (Houndmills, Macmillan, 1991); Carlo Guarnieri and Patrizia Pederzoli, *The Power of Judges* (Oxford, Oxford University Press, 2002).

[24] Glendon, above n 17, at 3.

on the ground, perhaps its more important effect was the way it vigorously signaled the unmitigated commitment of the secular, pro-Western liberal group to pushing forward its normative system in the struggle over the future cultural orientation of the country.

And yet, despite the immense importance of the law as both a symbolic and constitutive normative system, the renowned Israeli author Amos Oz was right when he noted that it is through the attractiveness of a culture's contents and practices, not through legal victories or legislation, that victory is won in a war of cultures. 'A cultural struggle is a struggle of seduction,' wrote Oz. 'It is a struggle over people's hearts and souls.... We need to make our version of Jewishness attractive.... We have to entice.'[25]

The Supreme Court has paid a heavy price for its identification with one of the two major groups contending in the struggle over the shaping of Israeli culture in the coming decades: unsurprisingly, it lost much legitimacy among the Jewish religious group, which feels very much alienated from the Court and regards it as a partisan institution that serves as a tool in the hands of the rival group for remedying their political and cultural losses.

The striking point, however, is that in recent years the Court has also lost legitimacy among the liberal former hegemons, the group that for some three decades provided it with unmitigated support for whatever it did. Yet whereas the reason for the Court's loss of stature among the Jewish religious group has to do with the Court's cultural identity, the reason for the Court's loss of stature among its supporters has to do with the erosion in the Court's standards of conduct, and in particular because of the Court's involvement in the appointment process of justices to its ranks.

The Israeli system, uniquely in the world, enables the Supreme Court to practically dominate the process of appointment of judges. But in spite of numerous claims on the part of the Court's justices that this has made the Israeli appointment procedure 'the best in the world' in fact exactly the opposite is true: the Court's involvement in the appointment process has exposed a highly unappealing political dimension in the Court's conduct, which, in turn, has undermined the Court's stature. One lesson that can clearly be drawn from the Israeli case is how destructive it is for courts to be involved in the process of appointment to their ranks.

The upshot of all of this is that at the beginning of the twenty-first century the Israeli Supreme Court finds itself in a highly precarious situation, having lost a substantial amount of legitimacy not only among its

---

[25] Amos Oz, 'A Struggle of Seduction: The War of Cultures on the Heart of Judaism', in Ruvik Rosenthal (ed), *The Heart of the Matter—Redefining Social and National Issues* (Jerusalem, Keter Publishing House, 2005) 15, 25 (Hebrew).

adversaries, the Jewish religious group, but also among its traditional supporters, Israelis that identify with the Western, secular, liberal cultural option for the state. This is a moment of crisis not only for the Court, but for Israeli liberalism, for since the establishment of the state the Court has played a crucial role in entrenching and cultivating Israel's liberal-democratic political culture. It may prove to be a turning point in the development of Israel's political culture in its entirety.

In addition to the schism within the Jewish group, there is an additional, profound schism between the Jewish group and the Arab group, which constitutes around 20 percent of the country's population. The Jewish group wishes to adhere to Israel's current definition as a 'Jewish and democratic state'. The Arab group perceives Israel differently. Some Arabs would like Israel to perceive itself as a bi-national state run in collaboration by the elites of the two national groups that compose its population. Others would rather Israel cease perceiving itself as the nation-state of the Jewish people, where they exercise their right of self-determination, and turn itself instead into a state that, modeling itself after the United States of America, does not have any clear national identity—'a state of all its citizens', as this option is known in Israeli parlance. The Arab group is also widely discriminated against in terms of the allocation of state resources; it is excluded from important political decisions; and by and large it lives in a separate civil society. Add to that the belief of the Arab group that the establishment of the state and its continued existence is based on the use of violence against them, plus the ongoing state of war between Israel and the Palestinian people in the Occupied Territories, and it is easy to see how explosive the situation is.

Israel certainly will need lots of goodwill, creative thinking and luck in the coming decades to overcome the profound schisms that exist both within the Jewish group and between the Jewish and Arab groups.

Despite Zionism's enormous, even unprecedented accomplishments, when the Israeli condition is looked at from the perspective of the country's cultural divisions, two unresolved issues stand out. The first is the cultural schism between secular and religious Jews, which has been a factor in Jewish life for the past 250 years, since the rise of the Jewish Enlightenment in the second half of the eighteenth century. For most of the twentieth century, the struggle between these two groups over the shaping of the culture of the Jewish society in Eretz Israel appeared to have ended with the decisive victory of the secular group. But with the eruption of the cultural struggle in Israel in the waning decades of the century, it became clear that the issue regarding the country's cultural orientation is far from resolved.

Zionism's second unresolved issue concerns the demography of Israel. The aim of Zionism was to establish a nation-state for the Jewish people in Eretz Israel. But by the time the Zionist endeavor began to take shape, an Arab society existed already in Palestine, and in the course of the twentieth century only a minority of world Jews responded affirmatively to the Zionist call to immigrate to Eretz Israel. As a result, not only did the Arabs constitute the majority of the population in Palestine throughout the first half of the twentieth century, and a sizeable minority of some 40 percent of the Jewish state that was supposed to be established under the 1947 United Nations 'Partition Resolution', but they continue to be a sizeable minority in Israel within its present borders. Israel officially defines itself as a 'Jewish and democratic state', but demographically it is a bi-national state. The discrepancy between the definition and the demography will continue to give rise to many of the problems Israel faces in the coming years.

These two unresolved issues are perhaps best summed up by the following data: In 1960, only 15 percent of the students in the Israeli primary-school system were either ultra-Orthodox Jewish students or Israeli Arabs. At present the figure stands at 46 percent, and it is expected that as early as 2020, ie, about a decade from now, the majority of primary-school students will be children from these two groups. The Western, secular, liberal Jewish group that led Israel in its first six decades will face major challenges in the coming years. The face of Israel is bound to change. How will all of this affect the country's regime, political culture and law?

CHAPTER 1

ZIONISM AND THE EVOLVING NEW CULTURE

In this chapter I will focus on the main trends in Zionist thought as to the culture of the new Jewish society that took shape in Eretz Israel (Palestine) in the first half of the twentieth century. I will also consider the key constitutive principles of the new culture.

This chapter has threefold significance for the discussion in the following chapters. First, in Chapter 2 I will discuss several early twentieth-century proposals for the structuring of the law of the new Jewish society, locating these proposals in the broader context of Zionist thought on the culture of the Jewish society developing in Eretz Israel, as discussed in this chapter. Second, in Chapter 2 I will examine the cultural characteristics of the jurisprudence of Israel's Supreme Court as it has developed since the establishment of the State of Israel. I shall locate these characteristics as well within the broader context of Zionist thought regarding the issue of culture, as discussed in this chapter. Third, in Chapter 5 I will argue that since the late 1970s two groups have been struggling over the stewardship of Israeli culture. One is a secular Jewish group that seeks to shape Israeli culture according to the values of liberalism and through strong contacts with Western culture. The other is a religious Jewish group that seeks to shape Israeli culture according to the Halakhah and traditional Jewish culture. I will further show in Chapter 5 that since the late 1970s the Israeli Supreme Court has been a central player in the struggle between these two groups. For the moment, I will show that the two cultural alternatives offered by these two groups have been present in the life of the Jewish people throughout the modern period, and in the life of the Zionist movement since it began.

A. THE RISE OF THE JEWISH ENLIGHTENMENT

In the course of the last two decades of the eighteenth century a Jewish Enlightenment movement [*Haskalah*] developed in Germany.[1] The Jewish Enlightenment challenged the confinement of Jewish culture[2] to its halakhic contents and the exclusivity of the leadership of the rabbis. The *maskilim*, as the supporters of this endeavor came to be known, strove to create a fusion between Judaism's religious legacy, on the one hand, and the philosophy, the sciences, and the secular culture of the European Enlightenment on the other. They sought to reshape Jewish culture, identity,[3] education and daily practices through reliance on elements borrowed from Western culture. Thus, unlike the European Enlightenment, the Jewish Enlightenment was not premised on a total denial of the authority of tradition. Only a century later did that happen, with secular Zionism's attempt to construct a novel and original Jewish culture from scratch in Eretz Israel (see below).

---

[1] Shmuel Feiner, *Haskalah and history: The emergence of a modern jewish historical consciousness* (Chaya Naor and Sondra Silverston trans, Oxford, Littman Library of Jewish Civilization 2002); Shmuel Feiner, *The Jewish Enlightenment in the Eighteenth-Century* (Jerusalem, Zalman Shazar Center, 2002) (Hebrew); Shmuel Feiner, *Moses Mendelssohn* (Jerusalem, Zalman Shazar Center, 2005) (Hebrew); Ehud Luz, *Parallels Meet: Religion and Nationalism in the Early Zionist Movement* (1882–1904) (Lenn J. Schramm trans, Philadelphia, Jewish Publication Society, 1988) chapter 1.

[2] The concept of culture is notoriously complex, with little or no agreement as to its content. William H. Sewell Jr, 'The Concept(s) of Culture' in Victoria E. Bonnell and Lynn Hunt (eds), *Beyond the Cultural Turn—New Directions in the Study of Society and Culture* (Berkeley, University of California Press, 1999) 35. I define culture as the contents of the mind by means of which human beings experience and express meaning as to what transpires in the course of their lives. Culture provides human beings with the collection of frames of reference through which they perceive and understand the world. Clifford Geertz, *The Interpretation of Cultures* (New York, Basic Books, Inc, 1973); Clifford Geertz, *Local Knowledge* (New York, Basic Books, Inc, 1983); Clifford Geertz, *After the Fact* (Cambridge, Harvard University Press, 1995); Clifford Geertz, *Available Light* (Princeton, New Jersey, Princeton University Press, 2000); David M. Schneider, 'Notes Toward a Theory of Culture', in Keith H. Basso and Henry A. Selby (eds), *Meaning in Anthropology* (Albuquerque, University of New Mexico Press, 1976) 197. Culture not only constitutes the minds of human beings and determines the meaning their lives have, but also shapes their practices and conduct. Theodor R. Schatzki, Karin Knorr Cetina and Eike von Savigny (eds), *The Practice Turn in Contemporary Theory* (2001); Pierre Bourdieu, *Outline of a Theory of Practice* (Richard Nice trans, 1977); Ann Swidler, *Talk of Love—How Culture Matters* (2001); Ann Swidler, 'Culture in Action: Symbols and Strategies' (1986) 51 Am Soc Rev 273. The building blocks of culture are cultural categories: Each culture is composed of a vast number of categories that not only organize the world for human beings, but also determine the normative value of things in the world. Richard A. Shweder and Robert A. LeVine (eds), *Culture Theory* (1984); James W. Stigler, Richard A. Shweder and Gilbert Herdt, *Cultural Psychology—Essays on Comparative Human Development* (1990); Dorothy Holland and Naomi Quinn (eds), *Language and Thought*, (1987).

[3] The term identity has come into use in recent decades in a series of contexts where it has acquired multiple meanings. Rogers Brubaker and Frederick Cooper, 'Beyond "Identity"' (2000) 29 Theory and Society 1. However, the term has today two main meanings. First, the identity of a person is the system of categories that she internalizes out of the culture in which she lives and that determines the way she perceives the world and gives meaning to what transpires in her life. The second meaning of identity refers to certain traits of a person that the culture in which she lives attaches meaning to as regards how that person should be treated. This last sense of the term is the one that has been in use in the context of 'the politics of identity' of recent decades.

The Jewish Enlightenment was an institutionalized and organized movement. It developed a distinctive agenda for intellectual and educational activity. It ran its own publishing houses and periodicals, and maintained a separate school system that followed distinctive curricula.

In the course of the nineteenth century the Jewish Enlightenment spread to central and Eastern Europe, reaching its apogee in Russia during the 1860s and 1870s. In the 1880s, many *maskilim* turned to Zionism.[4]

The rabbinic establishment understood the heresy embodied by the Enlightenment challenge to the exclusive role of Halakhah in the lives of the Jews. It also understood the threat that the Jewish Enlightenment posed to the rabbis' own status as leaders of the Jews and as their mentors in day-to-day conduct. Following the consolidation of the Jewish Enlightenment into an institutionalized movement, a persistent, bitter, and at times violent struggle erupted between the *maskilim* and the rabbis—a '*kulturkampf*'—over the shaping of the culture, education and daily practices of the Jews.

The Jewish Enlightenment, together with the spread of secularization practices in the course of the eighteenth century among Jews living in the urban centers of western and central Europe,[5] gave birth to a new kind of Jewish existence and identity, hitherto unknown in Jewish history, that of the secular Jew.

There have been many recurring manifestations of the schism between the Jewish Enlightenment and traditional halakhic Judaism in the history of the Jewish people in the 250 years that have elapsed since the dawn of the Jewish Enlightenment movement. The struggle that is currently being waged in Israel over the respective places of Western culture and of the Halakhah in Israel's culture and law is one further transmutation of this schism (Chapter 5 below).[6] Indeed, the term '*kulturkampf*,' which is used to describe the nineteenth century struggle between the *maskilim* and the rabbis, has also been applied to the relationship between secular and religious Jews in late twentieth century Israel (Chapter 7, below).

---

[4] Shmuel Feiner 'Out of Berlin: The Second Phase of the Haskalah Movement (1797–1824)', in Ezra Fleischer, Gerald Blidstein, Carmi Horowitz, Bernard Septimus (eds), *Me'ah She'arim—Studies in Medieval Jewish Spiritual Life* (Jerusalem, Magnes Press, Hebrew University, 1991) 403 (Hebrew); Immanuel Etkes (ed), *The East European Jewish Enlightenment* (Jerusalem, Zalman Shazar Center, 1993) (Hebrew); Mordechai Zalkin, *A New Dawn—The Jewish Enlightenment in the Russian Empire—Social Aspects* (Jerusalem, Magnes Press, Hebrew University, 1990) (Hebrew); Gideon Katzenelson, *The Literary War Between the Ultra-orthodox and the Enlightened* (Tel Aviv, Dvir, 1954) (Hebrew).

[5] Shmuel Feiner, *The Origins of Jewish Secularization in 18th Century Europe* (Jerusalem, Zalman Shazar Center, 2010) (Hebrew).

[6] Shmuel Feiner, '"They Look Like Jews But They Dress Like Cossacks": Pre-Zionist Origins of the Jewish Cultural Conflict', in Avi Sagi and Dov Schwartz (eds), *A Hundred Years of Religious Zionism*, (Ramat Gan, Bar Ilan University Press, 2003) vol 3, 375 (Hebrew).

B. ZIONIST THOUGHT ON THE CULTURE OF THE EVOLVING SOCIETY IN ERETZ ISRAEL

(a) Introduction

Zionism was not only a response to the distressing conditions of Jewish existence in Eastern and central Europe, but an answer to the grave cultural crisis that Jews faced in the nineteenth century. The crisis resulted from a combination of two developments. One was the decline in the power of religion and of the Halakhah to shape the lives of the Jews following the spread of the Enlightenment and secularism in the course of the nineteenth century. The other was the failure of the emancipation processes from which Jews living in various European countries benefited in the course of the nineteenth century, ie, the rejection of the Jews' attempt to be accepted as equals by the non-Jewish societies in which they lived.[7] Hence, Zionism was not only a political movement, but also, and to no lesser degree, a movement of cultural change.[8]

Furthermore, as a national movement Zionism was not driven by a stable, organic national culture that, at some point in its history, sought institutionalization as a nation-state. To the contrary, in the case of Zionism the national movement preceded the national culture: The new national culture of the Jewish people was largely the creation of the Jewish people's national movement. Zionism, then, was not only a movement of cultural change, but a movement for the creation of a new culture *ex nihilo*.[9]

As might be expected, the orientation and contents of the culture of the new Jewish society in Eretz Israel—'the heart of it all', as David Vital refers to it[10]—were in dispute among Zionists from the very beginning of their endeavor in the 1880s. For over two decades, until the early years

---

[7] Shlomo Avineri, *Herzl* (Jerusalem, Zalman Shazar Center, 2007) chapter 2 (Hebrew).

[8] Ehud Luz, above n 1; Shlomo Avineri, *The Making of Modern Zionism: The Intellectual Origins of the Jewish State* (London, Weidenfeld and Nicolson, 1981); Gideon Shimoni, *The Zionist Ideology* (Hanover, NH, University Press of New England, 1995); Jacob Katz, 'Zionism and Jewish Identity' in *Jewish Nationalism—Essays and Studies* (Jerusalem, The Zionist Library, 1979) 73 (Hebrew); Jacob Katz, *Out of the Ghetto—The Social Background of Jewish Emancipation 1770–1870* (Tel Aviv, Am Oved Publishers, 1985) (Hebrew). Shmuel Ettinger, 'The Uniqueness of the Jewish National Movement' in Ben-Zion Yehoshua and Ahron Kedar (eds), *Ideological and Political Zionism* (Jerusalem, Zalman Shazar Center, 1978) 9 (Hebrew); Yaacov Barnai, 'On the Beginning of Zionism', in Yechiam Weitz (ed), *From Vision to Revision: A Hundred Years of Historiography of Zionism* (Jerusalem, Zalman Shazar Center, 1997) 135; David Vital, *Zionism: The Formative Years* (Oxford, Oxford University Press, 1982) chapter 1.

[9] Yaacov Shavit, 'The Yishuv Between National Regeneration of Culture and Cultural Generation of the Nation', in Jehuda Reinharz, Gideon Shimoni, Yosef Salmon (eds), *Jewish Nationalism and Politics—New Perspectives* (Jerusalem, Zalman Shazar Center, 1996) 141 (Hebrew); Yaacov Shavit, 'The Status of Culture in the Process of Creating a National Society in Eretz-Israel: Basic Attitudes and Concepts' in Zohar Shavit (ed), *The History of the Jewish Community in Eretz-Israel since 1882* (Jerusalem, The Israeli Academy for Sciences and Humanities 1998) vol 1, 9 (Hebrew).

[10] Vital, above n 8, at 28.

of the twentieth century, Zionist leaders and activists engaged in bitter controversies over the issue of culture, which time and again threatened to break apart their newly established movement.[11] At the core of these controversies lay the question regarding the balance between the Halakhah and European culture in the life of the new Jewish society taking shape in Eretz Israel.

(b) Four approaches toward the issue of culture in early Zionism

Four main approaches are discernable in the writings of Zionist thinkers on the issue of the evolving Jewish culture in Eretz Israel.

(i) The cultural revival approach

It was in the Jewish Enlightenment movement of the second half of the eighteenth century that the cultural revival approach had its sources. According to this approach, Zionism was supposed to effect a revival of the waning religious Jewish culture by turning it into a national, secular culture. The culture evolving in Eretz Israel should therefore be a secular culture based on a fusion of elements derived from Judaism's religious legacy and from European culture. This approach, then, was premised on an unfavorable view of religious Jewish life in the Diaspora combined with deep appreciation of European culture.

At the end of the nineteenth century and the beginning of the twentieth century, the cultural revival approach was identified with the secular Jewish intelligentsia, the writers and the intellectuals of Eastern Europe active in the Zionist movement, and it enjoyed the broadest support among the Zionists of the time.[12] Its most prominent spokesman was Ahad Ha-Am.[13]

---

[11] Yosef Shalmon, *Religion and Zionism: First Encounters—Essays* (Jerusalem, The Zionist Library, 1990) (Hebrew); Yosef Shalmon, 'Zionism and Anti-Zionism in Traditional Jewry of East Europe', in Shmuel Almog, Jehuda Reinharz and Anita Shapira (eds), *Zionism and Religion* (Jerusalem, Zalman Shazar Center, 1994) 33 (Hebrew); Ehud Luz, 'The Limits of Toleration—On the Problem of the Partnership Between Ultra-Orthodox and Secular Jews in the Hibat Zion Era (1882–1895)', in *Zionism and Religion*, id, at 55; Israel Kolat, 'Religion, Society and State in the Era of Nationalism', in *Zionism and Religion*, id, at 329; Hedva Ben Israel, Book Review: 'Religion and Zionism: First Encounters by Yosef Shalmon', 2 Israel (2002) 189 (Hebrew); Luz, above n 1, chapter 3; Geula Refael, 'The Culture Question in the First Congresses' in Anita Shapira (ed), *The Religious Trend in Zionism* (Tel Aviv, Am Oved Publishers, 1983) 39 (Hebrew); Shmuel Almog, 'The Relation of Seculars to Religion in Early Zionism', in *The Religious Trend in Zionism*, id, at 31; Dov Schwartz, *Religious Zionism: History and Ideology* (Tel Aviv, Ministry of Defense, 2003) chapters 2, 3 (Hebrew).

[12] Avner Holtzman, 'Hebrew Literature and the "Cultural Controversy" in the Zionist Movement, 1897–1902', in Anita Shapira, Jehuda Reinharz and Jay Harris (eds), *The Age of Zionism* (Jerusalem, Zalman Shazar Center, 2000) 145 (Hebrew); Almog, id.

[13] Ahad Ha-Am was the pseudonym of Asher Ginsberg (1856–1927), a Jewish intellectual and thinker, one of the most prominent figures in the first and second generations of Zionism (the last decades of the nineteenth and first decades of the twentieth centuries). Ahad Ha-Am was opposed to Herzl's political Zionism and called for the establishment of a 'spiritual center' in Eretz Israel,

Ahad Ha-Am perceived Judaism as a national culture, and religion as only one of its components, albeit of central significance. 'Israel indeed has a national spirit that is not solely confined to religious beliefs,' he wrote.[14] In that spirit, he called for a reshaping of Jewish culture through the transformation of the religious contents of Jewish tradition into categories of a national culture. In his view, the traditional contents of Judaism should no longer be regarded as religiously binding, but treated instead as the embodiment of the culture and history of the Jewish people.

As part of the process of transforming Jewish religion into a national culture, Ahad Ha-Am proposed the selection of contents from Judaism's rich legacy and a restructuring of these contents by drawing on categories taken from modern, secular European culture. Ahad Ha-Am saw this not as a revolutionary process, but as one more stage in the sequence of Judaism's historical development. He therefore perceived the culture of the new Zionist society not as an antithesis to the Jewish culture of the Diaspora, but as another link in the chain of its historical development.

Ahad Ha-Am called for the establishment of a 'spiritual national center' in Eretz Israel (as opposed to the political conception of Zionism, which advocated the establishment of a Jewish state). He envisaged 'a center of Torah and wisdom, of language and books,'[15] where institutions of scholarship and research would work together with writers and thinkers to turn religious Jewish culture into a national culture. Ahad Ha-Am maintained that if the creation of a Jewish state was not preceded by a reshaping of Jewish culture, the result would be detrimental both to the Jewish state and to Judaism: The Jewish state would be just one more Western state, with a culture lacking genuine Jewish characteristics.

(ii) The Halakhic approach

The second approach concerning the character of the evolving Jewish culture in Eretz Israel was that endorsed by religious Zionists.

At the end of the nineteenth century, the religious Jewry of Eastern Europe was split between the ultra-Orthodox and the religious-Zionists.

in which a modern and secular Jewish culture would be fostered and spread among Jews in the world. See: *The Collected Writings of Ahad Ha-Am* (Tel Aviv, Dvir, 1954) (Hebrew); Leon Simon trans, ed, *Ahad Ha-Am, Essays, Letters, Memoirs* (Oxford, 1946); Leon Simon trans, ed, *Selected Essays of Ahad Ha'Am* (New York, Atheneum, 1970); *Nationalism and the Jewish Ethic: Basic Writings of Ahad Ha'Am* (Edited and introduced by Hans Kohn, New York, Schocken Books, 1962). See also: Steven J. Zipperstein, *Elusive Prophet—Ahad Ha'Am and the Origins of Zionism* (Berkeley, University of California Press, 1993).

[14] Ahad Ha-Am, 'Our National Morality', in *The Collected Writings of Ahad Ha-am*, id, at 159, 160.

[15] Ahad Ha-Am, *The Way of the Spirit*, id, at 41, 47. See also: 'A Spiritual Center', in *Ahad Ha-Am, Essays, Letters, Memoirs*, above n 13, at 201.

The ultra-Orthodox were hostile to Zionism because they viewed it as a secular movement the activities of which would only 'postpone the end'—delay the end of the exile and ingathering of the Diaspora by seeking to do so through human initiative, instead of waiting for it to be carried out by divine will. The ultra-Orthodox, therefore, were entirely indifferent to the issue of the culture of the new society in Eretz Israel.

Unlike them, the religious sectors that did support Zionism paid heed to this issue. They were suspicious of and hostile towards the cultural revival approach, advocating instead that the emerging culture in Eretz Israel should be a traditional Jewish culture founded on the Halakhah, in line with the motto 'Eretz Israel to the people of Israel according to the Torah of Israel.'[16] Religious Zionists, however, never succeeded in developing a detailed plan for their vision of a Jewish state governed by the Halakhah. Furthermore, this vision itself shattered against the reality that began to unfold in Eretz Israel in the first half of the twentieth century: Most Jewish immigrants were secularists who saw nationalism as an alternative to religion and as the primary source of their self-identity. A largely secular Jewish society emerged as a result (see below).

(iii) The European culture approach

On the third approach in Zionist thought, the evolving culture in Eretz Israel was perceived as a branch of European culture. In the early days of Zionism this approach was identified with the liberal Zionist intelligentsia of Western Europe. Perceiving Zionism primarily in material-political terms, proponents of this approach gave little thought to the cultural traits of the new Zionist society in Eretz Israel. When they did deal with the question of culture, they saw the cultures of central and Western Europe as the only ones worthy to serve as models for the culture of the new Zionist society.

The most prominent representative of the European culture approach was Theodor Herzl, the founder of the Zionist movement and the first president of the World Zionist Congress. Until the very end of his life Herzl remained alienated from the cultural revival approach, and hostile to the Halakhic approach. 'Culture for him was identical to European culture.'[17]

---

[16] Asher Cohen, *The Talit and the Flag—Religious Zionism and the Concept of a Torah State 1947–1953* (Jerusalem, Yad Ben Zvi, 1998) (Hebrew); Jacob Katz, *A Time for Inquiry—A Time for Reflection, An Historical Essay on Israel Through the Ages* (Jerusalem, Zalman Shazar Center, 1999) chapter 4 (Hebrew); Izhak Englard, 'Law and Religion in Israel', 35 Am J Comp L (1987) 185; Ehud Luz, 'The Failure of the Bridge', in Avi Sagi and Dov Schwartz (eds), *A Hundred Years of Religious Zionism* (Ramat Gan, Bar Ilan University Press, 2003) vol 3, 351 (Hebrew); Yosef Shalmon, 'Tradition and Modernity in Early Religious-Zionist Thought', in Ben-Zion Yehoshua and Ahron Kedar (eds), *Ideological and Political Zionism* (Jerusalem, Zalman Shazar Center, 1978) 21 (Hebrew); Eliezer Don-Yehiha, 'Ideology and Policy in Religious Zionism—Rabbi Yitzhak Ya'akov Reines' Conception of Zionism and the Policy of the Mizrahi Under his Leadership' (1983) 8 Zionism 103 (Hebrew).

[17] Almog, above n 11, at 74.

In 1896, Herzl published his book *The Jewish State: An Attempt at a Modern Solution of the Jewish Question*.[18] In it Herzl wrote that if the Jews do reach Palestine,

> we should there form a portion of a rampart of Europe against Asia, an outpost of civilization as opposed to barbarism. We should as a neutral State remain in contact with all Europe, which would have to guarantee our existence.[19]

Herzl expected the Jews in Eretz Israel to be like European Jews in their daily habits.

> There are English hotels in Egypt, and on the mountain-crest in Switzerland, Vienna cafes in South Africa, French theatres in Russia, German operas in America, and best Bavarian beer in Paris.

Hence, in Eretz Israel too, 'every man will find his customs again in the local groups, but they will be better, more beautiful, and more agreeable than before.'[20]

Concerning language, Herzl wrote a famous passage attesting to the fact that he saw no particular value in reviving Hebrew, the historical language of the Jewish people:

> We cannot converse with one another in Hebrew. Who amongst us has a sufficient acquaintance with Hebrew to ask for a railway ticket in that language? Such a thing cannot be done. Yet the difficulty is very easily circumvented. Every man can preserve the language in which his thoughts are at home...and the language which proves itself to be of greatest utility for general intercourse will be adopted without compulsion as our national tongue.[21]

As for the place of religion in the life of the future Jewish state, Herzl wrote that a synagogue would be visible from a distance in every neighborhood, for 'Faith unites us.' Reiterating this last statement again in another famous passage, he nonetheless vigorously opposes the idea of a theocracy:

> Faith unites us, knowledge gives us freedom. We shall therefore prevent any theocratic tendencies from coming to the fore on the part of our priesthood. We shall keep our priests within the confines of their temples in the same way as we shall keep our professional army within the confines of their barracks. Army and priesthood shall receive honors high as their valuable functions deserve. But they must not interfere in the administration of the State.[22]

Herzl also foresaw that freedom of religion and freedom from religion would prevail in the Jewish state: 'And if it should occur that men of other

---

[18] Theodor Herzl, *The Jewish State: An Attempt at a Modern Solution of the Jewish Question*, 4th edn, (Sylvie D'Avigdor trans, London, R. Searl, 1946). See also: Avineri, above n 7, chapter 5.
[19] Id, at 96.   [20] Id, at 135.   [21] Id, at 145–6.   [22] Id, at 146.

creeds and different nationalities come to live amongst us, we should accord them honorable protection and equality before the law.'[23]

In 1902, Herzl published his utopian novel *Altneuland*, which describes a visit to the future Jewish state in Eretz Israel.[24] The book is crammed with descriptions of Jewish society as resorting to the latest technology and science available in Europe and the United States. Yet the influences of Western culture are evident in *all* realms of life. The building style is mainly European. The schools teach European languages. Youths are busy with gymnastics, target shooting, tennis, cricket, and soccer. The same plays are being put on as in Berlin or Paris. Theater companies from France and Italy visit and stage their productions. Men attending the opera wear white gloves. Hotel orchestras are Hungarian, Romanian, and Italian. One of the novel's heroines sings lieder by Schumann, Rubinstein, Wagner, Verdi, and Gounod. Ladies discuss the latest Paris fashions. Universities promote studies in philosophy and art. There is a national academy on the French model. Women enjoy full equality of rights. Freedom of religion and freedom of access to the holy places of all religions are guaranteed. Jews, Moslems, and Christians live in harmony. The only manifestations of Jewish tradition are the adoption of the jubilee year and the construction of the Third Temple.

Ahad Ha-Am's sarcastic criticism of *Altneuland* was directed at the lack of any uniquely Jewish element in the life of Herzl's Jewish society. 'The Jews of *Altneuland* have not innovated anything, nor have they added anything of their own,' wrote Ahad Ha-Am. 'They have just imitated and put together scattered, disintegrated things they found among the enlightened peoples of Europe and America.' Therefore, *Altneuland* could serve as well as the recipe for the national revival of the Nigerian people, concluded Ahad Ha-Am.[25]

Another prominent representative of the European culture approach in early Zionist thought was Zeev Jabotinsky.[26] In a famous article published in 1926, Jabotinsky vehemently criticized Zionists who claimed that the Jews were an 'oriental people.' Jabotinsky argued that an

---

[23] Id, at 147.
[24] Theodor Herzl, *Altneuland—Old-New Land*, 3rd edn, (Paula Arnold trans, Haifa, Israel, Haifa Pub Co 1964). See also: Avineri, above n 7, chapter 7; Fania Oz-Salzberger, 'The Non-Israeli Herzl', in Avi Sagi and Yedidia Z. Stern (eds), *Herzl Then and Now: An Old Jew or a New Person?* (Jerusalem, Shalom Hartman Institute, 2008) 125 (Hebrew); Shmuel Feiner, *Jewish Secular Society and Culture in Herzl's Vision*, id, at 171 (Hebrew); Avi Sagi and Yedidia Z. Stern, *Expulsion of Identity: Altneuland in the State of the Jews*, id, at 257 (Hebrew).
[25] *The Collected Writings of Ahad Ha-Am*, above n 13, at 313.
[26] Zeev Jabotinsky (1880–1940) was a Zionist leader and distinguished Zionist thinker, writer, and poet. In 1925, he founded and led the 'Union of Zionist-Revisionists' within the World Zionist Congress, from which he seceded in 1935 to form the New Zionist Organization.

absolute bond (or sense of belongingness) linked the Jewish people to Western culture. 'We Jews have nothing in common with what is called "the Orient." We are going to Eretz Israel...to "expand the borders of Europe up to the Euphrates".' Citing in detail Judaism's vast contribution to European culture, Jabotinsky came to the conclusion that 'Europe is ours; we are among its foremost makers.' Even so, he held that Europe had equally influenced Judaism. Hence, more than any other people, Jews could say that '"Western" culture is our very own.' For Jews to become estranged from Western culture means 'to deny our own selves,' he concluded.[27]

For Jabotinsky, having deeply internalized Western humanism, human good was the supreme value. From this premise he developed his views concerning the relationship between the individual and the state. Jabotinsky was an ardent liberal; he perceived the state as an instrument for promoting human interests. 'In the beginning, God created the individual', he writes. 'Every individual is a king equal to his fellow. Society was created for the benefit of individuals, not vice-versa.'[28] As a liberal, Jabotinsky also held that the citizens of the state must be equipped with the civil and political rights that lie at the heart of liberal thought. Furthermore, he believed that the intervention of the state in the lives of its citizens must be kept to a minimum. Nevertheless, and in line with his instrumental view of the state, he held that the state must ensure its citizens a broad range of social rights. Jabotinsky's perception of the state was thus based on an interesting combination of libertarian traits together with an emphasis on the state's duty to ensure its citizens' social rights.[29]

---

[27] Zeev Jabotinsky, 'The East', in *Selected Writings* (Tel Aviv, S. Zaltzman, 1946) vol 3, 29, 30, 34, 35 (Hebrew); Mordechai Sarig (ed), *The Political and Social Philosophy of Ze'ev Jabotinsky: Selected Writings* (Shimshon Feder, trans, Portland Ore: Vallentine Mitchell, 1999).

[28] Zeev Jabotinsky, 'Diaspora and Assimilation', in *The Story of My Life, Part 1* (1947) 38 (Jerusalem, Eri Jabotinsky Publishing House) 38 (Hebrew). See also: Zeev Jabotinsky, 'The Wagon of the Klezmer', in *The Road to a State* (Jerusalem, Eri Jabotinsky Publishing House, 1953) 269, 271 (written in 1935) (Hebrew).

[29] On Jabotinsky's theory of the state see: Raphaela Bilski Ben-Hur, *Every Individual is a King—the Social and Political Thought of Ze'ev (Vladimir) Jabotinsky* (Tel Aviv, Dvir, 1988) (Hebrew); Raphaela Bilski Cohen, 'Introduction', in *The Essence Of Democracy In The Liberal-Democratic Philosophy Of Ze'ev Jabotinsky* (Tel Aviv, Zeev Jabotinsky Institute, 2001) 13 (Hebrew); Arye Naor, 'Jabotinsky's Constitutional Guidelines for Israel', in Avi Bareli and Pinhas Ginossar (eds), *The Eye Of The Storm—Essays On Ze'ev Jabotinsky* (Beer Sheva, Ben Gurion University, 2004) 49 (Hebrew); Michael Stanislawski, *Zionism And The Fin De Siecle—Cosmopolitanism And Nationalism From Nordau To Jabotinsky* (Berkeley, University of California Press, 2001) chapter 9; Shalom Ratzabi, 'Jabotinsky and Religion' (2004) 5 Israel 1 (Hebrew); Zvi Adiv, 'Zeev Jabotinsky's Zionist Thought' in Ben-Zion Yehoshua and Ahron Kedar (eds), *Ideological And Political Zionism* (Jerusalem, Zalman Shazar Center, 1978) 115 (Hebrew).

(iv) Negating exile: Hebrew culture as the antithesis of the Jewish culture in the Diaspora

The fourth approach to the evolving culture in Eretz Israel was founded on a concerted attempt to constitute it in opposition to the Jewish culture of the Diaspora. The most determined version of this approach was developed by Micha Yosef Berdyczewski.[30]

Berdyczewski was scathing in his criticism of Jewish life in the Diaspora (meaning Eastern Europe). He portrayed it as being stringently and rigidly ruled by the archaic prescriptions of the Halakhah, which prevented Jews from leading a free, earthly, natural, and full life. He therefore called upon Jews to return to their homeland to establish a normal life there, like that of other peoples.[31] 'Here the Zionist rejection of Galut [Exile] found its most radical interpretation,' writes Ehud Luz. 'The Exile, with all its negative connotations, was not the result of a political catastrophe, but was immanent within the very nature of Judaism. Consequently, redemption from Galut was bound up with rejection of historical Judaism.'[32]

Berdyczewski disagreed with Ahad Ha-Am, who had envisaged a smooth transmutation of halakhic Judaism into Jewish nationalism. Contrary to Ahad Ha-Am, Berdyczewski perceived the creation of a new Hebrew culture in Eretz Israel as a rupture in the history of the Jewish people, ie, as the beginning of an entirely new chapter in that history, and a radical departure from the halakhic Jewish culture of the Diaspora. The culture that had developed in the course of the people's abnormal existence in exile could not possibly be suited to the normal national life of a people in its land. For the purposes of this new chapter in Jewish history, Judaism would have to return to its ancestral, pre-exilic past, which had been choked by the exilic rabbinic tradition, and combine that with an extensive reliance on European culture. We must be the 'last Jews' and the 'first Hebrews,' Berdyczewski wrote.[33]

---

[30] Micha Yosef Berdyczewski (1865–1923) was a prominent Hebrew writer who greatly influenced Zionism, particularly the Labor movement in Eretz Israel, in the first decades of the twentieth century.

[31] *The Writings Of Micha Yosef Berdyczewski* (Tel Aviv, Dvir, 1960) (Hebrew).

[32] Luz, above n 1, at 166.

[33] Berdyczewski, n 31 at 33, 35, 36, 42. See also: Avner Holtzman, *Essays On Micha Josef Berdyczewski (Bin Gurion)* (Tel Aviv, Reshafim, 1993) (Hebrew); Avner Holtzman, *Literature And Life—Essays On M. J. Berdyczewski* (Jerusalem, Carmel, 2003) (Hebrew); Gideon Shimoni, 'The Theory and Practice of Shlilat Hagalut Reconsidered' in Anita Shapira, Jehuda Reinharz and Jay Harris (eds), *The Age Of Zionism* (Jerusalem, Zalman Shazar Center, 2000) 45 (Hebrew).

C. THE CULTURE THAT EVOLVED IN ERETZ ISRAEL IN THE FIRST HALF OF THE TWENTIETH CENTURY

(a) A culture 'from scratch' in negation of exile

While Zionist thinkers were still intensively debating the character of the evolving culture in Eretz Israel, that culture began actually to take shape. In the period from the 1880s until the establishment of the State of Israel in 1948, a new society was created in Eretz Israel with a specific culture, distinct from the Jewish culture of the ultra-Orthodox 'Old *Yishuv*' in Eretz Israel, as well as from the cultures of the Diaspora Jews.[34]

What characterized this culture was its construction from scratch, as a novel and original endeavor in both its contents and its establishments. (Even so, as I show below, a culture cannot possibly be created *ex nihilo*. The new culture thus drew extensively on contents borrowed from traditional Judaism and from European culture.) It was with a high level of awareness that the creators and disseminators of the new culture (intellectuals, educators, writers, artists, journalists, and so forth) took part in this process. They understood the magnitude of their endeavor—the creation from scratch of a comprehensive national culture that would offer a secular alternative to halakhic culture, and that would constitute the 'new Jewish man' of Zionism.

Though the creators and disseminators of the new culture were involved in many arduous disputes concerning the specific contents that were to become part of it, they did agree on the basic principle at the foundation of

---

[34] Itamar Even Zohar, 'The Emergence and Crystallization of Local Native Hebrew Culture in Eretz Israel 1882–1948' (1980) 16 Cathedra For The History Of Eretz Israel And Its Yishuv 165 (Hebrew); Yaacov Shavit, *Hebrew Culture and Culture in Hebrew*, id, at 190 (Hebrew); Itamar Even Zohar, 'Who is Afraid of Hebrew Culture' in Aharon Amir, Guy Ma'ayan and Amir Or (eds), *Ah'eret (Otherwise)—Miscelleneous Essays* (Jerusalem, Carmel, 2002) 38 (Hebrew); Ya'acov Shavit, *From Hebrew To Canaanite* (Tel Aviv, Domino, 1984) chapter 9; Yaacov Shavit, 'Culture and Cultural Status: Basic Developments in Hebrew Culture During the Second Aliya Period' in Israel Bartal (ed), *The Second Aliya—Studies* (Jerusalem, Yad Ben Zvi, 1997) 343 (Hebrew); Yaacov Shavit, 'Supplying a Missing System—Between Official and Unofficial Popular Culture in the Hebrew National Culture in Eretz-Israel' in Benjamin Z. Kedar (ed), *Studies In The History Of Popular Culture* (Jerusalem, Zalman Shazar Center, 1996) 327, 330 (Hebrew); Zohar Shavit, 'Introduction', in Zohar Shavit (ed),*The History Of The Jewish Community In Eretz-Israel Since 1882* (Jerusalem, Israeli Academy for Sciences and Humanities, 1998) vol 1, 1 (Hebrew); Benjamin Harshav, 'The Revival of Eretz Israel and the Modern Jewish Revolution: Reflection on the Situation', in Nurith Gertz (ed), *Perspectives On Culture And Society In Eretz Israel* (Tel Aviv, Open University Press, 1988) 7 (Hebrew); Baruch Kimmerling, *Immigrants, Settlers, Natives—The Israeli State And Society Between Cultural Pluralism And Cultural Wars* (Tel Aviv, Am Oved Publishers, 2004) chapter 2 (Hebrew); Yael Zerubavel, *Recovered Roots* (Chicago, University of Chicago Press, 1995) chapter 1; Moti Zeira, *Rural Collective Settlements And Jewish Culture In Eretz Israel During The 1920s* (Jerusalem, Yad Ben Zvi, 2002) (Hebrew); Charles S. Liebman and Eliezer Don-Yehiha, *Civil Religion In Israel* (Berkeley, University of California Press, 1983).

their endeavor, namely that the new culture should be the antithesis of the Jewish culture of Eastern Europe. The new culture, then, was founded on a series of such antitheses: Hebrew vs Yiddish, physicality vs spirituality, rootedness vs detachment, heroism vs impotence, old vs new. Accordingly, the chief constituent in the self-definition of those growing up in the new culture was that their identity was the opposite of the exilic Jew (of Eastern Europe).

As part of this contrast between the evolving culture of Eretz Israel and the Jewish culture of the Diaspora, Hebrew (in its Sephardic version, rather than the Ashkenazi idiom used in Eastern Europe) was adopted as the language of the new society. Moreover, the creators and disseminators of the new culture circumvented the Halakhah—the Jewish *oeuvre* of the exilic period—cultivating in its place identification with the pre-exilic legacy and granting primacy to the Bible, which was composed in Eretz Israel and presents an account of events that took place in Eretz Israel prior to the exilic chapter in the history of the Jewish people.[35] (For which reason novelist A.B. Yehoshua has defined Zionism as a 'backward-looking revolution').[36] Furthermore, they also anchored a self-perception of this culture through the category of 'Hebrewness': People who lived in the new society perceived themselves as living in a 'Hebrew culture' and as having a 'Hebrew' personal identity.

Consequently, the Jewish society coming together in Eretz Israel was called 'the Hebrew *Yishuv*,' as opposed to the Jewish people in exile. The Labor Federation (*Histadrut*) was called 'The General Federation of the Hebrew Workers in Eretz Israel.' The writers' association was called 'The Association of Hebrew Writers.' The literature created in the new society was called 'Hebrew literature.' Popular songs were called 'Hebrew songs.' The theater was called 'Hebrew theater.' The slogans of the period spoke of a 'Hebrew state,' 'Hebrew labor' and 'Hebrew youth.' The motto of 'The Young Laborer' (*Ha-Poel Ha-Tsa'ir*) (a key labor-affiliated party established in 1905) was: 'Our world stands on three things: Hebrew land, Hebrew labor, and the Hebrew language.' Tel Aviv was called 'the first Hebrew city.' The university in Jerusalem (established in 1925) was called 'The Hebrew University.' The national law that jurists sought to create for the emerging Jewish society was called 'Hebrew law' (see Chapter 2 below). When established, the Israel Defense Forces were known as the

---

[35] Anita Shapira, *The Bible And Israeli Identity* (Jerusalem, Magnes Press, Hebrew University, 2005) (Hebrew); Anita Shapira, 'The Religious Motives of the Labor Movement' in Shmuel Almog, Jehuda Reinharz and Anita Shapira (eds), *Zionism And Religion* (Jerusalem, Zalman Shazar Center, 1994) 301 (Hebrew).

[36] A.B. Yehoshua, 'A Revolution, Nonetheless' in Ruvik Rosenthal (ed), *The Heart Of The Matter—Redefining Social And National Issues* (Jerusalem, Keter Publishing House, 2005) 58 (Hebrew).

'Hebrew army.' And when the state was created, the first stamps bore the inscription 'Hebrew mail.'

Israel's Declaration of Independence adopted the distinction between the 'Jewish people' and the 'Hebrew *Yishuv*' (the pre-state new Jewish society formed in Eretz Israel), stating that those assembled to declare the establishment of the state were the 'representatives of the Hebrew *Yishuv*.' Although the Declaration referred to the 'Jewish people throughout the Diaspora,' it pointedly mentioned the contribution of the 'Hebrew *Yishuv*' to the defeat of Nazi evil in World War II. Extending the new state's hand in peace to the neighboring Arab states and their peoples, it called on them to cooperate with 'the sovereign Hebrew people settled in its land.'

Unquestionably, the highest point in the triumph of the evolving Hebrew culture over the Jewish culture of the Diaspora was the moment of Israel's establishment on May 14, 1948. Ever since the 1950s, however, the self-identity of those living in the new culture in terms of 'Hebrewness', and the 'negation of the exile' that was part of it, has been losing stature. Increasingly, room has been given to a self-identity in terms of Jewishness; to interest in traditional Jewish culture; and to the employment of cultural elements taken from this culture. The many causes for these developments have included information about the Holocaust; the encounter with Holocaust survivors; the Eichmann trial of 1961; the immigration to Israel during the 1950s of hundreds of thousands of Jews from Arab countries, who were deeply attached to the Halakhah and to Jewish culture and wished to go on defining themselves above all as Jews; the fact that the Hebrew culture created in Eretz Israel included many contents derived from Jewish tradition; and the encounter with the biblical territories of Judea and Samaria in the wake of the Six Day War of 1967. This process of strengthening the Jewish components in the culture and in the identity of those living in the culture at the expense of its Hebrew components has been ongoing since the creation of the State of Israel to the present day, so much so that for many years now few Israelis, if any, would define their identity as 'Hebrew'. Rather, they would perceive themselves as 'Jewish' and as 'Israeli'.[37] Also, it would not be an exaggeration to say that, striking

---

[37] Anita Shapira, 'Elements of the National Ethos in the Transition to Statehood' in Jehuda Reinharz, Gideon Shimoni and Yosef Salmon (eds), *Jewish Nationalism And Politics—New Perspectives* (Jerusalem, Zalman Shazar Center, 1996) 253 (Hebrew); Hanan Hever, 'An Imagined Native Community: Canaanite Literature in Israeli Culture', (1999) 2 Israeli Sociology 147 (Hebrew); Shmuel Almog, 'The Metaphoric Pioneer v. the Exilic Old Women', in Anita Shapira, Jehuda Reinharz and Jacob Harris (eds), *The Zionist Age* (Jerusalem, Zalman Shazar Center, 2000) 91 (Hebrew); Anita Shapira, 'Where has Negation of Exile Gone to?' 25 Alpaim (2003) 9 (Hebrew); Dan Laor, '"I am Hearing America Singing!"—On One Aspect in the Canaanite Worldview' 11 New Keshet (2005) 148 (Hebrew); Even Zohar, *The Emergence and Crystallization of Local Native Hebrew Culture*, above n 34; Zerubavel, above n 34, chapter 2; Harshav, above n 34; Shavit, *From Hebrew to Canaanite*,

as this may sound, for many years now, almost without exception, the only context in which the term 'Hebrew' has been in use in Israeli parlance is that of institutions established in the pre-state *Yishuv* period that are still extant and active (eg, the Hebrew University of Jerusalem).

(b) Borrowing contents from Jewish tradition and from European culture

I have noted that the culture of the new Jewish society in Eretz Israel was created from scratch in the context of creating a new society. Nevertheless, the new culture obviously could not rely only, or even mainly, on elements created within the new society. Creating a culture *ex nihilo* is impossible. Every culture is made up of a vast number of categories and practices, and the process of creating them requires the activity of many people over many centuries. Creating a rich, organic culture, therefore, cannot be accomplished in just a few years; it requires generations. Thus, in broad processes of 'cultural borrowing,'[38] the culture of the new Jewish society in Eretz Israel was fleshed out with many elements taken from the cultures with which the new Jewish society was in contact: Traditional Jewish culture, the cultures of Europe and English culture.

So even though the basic underlying principle of the new culture was its opposition to the Jewish culture of the Diaspora, in practice Jewish tradition, at all levels, was a key reservoir of cultural categories borrowed for the purpose of creating the new culture. In the spirit of Ahad Ha-Am's thought, these categories were given new, nationalist content.[39] A similar process is also evident at the linguistic level, where concepts taken from Jewish tradition, such as 'holiness,' '*mitzvah*' (commandment),

---

above n 34, at 292–7. S.N. Eisenstadt, *Changes In Israeli Society* (Tel Aviv, Ministry of Defense, 2004) chapter 9 (Hebrew).

[38] Cultural borrowing is a highly important source of cultural change. People living in one culture can come into contact with people living in another in a variety of ways—trade, regional trade associations, military conquest, the work of missionary religions, study abroad, tourism, immigration, multinational corporations, the work of NGOs, and current communication technologies. In the wake of such contacts, people may import cultural elements into their culture. See: Martinez, 'Cultural Contact: Archeological Approaches' (2001) 5 Int'l Encyclopedia Of The Social & Behavioral Sciences; Arjun Appadurai, 'Global Ethnoscapes—Notes and Queries for a Transnational Anthropology', in Richard G. Fox (ed), *Recapturing Anthropology—Working The Present* (Santa Fe, School of American Research Press, 1991); Adam Kuper, *Culture—The Anthropologist's Account* (Cambridge, Harvard University Press, 1999) 13, 63, 67; Sewell, above n 2, at 54–5. On cultural borrowing as a source of change in the law, see: Patrick H. Glenn, *Legal Traditions of the World: Sustainable Diversity in Law* (Oxford, Oxford University Press, 2000).

[39] Ram Fruman, 'What Do Secular Jews Do in the Holidays? Secular Jews and Jewish Holidays' in Aviad Kleinberg (ed), *Hard To Believe: Rethinking Religion And Secularism In Israel* (Tel Aviv, Tel Aviv University Press, 2004) (Hebrew); Liebman and Don-Yehiye, above n 34, chapter 2; Zerubavel, above n 34, chapter 2.

'Torah,' 'covenant' and 'sacrifice,' were given new content.[40] In the wake of these processes, the new culture was more of a 'culture in Hebrew' than a 'Hebrew culture.'[41]

At the same time, the new culture borrowed extensively from European cultures and English culture, as well, adopting many categories and practices in all realms of life: politics, education, academic life, literature, art, economics, architecture, leisure, the family, gender relationships, and so forth.[42] Needless to say, immigrants to the new society were unable to relinquish their former mental categories and behavioral practices all at once merely for having arrived. The continued link with European cultures was also supported by the culture's self-perception as a modern and European culture.[43] Also, since the British ruled over Palestine for three decades (between 1918 and 1948), the new culture had contacts with English culture, as well. As I shall show in the next chapter, this has had far-reaching implications for the political culture and law not only of the new society, but also for those of the state of Israel, until this very day.

The new Jewish culture that crystallized in Eretz Israel was a secular culture: the place of religion in the public sphere of the *Yishuv* was limited. Secularism was also congruent with the self-perception of the emerging culture as an alternative to the Jewish culture of the Diaspora, which was perceived as a religious culture. Moreover, most of the immigrants to the new society were secular—some of them even prior to their immigration, others only following it.

As a result of these processes, the day-to-day life of the people living in the new culture was composed of cultural elements taken from four main sources: Jewish culture, European cultures, English culture, and the local culture. The respective strength of these components in the lives of various people varied according to their social and professional affiliations, the spheres of their activity, their places of residence, and their cultures of origin. Thus, in addition to a shared, common cultural layer, the new culture also included a range of distinctive cultural elements, adopted and

---

[40] Liebman and Don-Yehiye, above n 34, chapter 2; Zeira, above n 34.

[41] Shavit, Hebrew Culture and Culture in Hebrew, above n 34.

[42] Anita Shapira, 'The Myth of the New Jew' in *New Jews, Old Jews* (Tel Aviv, Am Oved Publishers, 1997) 155, 171 (Hebrew); Yaacov Shavit, *Judaism In The Greek Mirror And The Emergence Of The Modern Hellenized Jew* (Tel Aviv, Am Oved Publishers, 1992) 396–7 (Hebrew); Shavit, *Culture and Cultural Status*, above n 34; Yaacov Shavit, 'National Society and National Culture in Hebrew—Two Perspectives' (1984) 9 Ha-Tzionut 111, 114 (Hebrew).

[43] Shapira, id; Even Zohar, 'Who is Afraid of Hebrew Culture' above n 34; Shavit, 'Culture and Cultural Status' above n 34; Shavit, 'National Society and National Culture in Hebrew' id, at 114; Shavit, 'Judaism in the Greek Mirror' above n 42, at 394, 396–7; Amir Ben-Porat, *The Bourgeoisie— The History Of The Israeli Bourgeoisies* (Jerusalem, Magnes Press, Hebrew University, 1999) (Hebrew).

practiced by many different subgroups.⁴⁴ To a great extent, these four main cultural sources have played a central role in constituting Israel's cultural scene until this very day, with several modifications, however: the place of European culture and English culture has been taken over by American culture, following massive processes of Americanization that Israeli culture has been going through since the 1970s, particularly in the spheres of business, law and the media.⁴⁵ Also, it should be borne in mind that since the establishment of Israel in 1948 the country has had an Arab minority constituting some 20 percent of the population, with its own national culture and several religious cultures (Muslim, Christian, etc), so that it is not only the case that there are two national cultures in Israel—one Jewish and one Arab; there is also a multiplicity of religious cultures (see Chapter 7, below).

(c) The problem of cultural thinness

As a young culture, the new Jewish culture in Eretz Israel suffered from 'thinness' by comparison to both the rich and longstanding Jewish halakhic culture and European culture. As Eliezer Schweid writes, 'the scope of the Hebrew culture in Eretz Israel was too narrow, and the depth of its absorption from its own sources relative to what it drew from external sources was too sparse to enable the existence of a rooted selfness.'⁴⁶ Note,

⁴⁴ For many years, anthropologists have dealt with the cultures of small and cohesive societies where cultural elements are shared by a relatively large number of people. As a result, culture was perceived as enjoying a high degree of internalization and acceptance among those living in a cultural group. In recent decades, however, a new understanding of culture has emerged, according to which culture is a divided entity, composed of a large number of subcultures, each internalized by only a small number of individuals living in society. This does not mean, however, that there is no shared, thick cultural layer in every society. The state educational system, the media, the law and the state's mechanisms of cultural dissemination (rituals, awarding prizes, etc) create a widely shared cultural layer (as well as linguistic partnership) among a vast number of people living in any state. This is particularly so in states controlled by hegemonies (see chapter 5 below). Furthermore, religious communities also manage to create a high level of cultural uniformity among those belonging to them. But a distinction should be made between awareness of cultural elements and acceptance of them. Many people may know what the meaning of 'democracy', 'capitalism' and 'globalization' is, but this does not mean that they all give these concepts the same meaning. And yet, it can be said that all these people share a single 'semiotic system' and live in a single, shared 'semiotic community'. Sewell, above n 2; Neil J. Smelser, 'Culture: Coherent or Incoherent' in Richard Munch and Neil J. Smelser (eds), *Theory Of Culture* (Berkeley, University of California Press, 1992) 3; Swidler, *Culture in Action: Symbols and Strategies*, above n 2; Pierre Bourdieu, 'Rethinking the State: Genesis and Structure of the Bureaucratic Field' in George Steinmetz, (ed), *State/Culture—State Formation After The Cultural Turn* (Ithaca, Cornell University Press, 1999) 53; J.L. Harouel, 'Culture, Sociology of,' in (2001) 5 Int'l Encyclopedia Of The Social & Behavioral Sciences.

⁴⁵ Tom Segev, 'Facing Elvis' Statue', in *The New Zionists* (Jerusalem, Keter Publishing House, 2001) 42 (Hebrew).

⁴⁶ Eliezer Schweid, *Toward A Modern Jewish Culture* (Tel Aviv, Am Oved Publishers, 1995) 310–1 (Hebrew). See also: Yonathan Shapiro, *An Elite Without Successors* (Tel Aviv, Sifriat Poalim Publishing House, 1984) chapter 4 (Hebrew) (the source of the malaise of the new culture was its isolation from foreign cultures); Amnon Rubinstein, 'The Rise and Decline of the Mythological Tzabar' in *Being A Free People* (Tel Aviv, Schocken Publishing House, 1977) 101 (Hebrew) (as a result of the radical

however, that this may be accepted as a description of the new culture, but not as a description of the culture of those living in Eretz Israel in the first half of the twentieth century who brought with them many cultural elements and practices from their former eastern and central European countries, including, for some, the contents of Jewish religious culture. Put differently, the culture of the *Yishuv*, and afterwards Israeli culture, has been far richer in contents and practices than the narrower Hebrew culture constructed from scratch in the first half of the twentieth century.

And yet, voices could be heard throughout the twentieth century claiming that the detachment of the new culture from religious Jewish culture has bred cultural thinness and a depletion of meaning among those living in the new culture. The renowned literary and cultural critic Baruch Kurtzweil wrote time and again that the idea of constructing a secular Jewish culture was doomed from the outset: a culture detached from religious Judaism could not be deemed a 'worthy' culture. Kurtzweil writes with sheer contempt for attempts to found the new culture on notions of nationalism, statism and militarism; on socialism; and even on Western humanism. These cultural options are utterly incapable of filling the void created by the new culture's severance of its ties with religious Judaism. Likewise, Kurtzweil vehemently opposed Ahad Ha-Am's infusion of nationalist, cultural contents into religious Judaism. Ahad Ha-Am would bring the new secular culture right to the verge of 'a wide, open abyss,' he wrote.[47]

Literary expression of Kurtzweil's pessimistic conclusions can be found in David Maletz's novel *Ma'agalot* depicting life in a new kibbutz in the 1920s.[48] One of the members, an intellectual leader of the group, claims that participation in the nation-building project cannot make up for the hollowness and meaninglessness experienced as a result of the transition from religiosity to secularism.

Apparently, many kibbutz members underwent a similar experience some forty years later, as well, in the late 1960s and early 1970s. These people speak in terms reminiscent of those used by Maletz's protagonist—'spiritual emptiness' and 'rootlessness' caused by their detachment from traditional Jewish heritage—and provide another reaffirmation of Kurtzweil's thesis.[49]

---

novelty of the new culture, those who grew up in it in the 1930s and 1940s were 'immature', 'childish', and 'egocentric' persons).

[47] Baruch Kurtzweil, *Our New Literature—Continuation Or Turn*, 2nd edn, (Tel Aviv, Schocken Publishing House, 1965) (Hebrew); Baruch Kurtzweil, *The Struggle Over The Values Of Judaism* (Tel Aviv, Schocken Publishing House, 1969) (Hebrew); Baruch Kurtzweil, *Facing The Spiritual Perplexity Of Our Time* (Tel Aviv, Schocken Publishing House, 1976) (Hebrew).

[48] David Maletz, *Ma'agalot* (Tel Aviv, Am Oved Publishers, 1945) 152–6 (Hebrew).

[49] Yona Hadari, *Messiah Rides A Tank—Public Thought Between The Sinai Campaign And The Yom Kippur War 1955–1975* (Jerusalem, Shalom Hartman Institute, 2002) 96, 148, 149, 150, 152 (Hebrew).

Literary depiction of the sense of meaninglessness experienced by secular Israelis reached its peak with Yaakov Shabtai's great book *Past Continuous*. Shabtai portrays the transition from a collectivist to an individualist worldview in the 1960s and 1970s as having bred that sense of aimlessness and meaninglessness among secular Israelis living in Tel Aviv.[50] (In Chapter 5 I shall show that those same years saw the rise in Israel of religious fundamentalism, which depicted secular life in more or less the same terms).

D. CONCLUSION

The new Jewish culture which developed in Eretz Israel in the first half of the twentieth century was modern, Western and secular. For decades, therefore, it seemed as if the 'halakhic approach' in Zionism towards the character of the new culture had been resoundingly defeated. In the 1970s, however, with the decline of the labor-led hegemony and the rise of religious fundamentalism among religious Zionists, proponents of the halakhic approach embarked on a renewed effort to anchor Israeli culture in the Halakhah, thereby reopening the struggle over the character of Israeli culture (Chapter 5, below).

In the course of a brief period during the second half of the twentieth century—only one or two generations—the new Jewish culture in Eretz Israel underwent three significant metamorphoses: first, from a self-perception of Hebrewness, alienated from the contents of the Jewish exilic heritage, to a self-perception of Jewishness, identifying with these very contents and almost totally neglecting the category of Hebrewness; second, from a collectivist worldview, which considers the good life to consist of contributing to the national project, to an individualistic worldview that sees life as a project of personal self-determination; and third, from faith in socialism and in the far-reaching involvement of the state in the economy, to a deeply entrenched neo-liberal belief in capitalism, the 'free' market and 'small' government. The secular Jewish group, then, which had coalesced in the context of a new culture in the first place, underwent three acute cultural and identity changes in the course of a short span of time. These processes—the creation of a new culture, which subsequently went through three metamorphoses—put the secular Jewish group on shallow, shaky and incoherent ground when it engaged in its *kulturkampf* with the religious Jewish group in the waning decades of the twentieth century. By contrast, its rival, the religious Jewish group, draws on a rich and enduring culture.

---

[50] Yaakov Shabtai, *Past Continuous* (Dalya Bilu trans, Philadelphia, Jewish Publication Society of America, 1985).

In the following chapters I will show that the law created and applied in Israel's courts, with its ties to the rich Western traditions of humanism, natural law, natural rights and liberalism, is the element of Israeli culture that provided the secular Jewish group with a wealth of contents, the depth and the continuity it needed for its struggle. However, being a liberal law, Israeli law has gone hand in hand with, and even paved the way for, trends in Israeli culture such as individualism, atomism, hedonism, consumerism, lack of social solidarity, and an entire plethora of phenomena attaching to the neo-liberal worldview, all of which has created among many Israelis a sense of cultural shallowness, which, in turn, has strengthened religious-fundamentalist, anti-Western and anti-liberal trends in Israeli culture, and thereby weakened the stature of liberal law in Israel.

CHAPTER 2

THE CULTURAL STRUGGLES OVER THE SHAPING OF THE LAW

Questions concerning the cultural character of the Jewish society taking shape in Eretz Israel (Palestine) preoccupied not only Zionist thinkers (Chapter 1, above), but Zionist jurists as well. In the first half of the twentieth century a 'Movement for the Revival of Hebrew Law' was active in Eretz Israel. Its members strove to revive the Halakhah, the traditional law of the Jewish people, as part of the Zionist national renaissance. Their efforts were therefore aimed at fashioning the law of the Jewish society in Eretz Israel and the law of the future Jewish state in accordance with the contents of the Halakhah, after adaptation to modern jurisprudence and to the unique conditions prevailing in Eretz Israel.

The development of the law in the State of Israel, however, followed an entirely different course from what the jurists of the Movement for the Revival of Hebrew Law hoped for. During the thirty years of the British Mandate over Palestine (1918–1948), the local legal community underwent an extensive process of Anglicization. In its wake, the law of the State of Israel developed in close association with Anglo-American law and with the political theory that underlies it—liberalism. Proponents of the idea of reviving Hebrew law were critical of this choice of direction and strove to arrest it. During the first thirty years of statehood, however, their voice had little resonance and their status in the legal field remained marginal, while the ties between Israeli law and Anglo-American law remained close and undisputed.

The call for a linkage between Israeli law and the Halakhah was reasserted following two legislative developments in the 1980s and 1990s. The first was the enactment of the Foundations of Law statute in 1980, stating that among the sources for filling lacuna in the law are 'the principles of freedom, justice, equity, and peace of Israel's heritage.' The second was the enactment, twelve years later, in 1992, of the Basic Law: Human Dignity and Liberty, and Basic Law: Freedom of Occupation. These two Basic Laws defined Israel as a 'Jewish and democratic state.' The grant of standing to 'Jewish heritage' in the country's law and definition of Israel as a 'Jewish state' served as the basis for a claim that it is the legislative intention to develop Israeli law in affinity with the Halakhah. The figure who most actively promoted this claim was Supreme Court Justice Menachem Elon, *the* leading Israeli academic in the area of Hebrew law in the last generation. Another Supreme Court Justice, Aharon Barak, contested this view. The two judges engaged in a vigorous debate over the cultural orientation to be adopted in the development of Israeli law in the ensuing decades. The debate shed light not only on the two options relevant to the future development of Israeli law, but also on the two main cultural options between which the Jewish people has vacillated in the modern era: Western culture and traditional Jewish culture.

A. THE ATTEMPT TO CREATE A LINKAGE BETWEEN ISRAELI LAW AND THE HALAKHAH: THE MOVEMENT FOR THE REVIVAL OF HEBREW LAW

The Movement for the Revival of Hebrew Law was active in Eretz Israel from the early 1920s until the end of the 1940s.[1] Its members, who were mostly secular, viewed the Halakhah as an expression of Jewish national culture rather than a religiously binding corpus. Hence, they sought to shape the law of the future Jewish state in accordance with the contents of the Halakhah, after adaptation to modern jurisprudence and to the special conditions of life prevailing in Eretz Israel.

---

[1] Ronen Shamir, *The Colonies Of Law—Colonialism, Zionism And Law In Early Mandate Palestine* (Cambridge, Cambridge University Press, 2000); Ronen Shamir, 'Lex Moriandi: On the Death of Israeli Law', in Menachem Mautner, Avi Sagi and Ronen Shamir (eds), *Multiculturalism In A Democratic And Jewish State* (Tel Aviv, Ramot Publishing House, 1998) 589 (Hebrew); Assaf Likhovski, *Law And Identity In Mandate Palestine* (Chapel Hill, University of North Carolina Press, 2006) Chapter 6; Assaf Likhovski, 'The Invention of "Hebrew Law" in Mandatory Palestine', (1998) 46 Am J Comp L 339; Assaf Likhovski, 'Hebrew Law and Zionist Ideology in Mandatory Palestine', in *Multiculturalism in a Democratic and Jewish State*, id, at 633; Assaf Likhovski, 'Between Two Worlds: The Legacy of the Mandatory Judicial System in the Early Years of the State of Israel' in Yehoshua Ben-Arieh (ed), *Jerusalem And The British Mandate* (Jerusalem, Yad Ben Zvi, 2003) 253; Menachem Elon, *Jewish Law, History, Sources, Principles* (Jerusalem, Magnes Press, Hebrew University, 1988) vol 3, 1329–37 (Hebrew). The main publications of the movement are: S. Eisenstadt and P. Dikstein (eds), *Hebrew Law* (Tel Aviv, Hebrew Law Society, 1918) (Hebrew); M. Eliash and P. Dikstein (eds), *Hebrew Law* (Tel Aviv, Hebrew Law Society, 1926) (Hebrew); Asher Gulak, 'On Our Legal Life in Our Country' in Jacob Bazak (ed), *The Jewish Law And The State Of Israel* (Jerusalem, Mosad Harav Kook, 1969) 28 (first published in 'Ha-Toren', 1921) (Hebrew); Elazar L. Globus, 'The Jewish Court' (1947) 4 Hapraklit 111 (Hebrew); Paltiel Dikshtein, 'Political Independence and Legal Independence' (1948) 5 Hapraklit 107 (Hebrew); Samuel Eisenstadt, 'The State and the Law' (1948) 5 Hapraklit 113 (Hebrew); Samuel Eisenstadt, *Zion In Justice* (Tel Aviv, Hamishpat, 1967) (Hebrew).

The Movement for the Revival of Hebrew Law was influenced by two sources:

The first was the thought of Ahad Ha-Am, who had proposed a cultural conception of Zionism, and called for a reshaping of Jewish culture by transforming its religious contents into categories of national culture (Chapter 1, above). Applying the thought of Ahad Ha-Am to the realm of the law, members of the Movement for the Revival of Hebrew Law suggested a conversion of the Halakhah's religious contents into legal, secular, and modern components. In that vein, they coined the concept of 'Hebrew law' in place of the Halakhah, so as to denote their intention to select and use only some sections of the Halakhah, which would also undergo secularization and updating.

The second source of influence on the Movement for the Revival of Hebrew Law was the historical school in jurisprudence, identified above all with its founder in German law, Friedrich Carl von Savigny.[2] Savigny, who was active in the first half of the nineteenth century, argued that the law is not a product of the conscious, rational planned processes of parliamentary legislation. Rather, in the spirit of Herder's view of nationalism, Savigny compared law to language, claiming that, like language, the law of a people develops gradually and spontaneously in the course of a people's history, and is embedded in the people's day-to-day practices. Thus, for Savigny law was something that comes into being, as opposed to being created, and the locus of law was not state legislation, but rather the daily customs and practices of a people and the notions and understandings prevalent among them.[3] Just as every people (*volk*) has a unique language of its own that embodies its unique spirit (*volkgeist*), so every people has a unique law of its own that embodies its spirit. It follows from this understanding that

---

[2] Carl von Savigny, 'On the Vocation of Our Age for Legislation and Jurisprudence' in H. S. Reiss (ed), *The Political Thought Of The German Romantics, 1793–1815* (Oxford, B. Blackwell, 1955) 203; Roger Berkowitz, *The Gift Of Science* (Cambridge, Harvard University Press, 2005) Chapters 6, 7; Edgar Bodenheimer, *Jurisprudence* (Cambridge, Harvard University Press, rev ed), 1974) 71–4; Hermann Klenner, 'Savigny's Research Program of the Historical School of Law and its Intellectual Impact in 19th Century Berlin' (1989) 37 Am J Comp L 67; Karl A. Mollnau, 'The Contributions of Savigny to the Theory of Legislation' (1989) 37 Am J Comp L 81; Mathias Reimann, 'The Historical School Against Codification: Savigny, Carter, and the Defeat of the New York Civil Code' (1989) 37 Am J Comp L 95; Mathias Reimann, 'Nineteenth Century German Legal Science' (1989) 31 BC L Rev 837; James E. Herget and Stephen Wallace, 'The German Free Law Movement as the Source of American Legal Realism' (1987) 73 Va L Rev 399, 405; Peter Fitzpatrick, *The Mythology Of Modern Law* (London, Routledge, 1992) 60, 114; H. S. Reiss, 'The Political Thought of the German Romantics' in H. S. Reiss (ed), *The Political Thought Of The German Romantics, 1793–1815* (Oxford, B. Blackwell, 1955) 1.

[3] In line with this view of law, Savigny regarded jurists as 'the people's guardians', whose task is not to substantively determine the contents of the law, but the more technical labor of distilling the people's law from its usages and customs and organizing it into a methodical system of concepts and rules to be enacted by the state's parliament. Thus, parliament was regarded by Savigny not as the creator of law, but merely as its legislator.

the law of one people cannot serve as the law of another, and that creating one universal law to serve all peoples is a misguided idea. (This stance was thus opposed to that of the modern natural law school, a product of the Enlightenment, and it developed out of controversy with the natural law school.)*

In that spirit, the Movement for the Revival of Hebrew Law held that, just as reviving the people's language, Hebrew, was part of the national renaissance of the Jewish people, the Jewish people should also return to its own law, the Halakhah, which embodies its unique spirit. By the same token, in the same way that one people cannot use the language of another, one people cannot use the law of another. Members of the movement therefore argued that the new Jewish society in Eretz Israel should not adopt English law (extensively introduced by the British in Eretz Israel in the first half of the twentieth century; see below) and make it its law.

In the 1920s, the Movement for the Revival of Hebrew Law established two periodicals and two publishing houses. It also held a series of academic conferences. Its activity reached its peak in 1935, when it established the Higher School of Law and Economics in Tel Aviv (which some 35 years later became the Faculty of Law at Tel Aviv University). One of the School's main aims was to train jurists who could work to promote the idea of reviving Hebrew law. Indeed, the curriculum at the School placed emphasis on the teaching of Hebrew law.

The Movement for the Revival of Hebrew Law declined in the 1940s, for several reasons. First, it encountered stubborn opposition from the rabbinic establishment and religious circles. These groups felt threatened by the Movement's perception of the Halakhah as embodying the culture of the Jewish people, as opposed to its being a religiously binding legal system regulating the lives of believers. Second, the movement encountered opposition in the legal community, which, as part of the Anglicization of the law of Eretz Israel, had become deeply committed to English law and held that the law of the new Jewish society should be developed in association

---

* The Enlightenment gave birth, in the course of the seventeenth and eighteenth centuries, to a resurgence of natural law doctrine. In the spirit of the Enlightenment, natural law advocates of the time argued that law should not be developed in close connection to particular local customs; rather, it needs to be developed in light of the universal dictates of human reason, so that the same law, a product of reason, would apply in all legal systems. This, in turn, sparked a codification movement in Europe. A code attempts to regulate social reality by applying human reason to the normative regulation of social interaction in advance, in a rational and abstract manner. The most famous code at the beginning of the nineteenth century was the French Code Civil of 1804, also known as the Code Napoleon. In the years subsequent to the enactment of the French Civil Code, suggestions were made in Germany that a similar code be enacted. Savigny came out against these suggestions. Following Savigny's position, throughout the nineteenth century German jurists studied the historical contents of German law, and it was only after the completion of this project that the German Civil Code (BGB) of 1896 was enacted.

with it. Third, since the Movement perceived Zionism in cultural terms, it failed to muster the support of the Zionist establishment, whose aim was the political fulfillment of Zionism by the establishment of a state. Fourth, the Movement's demand that the Halakhah, a law created in exile, should serve as the basis for fashioning the law of the new Jewish society in Eretz Israel, collided with a central principle of Zionism in the first half of the twentieth century, namely that the Jewish national renaissance must bypass the chapter of Jewish life in exile and identify itself instead with the biblical pre-exilic era in the history of the people (Chapter 1, above). Fifth, also active in the Movement were some religious jurists, who were opposed to the secularization and updating of the Halakhah and sought to apply it as is. Disputes between these jurists and the Movement's secular members adversely affected its options for action.

In the second half of the twentieth century, following the decline of the Movement for the Revival of Hebrew Law, the idea of reviving Hebrew law was exclusively appropriated by Jewish religious jurists. The demand to embrace the Halakhah in Israeli law, once identified with the cultural revival approach in Zionism, became increasingly identified with the halakhic approach. The proposals of these jurists never achieved more than marginal standing in Israel's legal field and political system.[5] Yet, as I shall show below, legislation enacted by the Knesset in the early 1980s and early 1990s instilled new life into the option of tying Israeli law to the Halakhah.

B. THE ANGLICIZATION AND LIBERALIZATION OF THE LAW

(a) The Anglicization of the law

Cultural borrowing is an important channel for cultural development and change.[6] One means of fostering intercultural contact and cultural borrowing is military occupation. In the course of the thirty years of the British Mandate over Palestine (1918–48), extensive borrowing from English law

---

[5] Likhovski, *Hebrew Law and Zionist Ideology in Mandatory Palestine*, above n 1, at 639; Mehachem Elon, 'More About the Foundations of Law Act' (1987) 13 Hebrew Law Annual 227, 252 (Hebrew); Mishael Cheshin, 'Jewish Heritage and the Law of the State' in Ruth Gavison (ed), *Civil Rights in Israel—Essays in Honor of Haim H. Cohen* (Jerusalem, The Association for Civil Rights in Israel, 1982) 47, 50 (Hebrew); Ahron Kirschenbaum, 'The Legal Foundation Law—Today and Tomorrow' (1985) 11 Tel Aviv U L Rev 117, 120 (Hebrew); Eliav Shochetman, 'Israeli Law and Jewish Law: Affiliation and Alienation' (1990) 19 Mishpatim 871, 876–7 (Hebrew); Ron Harris, 'Absent-Minded Misses and Historical Opportunities: Jewish Law, Israeli Law, and the Establishment of the State of Israel' in Mordechai Bar On and Zvi Zameret (eds), *On Both Sides Of The Bridge—Religion And State In The Early Years Of Israel* (Jerusalem, Yad Ben Zvi, 2002) 21 (Hebrew).

[6] On cultural borrowing see Chapter 1, above.

took place: the law in Eretz Israel and the local legal community underwent an intense process of Anglicization.

The British government in Palestine launched the process of Anglicizing local law in the early stages of its rule. Already in 1921, it founded a law school, the Jerusalem Law Classes.[7] The school's main aim was to serve as an institution for the professional training of Jewish and Arab jurists to assist the British in managing the local legal system. The school advocated a view of the law as an autonomous realm, distinct from society, which functions analytically and scientifically. In that spirit, a large part of the curriculum of the Classes was devoted to the study of English law (which was invalid in Palestine). The students were thus indoctrinated to think that English law was the most progressive of all laws and that it could be transplanted and applied without any problem in the Jewish and Arab societies of Palestine. At the time of the establishment of the State of Israel, graduates of the Jerusalem Law Classes made up a considerable part of the community of lawyers of the new state.

In 1935, a second law school was established in Eretz Israel: The Higher School of Law and Economics of Tel Aviv. As noted above, the founders of this school belonged to the Movement for the Revival of Hebrew Law and saw the law both as an organic product of a people's day-to-day practices, and as embodying that people's unique spirit. The agenda of this school thus challenged the central role played by English law in the local legal system and legal education, and sought instead to teach Jewish lawyers the fundamentals of Hebrew law. Because of this nationalist, anti-British stance, however, the School did not enjoy any support from the Mandate's administration, and obstacles were placed before its graduates' admittance to the bar. The School also failed to gain any support from the Zionist establishment or from the Hebrew University of Jerusalem (established in 1925). Thus, of the two law schools active in Eretz Israel during the Mandate period, the one with a distinctive British orientation—the Jerusalem Law Classes—enjoyed a clear advantage.

An important tool in the Anglicization process of the law in Palestine was Article 46 of the Palestine Order-in-Council.[8] Its wording served as

---

[7] Assaf Likhovski, 'Colonialism, Nationalism and Legal Education: The case of Mandatory Palestine', in Ron Harris, Alexander (Sandy) Kedar, Pnina Lahav and Assaf Likhovski (eds), *The History Of Law In A Multi-Cultural Society* (Aldershot, Ashgate, 2002) 75; Likhovski, *Law and Identity in Mandate Palestine*, above n 1; Issachar Rosen-Zvi, 'Constructing Professionalism: The Professional Project of the Israeli Judiciary' (2001) 31 Seton Hall L Rev 760, 765–70; Assaf Likhovski, 'Legal Education in Mandatory Palestine' (2001) 25 Tel Aviv U L Rev 291 (Hebrew).

[8] The text of the Article reads:

The jurisdiction of the Civil Courts shall be exercised in conformity with the Ottoman Law in force in Palestine on November 1st, 1914, and such later Ottoman Laws as have been or may be declared to be in force by Public Notice, and such Orders in Council, Ordinances and regulations

a source for the application of English law in the realm of civil law (in the case of lacuna). In practice, however, the courts of Palestine, and later the courts of the State of Israel, broadly applied English precedents in *all* areas of the law, not only in the realm of civil law. (After British rule over Palestine ended, Article 46 remained part of Israeli law for twenty-two years, until 1980; see below.) As Mishael Cheshin, who would eventually become a Supreme Court Justice, wrote:

> Before the establishment of the State of Israel and after our national independence—we would draw endlessly on English law, never saying enough... A stranger studying the ways of English law in our land would be surprised to find that the whole earth was full of its glory, far beyond what would have seemed justified by the legal analysis of the texts.[9]

Furthermore, following the application of English law, the courts also applied, though to a lesser extent, precedents taken from other common law countries, such as the United States, Canada, and Australia.[10]

Prior to the establishment of the state, then, the legal community in Palestine functioned in a professional culture that was largely influenced by English legal culture and maintained close professional contacts with the English legal community. This situation lasted for many years after the establishment of Israel. Thus, in 1958, ten years after independence, religious MK (Member of the Knesset, Israel's parliament) Zerah Warhaftig

---

as are in force in Palestine at the date of the commencement of this Order, or may hereafter be applied or enacted; and subject thereto and so far as the same shall not extend or apply, shall be exercised in conformity with the substance of the common law, and the doctrines of equity in force in England, and with the powers vested in and according to the procedure and practice observed by or before Courts of Justice and Justices of the Peace in England, according to their respective jurisdictions and authorities at that date, save in so far as the said powers, procedure and practice may have been or may hereafter be modified, amended or replaced by any other provisions. Provided always that the said common law and doctrines of equity shall be in force in Palestine so far only as the circumstances of Palestine and its inhabitants and the limits of His Majesty's jurisdiction permit and subject to such qualification as local circumstances render necessary.

[9] Cheshin, above n 5, at 77.

[10] In the period 1948–1994, almost all citations of foreign legal sources in Supreme Court opinions were from common law countries, and European legal sources were cited only rarely. In the first decades of Israel's existence, citations from English sources far surpassed those from American sources. The 1980s, however, marked a change, with fewer citations of English sources and a growing number of American ones. In 1986, 1993, and 1994, Supreme Court opinions cited American legal sources more often than English ones. A steady trend in the opinions issued since 1948, however, has been the growth in the number of citations from Israeli sources and a decline in the number of foreign sources in case law. Yoram Shachar, Ron Harris, and Meron Gross, 'Citation Practices of Israel's Supreme Court: Quantitative Analysis' (1996) 27 Mishpatim 119, 152–9 (Hebrew).

A further channel for the application of English law in the law of Eretz Israel, and later in the law of the State of Israel, were the Ordinances enacted during the Mandate, whose wording was based on English statutes or on English common law. Some of these Ordinances included an explicit provision compelling the application of English law for interpretation and completion purposes. Daniel Friedmann, 'The Effect of Foreign Law on the Law of Israel' (1975) 10 Israel L Rev 192, 193, 224. Some of these Ordinances have remained in force in Israeli law to this very day.

(who would later become chairman of the Knesset's Constitution, Law, and Justice Committee) said that

> by virtue of Article 46 of the Palestine Order-in-Council, large portions of English law, both quantitatively and qualitatively, have been introduced into Israeli law ... Even laws enacted by the Knesset are interpreted in light of English law, and, in this sense, we have in effect remained an English colony.

Warhaftig also commented sarcastically on an international conference of jurists convened several weeks previously in Jerusalem;

> The Hebrew jurists obsequiously attended to their honorable guests, the English lawyers, and assured them we go to great lengths when studying their decisions. We even advised them to study Hebrew so that they might see for themselves how well we interpret their precedents.[11]

In 1980, MK Warhaftig said that 'the State of Israel has remained, to some extent to this day, a legal province within the domain of English common law.'[12] And in the late 1980s, Supreme Court Justice Menachem Elon wrote that the recourse of Israeli jurists to English law 'was and is a daily occurrence, taking place as a matter of course.'[13]

(b) The courts as agents of liberal values

Since the creation of Israel, the Supreme Court has unquestionably perceived itself, above all, as an organ of the Zionist state. But the Court's great historical contribution has been to entrench some of liberalism's central values in Israel's state institutions, political culture and society.

Following the Anglicization process that the Jewish legal community in Eretz Israel underwent, Israeli law was applied by the Supreme Court and by the rest of the country's jurists (judges in other instances, lawyers, law professors, etc) out of deep attachment to English law, as well as to the laws of other common law countries. (Needless to say, neither the justices of the Supreme Court nor anybody else in the nascent legal system has taken a deliberate decision to apply the law in affiliation with Anglo-American law. Rather, the legal community acted within the context of the legal culture internalized by it in the course of its law studies and its practice in the legal field.) From the state's early days, therefore, being a jurist in Israel has implied a profound link not only to the legal doctrine of Anglo-American law, but also to the political theory of liberalism that lies at the foundation of this law and which its doctrines epitomize. Being a jurist in Israel has

---

[11] Motion of MK Zerah Warhaftig: Law for the Application of the Fundamentals of Hebrew Law, 1959, Divrei Ha-Knesset, 11.11.58, 231, 232.
[12] Fundamentals of Law Statute, 1978, Divrei Ha-Knesset, 11.2.1980, 1817, 1819.
[13] Elon, above n 1, at 1611.

meant internalizing, as well as applying in a practical, daily, ongoing fashion, a legal culture that embodies the principles of liberal political theory. Being a jurist in Israel has also implied academic exposure, through university courses on jurisprudence, political theory, sociology of law, and so forth, to the fundamentals of Western thought. The spectrum ranges from ancient Greece, through humanism, natural law and natural rights theories, to the liberalism of the last three hundred years, including the works of such thinkers as Plato, Aristotle, Thomas Aquinas, Grotius, Kant, Locke, Hobbes, Rousseau, Montesquieu, Bentham, Mill, Marx, Durkheim, Weber, and others. These processes of academic involvement with prominent Western thinkers have been greatly bolstered from the 1980s onward when Israel's legal academy, influenced by its American counterpart (again, through processes of cultural borrowing), underwent a paradigm shift, namely from the doctrinal study of the law to its evaluation in terms of its social implications and normative meaning, by drawing on all disciplines of the social sciences and the humanities.[14]

Applying Anglo-American legal doctrine, the Supreme Court instilled in the state's institutions, political culture, and society the perception that Israeli citizens are entitled to a series of 'basic rights' that create spheres protected from the reach of the state's power and that enable them to express their own views on the good life. As part of this endeavor, and following the realization in the early 1950s that the Knesset would not live up to the task of enacting a constitution, the Court began to present itself as the creator of 'an unwritten constitution,' ie, as the protector of a series of fundamental political and civil rights and liberties that presumably are at the disposal of the state's citizens, unless explicitly overridden by Knesset legislation.[15] Ruth Gavison, Professor of Jurisprudence at the Hebrew University of Jerusalem, rightfully notes that the achievements of Israel's Supreme Court 'in the absence of a constitution, are at times even more impressive than those of the American Supreme Court, in the presence of a constitution and a Bill of Rights.'[16] And Menachem Elon, formerly a Supreme Court Justice, rightfully asserts, following the use of the

---

[14] Menachem Mautner, *Legal Education* (Tel Aviv, Ramot Publishing House, 2002) (Hebrew); Menachem Mautner, 'Beyond Toleration and Pluralism: The Law School as a Multicultural Institution' (2002) 7 Int'l J Legal Profession 55.

[15] HCJ 112/77 *Fogel v Broadcasting Authority*, 31(3) PD 657, 664, Justice Landau (arguing that '[t]he development of our case law...is founded on the protection...of civil liberties, although these "are not written in a book." This is how we have achieved a kind of Bill of Legal Rights, resembling other similar Bills written in the constitutions of other countries'); HCJ 953/87 *Poraz v the Mayor of Tel Aviv-Jaffa*, 42(2) PD 309, 330, Justice Barak (arguing that fundamental values of the Israeli legal system 'derive from the very essence of Israel's democratic regime, and from the very essence of the individual as a free person...These values are part of our unwritten constitution').

[16] Ruth Gavison, 'Constitutional Law' (1990) 19 Mishpatim 617, 619 (Hebrew).

term 'constitutional revolution' to describe the changes in Israeli law in the 1990s (see below), that 'the revolution crown is the just due of the Supreme Court's founding fathers. They created and validated fundamental principles of human dignity and liberty through a vast and bold jurisprudence, *ex nihilo*, by virtue of profound belief and wondrous inspiration.'[17]

(c) 'Westwardness' v Judaism

It follows from the above discussion that Israel's legal community, headed by the Supreme Court, was a leading agent in the introduction of Western liberalism into Israel's state institutions, political culture and society. We could say that, according to the above mapping of the trends in Zionist thought regarding the character of the culture of the evolving new Jewish society in Eretz Israel, Israeli law was applied in adherence to the approach advocated by Herzl and Jabotinsky, who had envisaged a Jewish culture in Eretz Israel made in the image of European culture.

But just as secular Zionism has constantly had to confront the alternative offered by the rich religious Jewish culture of the last two and a half millennia, so Israel's secular liberal law has had to confront the Halakhah as a possible alternative for shaping state law. Indeed, there has been tension between the Supreme Court's Western law and Jewish law since the dawn of Israeli law, and the roots of this tension, as noted, date back to the early twentieth century, when the Movement for the Revival of Hebrew Law began its activities. From a broader perspective, this tension dates even farther back to the rise of the Jewish Enlightenment in the second half of the eighteenth century (Chapter 1, above).

Moshe Smoira, the first Chief Justice of the Supreme Court, speaking at the Court's inaugural ceremony, allowed only limited room for Jewish law in the future jurisprudence of the country's courts.[18] Smoira was well aware that Israeli law would develop in strong affinity with Anglo-American law, rather than with the Halakhah. Indeed, it is the overwhelming consensus among Israel's jurists that in six decades of statehood the influence of Jewish law has been little felt in Israeli law, particularly in the jurisprudence of the Supreme Court.[19] As noted by Ron Harris, a legal historian at Tel Aviv University, the status of Jewish law in the state's law has remained

---

[17] Menachem Elon, 'The Basic Laws: Their Enactment, Interpretation and Expectations' (1995) 12 Legal Research 253, 256–7 (Hebrew).

[18] Moshe Smoira, 'The Address of the President of the Supreme Court at the Opening Ceremony' (1949) 5 Hapraklit 187 (Hebrew).

[19] Motion of MK Zerah Warhaftig: Law for the Application of the Fundamentals of Hebrew Law, 1959, Divrei Ha-Knesset, November 11 1958, p 231; Sinai Deutch, 'Jewish Law in Israeli Courts' (1988) 6 Legal Research 7 (Hebrew); Cheshin, above n 5, at 50; Kirschenbaum, above n 5; Shochetman, above n 5, at 876–7.

'marginal,' a kind of 'thin husk of Judaism, evident more in the rhetoric and in the minority opinions of isolated judges.'[20]

As I will show further in the remainder of this chapter, however, Knesset legislation forced the Israeli legal community to contend, on two occasions, with the existence of the Halakhah as an alternative to Israeli law in its current form. This legislation honed the tension between these two large legal-cultural options, which had prevailed since the early twentieth century and the emergence of the Movement for the Revival of Hebrew Law.

C. THE FOUNDATIONS OF LAW STATUTE AND THE PLACE OF 'ISRAEL'S HERITAGE' IN ISRAELI LAW

In 1980, the Knesset enacted the Foundations of Law 5740-1980 statute. Section 2(a) revoked Article 46 of the Palestine Order-in-Council that dictated recourse to English law to fill any lacunae in Israeli law. Section 1 of the statute states:

> Where the court, faced with a legal question requiring decision, finds no answer to it in statute law or case-law or by analogy, it shall decide it in the light of the principles of freedom, justice, equity and peace of Israel's heritage.

In the three decades that have elapsed since the enactment of the Foundations of Law statute, whatever effect it may have had on the courts' mode of functioning has hardly been felt. The courts are deeply attached to Anglo-American law and understand the implied threat that Jewish law poses to the current identity of Israeli law. Also, the Foundations of Law statute tries to set a kind of 'recipe' for judicial decision-making processes, but these are highly complex intellectual processes, close to the practical wisdom model, which cannot be confined within the bounds of a procedure.

At the level of principle, however, the Foundations of Law statute is still highly significant. It has compelled the Israeli legal community to confront fundamental questions about Israeli identity in general, and about the identity of Israeli law in particular. The ensuing deliberations have clarified the cultural options available to Israeli law for its future development, and the sources from which it may draw inspiration.

The Foundations of Law statute generated intense controversy between two Supreme Court justices: Aharon Barak and Menachem Elon.

---

[20] Harris, above n 5, at 23, 55.

In Barak's view, the law was to be interpreted in such a way that recourse to the 'principles of Israel's heritage' would only rarely be required. He saw the law as made up of four cumulative layers: statutory law at the top, below it case law, below that analogy, and 'the principles of Israel's heritage' at the bottom. Furthermore, Barak gave broad meaning to each of the three upper layers, so that it would only seldom be necessary to dip into the bottom layer. Barak also interpreted the term 'principles of Israel's heritage' in a way that distanced it from the Halakhah.[21] In his view, the term does not directly refer to the Halakhah—a legal system 'whose provisions most of the public is not ready to live by.'[22] According to Barak, then, 'Israel's heritage' is:

a national concept that embraces the heritage of the nation, old and new together. It reflects the people's historical continuity. It includes the legacy of Maimonides and that of Spinoza; the legacy of Herzl and that of Ahad Ha-Am; the legacy of the time preceding the creation of the State of Israel and the legacy of the time that followed it; the legacy emerging from both halakhic and secular literature.[23]

Thus, by positing the principles of Israel's heritage as the lowest of four layers of legal sources, and by distancing the term 'principles of Israel's heritage' from Jewish law, Barak allocated a very limited role to Jewish law in the future development of Israeli law, even after the enactment of the Foundations of Law statute. In other words, Barak tried to maintain the future development of Israeli law on its traditional course, as a liberal system closely allied to Anglo-American law.

Menachem Elon perceived the Foundations of Law statute as intended to effect a radical change in the future development of Israeli law: Widespread invocation in Israeli law of contents drawn from the Halakhah. Elon's approach to interpreting the law was antithetical to that of Barak. He held there should be no impediment to having recourse to that layer of the law consisting of the principles of Israel's heritage. Elon also claimed that the

---

[21] Aharon Barak, *Judicial Discretion* (Tel Aviv, Papyrus Publishing House, 1987) 141 (Hebrew); Aharon Barak, 'The Foundation of Law Act and the Heritage of Israel' (1987) 13 Hebrew Law Annual 265, 270 (Hebrew); Aharon Barak, 'Judicial Creativity: Interpretation, the Filling of Gaps (Lacunae) and the Development of Law' (1990) 39 Hapraklit 267, 285 (Hebrew); Aharon Barak, 'Gaps in the Law and Israeli Experience' (1991) 20 Mishpatim 282, 315 (Hebrew).

[22] Barak, *Gaps in the Law and Israeli Experience*, id, at 320. A group of scholars supported Barak's view that the term 'principles of Jewish heritage' does not imply Jewish law: Guido Tedeschi, 'The Law of Laws' (1979) 14 Israel L Rev 145; G. Procaccia, 'The Foundation of Law Act 1980' (1984) 10 Tel Aviv U L Rev 145 (Hebrew); S. Z. Feller, 'The Application of the Foundations of Law Act in Criminal Law' in Aharon Barak et al (eds), *Sussman Book* (1984) 345 (Hebrew); Chaim Cohen, 'The Jewishness of the State of Israel' (1998) 16 Alpaim 9, 19 (Hebrew); Ruth Gavison, 'A Jewish and Democratic State—Political Identity, Ideology and Law' (1995) 19 Tel Aviv U L Rev 631, 635 (Hebrew).

[23] Barak, *Judicial Creativity*, above n 21, at 285.

notion of 'principles of Israel's heritage' should encompass elements drawn from the Halakhah. He argued that the term should be given legal content, ie, be seen as instructing the courts to apply the Halakhah as the main source for the future development of Israeli law.[24] Nevertheless, on one point he came close to Barak, acknowledging that 'Israel's heritage' may include 'the legacy of the movement of national renaissance.'[25]

Which of the Zionist approaches to the issue of culture is the most fitting rubric for Elon's stance? Prima facie, Elon's view would appear to belong to the halakhic approach. On closer scrutiny, however, it becomes apparent that Elon's outlook is closely associated with the cultural revival approach and the platform of the Movement for the Revival of Hebrew Law. For Elon, creating a linkage between Israeli law and Jewish law is a matter of cultural-national importance: further development of the unique law of the Jewish people—the Halakhah—and restricting the recourse of Israeli law to foreign sources, namely Anglo-American law.[26]

Justices Barak and Elon pursued their controversy over Israel's heritage as if Israel's population was exclusively Jewish. The fact that Israel's population includes a large Arab minority did not intrude into their dispute, nor did they consider the implications of applying 'Israel's heritage' to the Arab minority living in the country. This issue was first raised in 1938 by Moshe Silberg, who was appointed Supreme Court justice soon after the establishment of Israel. Silberg was opposed to turning the Halakhah into the law of the future state. One of his arguments was that the country has no 'moral right' to do so given that some of its citizens would not be Jewish.[27] The issue of Israel's non-Jewish citizens was raised in the deliberations following the enactment of the Foundations of Law statute by Ruth Gavison, who claimed that, since two national groups live in Israel, the country's legal system could not rely solely on the religion or the national legacy of one of them. Gavison also argued that the Foundations of Law statute increases the sense of inequality among Israel's Arab citizens because it more sharply delineates the country's Jewish national identity.[28] Silberg's and Gavison's comments point to an important characteristic of Israel,

---

[24] Elon, above n 5, at 233–41, 254 (Hebrew); Elon, above n 1, at 1547.

[25] Elon, above n 1, at 1548.

[26] Menachem Elon, 'Hebrew Law in the Law of the State' (1969) 25 Hapraklit 27, 51–3 (Hebrew); Elon, above n 1, at 1610–3, 1630–5; Elon, above n 17, at 285, 288; Elon, above n 5, at 227–30.

[27] Moshe Silberg, 'The Law of the Hebrew State' in *The Writings Of Moshe Silberg* (Jerusalem, Magnes Press, Hebrew University, 1998) 180 (Hebrew).

[28] Ruth Gavison, 'Introduction' in Ruth Gavison (ed), *Civil Rights In Israel—Essays In Honor Of Haim H. Cohen* (Jerusalem, The Association for Civil Rights in Israel, 1982) 9, 33–5 (Hebrew). This point was also raised by Shmuel Shiloh, who noted that Jewish law often applies different arrangements to Jews and non-Jews. Shiloh thus raised the question regarding how these provisions in Jewish law could be made part of the country's legal system. Shmuel Shilo, 'Comments and Some New Light on the Foundation of Law Act' (1987) 13 Hebrew Law Annual 351 (Hebrew).

'the zero sum game of Israel's multicultural situation': Any act meant to enhance the country's Jewish character will appeal to the religious Jewish group, but encroach upon the sensibilities of the Arab minority; and vice-versa, any dilution of the country's Jewish character will appeal to the Arab minority, but encroach upon the sensibilities of the religious Jewish group. (See also Chapter 7 below).

D. THE BASIC LAWS OF 1992 AND THE DEFINITION OF ISRAEL AS A 'JEWISH AND DEMOCRATIC STATE'

(a) Equating the status of the Jewish and Democratic-Liberal components in the future development of Israeli law

In 1992, twelve years after the enactment of the Foundations of Law statute, the Knesset enacted the Basic Law: Human Dignity and Liberty and Basic Law: Freedom of Occupation. These two Basic Laws stipulate that their purpose is 'to entrench in a Basic Law the values of the State of Israel as a Jewish and democratic state.'[29] The use of the formula 'the values of a Jewish and democratic state' in both Basic Laws was a further landmark, the second in a decade, requiring Israeli jurists to contend with fundamental questions touching on the cultural identity of Israeli law and the cultural identity of the country in general.[30]

The phrase 'Jewish and democratic state' led to a change in the relative weight of Jewish values in Israeli law. Until the enactment of the two Basic Laws, the courts and the legal community viewed themselves as operating within a liberal *Weltanschauung* balanced by another broad worldview, that of Zionism. Israel's legal community understood that Jewish law, with its rich lode of sophisticated materials, constitutes an option for the future

---

[29] Basic Law: Human Dignity and Liberty, section 1a: 'The purpose of this basic law is to protect human dignity and liberty, in order to entrench in a basic law the values of the State of Israel as a Jewish and democratic state.' Basic Law: Freedom of Occupation, Section 2: 'The purpose of this basic law is to protect freedom of occupation, in order to entrench in a basic law the values of the State of Israel as a Jewish and democratic state.'

[30] Dan Avnon, a political scientist from the Hebrew University of Jerusalem, writes that granting authority to the courts to determine the values of the State of Israel as a Jewish and democratic state, as was done in the two Basic Laws, 'constitutes a dramatic development in terms of Israel's political culture...The deepest ideological-political controversy splitting the Jewish public in Israel will henceforth be discussed in the courts as well.' Dan Avnon, '"The Enlightened Public": Jewish and Democratic or Liberal and Democratic?' (1996) 3 Mishpat Umimshal 417, 420 (Hebrew). Various scholars have been critical of the move of granting the courts the role of creating a balance between Israel's character as a Jewish state and its character as a democratic state: Ruth Gavison, *Can Israel Be Both Jewish And Democratic—Tensions And Prospects* (Tel Aviv, Hakibbutz Hameuchad Publishing House, 1999) (Hebrew); Gavison, above n 22; Ariel Rozen-Zvi, '"A Jewish and Democratic State": Spiritual Parenthood, Alienation and Symbiosis—Can We Square the Circle?' (1995) 19 Tel Aviv U L Rev 479 (Hebrew).

development of Israeli law, and worked to a large extent to limit its application in the law of the state. (This attitude towards Jewish law was exacerbated because, for their part, rabbinic courts applying the Halakhah hardly ever cited Knesset legislation and Supreme Court rulings in their opinions.[31] A kind of institutionalized 'acoustic separation'[32] was thus established between state law and Jewish law: State courts rarely applied Jewish law and rabbinic courts refrained from applying state law. See Chapter 7, below.)

The enactment of the two Basic Laws in 1992 led to a substantial change in the balance of power between liberalism and Judaism in Israeli law. Both Basic Laws state that, henceforth, the development of Israeli law should be guided by not only one pole of influence, liberalism, but two—liberalism and Judaism—requiring balances and compromises between them. In other words, the status of liberalism as the main source of inspiration in the development and fashioning of Israeli law has now been reduced, given the need to take into account another significant source of inspiration, Judaism.[33] Indeed, the term 'Jewish state' could possibly be used in the future as a basis for an argument that would require the Supreme Court to restrict the scope of application of basic rights in Israeli law when they clash with the element of Israel's Jewish identity, eg, when claims for equality are put forward by Arab citizens. (This obviously could have been the case even without the term 'Jewish state'. Any legal realist knows that the materials of the law are always so rich and complex that support may be found in them for any desired result. But the juxtaposition of the term 'Jewish state' beside 'democratic

---

[31] Supreme Court Justice Haim Cohen wrote in 1970: 'Rabbinic courts...are entirely oblivious to the laws of the country. Very seldom will you find any mention of a Knesset law in the decisions issued by rabbinic courts.' AH 23/69 *Yosef v Yosef*, 24(1) PD 792, 809. Itzhak Kahan, the former Chief Justice of the Supreme Court, wrote in 1976:

> The fact that the State of Israel exists has left no significant impression on the rulings issued by rabbinic courts, often giving the impression that a concerted effort is invested in ignoring the existence of the state.

Itzhak Kahan, 'Rabbinic and Secular Courts in Israel' (1976) 7 Dine Israel 205, 210 (Hebrew). Former Supreme Court Justice Mishael Cheshin has said: 'The rabbinical courts are running a state within a state. They don't recognize the state and they intentionally disregard its law.' Kobi Nachshoni, 'Cheshin: Expanding the Dayanim's Authority—The Road to Hell' (March 12 2010) Ynet.

[32] Meir Dan-Cohen, 'Decision Rules and Conduct Rules: On Acoustic Separation in Criminal Law' in *Harmful Thoughts* (Princeton, Princeton University Press, 2002) 37.

[33] Furthermore, Aharon Barak has said that:

> it is only natural that the provision concerning the values of the State of Israel as a Jewish and democratic state should not be exclusively limited to Basic Laws on human rights...The values of the State of Israel...anchored in the Basic Laws on human rights apply beyond the confines of these Basic Laws.

Aharon Barak, in Ron Margolin (ed), *Symposium: The State Of Israel As A Jewish And Democratic State* (Jerusalem, World Union of Jewish Studies, 1999) 8 (Hebrew).

state' would provide such a move with explicit legislative anchoring at the Basic Law level.)

Following the enactment of the two Basic Laws of 1992, a further dispute erupted between Justices Barak and Elon, this time concerning the meaning of the term 'Jewish state' and the relationship between Israel's Jewishness and its being a liberal-democratic state. (The term 'democratic state' has been widely perceived as referring not so much to democracy in the sense of a procedure, but rather to the substantive values of liberal-democratic political cultures.)[34] This dispute was a kind of 'second round' in the controversy between the two justices over the cultural orientation of Israeli law.

As expected, the significance of the phrase 'Jewish state' to Israeli law was not lost on Justice Elon, and he was quick to point it out. Elon emphasized that a new balance had been struck between the values identified with liberalism and democracy and those identified with Judaism.[35] Until the two Basic Laws, basic rights had been interpreted on the basis of the assumption that Israel was 'a democratic state, and only a democratic state,' wrote Elon.[36] Some judges had indeed referred to Jewish law in their decisions even before the enactment of the Basic Laws, but they had done so only due to their own personal recognition of the importance of applying Jewish law in the law of the Jewish state, rather than by virtue of any legal obligation. Following the enactment of the two Basic Laws, applying Jewish law became a legal duty incumbent on every judge, argued Elon.[37] This implied a 'revolutionary change' in the way the courts would henceforth have to act.[38] Elon also claimed that, since the term 'Jewish state' is mentioned first in the phrase 'Jewish and democratic state,' the Knesset had meant not only that the courts must henceforth develop Israeli law as Jewish law, but also that this duty is superior to that of developing the country's law as democratic law. Furthermore, Elon noted that in the case of the two Basic Laws—unlike that of the Fundamentals of Law statute, where Jewish values are a fourth legal layer preceded by three others—access to Jewish values is 'direct'. Hence, this time there was no validity to an interpretation such as the one suggested by Justice Barak to the

---

[34] Asher Maoz, 'The Values of a Jewish and Democratic State' (1995) 19 Tel Aviv U L Rev 547, 629 (Hebrew).
[35] Menachem Elon, in Ron Margolin (ed), *Symposium: The State Of Israel As A Jewish And Democratic State* (Jerusalem, World Union of Jewish Studies, 1999) 18 (Hebrew).
[36] Menachem Elon, 'Constitution by Legislation: The Values of a Jewish and Democratic State in Light of the Basic Law: Human Dignity and Liberty' (1993) 17 Tel Aviv U L Rev 659, 668 (Hebrew).
[37] Elon, above n 35, at 18. See also, Elon, id, at 659, 668, 677.
[38] Elon, above n 17, at 256–7.

Foundations of Law statute, which had precluded any possibility of applying Jewish law.[39]

Barak agreed with Elon concerning the essential change in Israeli law following the enactment of the two Basic Laws of 1992. In his view,

> in the past, the Supreme Court had dealt at length with the values of the State of Israel as a democratic state, but conducted no extensive discussion of the values of the State of Israel as a Jewish state.

After the enactment of the two Basic Laws of 1992, however,

> we are no longer allowed to confine ourselves to the democratic character of the State, and henceforth must also take into account both the character of the State of Israel as a democratic state and its character as a Jewish state.[40]

Furthermore, as I will show below, following the enactment of the two Basic Laws, the Halakhah became for Barak one of the two central components expected to instill content into the concept of a 'Jewish state' in the ongoing process of developing Israeli law.

It was in reference to the two Basic Laws of 1992 that Barak coined the term 'constitutional revolution.' His intention thereby was to demonstrate that the basic rights asserted in the Basic Laws had been raised to constitutional level, in a way enabling the Supreme Court to revoke Knesset laws found to violate these basic rights (see Chapter 3, below).[41] The enactment of the two Basic Laws, however, emerges as no less revolutionary in another context as well: whereas in the past the development of Israeli law had been expected to be governed by only one pole of inspiration—the secular, liberal pole of Anglo-American law—the two Basic Laws added an additional pole of inspiration for the future development of Israeli law, Judaism.

(b) A possible change in the contents of the concept 'Democratic State'

I have so far considered the first significant change that the phrase 'Jewish and democratic state' introduced into Israeli law: Equating the status of Judaism with that of liberalism as a source of inspiration for the future development of the law. A second significant change relates to the contents of the concept 'democratic state.'

Until the enactment of the two Basic Laws, it was clear that the law created and applied by Israel's courts serves as a means of introducing

---

[39] Elon, above n 36, at 672, 673.
[40] Aharon Barak, *Interpretation Of Law* (Vol 3, Constitutional Interpretation, Jerusalem, Nevo, 1994) 328 (Hebrew).
[41] Aharon Barak, 'The Constitutional Revolution: Protected Human Rights' (1992) 1 Mishpat Umimshal 9 (Hebrew). See also: David Kretzmer, 'The New Basic Laws on Human Rights: A Mini-Revolution in Israeli Constitutional Law?' (1992) 26 Israel L Rev 238.

liberal values into Israeli political culture. Following their enactment, claims began to be heard suggesting that the 'democratic state' concept entrenches the *formal* conception of democracy, which perceives it as a procedure for political decision-making, rather than its substantive conception, which is mainly concerned with ensuring citizens' fundamental liberal rights.[42] Should these voices find expression in the future jurisprudence of the Supreme Court, the Court will lose its most distinguishing feature among Israel's state institutions, namely its being a primary agent for the introduction of liberal values into the country's political culture. Thus, following the enactment of the two Basic Laws of 1992, the liberal values in Israeli law may not only be required to balance themselves against Jewish values, but find themselves exposed to far-reaching interpretations that seek to dilute them in the further development of the law.

(c) 'Jewish State'

The use of the phrase 'the values of a Jewish and democratic state' in the two Basic Laws of 1992 can be viewed as the 'official' conclusion of the conscious and deliberate endeavor by the Jewish society in Eretz Israel to create a Hebrew culture as a cultural entity distinct from the traditional Jewish culture of the Diaspora. It can also be viewed as recognition of the centrality that Israeli Jews attach to their identity and self-definition as Jews. (Note that the heyday of the idea of creating a Hebrew culture in Eretz Israel coincided with a legal document as well, the Declaration of Independence of the State of Israel on May 14, 1948; see Chapter 1, above.)

What content should be ascribed to the concept of a 'Jewish state'? This question lay at the core of the controversy between Justices Barak and Elon.

Aharon Barak proposed two components as contents of the 'Jewish state' concept. First, the values of the State of Israel as a Jewish state are

---

[42] Aviezer Ravitzky writes that:

[W]e need to talk about Israeli democracy in the narrow sense of the term: not as an embodiment of the basic values that prevail in a modern liberal society, but rather as a method of determination between conflicting and competing basic values.

Aviezer Ravitzky, 'On Israel as a Jewish and Democratic State' in Ron Margolin (ed), *Israel As A Jewish And Democratic State* (Jerusalem, World Union of Jewish Studies 1999) 50, 57–8 (Hebrew). The same approach has been suggested by Ruth Gavison. See: Gavison, above n 22, at 635–6; Gavison, above n 30, at 28–35. However, Gavison makes several important reservations. First, even formal democracy is a regime that embodies certain humanistic values. Second, formal democracy entails the existence of certain political rights. Third, and most importantly, a procedural perception of democracy does not mean giving up the commitment to human rights. Such rights should exist in any regime, so they should be protected even where a procedural perception of democracy has been adopted. For the counterargument that 'democratic state' means 'liberal state,' see: Maoz, above n 34, at 567; Barak, above n 40, at 336; Barak, above n 33, at 71.

the values derived from its being a 'a national home to the Jewish people.'[43] This claim may be viewed as a continuation of the stance adopted by Barak in the dispute surrounding the Foundations of Law statute, whereby the phrase 'the principles of Israel's heritage' is a 'national concept.'

Second, the values of the State of Israel as a Jewish state are the values derived from the Halakhah.[44] However, according to Barak the Basic Laws do not refer to the 'details of the laws,' but rather to the 'values,' 'worldviews' and 'basic principles' of the Halakhah.[45] 'The reference is to the abstract, rather than to the concrete. The reference is to the principle at the foundation of the rule, rather than to the rule itself,' wrote Barak.[46] These formulations seem intended to prevent the direct application of the Halakhah as part of Israeli law. In this context Barak mentioned the existence of Israel's Arab minority, writing: 'We should not forget that Israel has a considerable non-Jewish minority.'[47]

Despite Barak's reservations concerning the ways in which the Halakhah should be applied, he seems to have gone a long way toward positing a linkage between the Halakhah and the further development of Israeli law. Regarding the Foundations of Law statute, as noted above, Barak had proposed an interpretation that applies the principles of Israel's heritage in only a limited number of cases. He had also suggested a perception of the 'Israel's heritage' concept as a *national*, secular concept that includes the legacy of such figures as Spinoza, Herzl and Ahad Ha-Am, as opposed to a strictly *religious* concept. All the non-halakhic contents that Barak had ascribed to 'the principles of Israel's heritage' in the context of the Foundations of Law statute are no longer mentioned by him a decade later, when he turns to the contents of the 'Jewish state' concept. There is no trace of the immense effort that he had invested in his dispute with Elon on the Foundations of Law statute in order to restrict the place of the Halakhah in the future development of Israeli law. When filling the 'Jewish state' concept with content, Barak introduces the Halakhah into Israeli law as one of the two components that should play a key role in the continued development of the law, beside Zionism. At the same time, Barak disregards the rich output of Jewish creativity in non-halakhic realms throughout history, as well as the trove of secular Jewish creativity in recent centuries, particularly in the context of the Zionist endeavor. The striking difference between Barak in the 1980s and in the 1990s is unmistakable.

---

[43] Aharon Barak, 'The Enlightened Public' in Aharon Barak and Elinor Mazuz (eds), *Landau Book* (Tel Aviv, Bursi, 1995) 677, 692 (Hebrew). See also: Barak, above n 40, at 330; Barak, above n 41; Rozen-Zvi, above n 30, at 482.
[44] Barak, above n 40, at 330–1.
[45] Barak, above n 40, at 330. See also: Barak, above n 43, at 692.
[46] Barak, above n 40, at 330.   [47] Barak, above n 41, at 30–1.

As I will show in the discussion of Elon's approach in the following passages, due to the significant changes evident in Barak's approach, the gap between the two has considerably narrowed. Now Barak too, not only Elon, is ready to grant a central role to the Halakhah in the process of Israeli law's future development. Now Barak too, not only Elon, has confined the creative legacy of the Jewish people to the Halakhah, disregarding all other manifestations of Jewish, Hebrew, and Israeli creativity.

Continuing to maintain the view he had advocated in the dispute over the Foundations of Law statute, Menachem Elon writes that the 'Jewish state' concept must be filled with contents derived, first and foremost, from the 'enormous legal legacy'[48] of the Jewish people. Thus, whereas Barak thinks the Halakhah should be applied at the level of the 'values,' 'worldviews,' and 'fundamental principles,' Elon speaks of a *direct application* of the Halakhah as part of the 'Jewish state' concept.

Furthermore, Elon interprets the two Basic Laws as having prompted an essential change in the status of Jewish law within Israeli law. Henceforth, Jewish law is not supposed to be merely a source of inspiration and comparison, but a binding, active source in Israeli law. According to Elon too, then, as well as Barak, the other great revolution triggered by the two Basic Laws, beyond strengthening the constitutional layer in Israeli law, concerns the status of Jewish law within state law.

Like Barak, however, Elon also acknowledges the existence of a Zionist component within the 'Jewish state' concept. In his view, this concept includes 'values that have assumed special significance in the era of the national renaissance... that is, the values of Zionism.'[49]

(d) Reconciling the 'Jewish State' and 'Democratic State'

Justices Barak and Elon agree that the 'Jewish state' and 'democratic state' concepts should be interpreted as harmoniously as possible.[50] But what about cases of contradiction between the concepts 'Jewish' and 'democratic' (such as when Arab citizens argue that they are discriminated against because they cannot be included in the state's project of making Israel the nation-state of the Jewish people)?

---

[48] Elon, above n 17, at 259. See also: Elon, above n 36, at 670, 677.
[49] Elon, above n 17, at 260–1. See also: Elon, above n 35, at 17–8. Barak concluded the agreement between himself and Elon by writing:

> As far as Justice Elon...regards the values of a Jewish state as a complex of values, some religious-halachic ('Jewish heritage') and some Zionist ('Israel's heritage') I find myself in agreement with him.

Barak, above n 40, at 333–4.
[50] Barak, above n 40, at 338; Aharon Barak, 'Basic Law: Freedom of Occupation' (1994) 2 Mishpat Umimshal 195, 208 (Hebrew); Barak, above n 43, at 692; Barak, above n 33, at 12–4, 71; Elon, above n 36, at 663, 670; Elon, above n 17, at 258–69; Elon, above n 35, at 19.

Two main solutions for such cases emerge from Barak's writings. According to the first, in order to preclude contradiction between a 'Jewish state' and a 'democratic state,' the judge must choose sources from Zionism, the Halakhah, and democracy that are mutually compatible.[51] This approach, then, strives to find a shared area of overlap from among the wealth of contents encompassed by the concepts of 'Jewish state' and 'democratic state.'

The second solution is to apply the 'Jewish state' concept at a 'high level of abstraction...until it becomes compatible with the country's democratic character.'[52] In another formulation, Barak wrote that the values of a Jewish state are 'those universal values common to members of a democratic society, which grew out of Jewish history and tradition.' Barak mentions a series of such values: 'love of humanity, the sanctity of life, social justice, doing what is good and right, respecting human dignity, the rule of law.'[53] 'The reference to these values,' he writes, 'is at their universal level of abstraction, which is consistent with Israel's democratic character.'[54]

In this context Barak also mentions the fact that most of the population of Israel is secular and that some of its citizens are not Jewish. In his view, 'as long as the observant Jewish population is a minority among us...it is impossible to identify the values of the State of Israel as a Jewish state with those values of Judaism that are incompatible with a reality whereby the vast majority of the (Israeli and Jewish) public is not observant.'[55]

Barak's former solution—finding a common denominator for Jewish values and democratic values—is entirely different from the latter—applying the values of Judaism 'at a high level of abstraction.' The former solution necessitates finding an area of overlap between Jewish and democratic values. To judge by the latter solution, however, Barak appears to be placing himself within the democratic realm of values and gleaning compatible Jewish values. This is the 'cultural revival approach' in Zionism (Chapter 1, above), and it is also close to that of the Movement for the Revival of Hebrew Law (see above).

Menachem Elon was highly critical of Barak's latter solution. He opposed the application of only the 'Jewish state' concept at a high level of abstraction, but not the 'democratic state' concept. He also disputed Barak's claim

---

[51] Barak, above n 40, at 340.
[52] Barak, above n 41, at 30. See also: Barak, above n 43, at 692. John Rawls writes in a similar vein on the way to reach an 'overlapping consensus' that

> [s]ince we seek an agreed basis of public justification in matters of justice, and since no political agreement on those disputed questions can reasonably be expected, we turn instead to the fundamental ideas we seem to share.

John Rawls, *Political Liberalism* (New York, Columbia University Press, 1993) 150.
[53] Barak, above n 41, at 30. See also: Barak, above n 43, at 692.
[54] Barak, above n 41, at 30.   [55] Barak, above n 43, at 692.

that we should learn about the contents of Judaism 'out of what the entire world has accepted "at the universal level of abstraction", rather than out of the source that created them, that is, from the sources of Judaism and Israel's heritage.'

Why should we learn about the nature and essence of these fundamental rights in the world of Judaism from these values' mode of acceptance 'at their universal level', rather than as they emerged and developed in the jurisprudence and the literature that conceived them and in which they appeared to the entire world?

asks Elon.[56]

Elon also saw no reason why the concept of 'democratic state' should be awarded its 'full significance,' while the concept of 'Jewish state' be applied only 'as an appendix, a supplementary notion subject to the concept democratic.'[57] Quite the contrary, argued Elon: in the synthesis expected to emerge between the 'Jewish state' and the 'democratic state,' the former should dictate the contents of the latter.[58]

Following Elon's critique, Barak reconsidered his approach. In his new formulation, the 'Jewish state' and 'democratic state' concepts should be approached on equal terms. Both should be applied at the same level of abstraction. Barak also retreated from his claim that we should learn about the values of Judaism from the perspective of their universal acceptance. We should learn about both the values of Judaism and the values of democracy 'from "inside," according to the sources from which they were created and grew,'[59] he wrote. Barak, then, prescribed equality in the application of the values of Judaism and democracy for the purpose of determining the values of the State of Israel as a Jewish and democratic state.

E. CONCLUSION

The question regarding the cultural orientation of Israeli law has occupied Jewish jurists since the beginning of the twentieth century. In the first half of that century the claim was advanced by the Movement for the Revival of Hebrew Law that the Halakhah should be made a central element in the law of the Jewish state. That claim was rejected with the establishment of the State of Israel. Following the thirty years of British Mandate over

---

[56] Elon, above n 36, at 686.   [57] Id.

[58] Id, at 687. Several authors joined Elon's criticism. See: Gavison, *Can Israel be Both Jewish and Democratic*, above n 30, at 80; Rozen-Zvi, above n 30, at 496, 497, 508–10; Maoz, above n 34, at 624; Arye Edrei, 'Why Teach Jewish Law' (2001) 25 Tel Aviv U L Rev 467, 481 n 44 (Hebrew).

[59] Barak, above n 40, at 342–4. See also: Barak, above n 43, at 692. Ruth Gavison has written that 'in the dispute between Elon and Barak, Elon's arguments are fairly persuasive. Barak's position, even in its amended version, does not give any real meaning to the element of "Jewishness".' Gavison, above n 22, at 675.

Palestine, Israeli law developed in close association with Anglo-American law, with only a marginal place being accorded to the Halakhah. But two statutes enacted in the 1980s and 1990s gave new impetus to the claim that the Halakhah should play a central role in the future development of Israeli law.

As I shall show in Chapters 5 and 7, the 1970s witnessed the rise of religious fundamentalism among the religious-Zionist group in Israel. By implication, that undermined the legitimacy of the state's secular law, with its strong Anglo-American affiliation, and sparked a resurgence of the claim that the state's law should be founded on the Halakhah. Two additional developments have taken shape since the 1990s. First, religious-Zionist jurists have established a system of arbitration tribunals aimed at resolving civil disputes according to the Halakhah, in competition with the state's secular court system. Second, there have been calls for officially granting the Rabbinical Courts, which apply the Halakhah, the power to serve as arbitrators in civil disputes. These developments have also contributed to furthering the claim that the Halakhah should be made the prevailing law in the state.

CHAPTER 3

FROM JUDICIAL RESTRAINT TO JUDICIAL ACTIVISM

Three far-reaching changes were recorded in the jurisprudence of the Israeli Supreme Court during the 1980s and 1990s. The first was the rise of judicial activism, which will be discussed in this chapter. The second was the advent of a new style of reasoning, involving the open discussion of the law's normative meaning and distributive implications. Third, there was a change in the Court's perception of itself from playing a professional to playing a political role. The latter two changes will be discussed in Chapter 4. In Chapter 5, I will offer explanations for these changes tying them to the profound cultural and political changes that have taken place in Israel since the latter half of the 1970s.

A. THE CONCEPT OF JUDICIAL ACTIVISM AND THE RISE OF THE COURT'S ACTIVISM

The concept of judicial activism originated in the literature dealing with the jurisprudence of the American Supreme Court in the realms of constitutional and administrative law. This jurisprudence is often depicted as lying on a continuum between activism and restraint. The more the Court intervenes in decisions undertaken by other branches of state, ie, the greater the role it assumes vis-à-vis the other branches in determining the country's values and the allocation of its material resources, the more activist it is considered to be.[1]

---

[1] Kenneth M. Holland (ed), *Judicial Activism In Comparative Perspective* (Houndmills, Macmillan, 1991); Stephen C. Halpern and Charles M. Lamb (eds), *Supreme Court Activism And Restraint* (Lexington, Lexington Books, 1982); Obinna Okere, 'Judicial Activism or Passivity in Interpreting the Nigerian Constitution' (1987) 36 Int'l & Comp L Q 788; Clifford J. Wallace, 'The Jurisprudence of Judicial Restraint: A Return to Moorings' (1981) 50 Geo Wash L Rev 1; Phillip B. Kurland, 'Toward a Political Supreme Court' (1969) 37 U Chi L Rev 19; J. Skelly Wright, 'The Role of the Supreme Court in a Democratic Society—Judicial Activism or Restraint?' (1968) 54 Cornell L Rev 1; C. Neal Tate and Torbjorn Vallinder (eds), *The Judicialization Of Politics* (Oxford, Butterworth-Heinemann, 1995); Keenan D. Kmiec, 'The Origin and Current Meanings of "Judicial Activism"' (2004) 92 Ca

Looked at from this perspective, the Israeli Supreme Court in the 1980s and 1990s could be said to have been extremely activist. Indeed many scholars agree with this characterization, stopping at nothing short of extreme terms to describe the Court's conduct in the past three decades.[2] One of them, Martin Edelman, has gone so far as to write that since the 1980s the activism displayed by the Israeli Supreme Court has been more wide-ranging than its equivalent in any other democratic country.[3] In a similar vein, Robert Cooter and Tom Ginsburg report the findings of a survey conducted among a group of comparative law scholars who were asked to rank 'the degree of judicial daring in various countries.' Out of a list of 14 courts, the Supreme Court of Israel was ranked as the most daring, with an average score of 4.50 on a five-point scale. The United States Supreme Court came out second, with an average score of 4.42.[4]

About the Israeli Supreme Court led by Chief Justice Aharon Barak, Richard Posner has written:

What Barak created out of whole cloth was a degree of judicial power undreamed of even by our most aggressive Supreme Court justices... In Barak's conception of the separation of powers, the judicial power is unlimited.[5]

L Rev 1441; Shannon Ishiyama Smithey and John Ishiyama, 'Judicial Activism in Post-Communist Politics' (2002) 36 Law & Soc Rev 719.

[2] Moshe Landau, 'On Justice and Reasonableness in Administrative Law' (1989) 14 Tel Aviv U L Rev 5, 6 (Hebrew); Itzhak Zamir, 'Court and Politics' in Itzhak Zamir (ed), *Klinghoffer Book On Public Law* (Jerusalem, Institute for Legislative Research and Comparative Law, 1993) 209, 220 (Hebrew); Claude Klein, '*The Exemption of Yeshivot Students*' in David Cheshin et al (eds), *The Court Of Law—Fifty Years Of Adjudication In Israel* (Tel Aviv, Ministry of Defense, 1999) 152 (Hebrew); Yoav Dotan, 'Judicial Activism at the High Court of Justice' in Ruth Gavison, Mordechai Kremnitzer And Yoav Dotan, *Judicial Activism—For And Against* (Jerusalem, Magnes Press, Hebrew University, 2000) 5, 60 (Hebrew); Gad Barzilai, 'Who is Afraid of the Supreme Court' (January 1997) 1 Panim 36 (Hebrew); Gad Barzilai, 'Judicial Hegemony, Party Polarization and Social Change' (1998) 2 Politics 31, 32 (Hebrew).

[3] Martin Edelman, 'Israel' in C. Neal Tate and Torbjorn Vallinder (eds), *The Judicialization Of Politics* (Oxford, Butterworth-Heinemann, 1995) 403, 407. The rise of judicial activism in the jurisprudence of the Supreme Court is not a phenomenon unique to Israel, and has been noted in several countries in recent decades. This activism is mainly manifest in the judicial review of legislation in light of the constitution, as conducted by constitutional courts. For a review of these developments in various countries, see: *Judicial Activism in Comparative Perspective*, above n 1; *The Judicialization of Politics*, above n 1; Alec Stone Sweet, *Governing With Judges: Constitutional Politics In Europe* (Oxford, Oxford University Press, 2000); Carlo Guarnieri And Patrizia Pederzoli, *The Power Of Judges* (Oxford, Oxford University Press, 2002); Ran Hirschl, 'Beyond the American Experience: The Global Expansion of Judicial Review' in Mark A. Graber and Michael Perhac (eds), *Marbury Versus Madison—Documents And Commentary* (Washington DC, CQ Press, 2002) 147; Ran Hirschl, 'Resituating the Judicialization of Politics: Bush v Gore as a Global Trend' (2002) 15 Canadian J Law & Jurisprudence 191; Leslie Friedman Goldstein, 'From Democracy to Juristocracy' (2004) 38 Law & Soc Rev 611; Shannon Roesler, 'Permutations of Judicial Power: The New Constitutionalism and the Expansion of Judicial Authority' (2007) 32 Law & Soc Inq 545.

[4] Robert D. Cooter and Tom Ginsburg, 'Comparative Judicial Discretion: An Empirical Test of Economic Models' (1996) 16 Int'l Rev L & Econ 295, 300.

[5] Richard Posner, 'Enlightened Despot' The New Republic, April 23, 2007 (review of *The Judge in a Democracy* by Aharon Barak, Princeton University Press, 2006).

Elsewhere Posner has referred to Barak's approach as 'a world record for judicial hubris.'[6] At a conference held in Jerusalem, he also noted that the involvement of the Israeli Supreme Court in matters of national security is 'nothing short of striking, looked at from an American perspective.' 'I never imagined that there is a court more aggressive than the American Supreme Court,' he said in reference to the rulings of the Israeli Supreme Court under the leadership of Aharon Barak.[7] Similar observations have been made by Robert Bork, who said that Barak's judicial philosophy is 'activist through and through' and that Barak 'undoubtedly set a world record of judicial hubris.'[8] In summing up Aharon Barak's term as justice at the Court, Amnon Rubinstein, an Israel Prize recipient and one of Israel's most respected legal academics, wrote that the Court's intervention in decisions undertaken by other branches of state:

has effected a total revolution in the legal thought to which past generations of justices adhered and gave the Court a name as the most activist in the world... In fact, in many senses the Court, under Barak's leadership, has turned itself into an alternative government.[9]

In a study of the Court's activism, Eli Salzberger writes that the Court 'has moved center-stage in the collective decision-making process in Israel, affording an unprecedented degree of intervention in the conduct of the other branches of government.'[10] Salzberger writes about Aharon Barak that his writings on public law and legal and judicial theory have positioned him 'as one of the world's champions of legal activism.'[11]

In order to understand the activism of Israel's Supreme Court in the 1980s and 1990s, it will be useful to draw a distinction between doctrines that have to do with the jurisdiction of the Court, and substantive doctrines of administrative and constitutional law.

B. DOCTRINES REGULATING PETITIONING TO THE HIGH COURT OF JUSTICE

(a) Introduction

The Israeli Supreme Court fulfills two roles. One is that of the country's highest court of appeals. (The judicial system is comprised of three instances: the Magistrates Courts, the District Courts, and the Supreme

---

[6] Id.   [7] Yuval Yoaz, 'A Heavyweight Legal Fight' (December 20 2007) Haaretz,.
[8] Robert H. Bork, 'Barak's Rule', (Winter 2007) Azure 146, 149, 151.
[9] Amnon Rubinstein, 'Farewell to Barak', (September 15 2006) Maariv.
[10] Eli Salzberger, 'Judicial Activism in Israel' in Brice Dickson (ed), *Judicial Activism In Common Law Supreme Courts* (Oxford, Oxford University Press, 2007) 217, 218. See also: Brice Dickson, *Comparing Supreme Courts*, id, at 1. 16.
[11] Salzberger, id, at 219.

Court. There are also several tribunals, such as the religious tribunals, the labor tribunals and the military tribunals. In some circumstances, the Supreme Court is entitled to overrule decisions made by these tribunals). Its second role is as a High Court of Justice—an administrative court dealing with citizens' petitions against administrative authorities. The Supreme Court, then, heads the entire judicial system of the country and supervises all state tribunals. As a High Court of Justice, it functions as both a first and last instance—petitions are submitted only to this instance, and there is no instance to which the Court's decisions on these issues can be appealed. Due to its dual role, the legal, political, and public discourse refers to the Court sometimes as 'the Supreme Court' and sometimes as 'the High Court of Justice.'[12]

(b) Standing

The doctrine of standing determines who can submit a petition to the Supreme Court when it sits as a High Court of Justice. In the past, the Court required petitioners to show a personal, concrete interest in the issue that is the subject of the petition.[13] That approach was abandoned by the Court in the 1980s. Making 'dramatic changes'[14] in its jurisprudence, the Court ruled that petitioners need not point to any personal interest in order to acquire standing. Rather, standing may also be recognized in the case of a 'public petitioner', ie, when the petition raises a distinctively constitutional issue, an issue directly relevant to the rule of law, or an issue pointing to a violation of basic civil liberties; or when the petition blows the whistle on government corruption.[15] In regard to its judicial review process, then, the Court shifted from seeing it as designed to protect concrete, personal rights to seeing it as meant to ensure the realization of general public values.[16]

---

[12] Unlike equivalent institutions in other legal systems, the access to the Israeli High Court of Justice is extremely easy, and the relief is fairly quick and efficient. One does not need to go through lower instances, there are no witnesses or regular trial procedures, the application to the Court is inexpensive, and one does not even have to be represented.
Salzberger, above n 10, at 234.

[13] HCJ 90/49 *Nuchimowski v Minister of Justice*, 3 PD 4.

[14] Yoav Dotan, Ripeness and Politics in the High Court of Justice, (1996) 20 Tel Aviv U L Rev 93, 123 (Hebrew).

[15] HCJ 217/80 *Segal v Minister of Interior*, 34(4) PD 429; HCJ 1/81 *Shiran v Broadcasting Authority*, 35(3) PD 365; HCJ 243/82 *Zichroni v Executive Committee of the Broadcasting Authority*, 37(1) PD 757; HCJ 609/85 *Zucker v Mayor of Tel Aviv-Jaffa*, 40(1) PD 775; HCJ 428/86 *Barzilai v Government of Israel*, 40(3) PD 505; HCJ 852/86 *Aloni v Minister of Justice*, 41(2) PD 1; HCJ 910/86 *Ressler v Minister of Defense*, 42(2) 441.

[16] The liberalization of the standing rule not only led to an expansion of the Court's powers but significantly changed the public landscape and structure of civil society in Israel and gave a major impetus to the establishment of dozens of, if not hundreds, of public interest groups and associations whose access to the Supreme Court is almost always open.
Salzberger, above n 10, at 241.

(c) Justiciability

The doctrine of justiciability determines what issues are not appropriate for adjudication by the High Court of Justice. In a long series of opinions dating back to the 1950s, and in line with Anglo-American legal doctrine, the HCJ determined that petitions unsuitable for adjudication include those that raise politically or publicly controversial issues; those that raise issues that by their nature are the charge of other branches of government (first and foremost, issues of defense and foreign affairs); and those that raise issues that the Court has no legal criteria for determining.[17]

Just as it had in regard to the doctrine of standing, in the 1980s the Court changed its approach 'dramatically'[18] in this regard as well. It 'drastically reduced'[19] the scope of issues considered non-justiciable. As a result, petitions that in the past had been rejected out of hand as non-justiciable, 'petitions that in any other legal system would have been declared non-justiciable...are very frequently on the agenda of our High Court of Justice,'[20] and are decided 'on their merits.'[21]

The landmark case on justiciability was HCJ 910/86 *Ressler v Minister of Defense*.[22] Distinguishing between 'normative justiciability' and 'institutional justiciability', Justice Barak reduced the justiciability doctrine almost to the vanishing point.

Normative justiciability, according to Barak, refers to the question whether a legal norm exists that governs an action. Barak has used strong words to make the point that there is no such thing as 'normative non-justiciability': 'There is no such thing as a "legal void"... Law extends to all actions', he has written, for the reason that 'law is a system of prohibitions and permissions. Any action is either permitted or prohibited by the law.' Therefore, even political decisions, including such far-reaching ones as those concerning the initiation of war or conclusion of peace, are justiciable, for there will always be a norm that determines whether the decision is permissible or prohibited. Moreover, the norm of reasonableness (see below), argued Barak, is a super-norm that applies to the acts of all political and administrative authorities, and thus provides the courts with a standard for reviewing their conduct.

Institutional justiciability, according to Justice Barak, refers to the question whether the Court is the appropriate state institution for dealing

---

[17] HCJ 65/51 *Jabotinsky v President of Israel*, 5 PD 801; HCJ 186/65 *Reiner v Prime Minister*, 19(2) PD 485; HCJ 561/75 *Ashkenazi v Minister of Defense*, 30(3) PD 309.
[18] Zamir, above n 2, at 211.   [19] Dotan, above n 14, at 132–4.
[20] Ruth Gavison, 'Public Involvement of the High Court of Justice: A Critical View' in Ruth Gavison, Mordechai Kremnitzer And Yoav Dotan, *Judicial Activism—For And Against* (Jerusalem, Magnes Press, Hebrew University, 2000) 69, 86 (Hebrew).
[21] Zamir, above n 2, at 211–12.   [22] 42(2) PD 441.

with an issue. Barak discussed possible justifications for institutional non-justiciability and found them all meritless. 'Institutional non-justiciablity is a highly problematic doctrine,' he concluded: 'It is based on irrational justifications.' However, Barak was nonetheless prepared to give institutional non-justiciability some recognition, not because there are any good reasons for endorsing it, but rather for the fear that in some instances the Court's intervention in actions taken by other state authorities might undermine the public's trust in the Court. That would be the case if the Court intervenes in a decision by applying to it an abstract norm, such as reasonableness, which the Court has mustered for the sake of reviewing that particular decision. In such instances, the public may (mistakenly, according to Barak) hold that it is the Court and not the law that is making the determination whether the decision should be upheld. This may paint the Court as taking sides in contested political issues and, in turn, undermine the public's trust in the Court.[23]

Justices Shamgar and Elon opposed Justice Barak's approach.

Justice Shamgar suggested that the doctrine of institutional non-justiciability be maintained by the Court. What then are institutionally non-justiciable matters? Shamgar offered 'the dominant essence of the case' test: Matters that raise a predominantly legal question should be regarded as justiciable; all other matters should be left to the determination of other state authorities.[24]

Justice Elon took issue with Justice Barak's stance on normative justiciability.[25] The mere fact that the law treats an act as lawful or permissible does not mean that the law has anything substantive to say about it, argued Justice Elon. There are numerous human actions that the law does not refer to in any meaningful way and they are all therefore normatively non-justiciable. Elon also contested Barak's application of the standard of reasonableness to political actions: the distinction between reviewing the legal reasonableness of a political act and reviewing the political merit of such an act is thin, if not nonexistent, argued Justice Elon.

Justice Barak responded by offering a slightly modified version of his argument. Whereas he had initially argued that every human action is either permissible or prohibited, in the second round of the Court's discussion of justiciability Barak adopted the Hohfeldian-liberal notion of 'liberty',[26] claiming that since the law demarcates the boundaries of

[23] Id, at 475–6.
[24] Id, at 519. See also Justice Shamgar in HCJ 4481/91 *Bargil v Government of Israel*, 47(4) PD 210, 215.
[25] HCJ 1635/90 *Zharzevsky v Prime Minister*, 45(1) PD 749, 766–7, 770.
[26] Wesley Newcomb Hohfeld, 'Some Fundamental Legal Conceptions as Applied in Judicial Reasoning' (1913) 23 Yale L J 28.

protected human liberties, whatever people do within the confines of their liberties is governed by the law.[27]

Justice Barak subsequently reiterated his position on justiciability in several law review articles. In an article published in 1993[28] he began his analysis by declaring: 'The whole earth is full of law. Any human conduct is the object of a legal norm.' Barak's words alluded to Isaiah 6, 3: 'And one cried unto another, and said, Holy, holy, holy is the LORD of hosts: the whole earth is full of his glory.' Justice Elon reacted by vehemently criticizing the extension of the phrase from its Biblical context to the law.[29]

Barak's choice of strong words in which to couch his doctrine of justiciability has haunted him for many years thereafter, for it has been perceived as not only indicating his insistence on limitless justiciability, but also as epitomizing his entire project of ultra-activism. As to Barak's claim that every human conduct is normatively justiciable because it is either permissible or prohibited, and because it either falls within the confines of a certain legally recognized liberty or does not—obviously this way of thinking makes normative justiciability a formalistic and hollow concept: As rightly pointed out by Justice Elon, we cannot really say that a legal norm exists when all the law does is abstain from prohibiting a certain conduct. But while law professors would say that this formalistic notion of justiciability is either trivial or meaningless, for Barak and for his colleagues on the bench this, together with the strong words in which Barak kept insisting on couching his justiciability doctrine, made it acceptable and legitimate for the Court to review political and administrative decisions with almost no limits (see below).

Moreover, in order to understand the extent of the Court's activism, one needs to recall that the Court's justiciability doctrine went together with the Court's making reasonableness its prime instrument for the purpose of supervising government and administrative decisions (see below). Since reasonableness is a standard, ie, an abstract and open-ended norm (and this has been acknowledged by Barak in the context of his discussion of institutional justiciability), it is clear that the combination of the Court's

---

[27] *Zharzevsky v Prime Minister*, above n 25, at 855.
[28] Aharon Barak, *Judicial Philosophy and Judicial Activism*, (1993) 17 Tel Aviv U L Rev 475, 477. See also: Aharon Barak, 'The Limits of Law and the Limits of Adjudication' (2002) 2 Kiryat Hamishpat 5, 5, 6:

> Law has no limits. The whole earth is full of law. Every human conduct is the object of the law. There is no sphere to which law does not apply…Whatever has not been prohibited is permissible. Whatever has not been made permissible to the government is prohibited. Therefore, relations of friendship and love, thoughts, and so forth, are all within the sphere of the law, but they are within the purview of a norm that grants a general permission.

[29] Menachem Elon, 'The Basic Laws: Their Enactment, Interpretation and Expectations' (1995) 12 Legal Research 253, 300 (Hebrew).

almost limitless justiciability doctrine and its extensive application of the reasonableness standard has meant that the Court furnished itself with vast discretion as to whether and in what ways to intervene in political and administrative decisions.

Side by side with its radical modification of the justiciability doctrine, the Court also effected substantive changes in the way it presented the separation of powers principle. Whereas until the 1980s, in line with Montesquieu's famous formulation in book xi of *The Spirit of Laws*, the principle was presented as justification for the Court's abstention from intervention in decisions undertaken by other state authorities (see Chapter 4, below), in the new era of justiciability the separation of powers was presented as justification for the Court's intervention. It is the function of the Court, as guardian of the rule of law, to make sure that all state authorities act in accordance with the law, reasoned Justice Barak; therefore, when the Court scrutinizes the decisions of other authorities, it is merely fulfilling the function assigned to it under the separation of powers principle.[30]

(d) Application of the Court's expansive justiciability doctrine

In the years following *Ressler* the Court adopted Barak's expansive approach to justiciability, rather than Shamgar's and Elon's restrictive approaches.[31] This was manifest in the expansion of the Court's review power to many spheres that had hitherto been kept outside of its purview.

(i) Knesset's administrative decisions

Thus, whereas in the past all actions of the Knesset had been considered non-justiciable, in the 1980s the Court ruled that its reviewing powers extend also to the way in which the various Knesset administrative bodies exercise their legal authority, with the exception of the Knesset's authority to determine the contents of the country's binding legislation.[32] This expansion of the HCJ's reviewing powers was described as an 'unprecedented encroachment of the Court upon the affairs of the legislative branch (both in terms of the history of the State of Israel and in terms of what is

---

[30] *Ressler v Minister of Defense*, above n 22, at 462–4. See also: HCJ 680/88 *Schnitzer v Chief Military Censor*, 42(4) PD 617, 639–40.

[31] But see Justices Strassberg-Cohen and Cheshin in HCJ 3125/98 *Ayad v Commander of IDF Forces in the West Bank* (arguing for the application of Justice Shamgar's 'the dominant essence of the case' test); Justice Procaccia in HCJ 7712/05 *Polard v Government of Israel* (arguing that even though foreign policy matters are in principle institutionally justiciable, their 'dominant essence' may make them non-justiciable); Justice Rubinstein in HCJ 8902/05 *Amotat 'Shemesh' for Iraqi Jews v Prime Minister* (arguing that foreign policy matters are in principle institutionally justiciable, but their 'dominant essence may make them non-justiciable').

[32] HCJ 306/81 *Flatto-Sharon v Knesset Committee*, 35(4) PD 118; HCJ 652/81 *Sarid v Speaker of Knesset*, 36(2) PD 197; HCJ 325/85 *Miyari v Speaker of Knesset*, 39(3) PD 122; HCJ 142/89 *Laor Movement v Speaker of Knesset*, 44(3) PD 529.

acceptable in other western countries).'[33] Furthermore, the claim has been made that this development has 'no parallel in the democratic regimes known to us.'[34]

(ii) Defense

Departing from its previous rulings, the Court determined that the actions of bodies charged with the country's defense are also subject to its review, just like the actions of all other state authorities.[35] This decision was followed by a long series of rulings in which the Court subjected to its legal review the actions of the country's defense authorities, some in real-time, in a pattern probably unparalleled by any other legal system in the world.

Thus, the Court reviewed the legality of the IDF's (Israel Defense Forces) operational methods in the Occupied Palestinian Territories (OPT). In one case, it reviewed the legality of the 'neighbor procedure,' whereby IDF soldiers seeking to arrest a wanted person in the OPT force a local resident, chosen at random, to inform the wanted person that the IDF forces are after him, and that it's best to give himself up peacefully to avoid any unnecessary violence and casualties. The Court invalidated the procedure as illegal.[36]

The Court reviewed the legality of interrogation techniques used against detainees in situations involving a concrete danger of terrorist action ('the ticking bomb procedure'). It ruled that the use of these techniques had been unauthorized.[37]

In another case, the Court reviewed the legality of 'targeted killings,' a procedure that involves the killing of terrorists when there is credible information that they intend to commit terrorist acts. The Court ruled that this procedure cannot be sweepingly categorized as illegal.[38]

The Court reviewed the administrative detention of two Hezbollah members who were held not because they posed a danger to the country's security, but in order to be used as 'bargaining chips' for the release of Israelis imprisoned in enemy countries. It ruled that their detention was illegal.[39] The Court also considered the petition of these two Hezbollah

[33] Dotan, above n 14, at 123 n 65.
[34] Dotan, above n 2, at 41.
[35] HCJ 554/81 *Baransa v Commander of Central Command*, 36(4) PD 247; HCJ 393/82 *Jamayat Askhan v Commander of Judea and Samaria*, 37(4) 785; HCJ 428/86 *Barzilai v Government of Israel*, 40(3) PD 505; HCJ 68088 *Schnitzer v Chief Military Censor*, 42(4) PD 617; HCJ 4541/94 *Miller v Minister of Defense*, 49(4) PD 94; HCJ 1284/99 *Plonit v Chief of Staff*, 53(2) PD 62; CAP 7048/97 *Plonim v Minister of Defense*, 54(1) PD 721.
[36] HCJ 3799/02 *Adala v Commander of Central Command*.
[37] HCJ 5100/94 *Public Committee Against Torture v Government of Israel* 53(4) PD 817.
[38] HCJ 769/02 *Public Committee Against Torture v Government of Israel*.
[39] CAD 7048/97 *Plonim v Minister of Defense*, 54(1) PD 721. See also: AMM 5652/00 *Ubaid and Dirani v Minister of Defense*, 55(4) PD 913. See also: Salzberger, above n 10, at 251–2.

members against a decision by the authorities to deny them meetings with representatives of the International Red Cross. It ruled that in the balance between humanitarian and security considerations, the former override the latter, and therefore the Red Cross representatives should be allowed to visit the detainees.[40]

In the course of Operation Defensive Shield in the West Bank in April-May 2002 the Court dealt with a series of petitions submitted by Israeli and Palestinian human rights organizations, Knesset members and residents of the OPT, challenging various actions undertaken by the IDF in the course of the fighting.[41] In 2004, amidst fighting by the IDF in Gaza, the Court dealt with a petition that had to do with the provision of water, food and medical supplies to Gaza residents, as well as with the evacuation of the injured and the burial of the dead.[42] In 2008, amidst ongoing violent clashes between Gaza militants and Israeli forces, the Court dealt with a petition challenging a decision made by the government's political-defensive cabinet to restrict the supply of fuel and electricity to Gaza.[43] In the course of Operation Cast Lead in Gaza, in December 2008-January 2009, the Court dealt with petitions submitted by Israeli human rights organizations aimed at ensuring that Palestinian medical crews could continue to operate uninterruptedly among the local civilian residents of Gaza, as well as to guarantee the supply of electricity to Gaza residents.[44]

During the Gulf War of 1991, the Court ordered the IDF to distribute protective gas masks to Palestinian residents of the OPT after such masks were given to Jews living in the same areas.[45]

The Court has dealt with over one-hundred petitions submitted by residents of the OPT against the 'security wall,' which Israel has been building since 2002 to separate itself from the OPT and seal itself off from potential terrorist attacks emanating from there. The petitions challenged the legality of erecting the wall and the legality of various sections of its route. On several occasions, the Court has ordered the defense authorities to change

---

[40] HCJ 794/98 *Ubaid and Dirani v Minister of Defense*, 55(5) PD 769.
[41] HCJ 2936/02 *Physicians for Human Rights v Commander of IDF Forces in the West Bank*, 56(3) PD 3; HCJ 2977/02 *Adala v Commander of IDF Forces in the West Bank*, 56(3) PD 6; HCJ 3022/02 *Law—Palestinian Human Rights Organization v Commander of IDF Forces in the West Bank*, 56(3) PD 9; HCJ 3114/02 *Barakha v Minister of Defense*, 56(3) PD 11; HCJ 3117/02 *Hamoked Center for the Defense of the Individual v Minister of Defense*, 56(3) PD 17; HCJ 2901/02 *Hamoked Center for the Defense of the Individual v Commander of IDF Forces in the West Bank*, 56(3) 19; HCJ 3436/02 *Custodia International de Terra Santa v Government of Israel*, 56(3) PD 22; HCJ 2117/02 *Physicians for Human Rights v Commander of IDF in Gaza*, 56(3) PD 26; HCJ 3451/02 *Almadani v Minister of Defense*, 56(3) PD 30.
[42] HCJ 4764/04 *Physicians for Human Rights v Commander of IDF Forces in Gaza*, 58(5) PD 385.
[43] HCJ 9132/07 *Albasiouni v Prime Minister*.
[44] HCJ 201/09 *Physicians for Human Rights v Prime Minister*.
[45] HCJ 168/91 *Morcos v Minister of Defense*, 45(1) PD 467.

the route they had planned, or even to tear down and reroute a section already built.[46]

The Court has dealt with a petition submitted on behalf of Gilead Shalit, an Israeli soldier kidnapped to Gaza, in which it was asked to order the government not to make certain concessions to the Hamas government in Gaza until Shalit is released.[47]

The Court has dealt with a writ issued by the military commander of the West Bank that banned Palestinian residents of the West Bank from using a certain road, mostly located in the West Bank, which connects central Israel and Jerusalem. Some of the road was constructed on lands confiscated from West Bank residents. Until 2000 the road was in use by both Israelis and Palestinians. Then, in the course of the Second Intifada (Palestinian uprising), Israelis were attacked on the road and suffered a number of casualties. Subsequently, the military commander issued the writ banning Palestinian residents of the West Bank from using the road, which remained in force for almost a decade. The Court held that the writ was unlawful and ordered the military commander to allow Palestinians to use the road again. The Court reasoned that in issuing the writ, the military commander had both breached his duty to act for the welfare of the residents of the West Bank and also acted disproportionately.[48]

(iii) Foreign affairs

Departing from previous rulings,[49] the Court has determined that government decisions concerning the country's foreign relations are also subject to its judicial review. Thus, in one of the most activist moves in its history, the Court dealt with a petition seeking to prevent Prime Minister Benjamin Netanyahu from deploying military forces in the 'Orient House'

---

[46] The leading case is HCJ 2056/04 *Board of Beit Sureik Village v Government of Israel*, 58(5) PD 807. See also: HCJ 7957/04 *Maraba v Prime Minister of Israel*, 60(2) PD 477; HCJ 5488/04 *Elram v Government of Israel*; Salzberger, above n 10, at 255–6.

[47] HCJ 5551/08 *Shalit v Government of Israel*.

[48] HCJ 2150/07 *Abu Tsafia v Minister of Defense*.

[49] In 1965 Israel entered into diplomatic relations with the Federal Republic of Germany. Germany nominated as its first ambassador to Israel a person who had served as an officer in the German army in World War II. A petition was submitted to the HCJ to order the government not to accept this nomination. Justice Sussman denied the petition with one brief passage:

> It is well known that there is disagreement in the public as to whether it is desirable to enter diplomatic relations with Germany. The government has made its decision and brought it to the Knesset which, in turn, endorsed the government's decision. This is not a legal matter; it is clearly a political matter. It cannot be determined by legal criteria. By the same token, the question of the confirmation of the ambassador of a foreign state is a political issue...It is not a legal issue to be resolved by a court. The relevant considerations are not legal considerations, but rather those of foreign policy and considerations having to do with the fitness of the candidate for the job. These considerations fall beyond the jurisdiction of the Court and it is impossible for the Court to make any decision with regard to them.

HCJ 186/65 *Reiner v Prime Minister*, 19(2) PD 485.

(the headquarters of the Palestinian Authority in East Jerusalem) and issued an interlocutory order against it.[50] In that case, the election of Ehud Barak as Prime Minister several days later preempted any need to discuss the petition on its merits.

The Court dealt with a petition against Ehud Barak's government's conducting political negotiations with the Palestinian Authority after it had resigned and a date had been set for new elections. One of the judges in the panel held that it would be inappropriate for the Court to intervene in such cases, but without explicitly mentioning 'non-justiciability.'[51]

The Court has discussed the question whether the government is allowed to conduct peace talks with Syria.[52] It has reviewed a government decision to send members of the Israeli Police to join a multinational force operating in Haiti following a Security Council resolution.[53]

However, in a case having to do with the government's policies regarding the Temple Mount, Justice Zamir said that given the sensitivity of the site, the way the government manages it should be regarded as institutionally non-justiciable.[54]

(iv) Socio-economic policies

On several occasions, the Court has reviewed government social-economic policies. In two decisions with far-reaching budgetary implications, the Court ordered the government to allocate funds for the integration of Down syndrome children[55] and children with special needs[56] in regular school classes. The Court reviewed Knesset legislation and government decisions that reduced the support provided by the state to the needy. It was claimed that these measures violated the right of the needy to human dignity in their lives. The Court, by a majority of six to one, dismissed the petition, holding that since the state provides the needy with a varied package of other support measures, it had not been proved that the particular measures petitioned against were responsible for taking the needy below the standard of dignified living.[57] These proceedings sparked widespread criticism of the Court. The Knesset held a special session on 'The Latest Interventions of the

---

[50] HCJ 3123/99 *Hilman v Minister of Internal Security*.
[51] HCJ 5167/00 *Weiss v Prime Minister*, 55(2) PD 455.
[52] HCJ 4354/92 *Temple Mount and Eretz Israel Loyalists Movement v Prime Minister*, 47(1) PD 37.
[53] HCJ 5128/94 *Federman v Minister of Police*, 48(5) PD 647.
[54] HCJ 8666/99 *Temple Mount Loyalists Movement v Attorney General*, 54(1) PD 199, 203.
[55] HCJ 2599/00 *Yated—Parents of Down Syndrome Children v Ministry of Education*, 56(5) PD 834.
[56] HCJ 6973/03 *Martziano v Minister of Treasury*, 58(2) PD 270; HCJAD 247/04 *Minister of Treasury v Martziano*.
[57] HCJ 366/03 *Commitment to Peace and Social Justice v Minister of Treasury*.

High Court of Justice in the State's Budget,' and adopted a resolution stating that

> The Knesset views with concern the Supreme Court's slippage to subjects that unequivocally fall within the jurisdiction of the executive and legislative branches... The Knesset cautions against this tendency which may develop into a constitutional crisis.[58]

Chief Justice Aharon Barak's response to the Knesset session was: 'The dialogue between the branches of the state ceases to exist. Power takes over reason. Tools are broken.'[59] *Haaretz*, the daily newspaper that for many years has been providing the Court with blanket support (see below, Chapter 5), came out with an editorial critical of the Court, as well.[60]

In another instance, the Court ordered the Prison Authority to provide all prisoners with beds, and not only mattresses, to sleep on.[61]

(v) Political agreements

The Court has expanded the scope of its judicial review to cover political agreements—agreements signed between political parties concerning the operation of political coalitions and the staffing of specific executive positions. Until the 1980s these agreements had been viewed as being outside the Court's purview,[62] but at that time it held that political agreements are justiciable and developed a new doctrine purporting to govern them.[63]

(vi) Appointments

The Court has expanded its judicial review to the legality of the appointment of ministers and deputy ministers, ruling that ministers or deputy ministers who have been indicted cannot remain in office.[64]

The Court has intervened in the appointment of senior state officials. It overruled the government's decision to appoint a person charged with severe obstruction of justice to the post of director-general of the Ministry of Construction and Housing.[65] It overruled the government's decision

---

[58] Divrei Ha-Knesset (Knesset Minutes), January 13 2004.

[59] 'The Confrontation between the Knesset and the Supreme Court Escalates' (January 14 2004) Haaretz. Yedioth Ahronoth titled its report of the confrontation *'On the Road to Explosion'* (January 15 2004) Yedioth Ahronoth.

[60] 'With All Due Respect, Not Within the Court's Jurisdiction' (January 12 2004) Haaretz.

[61] HCJ 4634/04 *Physicians for Human Rights v Homeland Security Minister*.

[62] HCJ 313/67 *Axelrod v Minister of Religious Affairs*, 22(1) PD 80.

[63] HCJ 669/86 *Rubin v Berger*, 41(1) PD 73; HCJ 1523/90 *Levy v Prime Minister of Israel*, 44(2) PD 213; HCJ 1601/90 *Shalit v Peres*, 44(3) PD 353; HCJ 1635/90 *Zharzevski v Prime Minister*, 45(1) PD 749; HCJ 5364/94 *Welner v Chairman of Israel Labor Party*, 49(1) PD 758.

[64] HCJ 3094/93 *Movement for Quality of Government in Israel v Government of Israel*, 47(5) 404; HCJ 4267/93 *Amitai v Prime Minister of Israel*, 47(5) PD 441; HCJ 1993/03 93 *Movement for Quality of Government in Israel v Government of Israel*, 57(6) PD 817.

[65] HCJ 6163/92 *Eisenberg v Ministry of Construction and Housing*, 47(2) PD 229.

on the appointment of the director-general of the Ministry of Science and Technology, for the reason that the appointee lacked adequate qualifications.[66] The Court aborted the appointment of the director-general of a government corporation due to charges of corruption against the appointee[67]; the appointment of the head of the Terror-Fighting Staff in the Prime Minister's Office because the appointee had been involved in severe obstruction of justice[68]; and the promotion of a brigadier general in the IDF to the rank of general for his having had inappropriate relations with a female soldier on his staff.[69]

(vii) The Attorney General and the President

Again departing from its jurisprudence since the establishment of the State of Israel until the 1980s, the Court has ruled that the decisions of the Attorney General are subject to the same tests that apply to the decisions of any other administrative body.[70]

The Court has extended its review to the authority of the President of Israel to issue pardons.[71]

(viii) Government agenda

The Court issued a temporary injunction of six days prohibiting 'any governmental forum' (including the government) from dealing with proposed legislation that was meant to effect far-reaching changes in Israel's zoning law. The injunction was issued at the request of several environmental protection organizations which claimed that they had not been given adequate time to study the 241 page proposed legislation.[72] Yoav Dotan, a professor of administrative law at Hebrew University, called the Court's injunction 'one of the most far-reaching decisions in the Court's history.' 'This is the first time in the history of Israel's judicial branch that an injunction bars the government from dealing with a matter on its agenda,' wrote Dotan.

It is not only the case that the Israeli Supreme Court has never come out with such a ruling; the ruling is a precedent in the history of judicial activism in general. It is doubtful whether a court in any country ever dared to order its government what should and what should not be on its agenda.[73]

---

[66] HCJ 5657/09 *The Movement for the Quality of Government in Israel v Government of Israel.*
[67] HCJ 932/99 *The Movement for the Quality of Government in Israel v Chairperson of the Appointments Review Committee*, 53(3) PD 769.
[68] HCJ 4668/01 *Sarid v Prime Minister*, 56(2) PD 265.
[69] HCJ 1248/99 *Plonit v Chief of the General Staff*, 53(2) PD 62.
[70] HCJ 329/81 *Nof v Attorney General*, 37(4) PD 356; HCJ 223/88 *Sheftel v Attorney General*, 43(4) PD 356; HCJ 943/89 *Ganor v Attorney General*, 44(2) PD 485.
[71] HCJ 428/86 *Barzilay v Government of Israel*, 40(3) PD 515.
[72] HCJ 1658/10 *Israel Union for Environmental Defense v Government of Israel.*
[73] Yoav Dotan, 'A Dubious Constitutional Revolution' (March 3 2010) Yedioth Ahronoth.

(e) Conclusion

Through the considerable expansion of standing and reduction of the issues considered non-justiciable, the types of cases in which the petitioning of the Court is allowed were substantially increased. The Court, then, granted itself broad powers to discuss petitions requesting judicial review of actions undertaken by the government, the public administration, and the Knesset. Indeed, the Court not only granted itself these powers, but also made extensive use of them.[74]

C. SUBSTANTIVE LAW DOCTRINES

(a) Reasonableness

Until the 1980s, the central principle of Israeli administrative law had been the 'administrative legality principle,' stating that an administrative body could only exercise the authority it had been granted by law, so that when a body acted beyond its authority (*ultra vires*), its actions were considered invalid.[75] The administrative legality principle stood at the basis of the HCJ's perception of its role in the area of administrative law. The Court did not view itself as charged with reviewing the decisions of administrative bodies on their merit. Rather, it saw its duty as consisting of identifying the *scope* of the legal authority granted to an administrative body and determining whether in taking a certain decision it had acted within its authority, or exceeded it. The Court, then, acted as the 'border patrol' of the authority granted to the state's administrative bodies. When it invalidated an administrative decision, it did so not on grounds having to do with the decision's substantive contents, but for the reason that in taking the decision, the administrative body had exceeded the scope of its authority.[76]

In its jurisprudence since the early 1980s, the Court completely abandoned this approach, developing the 'reasonableness test' in its stead and

---

[74] See also: Itzhak Zamir, 'Public Law' (1990) 19 Mishpatim 563, 567 (Hebrew).
[75] Baruch Bracha, *Administrative Law* (Tel Aviv, Schocken Publishing House, 1986) 35 (Hebrew).
[76] As the Court stated in one of its initial decisions:

> The Supreme Court, sitting as a High Court of Justice, is not an appeal court for appealing against the actions of government institutions or government officials...As long as the executive branch acts within the boundaries set by the law, it is not within the Court's authority to examine the nature of the action.

HCJ 16/48 *Baron v Prime Minister*, 1 PD 109, 112, 113. And in another early opinion:

> This Court will necessarily confine itself exclusively...to the question of whether the agency has exceeded the scope of its authority as determined by the law...The efficiency of the exercise of the agency's discretion and its wisdom—as opposed to its legality—cannot be reviewed by this Court.

HCJ 311/60 *Miller v Minister of Transportation*, 15 PD 1989, 1996.

making that its main tool for reviewing the actions of the government and the state's public administration. The reasonableness test was developed by Justice Aharon Barak, who stated its contents in the ruling that paved the way for the Court's new approach. On the one hand, an administrative body has to base its actions on appropriate considerations and to strike a proper balance among them, ie, it must give each of the relevant considerations its appropriate relative weight. On the other hand, a 'range of reasonableness' exists in any event, that is, a range of decisions that are all based on striking a proper balance among the relevant considerations, and hence reasonable. Only such decisions as fall beyond this range of reasonableness would be invalidated, stated Barak.[77] (Barak thus adopted a rhetoric of borders—'range'—taken from the previous era, to legitimize an entirely new tool for judicial review of administrative decisions, one involving substantive review of the considerations that underlie them.)[78]

The Court applied the reasonableness test in two ways. Usually, the test is concerned with what might be called 'legal reasonableness.' In some cases, however, it is concerned with what might rather be called 'professional reasonableness.'

When the Court applies the *legal* reasonableness test, it identifies a series of *principles* that are embedded in the law and strikes a balance among them by granting each its appropriate weight. In adopting this procedure, ie, in concretizing the bearing of the relevant principles to the facts of the case at hand, the Court actually created a new legal norm *ex nihilo*. Since the early 1980s, the Court has applied the reasonableness test in this way

---

[77] HCJ 389/80 *Yellow Pages Ltd v Broadcasting Authority*, 35(1) PD 421.

[78] Justice Barak's position was not accepted without objection; it was opposed by Justices Landau and Elon. Justice Landau argued, in the spirit of the traditional conception underlying the administrative legality principle, that applying the reasonableness test as suggested by Justice Barak 'would soon lead to a *de novo* examination of the decision on its merits, as if the Court were engaging in a repeated discussion of the decision's propriety.' In other words, the Court would take it upon itself 'to redo the job of the public administration,' although 'the Court has never assumed such a role until now.' HCJ 389/80 *Yellow Pages Ltd v Broadcasting Authority*, 35(1) PD 421. Justice Landau argued that 'the sanction for [the administration's] unwise and inefficient decisions lies in the parliamentary responsibility of the government and its ministers to the Knesset and, ultimately, to the public as a whole.' HCJ 112/77 *Fogel v Broadcasting Authority*, 31(3) PD 657, 666. An additional argument raised by Justice Landau against expanding the application of the reasonableness test reflects the tension that has prevailed throughout the history of the Zionist endeavor between the dynamism of 'action' and the reins of 'legality.' Expressing a concern that 'legality' might excessively restrain 'action,' Justice Landau claimed that subjecting the administration to the reasonableness test 'might, due to too many legal limitations, impair the efficiency of the public administration and its ability to act without delay.' HCJ 389/80 *Yellow Pages Ltd v Broadcasting Authority*, 35(1) PD 421, 431, 432. Justice Elon endorsed this argument in HCJ 840/79 *Builders and Contractors Center v Government of Israel*, 34(3) PD 729. The Supreme Court, however, adopted Justice Barak's stance. Since the 1980s, then, the Court has turned the reasonableness test into its main, albeit not the only, criterion when reviewing the government's and the public administration's use of their authority.

in thousands of cases and annulled administrative decisions in only a small fraction of them.[79]

When the Court applies the *professional* reasonableness test, it examines, on their merits, the professional considerations that come within the expertise and professional knowledge of the administrative body. Judges applying the reasonableness test in this fashion actually use their 'common sense' to examine the extent to which the administrative body's use of its authority is reasonable,[80] ie, they do not draw on any skill specific to them as jurists or judges. In some cases, the Court ruled that the decision of the administrative body, although found to be within the range of its knowledge and expertise, had been unreasonable.[81]

---

[79] For instance, the HCJ annulled a decision of the Broadcasting Authority to refrain from initiating and broadcasting interviews with public leaders identified with the PLO in the OPT. The Court ruled that the Broadcasting Authority had failed to strike a proper balance between the principle of freedom of expression and the need to protect the welfare of the public and the security of the country. HCJ 243/82 *Zichroni v Executive Board of Broadcasting Authority*, 37(1) PD 757. The HCJ annulled a decision by a police district commander to forbid a political demonstration and a parade. It found that the district commander had failed to strike a proper balance between the basic freedom to demonstrate and the need to preserve the public's safety. HCJ 153/83 *Levy v Commander of Southern District*, 38(2) PD 393. The HCJ annulled a decision by the Films and Plays Censorship Board to forbid the performance of a play. It ruled that the Board had failed to strike a proper balance between the principle of freedom of expression and the need to protect the public order. HCJ 14/86 *Laor v Censorship of Films and Plays Board*, 41(1) PD 421. The HCJ cancelled the decision of the Broadcasting Authority to impose limitations on broadcasts related to the ultra-rightist Kach movement headed by Rabbi Meir Cahana. It ruled that the Broadcasting Authority had failed to strike a proper balance between the value of freedom of expression and the need to prevent harm to the public order. HCJ 399/85 *Kahane v Executive Board of Broadcasting Authority*, 41(3) PD 255. The HCJ annulled the decision of the Chief Military Censor to censor passages included in a journalistic piece on the Mossad. It found that the censor had failed to strike a proper balance between the principle of freedom of expression and the need to protect the country's security. HCJ 680/88 *Schnitzer v Chief Military Censor*, 42(4) PD 617. The HCJ instructed the Prime Minister to dismiss a minister and deputy minister after both had been indicted. It ruled that this decision was compelled by the consideration of preserving the public's trust in the government. HCJ 3094/93 *Movement for Quality of Government in Israel v Government of Israel*, 47(5) PD 404; HCJ 4267/93 *Amitai v Prime Minister of Israel*, 47(5) PD 441.

[80] Clifford Geertz, 'Common Sense as a Cultural System' in *Local Knowledge* (New York, Basic Books Publishers, 1983) 73.

[81] For instance, the HCJ annulled a decision by Tel Aviv's mayor not to allow the owner of a café to set up tables and chairs on the pavement. It ruled that the mayor had failed to strike a proper balance between the extent of the injury to the interests of the café owner and the injury that would have been inflicted upon the neighboring residents due to the noise caused by the patrons of the café. HCJ 127/80 *Odem v Mayor of Tel Aviv*, 35(2) PD 118. The HCJ annulled the Ministry of Labor's guideline to limit the ministry's contribution to kindergarten fees only to children of salaried mothers, and not extend this measure to self-employed mothers. The rationale for this guideline had been that the ministry could not verify the declarations of self-employed mothers concerning their income. The HCJ ruled that the goal of encouraging mothers to go out to work overrides any concern about verifying their income. HCJ 281/82 *Shilo-Askenazi v Minister of Labor and Welfare*, 37(1) PD 95. The HCJ annulled a decision of the Minister of Defense concerning inscriptions on soldiers' tombs. AHCJ 3299/93 *Wichselbaum v Minister of Defense*, 49(2) PD 195. The HCJ annulled a tender of the Israel Land Authority for the marketing of building plots, because it found the tender's provisions unreasonable. HCJ 1444/93 *Municipality of Eilat v Board of Israel Lands*, 49(3) PD 749. The HCJ invalidated the discretion of the Minister of Health in his refusal to grant a license for the operation of medical equipment. HCJ 29/94 *Tzarfati v Minister of Health*, 49(3) PD 804.

A case in which the Court applied the professional reasonableness test marks one of the most activist decisions in the Court's history. Since 2002 thousands of Qassam rockets and mortar shells have been fired from Gaza at neighboring settlements in Israel. In 2006 the government adopted a plan devised by IDF experts for shielding the schools in these settlements. The plan was premised on the creation of 'protected spaces' in the vicinity of school classes. The Court held that the government's plan failed to provide schoolchildren with adequate protection and was therefore unreasonable. The Court ordered the government to adopt instead a 'full protection' scheme whereby school classes themselves would be shielded. (The cost of 'full protection' was over twice as much as 'protected spaces').[82]

It should be noted, however, that in a 2007 case[83] Justice Asher Grunis took the most critical stance against the Court's reasonableness doctrine in three decades. Justice Grunis suggested that instead of applying the reasonableness test, the Court should opt for its traditional, less abstract, neglected tests of ulterior motives, *ultra vires* and discrimination. That would reduce the Court's scope of discretion and thereby increase legal certainty. Reasonableness should be kept as a test of last resort, suggested Justice Grunis. Justice Grunis' remarks amounted to nothing short of an attempt to roll back the reasonableness doctrine to its status in 1979! Additionally, Justice Grunis claimed that in many cases the application of the reasonableness test means the substitution of the Court's discretion for the administrative authority's discretion. Justice Procaccia joined with Justice Grunis in this last point, saying that it was a real concern that application of the reasonableness test may amount to substituting the Court's discretion for the administrative authority' discretion, and that it could not be disregarded.

(b) *Proportionality*

In the 1990s, the Supreme Court developed an additional new test to be applied in its review of administrative decisions—the proportionality test. In applying this test, the Court assumes that the administrative decision is reasonable, yet examines both the suitability of the means chosen by the administrative body and the end meant to be achieved.[84]

---

[82] HCJ 8397/06 *Wasser Eduardo v Minister of Defense*.
[83] HCJ 5853/07 *Emunah—National Religious Women's Organization v Prime Minister*.
[84] AHCJ 4466/94 *Nusseiba v Minister of Treasury*, 49(4) PD 68; HCJ 3477/95 *Ben-Atiyah v Minister of Education*, 49(5) PD 1; HCJ 5434/96 *Horev v Minister of Transportation*, 51(4) PD 91; HCJ 1715/97 *Board of Investment Directors in Israel v Minister of Treasury*, 51(4) PD 367; HCJ 3648/97 *Stamka v Minister of Interior*, 53(2) PD 728.

The proportionality test is comprised of three subtests.[85] The first examines the extent to which the means chosen to achieve an end can indeed do so. 'The means must rationally lead to the attainment of the end.'[86] The second subtest examines whether the means 'is not harmful, beyond the required measure, to values worth protecting,'[87] ie, the means 'must cause the least possible harm to values and principles worth protecting.'[88] The third subtest examines the balance between the harm inflicted on a particular individual and the benefit purportedly accruing to the public at large as a result of the administrative decision. An inadequate ratio will be deemed disproportionate and the decision invalidated.[89]

The Supreme Court has applied the proportionality test in its review of the administrative decisions in a long list of cases. At times, its application has resulted in the invalidation of administrative decisions.[90]

---

[85] HCJ 4541/94 *Miller v Minister of Defense*, 49(4) PD 94; CA 6821/93 *United Mizrahi Bank Ltd. v Migdal*, 49(4) PD 221; HCJ 3477/95 *Ben-Atiyah v Minister of Education*, 49(5) PD 1; HCJ 4330/93 *Ganem v Committee of Tel Aviv District, Israeli Bar Association*, 50(4) PD 221; HCJ 3648/97 *Stamka v Minister of Interior*, 53(2) PD 728; HCJ 6268/00 *Ha-Chotrim Kibbutz v Board of Israel Lands*, 55(5) PD 639; HCJ 1715/97 *Board of Investment Directors in Israel v Minister of Treasury*, 51(4) PD 367; HCJ 5434/96 Horev *v Minister of Transportation*, 51(4) PD 91.
[86] HCJ 3477/95 *Ben-Atiyah v Minister of Education*, 49(5) PD 1.
[87] HCJ 4330/93 *Ganem v Committee of Tel Aviv District, Israeli Bar Association*, 50(4) PD 221.
[88] Id.
[89] AHCJ 4466/94 *Nusseiba v Minister of Treasury*, 49(4) PD 68.
Of these three subtests of proportionality, only the second involves a legal question. The first subtest, like the test of professional reasonableness, is mainly non-legal. Judges applying this subtest are chiefly using their common sense as people rather than any knowledge or qualifications specific to them as jurists or judges. When applying the third subtest, the Court places itself in the position of weighing considerations as to the extent that decisions promoting the public benefit should be endorsed.
[90] For instance, a demolition order was issued concerning a terrorist's house. The terrorist's family, including his elder brother and his family, also lived in the house. The HCJ decided that demolishing the *entire* house would constitute a disproportionate measure, as punishing the terrorist's actions needed to be weighed against the suffering that would be inflicted on the family of his elder brother. It therefore ordered that two rooms in the house be sealed off, as an alternative to the demolition, in a way that would enable the elder brother and his family to go on living in the rest of the house. HCJ 5510/92 *Turkeman v Minister of Defense*, 48(1) PD 217. Another case dealt with the policy of the Ministry of the Interior concerning marriages between illegal non-Jewish foreign workers and Israeli citizens. The Ministry would order the non-Jewish partner in such marriages to leave Israel for a period of several months to enable the Ministry to test whether the marriage was genuine. The HCJ determined that the policy of the Ministry of the Interior lacked proportionality, since it failed to meet any of the three subtests of the proportionality test. HCJ 3648/97 *Stamka v Minister of Interior*, 53(2) PD 728.
Moreover, when the Court has annulled provisions in Knesset laws (see below), it has done so because these provisions failed the proportionality test established through the 'limiting clauses' of the 1992 Basic Laws. HCJ 1715/97 *Board of Investment Directors in Israel v Minister of Treasury*, 51(4) PD 367; HCJ 6055/95 *Tzemach v Minister of Defense*, 53(5) PD 241; HCJ 1030/99 *Oron v Speaker of the Knesset*, 56(3) PD 640; HCJ 1661/05 *Local Municipality Gaza Beach v Government of Israel*, 59(2) PD 481; HCJ 8276/05 *Adala v Minister of Defense*.

(c) The Pinnacle of activism—annulling Knesset laws

During the 1980s, the judicial activism of the Supreme Court focused mainly on the state's public administration. All the innovations—abolishing the requirements of standing, narrowing the non-justiciability doctrine almost to the vanishing point, and developing reasonableness as the main tool for reviewing administrative decisions—were meant to allow the Court far-reaching intervention in governmental and administrative decisions. The Court also applied its judicial review to the Knesset's non-legislative decisions. Despite the Court's broad activism, however, one central decision-making capacity of another branch of the state remained beyond its reach: Knesset legislation. Subjecting this capacity also to the Court's review was the most significant plank of the Court's activist stance of the 1990s, as well as the most important development in the Court's activism in general.

In the 1995 ruling of *United Mizrahi Bank v Migdal*,[91] the Supreme Court held that it is authorized to annul Knesset legislation if it finds it to contradict the provisions of the Basic Law: Human Dignity and Liberty and the Basic Law: Freedom of Occupation enacted in 1992. The Court came to this conclusion even though neither of these two Basic Laws nor any other source in Israeli law give it any such power, and even though in debating the two Basic Laws the Knesset never expressed any intention to legislate at the constitutional level. Two justices, Meir Shamgar and Aharon Barak, went even further and held that the Court is authorized to annul Knesset legislation that contradicts the provisions of *any* of the Basic Laws enacted by the Knesset since the 1950s.[92]

In the years since *United Mizrahi Bank*, the Court has annulled Knesset legislation seven times. In most cases, the annulled legislation has not involved far-reaching violations of constitutional principles. The Court annulled a provision that, with the establishment of a new licensing regime in the investment industry, failed to give due credit to the experience gained by investment directors who had practiced their trade prior to the new regime.[93] The court annulled a provision that allowed the arrest of a soldier without a court order for a period of 96 hours. The Court held this

---

[91] CA 6821/93 *United Mizrahi Bank Ltd. v Migdal*, 49(4) PD 221.

[92] Moshe Landau, former Chief Justice of the Court, who was an unswerving critic of the Court's activism, rightfully noted that 'a straight line' links the activism of the 1980s (development of the reasonableness test) with that of the 1990s (annulment of Knesset legislation). Moshe Landau, 'On Judicial Activism' (2002) 12 Hamishpat 83, 83–4 (Hebrew); Moshe Landau, 'The Supreme Court as Constitution Maker for Israel' (1996) 3 Mishpat Umimshal 697, 702–10 (Hebrew).

[93] HCJ 1715/97 *Board of Investment Directors in Israel v Minister of Treasury*, 51(4) PD 367.

period to be too long.⁹⁴ The Court annulled a provision that legalized a pirate radio station.⁹⁵ The Court intervened in the compensation granted to Jewish settlers in Gaza who were evacuated from their homes following the 'disengagement' of 2005. (See Chapter 7, below).⁹⁶ The Court annulled a provision that exempted the state from tort liability for certain damages caused by the IDF to residents of the OPT.⁹⁷ In what is the most constitutionally significant annulment decision, the Court annulled legislation that authorized the establishment of private prisons. The Court held that the state is not allowed to divest itself of its responsibility to run prisons, and that prison privatization amounts to a commoditization of inmates in violation of their human dignity.⁹⁸ The Court annulled a provision that allowed court extension of the arrest period of a person interrogated for security crimes without the presence of the arrestee.⁹⁹

---

⁹⁴ HCJ 6055/95 *Tzemach v Minister of Defense*, 53(5) PD 241.
⁹⁵ HCJ 1030/99 *Oron v Speaker of the Knesset*, 56(3) PD 640.
⁹⁶ HCJ 1661/05 *Local Municipality Gaza Beach v Government of Israel*, 59(2) PD 481.
⁹⁷ HCJ 8276/05 *Adala v Minister of Defense*.
⁹⁸ HCJ 2605/05 *Human Rights Unit v Minister of Treasury*.
⁹⁹ HCJ 8823/07 *Ploni v State of Israel*.

Ron Harris has argued that the seeds of the process of judicialization of the Israeli public sphere were planted in the 1970s. Harris identified a growth in the number of petitions submitted to the HCJ in this decade; changes in the Court's jurisprudence toward expansion of its jurisdiction; extension of the Court's jurisdiction to the conduct of the Israeli government in the OPT; changes in the functioning of two successive attorney generals (Meir Shamgar and Aharon Barak) that substantially increased the power and status of that institution; and increased use of investigative committees. Ron Harris, 'Judicialization of the Public Sphere in the Third Decade' in Zvi Zameret and Hanna Yablonka (eds), *The Third Decade* (Jerusalem, Yad Ben Zvi, 2008) 251 (Hebrew).

CHAPTER 4

THE DECLINE OF FORMALISM AND THE RISE OF VALUES

In the previous chapter, I discussed the adoption of a sweeping activist stance by Israel's Supreme Court in its jurisprudence in the 1980s and 1990s. In the present chapter, I will discuss a second significant change discernible in the Court's jurisprudence: The shift to a style of reasoning that exposes the normative meaning and distributive implications of the law. At the end of the chapter, I will discuss still a third significant change in this jurisprudence: the shift from the Court's view of itself as a professional institution whose role is to settle disputes, to a view of itself as a political institution that participates in determining the values that prevail in the country and the distribution of its material resources.

A. LEGAL FORMALISM

(a) The principles of legal formalism

In the course of the twentieth century a rich body of literature grew around the concept of legal formalism, mainly in three contexts.[1] First, since formalism is a key concept in Max Weber's theory of law and modernity, it has been discussed extensively in the literature dealing with the sociology of law.[2] Second, formalism was an important principle in the 'legal

---

[1] Wolfgang Schluchter, *The Rise Of Western Rationalism* (G. Roth trans, Berkeley, University of California Press, 1981, 1985); R. Brubaker, *The Limits Of Rationality* (London, Routledge, 1984); Anthony T. Kronman, *The Lost Lawyer—Failing Ideals Of The Legal Profession* (Cambridge, Harvard University Press, 1993); Roscoe Pound, 'Mechanical Jurisprudence' (1908) 8 Colum L Rev 605; Fredrick Schauer, 'Formalism' (1988) 97 Yale L J 509; Duncan Kennedy, 'Legal Formality' (1973) 2 J Leg Stud 351; Brian Leiter, 'Positivism, Formalism, Realism' (1999) 99 Colum L Rev 1138; Ernest Weinrib, 'Legal Formalism: On the Imminent Rationality of the Law' (1988) 97 Yale L J 951; Larry Alexander, '"With Me, It's All or Nothing": Formalism in Law and Morality' (1999) 66 U Chi L Rev 530.

[2] Max Weber in Guenther Roth and Claus Wittich (eds), *Economy and Society* (Berkeley, University of California Press, 1978) Vol 2; Anthony T. Kronman, *Max Weber* (Stanford, Stanford University Press, 1983); Donald N. Levin, 'Rationality and Freedom: Weber and Beyond' (1981) 51 Soc Inq 5; Stephen Kalberg, 'Max Weber's Types of Rationality: Cornerstones for the Analysis

science' school that dominated German law in the closing decades of the nineteenth century. The history of German law in the nineteenth century, therefore, deals with the concept of legal formalism.[3] Third, the history of American law since the nineteenth century is usually presented in terms of the shift from a formalist to an instrumentalist approach towards law. According to this depiction, a formalist worldview became dominant in the mid-nineteenth century, but in a process that began near its end and continued throughout the twentieth century, the instrumentalist perception of law attained a position of dominance in American law. The turning point in this process dates back to the 1920s when the school of legal realism exposed the fallacies of formalism, both as a description of what actually happens in judicial decision-making processes, and as a normative stance towards legal decision-making and the social function of law in general.[4]

The concept of legal formalism that emerges from the literature in these three contexts rests on four principles:

(i) The organization of legal norms into a system ruled by an inner logic

Legal formalism strives to make the factual situation at the root of every legal dispute amenable to classification into a legal category which contains the solution purported to solve the dispute. Formalism, therefore, strives to organize all legal norms into a system built according to an inner logic which is both horizontal and vertical.

Horizontally, legal norms are supposed to be arranged according to defined legal categories (contracts separate from torts; civil law from public law; substantive law from procedural law, and so forth). The purpose of this structure is to enable the jurist to identify the relevant legal characteristics in each and every factual case and then place it in the single legal category that is supposed to resolve it. Jurists who adopt a formalist worldview devote a great deal of intellectual energy to the prevention of any overlapping between legal categories.

---

of Rationalization Processes in History' (1980) 85 Am J Soc 1145; Ronen Shamir, 'Formal and Substantive Rationality in American Law: A Weberian Perspective' (1993) 2 Soc & Leg Stud 45; Schluchter, id; Brubaker, id.

[3] Mathias Reimann, 'Nineteenth Century German Legal Science' (1990) 31 BC L Rev 837; James E. Herget and Stephen Wallace, 'The German Free Law Movement as the Source of American Legal Realism' 73 (1987) Va L Rev 399; Roger Berkowitz, *The Gift of Science* (Cambridge, Harvard University Press, 2005).

[4] Morton Horwitz, 'The Rise of Legal Formalism' (1975) 19 Am J Leg History 251; Robert S. Summers, *Instrumentalism And American Legal Theory* (Ithaca, Cornell University Press, 1982); Morton Horwitz, *The Transformation Of American Law 1870–1960* (Oxford, Oxford University Press, 1992) chapter 1.

Vertically, underlying every legal branch there should be several fundamental general principles, from which more detailed minor principles and rules can be derived, so that the system is governed by a logical hierarchy of norms. This structure is supposed to allow jurists to derive specific legal solutions from higher norms, in cases in which no readymade solution unequivocally exists for a legal problem that may arise in the system.

(ii) Law as an autonomous system: Detaching law from its normative and distributive dimensions

Legal formalists think that law should operate as if it were an autonomous system detached from social reality. Legal formalism holds that neither judicial decision-making processes nor the academic discourse on the law are supposed to deal directly with social reality. The concern of lawyers should be with the legal norms found in the legal system, not the normative goals or distributive outcomes that can be realized by means of the law. Lawyers should not be asking what values and which distribution of resources will be effected in society if this or that legal norm were to be adopted, but what norm should be chosen to apply according to the inner logic of the existing normative system.

Formalists, then, do not perceive lawyers and judges as participating in processes that determine the normative character of their societies or affect the distribution of material resources in their societies. Rather, formalists see lawyers as professionals whose main activity is the application of expert knowledge in the service of clients for the legal realization of the aims determined by the clients. Similarly, formalists see judges as professionals whose main activity is the application of expert knowledge for the purpose of settling legal disputes. Thus, at the basis of formalism lies a distinction between politics and law which overlaps (on both sides of the distinction) the distinction between legislators and courts, as well as the distinction between politics and professionalism.

In that spirit, formalists view law schools as professional schools—institutions whose primary role is to train students to join the existing legal practice and function successfully within it. Formalist jurists and formalist teachers, then, devote their intellectual energies to honing their students' skills in the application of legal doctrine, by helping them master the details of legal doctrine and teaching them to 'think like lawyers', ie, to identify in daily events factual components that are considered legally relevant; to place daily factual events in the legal categories containing the legal solutions that purportedly apply to them; and to apply inductive and deductive reasoning in resolving cases for which no clear legal rule can be found.

(iii) Limited creativity in judicial decision-making processes

An ideal model of legal formalism assumes that judges will usually find an appropriate norm within the system, providing a direct solution to the case at hand and readily available for application. If the system fails to offer such a norm, it should be assumed that the norm exists implicitly, and it is the task of the judge to reveal it through an inductive and deductive process of legal reasoning that relies on existent legal norms as its raw material.

In *inductive* reasoning, the legal norm is formulated according to the contents of 'neighboring norms' whose relevance to the problem can be pointed out. In *deductive* reasoning, the legal norm providing the solution is derived from principles and rules in the system. The law, then, is supposed to develop not by considering the normative meaning and distributive implications of potential alternatives, but from within the system of norms. Furthermore, it is supposed to be a technical-mechanistic process, invariably leading to one agreed norm at which all users of the system are necessarily expected to arrive, as long as they apply it correctly.

(iv) Certainty and planning ability as central goals of the legal system

According to legal formalism, legal norms are thought to be found in the legal system, whether explicitly or implicitly, as the product of a technical-mechanistic process of exposure. Hence, decision-makers operating within the system can view norms as part of the world's factual circumstances, on which they can rely when they plan to achieve certain aims. Legal norms, then, are deemed to enable legal consumers to operate with a high level of certainty, that is, with a high degree of immunity from unexpected external interference in the actions they have taken in order to attain their legal aims.

B. LEGAL FORMALISM IN ISRAELI LAW

(a) Outline of the argument

In this chapter I will argue that until the 1980s Israeli law operated in the context of a formalistic legal culture. This was evident, above all, in the reasoning employed in the opinions of the Supreme Court. The canonical reasoning in the Court's opinions from the establishment of the State of Israel in 1948 until the 1980s was formalistic. It is true that the opinions from this period offer a mixture of formalistic and non-formalistic arguments in different opinions issued by various justices, and often in a single opinion issued by one justice (indeed, a legal system that does not simultaneously resort to formalistic and non-formalistic reasoning can hardly be imagined).[5] Nevertheless, formalistic reasoning enjoyed canonical status, non-formalistic reasoning marginal status only. In the 1980s and 1990s, however, a new, value-laden jurisprudence, which exposes the normative meaning and distributive implications of the law, gained ascendancy in the Court's opinions, and the earlier formalistic legal reasoning, while still discernible in the Court's opinions, lost much of its former status.[6]

Three points deserve emphasis. First, as noted above, it would be wrong to present the non-formalistic elements in the Court's opinions of the 1980s and 1990s as an entirely new phenomenon, and not only because some value-laden reasoning may be found in its opinions even before the 1980s. Cultural paradigms develop gradually, rather than through revolutionary or radical departure from the past, and the seeds of every new cultural paradigm lie dormant in its predecessor:[7] A truly new cultural paradigm, indiscernible in the context of the current one, will be rejected, as would a transplanted organ completely foreign to the genetic environment into which it is transplanted.[8] Thus, though some non-formalistic reasoning can be found in opinions of the Court issued before the 1980s, in that period it still served only a marginal purpose; in the 1980s and 1990s, however, such reasoning became canonical and rose to prominence.

Second, formalistic reasoning is also value-laden, that is, it also embodies normative and distributive determinations. The difference between formalistic and value-laden reasoning, however, is that in the framework of

---

[5] Patrick S. Atiyah and Robert M. Summers, *Form and Substance in Anglo-American Law* (Oxford, Clarendon Press, 1987) 2–3.

[6] This argument could also borrow Thomas Kuhn's notion of 'scientific paradigm.' Thomas S. Kuhn, *The Structure of Scientific Revolutions*, 2nd edn, (Chicago, University of Chicago Press, 1962). According to Kuhn, most scientists' scientific research is conducted in the context of an accepted and stable scientific paradigm, namely a shared set of presumptions as to the questions to be investigated, together with the criteria for determining the answers to these questions. The nature of such paradigms, according to Kuhn, is that they ultimately encounter a 'crisis' and, in a process of scientific revolution, are replaced by other, purportedly better ones. Borrowing Kuhn's terminology, legal formalism could be said to have been the paradigm of Israeli law until the 1980s. Formalism dictated the way law should be done: What questions the jurist should contend with—various factual situations that raise legal questions—and how to contend with them—the formalistic techniques of legal reasoning. In the 1980s, the formalistic paradigm was replaced by a non-formalistic paradigm. The change was evident in the prominence given a series of new questions that jurists were expected to address, namely about the normative meaning of the law and about the distribution of the resources created by the law.

[7] Itamar Even-Zohar, 'Introduction' (1980) 11 Poetics Today 1, 4 ('this is a regular process in attitude change in culture: We do not understand or accept anything new except in the context of the old.').

[8] Zohar Shavit, 'The Entrance of a New Model into the System', in Karl Eimermacher et al (eds), *Issues in Slavic Literary and Cultural Theory* (Bochum, Universitasverlag Dr. N. Brockmeyer, 1989) 593, 594–6 ('A new model enters the system in a slow process in which the new elements and functions distinguishing between this model and the previous one are only gradually structured... [T]he new model does not and can not enter the system as a global novelty... As in the case of a new transplanted organ, the organ needs to be regarded as already part of the system, to be covered by an already known entity so that it will not be rejected.').

the former normative and distributive implications are concealed, whereas in that of the latter they are exposed and openly discussed. Furthermore, whereas formalistic reasoning contends with the normative and distributive implications of legal decisions at a low level of awareness and in keeping with the judges' common sense intuitions,[9] value-laden decisions seek to deal with these implications at a high level of awareness (preferably by openly applying theoretical and academic knowledge borrowed from the various disciplines of the social sciences and the humanities).[10]

Third, although I maintain that the kind of legal reasoning employed by the Supreme Court has changed, it is not my contention that the normative contents of the Court's opinions since the establishment of Israel to the present day have changed. Throughout Israel's six decades of statehood, the Court has promoted a liberal value system at whose core lies the concept of human rights.

In the rest of this chapter, then, I divide the history of the jurisprudence of Israel's Supreme Court into two periods: the first from the establishment of Israel until the 1980s, and the second from the 1980s to the present day. Nevertheless, I focus mainly on two decades, the 1950s and the 1980s, which I consider the most formative in the history of the Court.

(b) Anglicization and formalism

Until the closing decades of the twentieth century, the professional culture of lawyers, judges, and law teachers in England was founded on the bedrock of legal formalism. Ronald Dworkin describes the approach that dominated English jurisprudence in the mid-twentieth century:

> [T]he subject was taught out of standard textbooks like *Salmond on Jurisprudence* and *Paton on Jurisprudence*. Most of these texts were devoted to what they called analytical jurisprudence, which they carefully distinguished from 'ethical jurisprudence' or the study of what the law ought to be. By analytical jurisprudence they meant the careful elaboration of the meaning of certain terms (like 'fault', 'possession', 'ownership', 'negligence', and 'law') that are fundamental to law in the sense that they appear not just in one or another branch but throughout the range of legal doctrine.[11]

Unlike American law, then, English law was spared the intellectual confrontation between formalism and instrumentalism, and thus until the closing decades of the twentieth century it remained mainly formalistic.[12]

---

[9] Clifford Geertz, 'Common Sense as a Cultural System' in *Local Knowledge* (New York, Basic Books, Inc., Publishers, 1983) 73.
[10] Bruce Ackerman, *Property Law and the Constitution* (New Haven, Yale University Press, 1977).
[11] Ronald Dworkin, *Taking Rights Seriously* (Cambridge, Harvard University Press, 1977) 2.
[12] P. S. Atiyah, *The Rise and Fall of Freedom of Contract* (Oxford, Clarendon Press, 1979) 660–71; Atiyah and Summers, above n 5.

In Chapter 2 I argued that over the course of the thirty years of the British rule over Palestine the local legal community underwent a profound and extensive process of Anglicization. As part of this process, lawyers, judges, and law teachers in Eretz Israel, and subsequently in the State of Israel, internalized legal formalism as the bedrock of their professional culture. That was the situation until the 1980s: The formalistic worldview was shared by everyone active in the legal field in Israel—primarily judges, but also lawyers and law teachers.

Shimon Agranat, the third Chief Justice of the Supreme Court, described the dominant legal worldview at the end of the British Mandate in terms borrowed from the world of legal formalism. According to Agranat, at that time the law was perceived as:

a 'closed system' that requires all answers to all questions to be reached by way of logical deduction out of a predetermined set of written rules... Such a system differs from an 'open system' that allows for gradual filling up of legal lacunas... by drawing on natural justice principles and on considerations of public policy.[13]

Agranat received his legal education at the University of Chicago Law School in the latter half of the 1920s. When Agranat was a young judge in Eretz Israel in the 1940s, writes his biographer Pnina Lahav:

[t]he more he reflected on the nature of the judicial process, the more critical he became of the Mandatory system, which appeared to him as excessively formalistic, and the more he tried to show, in as discrete and inoffensive a way as he could, that a legal opinion need not be full of what Felix Cohen called 'transcendental nonsense'.[14]

Eli Salzberger and Fania Oz-Salzberger offer an additional explanation, besides the Anglicization of the law of Eretz Israel, for the centrality of formalism in Israel's legal culture during the early decades. In the first twenty-five years of the Supreme Court (that is, until the mid-1970s), fully half of its judges were of German extraction or had received their legal education at German universities. These judges, appointed to the Court in the 1950s, constituted the largest group among the Court's judges at the time. The 'German judges' had studied in the Weimar republic during the 1920s and had internalized, in the course of their studies, a formalistic approach to law that was a product of late nineteenth-century German Legal Science, viewing law 'as an exact science... whose practical application is merely a

---

[13] Pnina Lahav, 'Traits in Justice Agranat's Legal Worldview' in A. Barak et al (eds), *Essays in Honor of Shimon Agranat* (Jerusalem, 1988) 9, 15–6 (Hebrew). Lahav describes her disappointment when, in the mid-1960s, she began her law studies at the Faculty of Law of the Hebrew University in Jerusalem. At the time, according to Lahav, the study of law was conducted in a formalistic mode, as something arid and cold, ignoring the law's historical, social, and human aspects. Id.

[14] Pnina Lahav, *Judgment In Jerusalem—Chief Justice Simon Agranat And The Zionist Century* (Berkeley, University of California Press, 1997) 69.

matter of technical skill.' In that vein, law professors at Weimar, according to Salzberger and Oz-Salzberger, saw themselves as professionals whose task was to teach merely the positive contents of the law, without offering any critical or theoretical explications of the law's normative meanings and distributive implications. They therefore attempted

to cast out the new social sciences from the threshold of the law faculties. Attempts to bridge between law and economics, sociology, and psychology usually remained outside the traditional curriculum.[15]

A formalistic perception of the law, then, was a key element in the legal approach that the Jewish students of these professors brought with them to Eretz Israel. Salzberger and Oz-Salzberger also note that, in the wake of their immigration to Eretz Israel, these Jewish jurists enthusiastically endorsed the formalistic English legal culture and doctrine.

(c) *Judicial reasoning in the 1950s*

Opinions from the 1950s, also from the 1960s and 1970s, reveal a legal culture dominated by the norms of legal formalism, as manifested by several typical patterns of thought and reasoning:

(i) Focus on language

The jurisprudence of this period points to the belief that the solution to legal problems lies mainly in the language of legal norms. The opinions of the Court exhibit a considerable effort to engage in the conceptual analysis of relevant norms and to contrast the wording of these norms with, or distinguish it from, that of similar norms within the same piece of legislation or that of similar norms in other pertinent legislation, whether extant or revoked, in Israel, England, or other common law countries.

One example is HCJ 95/49 *Al Khuri v Chief of Staff.* An administrative writ of detention issued by the Chief of Staff in September 1949 ordered that the petitioner be 'detained and held for a period of twelve months at a place within the territory of the State of Israel, to be determined by the Police Commissioner.' The writ was issued after information had been received about acts of murder and violence against Jews committed by the petitioner in the 1940s, and in reliance on Ordinance 111(1) of the Defense (Emergency) Regulations, 1945, which stated:

A Military Commander may by order direct that any person shall be detained for any period not exceeding one year in such a place of detention as may be specified by the Military Commander in the order.

---

[15] Eli Salzberger and Fania Oz-Salzberger, 'The Hidden German Origin of the Israeli Supreme Court' in Daniel Gutwein and Menachem Mautner (eds), *Law And History* (Jerusalem, Zalman Shazar Center, 1999) 357, 370, 372 (Hebrew).

The petitioner questioned the legality of the writ issued against him, inter alia claiming that Ordinance 111(1) requires the detention writ to specify a particular venue, whereas the writ against him had failed to do so, instead transferring to the Police Commissioner the authority to determine the place of detention.

Justice Agranat accepted the petitioner's claim and ordered his release:

> Due to the failure to set a specific place of detention in the body of the writ... this writ is null and void and hence lacking any legal validity whatsoever.

A large part of Justice Agranat's reasoning was formalistic. He discussed the wording of Ordinances 111(1), 111(3), and 111(6) of the Defense Regulations; the difference between the wording of the latter Ordinances and that of Ordinance 111(1); the parallel ordinance in England; and he also analyzed the concept 'detention' as used in Ordinance 111(1): 'A person is not detained in an empty space. The very concept of "detention" implies that a person is held in a known physical space, which is entirely delimited and defined.'[16]

(ii) Belief in a strict division of powers between the Knesset and the Court

The jurisprudence of the 1950s, 1960s, and 1970 contains many statements revealing an entrenched belief in a strict separation of powers between the Knesset and the courts. The Supreme Court repeatedly warned itself that making normative and distributive decisions is the Knesset's task, whereas the courts are charged with the secondary, and relatively passive, role of applying existing norms. In a typical pronouncement, Justice Moshe Silberg wrote that judges should be cautious 'not to exceed the bounds of their authority and not to don the legislator's garb,' lest a situation arise in which 'the judge is the one who created the law, rather than the sovereign legislator, and no such thing will be done in our land.'[17]

Furthermore, that approach also applied to cases obviously pointing to a legislative lacuna. The Court repeatedly emphasized that, even in such cases, it lacks authority to intervene in the existing law and correct it, and must leave this task to the legislator. In a characteristic statement, Justice Moshe Landau asserted that the Court must 'validate the clear wording of the law, and should the ensuing result prove undesirable, changing it is not within our powers.'[18]

---

[16] HCJ 95/49 *El Khouri v Chief of Staff,* 4 PD 34, 41, 42.
[17] HCJ 188/63 *Batzul and Elazhari v Minister of Interior,* 19(1) PD 337, 346.
[18] HCJ 99/52 *Palmoni v Trustee of Absentees Assets,* 7 PD 836, 840.

(iii) Administrative law: Dealing with authority rather than contents

In the realm of administrative law, as noted in Chapter 3, the Court's jurisprudence focused on whether the State's public administration had acted within its jurisdiction, with only limited reference to the specific contents of its action.

(iv) Stressing the division into legal categories

The opinions of the 1950s, as well as those of the ensuing decades, emphasized the division into various legal categories. They dealt at length and in great detail with the assignment of factual situations to possible legal categories, and with comparisons between various legal categories regarding the factual and legal elements that are required for their application. In that spirit, the emphasis was on the attempt to apply each legal category only when all the anticipated factual conditions prevail.[19]

(v) Emphasis on the value of legal stability

The jurisprudence of this early period emphasized the values of legal stability and legal certainty.[20]

(vi) Meticulous reading of precedents

Cass Sunstein draws a distinction between the kind of reasoning that discloses its underlying normative theories and the kind that does not. Sunstein writes that, in a society fraught with profound normative disputes, courts should endorse modes of reasoning that do not disclose the normative theories underlying their decisions, and he lists several such modes. One is the application of precedents: When a court relies on precedent, it falls back on a previous decision and is not required to clarify the normative theory that supports its ruling.[21]

Following Sunstein, it can be said that the jurisprudence of the Supreme Court in the 1950s, 1960s, and 1970s was generally based on a close reading of precedents, and the avoidance of any open discussion of the precedents' normative grounds. Moshe Landau, the fifth Chief Justice of the

---

[19] See eg CA 47/48 *Agushevich v Puterman*, 5 PD 4; CA 76/51 *Bar-On v Topol*, 8 PD 1065; Cr App 99/51 *Podamski v Attorney General*, 6 PD 341; Cr App 35/52 *Rotenshtreich v Attorney General*, 7 PD 58; Cr App 208/51 *Haker v Barash*, 8 PD 566.

[20] HCJ 287/51 *Reem v Ministry of Treasury*, 8 PD 494, 503; CA 376/46 *Rosenbaum v Rosenbaum*, 2 Psakim 5, 18, 19.

[21] Cass R. Sunstein, *Legal Reasoning and Political Conflict* (Oxford, Oxford University Press, 1996).

Supreme Court, wrote that the Court's jurisprudence in that period was characterized by:

advance from the particular to the particular, adherence to the facts of the case, and rigorous textual interpretation of previous opinions, recoil from theoretical generalizations, and the inductive, organic growth of the law.[22]

(c) *Non-formalistic elements in the Court's jurisprudence*

Law is a rich cultural system made up of a large number of elements, some mutually contradictory (this profusion of contents and contradictions is a characteristic of all cultural systems).[23] As noted above, since the foundation of Israel the Supreme Court has included both formalistic and non-formalistic reasoning in different opinions, and sometimes in the same opinion, even by the same judge. Nevertheless, formalistic reasoning enjoyed primacy until the 1980s, whereas non-formalistic reasoning was marginal.

The most famous example of a non-formalistic opinion from the 1950s is HCJ 73/53 *'Kol Ha-Am' Co. Ltd. v Minister of the Interior*. In that opinion, Justice Agranat spoke about the centrality of the principle of freedom of expression in democratic regimes. In his view, in order to understand the limitations that can be imposed on freedom of expression, 'we must first of all consider the values involved in the exercise of that important right. It is important that we should first acquaint ourselves with the interests that that right is designed to protect.'

Freedom of expression, however, should be balanced against other values, wrote Justice Agranat, in a process whereby 'we weigh various competing interests and, after reflection, select those which, in the circumstances, predominate.'

In another section of his opinion, speaking about the role of the Declaration of Independence of the State of Israel in interpretive processes, Justice Agranat wrote that

insofar as the Declaration 'expresses the vision of the people and its faith'... we are bound to pay attention to the matters set forth in it when we come to interpret

---

[22] Moshe Landau, 'Trends in the Decisions of the Supreme Court', (1982) 8 Tel Aviv U L Rev 500, 502–3 (Hebrew).

[23] R. A. Shweder, 'Culture: Contemporary Views' (2001) 5 Int'l Encyclopedia Of The Social And Behavioral Sciences; U. Hannerz, 'Anthropology' (2001) 1 Int'l Encyclopedia Of The Social And Behavioral Sciences; T. H. Eriksen, 'Anthropology, History of', id; William H. Sewell Jr., 'The Concept(s) of Culture' in Victoria E. Bonnell and Lynn Hunt (eds), *Beyond The Cultural Turn—New Directions In The Study Of Society And Culture* (Berkeley, University of California Press, 1999) 35; Robert Brightman, 'Forget Culture: Replacement, Transcendence, Relexification' (1995) 10 Cultural Anthropology 509; Paul DiMaggio, 'Culture and Cognition' (1997) 23 Ann Rev Sociol 263.

and give meaning to the laws... For it is a well-known axiom that the law of a people must be studied in the light of its national way of life.[24]

As Pnina Lahav, Agranat's biographer, has written:

The jurisprudence utilized by Agranat in Kol Ha-Am was distinctively American, rooted in an upswing in Progressive thinking and politics. *Kol Ha-Am* rejected legal formalism and rigid positivism and recognized law as a social system and the judicial process as an enterprise engaged in balancing political interests. In short, Agranat's opinion in *Kol Ha-Am* vindicated sociological jurisprudence.[25]

C. THE 1950S JURISPRUDENCE OF THE SUPREME COURT IN A CULTURAL CONTEXT

(a) *The collectivism of the 1950s*

Since the establishment of Israel, following the Anglicization of the law of Palestine in the Mandate period, the Supreme Court has applied and developed Israeli law in close association with English law and with the laws of other common law countries. Since the establishment of the state the Court has served therefore as the state organ most closely affiliated with the liberal worldview and as the prime agent in entrenching liberal values in Israel's political culture. This has meant that in the early years of statehood there was a tension, if not a contrast, between the central values of Israeli culture of the time and the cultural values embodied in the jurisprudence of the Court.

In the 1950s, the central values of the hegemonic culture in Israel were collectivistic,[26] asserting the primacy of the state over the citizen. A life

---

[24] 7 PD 871, 876, 879, 884.
[25] Lahav, above n 14, at 108.
[26] On the distinction between cultures of collectivism and cultures of individualism see: Harry C. Triandis, et al, 'Multimethod Probes of Individualism and Collectivism' (1990) 59 J Personality & Soc Psych 1006; Harry C. Triandis, 'The Self and Social Behavior in Differing Cultural Contexts' (1989) 96 Psych Rev 506; Ladd Wheeler, Harry T. Reis & Michael Harris Bond, 'Collectivism—Individualism in Everyday Social Life: The Middle Kingdom and the Melting Pot' (1989) 57 J Personality & Soc Psych 79; Harry C. Triandis et al, 'Individualism and Collectivism: Cross-Cultural Perspectives on Self-Ingroup Relationships' (1988) 54 J Personality & Soc Psych 323. For depictions of Israeli culture of the 1950s as collectivist see: Anita Shapira, 'Elements of National Ethos in the Transition to Statehood' in Jehuda Reinharz, Gideon Shimoni, Yosef Salmon (eds), *Jewish Nationalism and Politics: New Perspectives* (Jerusalem, Zalman Shazar Center, 1996) 253 (Hebrew); Yaron Ezrahi, *Rubber Bullets* (Berkeley, University of California Press, 1997) 11, 29–30, 82–3. On the roots of collectivism in the culture of the Yishuv see: Dan Horowitz And Moshe Lissak, *Trouble in Utopia* (Tel Aviv, Am Oved Publishers, 1990) 153–4 (Hebrew); Zeev Sternhell, *Nation-Building or a New Society?* (Tel Aviv, Am Oved Publishers, 1995) (Hebrew); S. N. Eisenstadt, 'The Struggle Over the Symbols of Collective Identity and its Boundaries in the Post-Revolutionary Israeli Society' in Pinhas Ginossar and Avi Bareli (eds), *Zionism—A Contemporary Controversy* (Sede Boqer, Ben-Gurion Research Center, 1996) 1 (Hebrew); Yonathan Shapiro, 'The Historical Origins of Israeli Democracy' in Ehud Sprinzak and Larry Diamond (eds), *Israeli Democracy under Stress* (Boulder, Lynne Rienner Publishers, 1993) 66–8; Anita Shapira, 'The Land Generation' in *New Jews Old Jews* (Tel Aviv, Am Oved Publishers, 1997) 130, 136 (Hebrew).

well spent was one in which the individual contributed to the advancement of the state's collective good. Individuals were expected to contribute, to the best of their ability, to the success of the Zionist endeavor. The culture's pivotal values were 'sacrifice'—the sacrifice of one's life for the general good (as was the case, most tragically, during the War of Independence)[27]—and *'hagshamah'* [realization, or fulfillment]—devoting one's life to the service of the collective in such areas as settlement, defense, immigrant absorption, and so forth.[28] Operating in the context of this hegemonic culture, the state's institutions promoted extensive processes of 'nation building.'[29]

The dominant collectivistic culture in Israel in the 1950s was closely related to the dominant approach at the time concerning the relative standing of public and private forces in the economy. During the 1950s, the prevailing sentiment among Israeli decision-makers was a deep distrust of the market, together with a faith in extensive government intervention in the economy.[30]

In every culture, however, there are many and contradictory elements. It therefore bears emphasis that certain elements within the Israeli culture of the 1950s stood in opposition to those representing the hegemonic culture, and widespread practices deviated from that culture's key values.[31] Moreover, no hegemonic culture ever succeeds in imposing itself absolutely on all its subjects. In the Israeli culture of the 1950s, then, there were also groups who lived by values that were opposed to the central values of the hegemonic culture (eg, the ultra-Orthodox and Israeli Arabs).

(b) Legal formalism and downplaying the gap between the legal culture and the general culture

It is my contention in this chapter that the jurisprudence of the Supreme Court in the 1950s and the ensuing decades was characterized by a relatively high level of formalism. Legal formalism was not the product of a

---

[27] Oz Almog, *The Sabra—a Profile* (Tel Aviv, Am Oved Publishers, 1997) 74, 121, 130, 138, 142–3 (Hebrew).

[28] Almog, id, at 110, 115–8, 233–4, 320, 323; Amos Oz, *Under This Blazing Light* (Nicholas de Lange trans, Cambridge, Cambridge University Press, 1979) 125–33; Yonathan Shapiro, *An Elite Without Successors* (Tel Aviv, Sifriat Poalim Publishing House, 1984) 73–83 (Hebrew); Avraham Shapira, 'The 1948 Generation and the Legacy of Jewish Culture' in Mordechai Bar-On (ed), *The Challenge Of Independence—Ideological And Cultural Aspects Of Israel's First Decade* (Jerusalem, Yad Ben Zvi, 1999) 167, 188, 189, 193 (Hebrew).

[29] Charles S. Liebman And Eliezer Don-Yehiya, *Civil Religion In Israel* (Berkeley, University of California Press, 1983) chapters 4, 5; Daniel Gutwein, 'Left and Right Post-Zionism and the Privatization of Israeli Collective Memory' (2001) 20 J Israeli History 9, 37.

[30] Yair Aharoni, 'The Changing Political Economy in Israel' (1998) 555 Annals Of The American Academy Of Political Science 127.

[31] Orit Rozin, *Duty And Love—Individualism And Collectivism In 1950s Israel* (Tel Aviv, Am Oved Publishers, 2008) (Hebrew); Avi Bareli, *Mapai In Israel's Early Independence 1948–1953* (Jerusalem, Yad Ben Zvi, 2007) chapters 8, 9 (Hebrew).

conscious choice by the Supreme Court justices, but rather a central component of their professional culture, which the British had imparted in the course of their thirty-year rule in Eretz Israel. However, legal formalism served the needs of the Court well, given the Court's problematic status as a 'cultural alien' operating as an agent of liberal values in a state whose hegemonic culture was collectivistic. Formalism enabled the Court to downplay the normative dimension of its decisions and present the judicial decision-making process as a professional, mechanistic course of action rather than one that involves normative choices. The Court was thus able to downplay the cultural gap that prevailed at the time between the central values of the legal culture and those of the country's hegemonic culture.[32]

An example is HCJ 1/49 *Bezerano v Minister of Police*, one of the most important constitutional decisions in the history of Israeli law. The case dealt with the ban imposed on 'middlemen' who represented clients before the Ministry of Transportation and the Police. The state claimed that the petitioning middlemen had no acquired right to pursue their occupation, and there was no obligation incumbent on the state to enable them to do so. Justice Shneor Zalman Cheshin rejected the state's claim. Laying the foundations for the liberal edifice of Israel's administrative and constitutional law, Justice Cheshin wrote that when citizens want the state's administration to do something for them, they must point to the legal source imposing a duty on it to perform this action. Similarly, when the administration wishes to forbid the performance of a certain action by a citizen, it must point to the legal source for the prohibition it wishes to impose. Justice Cheshin added:

> It is a fundamental principle that every person has a natural right to engage in any work or profession of his choice, as long as his pursuit of this work or profession is not legally forbidden... As long as the law does not forbid the [middlemen] to engage in the craft they have chosen for themselves... their right is a right, and they cannot be banned from exercising this right except for reasons specified in the law.[33]

In the collectivist era, when the state demanded '*hagshamah*' and even 'sacrifice' from its citizens, Justice Cheshin found it hard to emphasize the importance of the natural right to freedom of occupation, often associated

---

[32] When Israel was established, the Court was required to instill in the government bodies of the young state values of legalism, that is, of action according to preset rules. Legal formalism, which was then dominant in the legal culture of the Court, served this purpose well: it made it possible to inculcate the government with respect for the rule of law in the formal sense. For a classic statement of this argument see: Alfred Witkon, 'The Law in a Developing Land' in *Justice And The Judiciary* (Jerusalem and Tel Aviv, Schocken Publishing House, 1988) 39 (Hebrew). See also: Tom Segev, *1949—The First Israelis* (Jerusalem, Domino Publishing, 1984) 83–104 (Hebrew).
[33] 2 PD 80, 82–3.

with the value of personal self-realization. Hence, his conclusion is cloaked in the conceptual language of 'right', 'duty' and 'prohibition', while creating a distinction between two factual situations that are governed by two distinct rules that necessarily follow: When citizens ask the state's administration to act in their benefit, they must point to a law granting them a right to this requirement from the administration; when citizens want the administration to refrain from a specific action toward them, the administration must point to a law granting it a right to persist in that action.

(c) The 1950s: A comparison between law and literature

A comparison with the Israeli literature of the 1950s may shed light on the Supreme Court's jurisprudence and unique contribution during that period. In the 1950s, as noted above, the Court introduced liberal values into a society and culture whose pivotal values were collectivistic. The Supreme Court was repeatedly required to resolve conflicts between individuals and the collective's state authorities. On some occasions, it did so by granting preference to the rights of individuals over the requirements of the collective. In doing that, the Court was acting within the professional culture of Israeli law of the time, which was premised on the blend of a formalistic style of reasoning together with the substantive values of the political theory of liberalism.

Israeli literature in the 1950s contended with a conflict similar to the one that faced the Court. Generally, however, it resolved the conflict by subordinating the individual to the needs of the collective. The writings of the dominant group of authors in the literary field of the 1950s express 'a basic tension between the individual and the collective,' writes Avner Holtzman:

> The individual's longing for self-expression and self-realization is presented in this fiction against a background of the need to consent, willingly or under duress, to the imperatives of the collective framework—the kibbutz, the army, the state, Zionist ideology or the Jewish historical legacy.[34]

Conflicts between the individual and the collective, however,

> are usually solved in a way that meets the demands of the Zionist narrative... The personal identity of the Israeli is subordinate to and derived from... his existence in a collective.[35]

Clearly, Israeli literature of the 1950s was well integrated in the hegemonic culture of the time and played an important role in its dissemination.

---

[34] Avner Holtzman, 'The Literature of the "In Land Generation"' in Zvi Tzameret and Hanna Yablonka (eds), *The First Decade, 1948–1958* (Jerusalem, Yad Ben Zvi, 1997) 263, 268 (Hebrew).

[35] Hanan Hever, *Literature Written From Here* (Tel Aviv, Miskal-Yedioth Ahronoth Books, 1999) 16, 17 (Hebrew).

Moreover, throughout the 1950s writers and poets were engaged in a dialogue among themselves and with the country's political leadership as to the ways in which the literary community might contribute to the project of nation-building. In the early 1950s, Israel's literary community had endorsed the notion of '(ideologically) mobilized literature'—an approach that judged literature by its contribution to the nation-building effort and the extent to which it described that effort in positive, encouraging, and uncritical terms.[36]

By contrast, the actions of the Supreme Court in the context of a liberal legal culture contradicted those elements of the hegemonic culture that were founded on the primacy of collectivist values (insofar as the Court's identification with Zionism was concerned, however, its actions were entirely in accord with the hegemonic culture). The relationship between the professional culture of Israel's legal community and the country's hegemonic culture in the 1950s, then, was clearly the antithesis of the relationship between the culture of the literary community and the country's hegemonic culture during the same decade.

It was the formalistic professional culture of the legal community in the 1950s, which perceived law as an autonomous and apolitical set of rules and conceptions operated by professionals according to its inner logic, that enabled the legal community to maintain and develop the evolving values of Israeli law, which were in tension with, if not in contradiction to, some of the central values of the hegemonic culture.

D. THE 1980s AND THE 1990s: THE DECLINE OF FORMALISM AND THE RISE OF VALUES IN ISRAELI LAW

In the 1980s and 1990s the use of value-laden reasoning in the opinions of the Supreme Court dramatically increased at the expense of the formerly dominant formalistic reasoning. This is manifest in the rise of several new

---

[36] It was only at the end of the 1950s and during the 1960s that a new type of literature, focusing on individual topics or on universal topics not necessarily related to the Israeli experience, arose and became dominant. Only then did Israeli literature begin to be perceived as an autonomous sphere, to be judged by literary criteria and not necessarily by the extent of its contribution to the collective endeavor. Hanna Herzig, *The Voice Saying I—Trends In Israeli Prose Fiction Of The 1980s* (Tel Aviv, Open University Press, 1998) chapter 1 (Hebrew); Gershon Shaked, 'Introduction' in G. Shaked and J. Yaron (eds), *Life On The Razor's Edge* (Tel Aviv, Hakibbutz Hameuchad Publishing House, 1979) 9 (Hebrew); Nurith Gertz, *Generation Shift In Literary History—Hebrew Narrative Fiction In The Sixties* (Tel Aviv University, Porter Institute for Poetics and Semiotics, 1983) chapter 1 (Hebrew); Dan Miron, 'From Creators and Builders to Homeless' in *If There Is No Jerusalem…* (Tel Aviv, Hakibbutz Hameuchad Publishing House, 1987) 9 (Hebrew); Yaacov Shavit, 'The Status of Culture in Processes of Creating a New Society in Eretz Israel' in Zohar Shavit (ed), *The History Of The Jewish Community In Eretz Israel Since 1882* (Jerusalem, The Israeli Academy for Sciences and Humanities, 1998) Vol 1, 9 (Hebrew).

modes of reasoning, which were formerly almost wholly unrecognized in the Court's jurisprudence.

(a) Emphasizing the Court's role in determining the normative contents of the law

In a long series of opinions, the Court began speaking about the 'basic values' of the legal system, presenting them as 'fundamental principles' to be applied when interpreting existing legal norms, or even casting new legal norms ex nihilo. For instance, when imposing a duty of loyalty to the company on a holder of controlling shares, Justice Barak wrote:

Indeed no formal specific recognition of this duty of loyalty on the part of a shareholder has yet been made in our legal system, but the fundamental principle upon which it is based has been part of our system for years. On the basis of this well-known, recognized fundamental principle, we are fully entitled to deduce new secondary duties, to suit our needs.[37]

In other cases, the Court presented the system's basic values as a 'normative umbrella,' which enfolds the system as a whole and serves for the purposes both of interpreting its existing contents and of creating new contents. Justice Barak argued in one opinion that the Court is superior to the legislator, since in applying the system's basic principles to any specific statute the Court may ascribe goals to it that the legislator had not thought of.[38]

In these opinions, the Court presented itself as acting contrary to important principles of legal formalism, according to which courts are not expected to participate in determining the normative contents of the law and in creating norms of law. Rather, legal formalism views the courts' role as being merely to identify an (explicitly or implicitly) extant legal norm and apply it to the case at hand.

(b) Balancing clashing values

The Court has recurrently presented the principles it applied in its decisions as being mutually competitive and, as such, amenable to being balanced in several ways. In order to strike a balance between competing principles, it is necessary to exercise discretion in ranking the values they

---

[37] CA 817/79 *Edward Kossoy v Bank Y. L. Feuchtwanger Ltd*, 38(3) PD 253. For many additional examples, see: Menachem Mautner, *The Decline Of Formalism And The Rise Of Values In Israeli Law* (Tel Aviv, Maagalai Daat, 1993) 77 n 41 (Hebrew).
[38] HCJ 693/91 *Efrat v Director of Population Registrar, Ministry of the Interior*, 47(1) PD 749, 764.

represent according to their relative weight. In a typical pronouncement, Justice Barak writes about the fundamental principles of the system:

> The list of these principles is never closed...At times they lead in opposite directions. In such circumstances, the Court...must juxtapose the competing values, assigning each of them its appropriate weight in the circumstances of the case. Put differently, the Court must balance between different values.[39]

Elsewhere, Justice Barak has written:

> Balancing constitutes a normative act. The judge must locate the clashing values. He must determine their relative social importance. When the legal system holds that the values are of equal status, the judge must determine—in the absence of a statutory guideline—the extent of the mutual concession each value must make to the other so as to enable them to coexist ('horizontal balancing')...At times, the clashing values are not equal in status. In cases of this type, the court must...consider what would justify preferring one value over another ('vertical balancing')...Barring any possibility of reconciling the clashing values, it is unavoidable to prefer...one value to another.[40]

Presenting the system's fundamental principles and values as mutually competitive and as requiring the attribution of weights to strike a balance among them contradicts important principles of legal formalism. One of formalism's fundamental distinctions is that between the legislative process—which generates compromises that strike a balance between competing normative worldviews—and judicial decision-making—which involves the assignment of factual cases to their appropriate legal categories and application of the pertinent solutions found within the categories. In the words of Yitzhak Englard, later a Supreme Court Justice, the process of balancing principles and values 'involves elements typical of legislation, due to the pre-weighing of interests and the normative determination of their priorities for the purpose of formulating a legal norm.'[41]

The Court thus deviated from the formalistic perception of its role. Furthermore, striking a balance among principles and values runs counter to another fundamental assumption of legal formalism, namely that every legal problem has only one correct solution, reachable by anyone appropriately addressing the problem.

However, the Court's recurrent recourse to the 'balancing' phrase helped it to play down the innovative dimension of its reasoning.[42] The balancing

---

[39] Cr. App. 677/83 *Borochov v Yeffet*, 39(3) PD 205, 218.

[40] CA 105/92 *Reem Engineers and Constructors Ltd. v Upper Nazareth Municipality*, 47(5) PD 189, 204. For many additional examples, see Mautner, above n 37, at 80 n 45.

[41] Yitzhak Englard, 'The Role of Court in the Recent Developments of Tort Law—Self Image and Reality' (1985) 11 Tel Aviv U L Rev 67, 90 (Hebrew). See also: Patrick M. McFadden, 'The Balancing Test' (1988) 29 BC L Rev 641.

[42] The source of the 'balancing interests' formulation in Israeli law is the ruling of Justice Agranat in HCJ 73/53 *Kol Ha-Am v Minister of the Interior*, 7 PD 871, 876, 879, 884. Eight years

metaphor in regard to the law is perhaps the one most frequently employed in Western culture.[43] The Court, then, resorted to a widespread metaphor to introduce a wholly new mode of reasoning into its jurisprudence.

(c) The rise of purposive interpretation

Purposive interpretation was not common in the Supreme Court's jurisprudence until the 1980s.[44] As in the past, the jurisprudence from the 1980s onward continued to make use of the 'language test' in interpreting legislation. In a departure from past custom, however, many of these opinions noted that the language of legal norms is limited in its ability to provide clear and unequivocal solutions: it often admits of more than one solution. The Court therefore emphasized the superiority in such cases of the 'purpose test' over the 'language test' as the decisive interpretive tool. The language of the law, wrote Justice Shoshanna Netanyahu, is 'only the starting point of interpretation, not its ending... We must still examine the aim of the legal provision and its purpose, and choose from among the various options sustainable by the provision's language the interpretation leading to the realization of its aim.'[45]

And Justice Barak wrote: 'The judge is not allowed to confine himself to the language test, since the law is not merely a linguistic text. The law is a normative creation meant to realize a social purpose and express a policy. The interpreter must expose, from the range of linguistic possibilities, the meaning that will realize the purpose of the law.'[46]

The superiority of the 'purpose test' over the 'language test' was also established in the realm of criminal law, where linguistic and literal interpretation had traditionally been dominant. 'Criminal law, like any other

elapsed from the time this opinion was published in 1953 until the next mention of this formulation. Subsequently it received seven additional mentions until 1977, mostly marginal. The opinion attained a more central and prominent status only in 1983–1984.

> From then on, mentions have become increasingly frequent, becoming gradually cloaked in expressions reserved for Scripture in faith traditions. Given this chronology, Justice Agranat's ruling in HCJ Kol Ha-Am may be viewed as a prophecy that preceded its time by three decades... Agranat and his contemporaries were not aware of its importance, hardly issuing any rulings in its spirit.

Yoram Shachar, Miron Gross and Chanan Goldsmidt, '100 Leading Precedents of the Supreme Court—Quantitative Analysis' (2004) 7 Mishpat Umimshal 267–8 (Hebrew). In the United States as well, the rise in the 'balancing interests' reasoning was identified with the decline of legal formalism. This reasoning first appeared in the constitutional jurisprudence of the American Supreme Court in the late 1930s, and has been claimed to reflect the rise of the instrumentalist approach in the Court's opinions. Alexander Aleinikoff, 'Constitutional Law in the Age of Balancing' (1987) 96 Yale L J 943, 943–4, 948, 949, 959, 960.

[43] Dennis Curtis and Judith Resnik, 'Images of Justice' (1987) 96 Yale L J 1727.
[44] Nir Kedar, 'Interpretive Revolution: The Rise of Purposive Interpretation in Israeli Law' (2002) 26 Tel Aviv U L Rev 737, 741 (Hebrew).
[45] IBA App 11/86 *Ben-Haim v Tel Aviv District Committee, Israel Bar Association*, 41(4) PD 99, 103.
[46] AD 40/80 *Kenig v Cohen*, 36(3) PD 701, 715.

law,' wrote Justice Barak, 'should be interpreted neither restrictively nor expansively, but with the aim of realizing the purpose of the legislation.'[47]

In these opinions, too, the Court contested several principles of legal formalism: the assumption that the meaning of legal norms is exhausted by their language; and the perception of the law as an autonomous system, whose application by the Court does not require the latter to strike out beyond the confines of language into the domain of purposes, which are supposed to be the exclusive purview of the legislator.

(d) Lessening the importance of the distinction between categories

In a series of opinions in the 1980s and 1990s, the Supreme Court expressed its opposition to meticulous distinctions between the various categories of which the law is comprised. 'Superfluous categorization and the creation of distinctions hard to justify and implement should be avoided,' wrote Justice Barak.[48] Instead, the Court recommended that relevant principles should be clarified and specific legal solutions derived from them.

In these opinions, the Court went against the attempt of legal formalism to create clearly delimited legal categories that allow the classification and assignment of every factual case to the one legal category that purportedly contains its solution.

(e) A 'jurisprudence of values' instead of a 'conceptual jurisprudence'

In another series of opinions, the Court declared it had abandoned conceptual jurisprudence, in which legal decisions are based on clarifying the contents of legal concepts, and shifted instead to normative jurisprudence, where legal decisions rest on the weighing of relevant normative considerations. 'We must draw away from conceptual jurisprudence,' wrote Justice Barak: 'We must aspire to a jurisprudence of values.'[49] Similarly,

> We would not wish to get back to a jurisprudence of concepts (*Begriffsjurisprudenz*) in which the conclusion was presented as popping up out of objective considerations. We prefer a jurisprudence of interests (*Interessenjurisprudenz*) and a jurisprudence of values (*Wertungsjurisprudenz*)... We prefer substance over form.[50]

And elsewhere, Justice Barak wrote:

> We do not live in a world of concepts. The essence is the social purpose that the law is meant to accomplish, not the concepts in which the law enfolds itself... The

---

[47] Cr App *Mizrahi v State of Israel*, 35(4) PD 421, 427. For many additional examples, see: Mautner, above n 37, at 82 n 49.

[48] CA 862/80 *Hadera Municipality v Zohar*, 37(3) PD 757, 770. For many additional examples, see: Mautner, above n 37, at 85 n 54.

[49] Cr AD 4603/97 *Meshulam v State of Israel*, 51(3) PD 160, 182.

[50] CA 6024/97 *Shavit v Rishon Le'zion Jewish Burial Society*, 53(3) PD 600, 658.

approach we endorse views the law as a social tool. The concepts of the law are meant to realize social aims. They are tools for achieving social goals. They express the suitable balance between clashing values and interests.[51]

(f) Emphasizing choice in judicial decision-making

In several opinions, the Court presented its role as being to choose between various solutions, all of which are possible and plausible in the context of the system. Thus, in one case Justice Barak wrote:

> The language of the legislation, against the backdrop of its purpose, can be interpreted in two different ways. Each of them seems to me to be lawful and possible. Once more, we face a hard case wherein the judge must apply what Justice Holmes called the sovereign prerogative of choice... As in the areas of administrative law, a range of judicial reasonableness has been created here. Within this range are several options, from which the reasonable judge is allowed to choose. Two reasonable judges may reach different results.[52]

In these opinions, the Court rejected the assumption of legal formalism that every legal problem has only one solution reachable through appropriate legal reasoning.

(g) Emphasizing creativity in judicial decision-making

In a series of opinions, the Court presented itself as being engaged in the task of developing the law by providing new solutions, *ex nihilo*, to problems to which no solutions exist in the extant body of law. 'Frequently the court creates, by its very ruling, the right itself. Judging is not merely declarative; it also involves creativity,' wrote Justice Barak.[53]

By emphasizing the creativity involved in judicial decision-making, the Court rejected the distinction that legal formalism makes between the legislature, which is supposed to determine the contents of the law, and the judiciary, which is supposed to apply the existing law to the factual cases submitted to it for resolution.[54]

---

[51] HCJ AD 4601/95 *Sarusi v National Labor Court*, 52(4) PD 817, 826–7. For many additional examples, see: Mautner, above n 37, at 85 n 54.

[52] HCJ 547/84 *Valley Chicken v Ramat Yishai Local Government*, 40(1) PD 113, 141. For many additional examples, see: Mautner, above n 37, at 86 n 58.

[53] HCJ 910/86 *Major (Res) Yehuda Ressler, Advocate v Minister of Defence*, 42(2) PD 441, 464. Moshe Landau, the former Chief Justice of the Supreme Court, described another dimension of the phenomenon when he wrote that, since the 1970s, the 'codifying opinion' emerges in the jurisprudence of the Court, ie, an opinion that resolves a case 'not only as far as required for the decision in the concrete case at stake', but rather one that 'seeks to formulate in advance rules for problems that have not actually emerged, as if the judge was required to write a summary chapter of a statute as a guide to the public administration officers or to the public in general.' Landau, above n 22, at 502–3.

[54] The decline of formalism and the rise of values in the jurisprudence of the Supreme Court since the 1980s were also evident in the Court's readiness to state that legal results would apply

E. CHANGES IN THE PERCEPTION OF THE COURT'S ROLE IN THE 1980S AND 1990S

I have already pointed out two significant changes in the jurisprudence of the Supreme Court in the 1980s and 1990s: The rise of a sweeping activism in the Court's jurisprudence, and the rise of a new model of reasoning, characterized by extensive exposure of the values that underlie the law and the law's distributive implications. These two changes led to a third change, namely a change in the Court's perception of its role among the branches of the state.

From the establishment of Israel until the early 1980s, the Supreme Court operated in accordance with a worldview postulating a sharp distinction between politics and the law. Contentions over the dominant values in society and over the allocation of material resources were considered political in nature, their place the Knesset. Law, by contrast, was perceived as a non-political realm where professionals—lawyers and judges—apply their expert knowledge. The Knesset and politics stood on one side of this distinction, then, judges, lawyers, and professionalism on the other. In the context of this worldview, the role of lawyers was perceived as being to promote their clients' goals by applying legal knowhow, and that of judges to resolve legal disputes. Insofar as judges were perceived as dealing with the creation of the law, they were seen as doing so interstitially and by filling any lacunas left in the law after the Knesset's action.

Benjamin Aktzin, the former dean of the Faculty of Law at the Hebrew University of Jerusalem, expressed this view of the relationship between politics and the law in a book read by generations of law students in Israel in the 1950s, 1960s, and 1970s. Aktzin depicted the state apparatus as a hierarchical pyramid of institutions wielding their powers in the context of a parallel hierarchical pyramid of legal norms. When Aktzin drew the pyramid of the country's institutions of government, he included in it the legislative branch and, subordinate to it, the executive branch. Aktzin located the courts entirely *outside* the pyramid of the country's institutions. Similarly, he located the courts' opinions *outside* the pyramid of legal

---

although the procedures stipulated by the law as the proper way to attain those results had not been implemented. For an extensive discussion, see Mautner, above n 37, at 52–6; Menachem Mautner, 'Judicial Intervention in the Contents of Contracts and the Question of the Future Development of Israeli Contract Law' (2005) 29 Tel Aviv U L Rev 17 (Hebrew). The Court's broad use of the good faith standard in contract cases may also be viewed as part of this process. For further discussion, see: Menachem Mautner, 'Good Faith and Implied Warranties' in Daniel Friedmann and Nili Cohen (eds), *Contracts* (Vol 3, Tel Aviv, Aviram, 2003) 313 (Hebrew). Guy Mundlak writes that a shift from formalism to overt exposure of the judges' ideological assumptions and values can be discerned in the rulings of the Labor Courts in recent decades. Guy Mundlak, 'The New Labor Law as a Social Text: Reflections on Social Values in Flux' (2005) 3 Israel Studies 119, 137.

norms that apply in the country. Aktzin presented the courts and their opinions in this manner because he held that judging is:

> an action whose essence is to provide a compelling and binding determination as to whether a particular behavior meets the requirements of a normative system or as to the legal results of some behavior.[55]

In this perception of the law and of the role of the courts, then, the latter were not expected to make any substantive contribution to the law that applies in the country. Rather, the law was viewed as a product of the Knesset's action, which reflects the will of the people. The Supreme Court's definition of the limits of its authority vis-à-vis the country's public administration also derived from this view. The public administration was perceived as acting by virtue of a series of Knesset authorizations, and subject to its review. Hence, the Supreme Court considered it was not authorized to review the contents of decisions taken by the public administration; this review was perceived as reserved to the Knesset (see Chapter 3, above). Rather, the Supreme Court saw its role as being to review the extent to which decisions taken by the state's public administration were within the scope of the powers granted to decision-makers by the law.

In the 1980s, however, the Supreme Court turned to presenting itself as being charged with an entirely different set of roles among the institutions of the state. The Court's jurisprudence during this period clearly emphasized the view that the Supreme Court, as well as the lower courts, is to take part in determining the contents of the law, that is, in determining the values that apply and the distribution of material resources in the country. The Court no longer presented itself as an institution whose main role was to apply the existing law in the course of resolving disputes, but as one expected to make its own contribution, beside the Knesset, in determining the valid law in the country.[56]

The process reached its peak in the mid-1990s, when the Court stated it was qualified to annul Knesset laws if they failed to abide by the criteria of the Basic Law: Human Dignity and Liberty and the Basic Law: Freedom of Occupation (and perhaps also by the criteria of all the other

---

[55] Benjamin Aktzin, *Regimes Theory* (Jerusalem, Academon, 1967) 321 (Hebrew).
[56] See also: Moshe Landau, 'On Judicial Activism' (2001) 12 Hamishpat 83, 84 (Hebrew) (some of the judges in the 1980s and 1990s purported 'to deal with general problems in the realms of philosophy and sociology, in order to serve as beacons to the entire society. This role appeared to the judges as more important than the decision on a dispute brought before them'); Ruth Gavison, *The Constitutional Revolution—Depiction Of Reality Or A Self-Fulfilling Prophecy* (Jerusalem, Israel Democracy Institute, 1998) 122 (Hebrew) (although some judges 'pay lip service to the principle that the judge's chief role is to decide on the issues brought before him and do justice to the parties,' one cannot avoid the impression that another role has begun to take center stage—'a quasi-legislative role or a role of "repairing the world" and instituting worthy norms in the society.')

Basic Laws enacted by the Knesset since the late 1950s) (see Chapter 3, above). Abandoning the conception it had endorsed since the foundation of the state, which grants the Knesset absolute sovereignty to determine the contents of the law, and no authority to the Court to review that content, the Court thereby positioned itself not only as authorized to participate in determining the values that apply and the allocation of the resources available for distribution in the country *beside* the Knesset, but even *above* the Knesset.

CHAPTER 5

FROM HEGEMONY TO WAR OF CULTURES

In the previous two chapters, I discussed three significant changes that occurred in the jurisprudence of Israel's Supreme Court during the 1980s and 1990s: The rise of a sweeping judicial activism; the advent of a new style of reasoning that exposes the normative and distributive dimensions of law; and a change in the Court's perception of its role—from an institution that resolves disputes to a political institution that participates in determining the normative and distributive arrangements that apply in the country.

In this chapter, I will suggest an explanation for these changes and argue that they should be understood in the context of the great historical process that Israel has been going through since the end of the 1970s, namely the decline of the political and cultural hegemony of the labor movement. I will argue that in the wake of that decline, two social groups have been offering their competing comprehensive visions as to the shaping of Israeli culture in the coming decades: a Jewish secular-liberal group and a Jewish religious group. The Supreme Court, which since Israel's foundation has been the state institution most closely identified with the project of promoting liberalism, has cooperated with the former group in its struggle against the latter. By so doing, in the closing decades of the twentieth century the Court turned itself into a highly significant arena for the struggle over the country's cultural identity, a struggle that has been ongoing within the Jewish people for the past two hundred and fifty years, since the rise of the Jewish Enlightenment in the latter half of the eighteenth century.

A. INTRODUCTION

(a) *Explaining the changes in the Supreme Court's jurisprudence*

Of the three significant changes that took place in the jurisprudence of the Supreme Court in the 1980s and 1990s, Israel's legal literature has attempted to explain only *one*—the Court's increased activism.

One such explanation, focusing on the state of the rule of law in the country, has been suggested by former Supreme Court Justice Yitzhak Zamir. According to this explanation, compliance with the law deteriorated in Israel in the 1980s, and the Supreme Court found itself forced to respond to public expectations, adopt an activist approach, and come to the rescue of the rule of law. By so doing the Court jeopardized its status, but it was aided by the experience and the prestige it had accumulated over the years on one hand, and by the weakening of the government and the Knesset on the other.[1] This explanation, then, presents the Court as a body that was *forced into* judicial activism against its will and against its better interest, in order to serve the country by defending the rule of law.

A second explanation focuses on the weakness of the government and the Knesset. It holds that, in the 1970s and 1980s the public mistrusted the ability of these branches of state to cope successfully with the country's problems. Among the reasons for this mistrust were the 1973 Yom Kippur War; the double—and triple-digit inflation of the late 1970s and early 1980s; the First Lebanon War of 1982; the rift between secular and religious Jews; and the divide between Ashkenazi and Sephardic (*Mizrahi*) Jews. Key problems were therefore shifted from the political arena to the Supreme Court, which at the time was perceived as a non-political body. For its part, the Court reacted by developing doctrines that enabled its broad intervention in the actions of the other branches of government.[2]

A third explanation, close in spirit to the previous one, focuses on the emergence in Israeli politics during the 1980s of two political blocs of equal power, leading to a state of polarization. According to this explanation, Israel's party structure until the late 1970s was centralized, with one dominant party (Mapai, and later the Alignment-Labor party) at the center of the political field, and several significantly weaker parties beside it. This structure allowed the political system to tackle pivotal public issues successfully, without any need for the Court's intervention in political matters.

---

[1] Itzhak Zamir, 'Public Law' (1990) 19 Mishpatim 563, 570–1 (Hebrew); Itzhak Zamir, 'Law and Politics' in Itzhak Zamir (ed), *The Klinghoffer Book On Public Law* (Jerusalem, Institute for Legislative Research and Comparative Law, 1993) 209, 221 (Hebrew).

[2] Eli Salzberger, 'Judicial Activism in Israel' in Brice Dickson (ed), *Judicial Activism In Common Law Supreme Courts* (Oxford, Oxford University Press, 2007) 217, 223 ('the unprecedented judicial activism in Israel in recent decades is the result of...a decreasing ability of the political branches to reach coherent and far-sighted or long-term collective decisions, thereby leading to the delegation of decision-making powers to the courts'); Zeev Segal, 'The Supreme Court (Sitting as a High Court of Justice) Within the Framework of the Israeli Society—After 50 Years' (2000) 5 Mishpat Umimshal 235, 245 (Hebrew); Zeev Segal, 'The Supreme Court as a Social Constructor' in Hanna Herzog (ed), *Reflection Of A Society* (Tel Aviv, Ramot Publishing House, 2000) 297, 309 (Hebrew). See also: Shannon Ishiyama Smithey and John Ishiyama, 'Judicial Activism in Post-Communist Politics' (2002) 36 Law & Soc Rev 719; Martin Edelman, 'Israel' in C. Neal Tate and Torbjorn Vallinder (eds), *The Judicialization Of Politics* (New York, New York University Press, 1995) 403; Itzhak Galnoor, 'The Judicialization of the Public Domain in Israel' (2004) 7 Mishpat Umimshal 355 (Hebrew).

Following the political turnabout of 1977 (the defeat of the Alignment-Labor party and the transfer of power to the right-wing Likud party), two blocs of equal size emerged in Israeli politics, a left-wing bloc (headed by the Alignment-Labor party) and a right-wing bloc (headed by Likud). The polarization between them eroded the political system's effectiveness, and the Supreme Court became the institution to which demands for settling conflicts were addressed. In response, the Court developed doctrines that enabled its extensive intervention in the actions of other branches of government.[3]

(b) The explanation proposed in this chapter

In this chapter, I propose an explanation for *all three changes* that have taken place in the jurisprudence of the Supreme Court since the 1980s. This explanation links the changes to the great historical process that began in Israel at the end of the 1970s, namely the decline of the political and cultural hegemony of the labor movement.

Legal literature offers different approaches towards the link between the law created and applied in the courts, on the one hand, and the society, politics and culture 'outside the law', on the other.[4] At one end of the spectrum we find the vulgar Marxist outlook that views everything that happens in the law as a reflection of processes evolving in society and, consequently, also in politics and in culture. At the other end is the doctrinal-formalist approach that views everything that happens in the law as a product of internal processes unfolding within it. In the middle are various approaches that acknowledge the 'thickness' of the law, ie, they recognize

---

[3] Menachem Hofnung, 'The Unintended Consequences of Unplanned Constitutional Reform: Constitutional Politics in Israel' (1996) 44 Am J Comparative L 585; Nir Kedar, 'Interpretive Revolution: The Rise of Purposive Interpretation in Israeli Law' (2002) 26 Tel Aviv U L Rev 737, 767 (Hebrew). See also: Oz Almog, 'From "Our Right to Eretz Israel" to "Civil Rights" and from "a Jewish State" to "the Rule of Law": The Legal Revolution in Israel and its Cultural Meanings' (1999) 18 Alpaim 77, 98 (Hebrew); Yoash Meisler, '"The Constitutional Revolution" Just Over a Decade Later—Law and Disorder' (2003) 7 Democratic Culture 131, 152 (Hebrew).

[4] One of the main approaches is the instrumentalist approach, with its roots in American legal realism. On this approach, the law is perceived as a tool for tinkering with society and, therefore, society and the law are seen as two separate entities. Another is the constitutive approach, with its roots in the cultural studies movement that began to develop in England at the end of the 1950s. On this approach, the law is perceived as constitutive of culture, people's consciousness and their practices, and hence as embedded in social interactions. Law and society on this approach, therefore, are one inseparable entity, the social and legal components of which cannot be separated. On the constitutive approach, see: Robert W. Gordon, 'Critical Legal Histories' (1984) 36 Stan L Rev 57; Pierre Bourdieu, 'The Force of Law: Toward a Sociology of the Juridical Field' (1987) 38 Hastings L J 805; Austin Sarat and Thomas R. Kearns, (eds), *Law In Everyday Life* (Ann Arbor, University of Michigan Press, 1993); Bryant G. Garth and Austin Sarat (eds), *Justice And Power In Sociolegal Studies* (Evanston, Northwestern University Press, 1998); Austin Sarat and Thomas R. Kearns (eds), *Law In The Domains Of Culture* (Ann Arbor, University of Michigan Press, 1998); Naomi Mezey, 'Law as Culture' (2001) 13 Yale J L & Human 35.

that processes unfolding within the law are dictated by the law's content, but also appreciate that the law's development is affected in various and complex ways by social, political, and cultural processes beyond the law.

I hold that, usually, the development of the law of the courts must be understood as the product of three elements in combination: processes internal to the law (law as an enabling and constraining cultural system); processes external to the law (the political, social, and cultural conditions of the law's development and implementation); and the personalities, biographies, character dispositions, and unique life experience of the judges who implement and develop the law. The approach I propose to employ in this chapter, however, will focus only on the second of these three factors. I will seek to ascribe the changes evident in the jurisprudence of the Supreme Court during the 1980s and 1990s to far-reaching processes that unfolded at the time in the politics, society, and culture of Israel. As I have shown in Chapters 3 and 4, the changes in the Court's jurisprudence recorded in that period were far-reaching, and, as I show in the current chapter, so were the changes in the politics, society, and culture of Israel. I hold that the link between the two types of changes is so close that it justifies an explanation that binds them together.[5]

I will therefore argue that the changes in the Supreme Court's jurisprudence in the 1980s and the 1990s should be understood as a reaction of the Court and the socio-cultural group identified with it to processes then transpiring in Israel. These processes began to unfold following the decline in the political, social, and cultural hegemony of the labor movement at the end of the 1970s, and the ensuing transition, several years later, from that hegemonic domination to a state of acute political and cultural polarization, which would be conceptualized in the 1990s as multiculturalism. I will also argue that, in the context of these processes, the Supreme Court's actions reflected its association with one of the two groups involved in the cultural struggle that erupted in Israel following the decline of the hegemony—the Jewish secular-liberal group. The Court turned itself into a significant venue for the promotion of the cultural worldview and political aims of that group in its struggle to shape the character of Israel in the decades following the hegemony's decline.

---

[5] I certainly do not mean to underestimate the contribution of particular individuals to the development of historical processes and changes. Concerning changes in Israeli law in the closing decades of the twentieth century, Aharon Barak played a decisive role. Barak was a Supreme Court justice for twenty-eight years, from 1978 to 2006, and Chief Justice for eleven years, 1995–2006. He is a man of exceptional personal qualities and rare legal talents. I leave to others, however, the task of writing Barak's personal and intellectual biographies, and focus on the unique cultural, social, and political conditions that set the stage for the actions of Barak and other Supreme Court justices—conditions that restrained them on the one hand, and opened up enabling options on the other.

I will also argue that, following the hegemony's decline and the onset of the struggle over the character of Israel, members of the Jewish secular-liberal group were struck by anxiety. Anxiety dictated the group's political conduct during the 1980s: The increasing recourse to the Supreme Court as a venue of political action; the Court's broad support for the group; and, for many years, the group's abstention from any criticism concerning the far-reaching changes in the Court's jurisprudence during the 1980s.

B. THE DECLINE IN THE HEGEMONY OF THE LABOR MOVEMENT

(a) The concept of hegemony according to Antonio Gramsci

The concept of hegemony[6] developed in Marxist literature at the end of the nineteenth century. In the 1920s and 1930s, the prominent Italian Marxist thinker Antonio Gramsci gave it new content, which gained wide diffusion in the closing decades of the twentieth century through the writings of political scientists, scholars of cultural and media studies, and anthropologists.

Gramsci's writings, however, hardly offer a single clear definition of the concept of hegemony. There are at least three different, though allied, versions of it. In the latter half of the twentieth century, for many authors this vagueness served as a basis for developing the concept and enriching it with content, though not necessarily identical. In what follows I trace what seems to me the most accurate interpretation of the concept of hegemony according to Gramsci.

A hegemonic situation prevails in a country when one social group (the hegemonic group) succeeds in controlling three foci of power. The first are the central institutions of the state. The second are the main institutions of civil society: economic institutions, the educational system,

---

[6] On the concept of hegemony, see: Antonio Gramsci, in Quintin Hoare and Geoffrey Nowell Smith trans (eds), *Selections From The Prison Notebook* (London, Lawrence and Wishart, 1971); Chantal Mouffe, 'Hegemony and Ideology in Gramsci' in Chantal Mouffe (ed), *Gramsci And Marxist Theory* (London, Routledge & Kegan Paul, 1979) chapter 5; Jean Comaroff And John Comaroff, *Of Revelation And Revolution Vol 1* (Chicago, University of Chicago Press, 1991); Terry Eagleton, *Ideology* (London, Verso, 1991) 112–23; Dick Hebdige, 'From Culture to Hegemony' in Simon During (ed), *The Cultural Studies Reader* (London, Routledge, 1993) 357; Tony Bennett, 'Introduction: Popular Culture and "The Turn to Gramsci"', in Tony Bennett, Colin Mercer and Janet Woollacott (eds), *Popular Culture And Social Relations* (Philadelphia, Open University Press, 1986) xi; Tony Bennett, *Culture—A Reformer's Science* (London, Sage Publications, 1998) chapter 3; Fred Inglis, *Cultural Studies* (Oxford, Blackwell, 1993) chapter 3; Jeff Lewis, *Cultural Studies* (London, Sage Publications, 2002); S. Kim, 'Hegemony: Cultural' (2001) 10 Int'l Encyclopedia Of The Social And Behavioral Sciences; D. V. Kurtz, 'Hegemony: Anthropological Aspects' (2001) 10 Int'l Encyclopedia Of The Social And Behavioral Sciences; Robert Wuthnow, *Communities Of Discourse* (Cambridge, Harvard University Press, 1989) chapter 17; Raymond Williams, *Marxism And Literature* (Oxford, Oxford University Press, 1977) chapter 6.

press, radio, electronic media, publishing houses, religious institutions, trade unions, and so forth. Third, through its ability to place its people at the foci of power of the state and of civil society, the hegemonic group is also able to control the shaping of key elements in the country's culture, ie, it succeeds in implanting certain elements in the consciousness of many citizens—first and foremost the fundamental principles ('rules of the game') that determine how the country should be run, ie, its regime, political culture and economic order. These elements also relate to the people's historical memory.

The cultural elements and the consciousness that the hegemonic group succeeds in imparting and disseminating determine the boundaries of what is considered plausible, acceptable, reasonable, worthy, and so forth in regard to how the country should be run and the relationships that should prevail between the state and its citizens. These elements reflect the worldview of the hegemonic group and serve its interests. Due to the broad diffusion of these elements, however, they are incorporated into the worldview of many citizens, who come to view them as serving their own interests as well. This emphasis on the hegemonic group's control over the central components in the dominant culture represents Gramsci's main contribution to the concept of hegemony.[7]

According to Gramsci, it is not only its own interests that the hegemonic group works to promote. Instead of seeking to destroy other social groups, it rules by standing at the center of a coalition—the 'hegemonic bloc.' Within this coalition, the hegemonic group cooperates with other social groups in ways that enable them to promote their own interests and to express the cultural elements unique to them within the context of the hegemonic culture. The broad diffusion of the hegemonic culture also leads all the other social groups that participate in the hegemonic bloc to define themselves and articulate their worldview and their interests in the conceptual terms that the hegemonic group has succeeded in imposing.

The cultural package that the hegemonic group successfully disseminates is a conceptual web composed of many elements, often mutually

---

[7] According to the classic Marxist view, the key to social control is control over the means of production: the social group that controls the means of production ('the base') will consequently control social relations in general as well as the 'superstructure,' implying the country's institutions, the law, the dominant culture, and so forth. Control of culture, culture per se, then, is not a significant instrument in attaining social control. Gramsci's outlook represents a radical deviation from this approach. He posited control of the culture as a primary element in the ability to exercise power: Control of the culture enables control of society and country, not through coercion and violence (by means of the army, the police, and so forth), but through the creation of wide acquiescence with the worldview of the hegemonic group. Many scholars have pointed out that this form of control—agreement to the dominance among the dominated—is more sophisticated, more effective, and also 'cheaper' than control based on coercion. It is, in fact, the ultimate form of control.

contradictory. The relationship between these elements, however, is not static. The various groups comprising the hegemonic bloc wage a ceaseless struggle over the extent to which different elements will carry more or less weight than others in the context of the hegemonic culture. Because of human creativity, as well as processes of cultural borrowing, social, cultural, and ideological life is also constantly changing, even if in a gradual rather than revolutionary way, leading to changes in the contents of the hegemonic culture as well, or at least in the relative weight ascribed to its various components.

Hegemony never succeeds in imposing its control over all citizens to an equal extent, and certain social groups will adopt more elements of the hegemonic culture than others. Also, no hegemony ever manages to assert perfect control over *all* the citizens of a state: there will invariably be some social groups that refuse to accept the principles of the hegemonic culture and seek to promote contrary political and economic approaches, as well as a different historical memory. The control of the hegemonic group is weakened, then, by the growth of the political, economic, cultural, organizational, and demographic power of the social groups that do not accept the basic political and economic principles of the hegemonic group, as well as the historical memory imparted by it.

Another of Gramsci's significant contributions to the development of the concept of hegemony was his emphasis on the importance of day-to-day behavioral practices as a significant tool for shaping the citizens' consciousness in ways befitting the interests and worldview of the hegemonic group. According to Gramsci, the citizens internalize the hegemonic group's *Weltanschauung* by sharing in day-to-day practices in many spheres of their lives. In other words, the citizens encounter manifestations of the hegemonic culture all the time and in many locations. Thereby, argues Gramsci, the worldview of the hegemonic group becomes part of the citizens' 'common sense': a set of categories for perceiving reality that people unconsciously internalize on an ongoing basis, and which works upon them as if it were transparent, making it hard to contest. The citizens' participation in many daily practices that embody values matching the worldview and interests of the hegemonic group reaffirms that worldview and impairs the citizens' ability to resist it.

Gramsci, then, gave new meaning not only to the concept of hegemony, but also to the concept of ideology. Ideology, in the sense of a comprehensive framework of thought widely imparted to the citizens, is for Gramsci an important means of preserving the hegemony. He views ideology not as a set of ideas developed by a group of theoreticians and disseminated through deliberate and conscious teaching, but as a collection of ideas, understandings, dispositions, feelings, and so forth, which are internalized through participation in daily practices that embody the ideology. A high correlation thus exists between ideology and the daily practices and experiences of the citizens, who are minimally aware of its existence. Moreover, the ideology is not a coherent and static set of ideas; it is a collection of meanings, those at the core of it reflecting the worldview of the hegemonic group.

(b) The hegemony of the Labor Movement

Mapai, the main political party within the labor movement, took over the World Zionist Organization and its institutions in 1933.[8] Subsequently, the labor movement headed by Mapai stood at the center of a political and cultural hegemony whose subordinate partners were the religious-Zionist group and the 'civic bloc' (property owners in the cities and in agricultural settlements who held liberal views in economic and social matters).[9] This hegemony ended in the late 1970s, when the 'Alignment' (a party formed in 1965 through the merger of Mapai and another party within the labor movement) conceded the power it had held unbrokenly for twenty-nine years to the right-wing Likud party. The hegemony of the labor movement, then, extended from the time of the *Yishuv* (the pre-state Jewish society) until well into statehood, a total of four and a half decades.[10]

From Israel's foundation until 1977, Mapai (after 1965, the Alignment) controlled the prime minister's office, the ministry of defense, the ministry of finance, the ministry of education, and the foreign ministry. Mapai was the largest political party throughout this period, also controlling several other government ministries, as well as the central institutions of the Zionist movement. During these years, the prime minister's office also controlled the state radio channels, and the ministry of defense controlled

---

[8] Avi Bareli, *Mapai In Israel's Early Independence 1948–1953* (Jerusalem, Yad Ben Zvi, 2007); Yoav Peled And Gershon Shafir, *Being Israeli—The Dynamics Of A Multiple Citizenship* (Cambridge, Cambridge University Press, 2002) chapter 1.

[9] The historical alliance between Mapai and religious Zionism was established in 1935 and lasted for 42 years until 1977. See: Baruch Kimmerling, *Immigrants, Settlers, Natives—The Israeli State And Society Between Cultural Pluralism And Cultural Wars* (Tel Aviv, Am Oved Publishers, 2004) chapter 3 (Hebrew); Dov Schwartz, *Religious Zionism: History And Ideology* (Tel Aviv, Ministry of Defense, 2003) chapter 10 (Hebrew); Amir Ben-Porat, *The Bourgeoisie—The History Of The Israeli Bourgeoisies* (Jerusalem, Magnes Press, Hebrew University, 1999) (Hebrew); Menachem Friedman, 'Religious-Secular Relations' in Anita Shapira (ed), *The Religious Trend In Zionism* (Tel Aviv, Am Oved Publishers, 1983) 69.

[10] Since hegemony rests on a combination of control over the political and social institutions, including control of the culture, this hegemony is hard to periodize exactly. The accepted view dates the beginning of the labor hegemony to 1933, when Mapai took over the institutions of the Zionist movement, and its end in 1977, when the Likud formed the government after the 1977 elections. See: Baruch Kimmerling, *The End Of Ashkenazi Hegemony* (Jerusalem, Keter Publishing House, 2001) 16 (Hebrew); Kimmerling, 'Immigrants, Settlers, Natives' id, at 164, 499.

the army radio. In the late 1960s, when a state television channel was established, it was put under the control of the prime minister's office and the ministry of information.

The labor movement, headed by Mapai, controlled the chief institutions of civil society, first in the *Yishuv* and later in the state: The *Hagannah* (the largest underground organization during the British Mandate period), the *Histradrut* (the strong central federation of trade unions, which controlled a large number of economic enterprises and operated many cultural and social organizations), the press, publishing houses, the *Histadrut's* healthcare organization (by far the largest in the country), the settlement movements, agricultural supply companies, cultural enterprises, youth movements, soccer and many other sports clubs.

The labor movement, headed by Mapai, succeeded in imposing the hegemonic cultural package on large segments of the Jewish population, first in the *Yishuv* and then in the state. That package represented a comprehensive scheme of ideas about the aims of Zionism in general and the State of Israel in particular; about the relationships between the citizen and the state; and about the meaning of life for a Jewish person living in Eretz Israel and in the State of Israel. The scheme also included a historical memory and narrative about the Jewish people, about Zionist settlement in Eretz Israel, and about the creation of the State of Israel.

Various elements are discernible in this scheme of thought, of which three are significant in the present context. First, a new society based on healthy and productive foundations was being built in Eretz Israel, the opposite of Jewish existence in exile. Within this society, a 'new Jew' was being created, as an antithesis to the Jew in exile. Second, Israel was to be a secular, democratic, modern state, closely linked to Western culture and technology. Third, Jewish individuals could do no better than devote their lifetimes—and, if necessary, their very lives—to the realization of the central aims of the Jewish group in Eretz Israel: the creation of a Jewish state, its defense, and its development.

The fundamental principles of the hegemonic culture were widely internalized by Jews living in Eretz Israel during the British Mandate, most of them immigrants from Eastern and Central Europe, and by their descendants after Israel's foundation. Members of this group thus became the bearers of the hegemonic culture. Indeed, they perceived themselves and were also perceived by immigrants arriving in Israel in the 1950s as the epitome of Israeli culture and identity.[11]

During the 1950s, through its control of the state's and society's paramount institutions (particularly the army and the secular educational

---

[11] Kimmerling, above n 9, at 13–14; Peled and Shafir, above n 8, chapter 2.

system), the labor movement implemented 'melting pot' and 'nation-building' processes that served in the broad dissemination of the hegemonic culture among the recently arrived immigrants. Politicians, educators, writers, poets, journalists, and academics belonging to the hegemonic group played a significant role in the spread of these principles.[12]

But these processes succeeded only to a partial extent. In the same years that the state was involved in 'melting pot' and 'nation-building,' it also adopted a policy of 'population dispersal', ie, settling the 1950s immigrants in development towns and *moshavim* (agricultural settlements) located in the country's geographical periphery—the new territories captured in the course of the Independence War of 1948. This last policy was applied mainly to 1950s immigrants from Arab countries (more specifically from North Africa); the absorbing hegemonic group largely remained in the center of the country, where it had settled prior to 1948.

The contradiction between 'melting pot' and 'population dispersal,' however, is self-evident. Indeed, the geographical marginalization of the immigrants has had far-reaching implications in terms of their absorption into the hegemonic mainstream society. Sixty years after the foundation of Israel, the Ashkenazi group (descendants of immigrants from Eastern and Central Europe; bearers of the hegemonic culture) still enjoys a clear superiority over the Sephardic (*mizrahim*) group (people who immigrated to Israel after 1948 from Arab countries) by all socioeconomic indicia. The economic income (income derived from work and capital) of the Ashkenazi group is substantially higher than that of the Sephardic group (since the 1970s the gap between rich and poor in Israel has been one of the highest in the West, and it is close to that of the most inegalitarian countries in South America). An important key to this inequality is the gap in the educational achievements of members of the two groups—Israel is the most polarized country in the West in terms of the achievements of its students of all ranks, from elementary school to university. These processes of inequality in the standards of income and education have been greatly exacerbated since the 1990s, when Israel became a cultural capital-based economy that generously rewards professional know-how (particularly in the hi-tech and financial sectors). The Ashkenazi group also enjoys superior medical services, the result of better access to such services in the center of the country and the ability of members of the group to purchase health services in the market. (Israeli sociologists usually contrast the Ashkenazi group not only to the Sephardic group, but to the Arab group as well, which fares

---

[12] Kimmerling, above n 9, chapters 3, 7.

the worst by all socioeconomic indicia. For more extensive discussion, see Chapter 7, below).[13]

(c) The decline of the hegemony

Toward the end of the 1970s, the hegemony of the labor movement declined.[14]

(i) The state

In the general elections of 1977, the labor movement (headed by the Alignment) lost control over Israel's political system for the first time in 29 years, since the establishment of the state, and the Likud became the central party in Israeli politics to this very day. 'The political turnabout is a turning point in the development of Israeli society', writes sociologist S.N. Eisenstadt.

It involved not only a political shift from 'left' to 'right', but also the disintegration of the hegemonic regime of one dominant party. It brought about immense transformations in Israeli society in its entirety.[15]

In the wake of the 1977 political turnabout, the labor movement lost control of Israel's central state institutions. Although three further elections were held during the 1980s (in 1981, 1984, 1988), the labor movement failed to regain its former sway.[16] Only in 1992, fifteen years(!) after the 1977 'turnabout,' did the labor movement manage to return to power on its own, and then too for only four years. The hegemonic group's control of the foci of state power was thus considerably reduced, together with its

---

[13] Momi Dahan, 'Income Distribution' in Uri Ram and Nitza Berkovitch (eds), *In/Equality* (Beer Sheva, Ben-Gurion University of the Negev Press, 2006) 189 (Hebrew); Yinon Cohen, 'National, Gender and Ethnic Income Gaps' id, at 339 (Hebrew); Yehuda Gardos, 'Geography of Center and Periphery' id, at 73 (Hebrew); Barbara Svirsky, 'Health' id, at 64 (Hebrew); Hanna Ayalon, 'Higher Education' id, at 148 (Hebrew); Gal Levy, 'Education' id, at 181 (Hebrew); Noah Levin-Epstein, 'Mobility' id, at 291 (Hebrew).

[14] Baruch Kimmerling, *The Invention And Decline Of Israeliness* (Berkeley, University of California Press, 2001) chapter 4; Kimmerling, above n 10; Kimmerling, above n 9; Uri Ram, *The Changing Agenda Of Israeli Sociology* (Albany, State University of New York Press, 1995) 14; Menachem Mautner, 'Invisible Law' (1998) 16 Alpaim 45 (Hebrew); Menachem Mautner, 'The 1980s: The Fourth Decade' in David Cheshin et al (eds), *The Courts Of Law: Fifty Years Of Adjudication In Israel* (Jerusalem, Ministry of Defense, 1999) 132 (Hebrew); Menachem Mautner, 'Law and Culture in Israel: The 1950s and the 1980s' in Ron Harris, Alexander Kedar, Pnina Lahav and Assaf Likhovski (eds), *The History Of Law In A Multi-Cultural Society: Israel 1917–1967* (Aldershot, Ashgate, 2002) 175; Menachem Mautner, 'The 1980s—Years of Anxiety' (2003) 26 Tel Aviv U L Rev 645 (Hebrew).

[15] S.N. Eisenstadt, *Changes In Israeli Society* (Tel Aviv, Ministry of Defense, 2004) 10 (Hebrew).

[16] In the 1977 elections, the Likud won 45 Knesset seats, the Alignment (Labor) 32, and the Democratic Movement for Change (DMC or DASH in its Hebrew acronym) 15. In the 1981 elections, the Likud won 48 Knesset seats and the Alignment 47. Menachem Begin, the Likud leader, was Prime Minister from 1977 to 1984. In the 1984 elections, the Alignment won 44 seats and the Likud 41. The Alignment and the Likud formed a national unity government, with Shimon Peres serving as Prime Minister during the first two years and Yitzhak Shamir during the next two. A national unity government was also formed after the 1988 elections, which lasted until 1990.

ability to place its people in all echelons of the state's public administration. (Nevertheless, as I shall show later on, one subgroup of the former hegemonic group, the liberal former hegemons, successfully preserved and even greatly strengthened their power in one state institution, namely the Supreme Court, during the last three decades of the twentieth century.)

(ii) Civil society

During the 1980s and 1990s, the institutions of civil society that had for decades been controlled by the labor movement lost much of their power. The *Histradrut* was greatly weakened; the labor movement's publishing houses lost much of their market share; *all* its daily newspapers ceased publication; a theater that had been identified with the labor movement closed down; in the mid-1990s, the *Histadrut's* healthcare organization underwent de facto nationalization, and the *Histadrut* consequently lost three-quarters of its members; the economic enterprises controlled by the *Histadrut* underwent broad privatization; the labor movement's youth movements lost much of their influence over young people; its sports associations were extensively privatized; the agricultural supply corporations it controlled went into decline.

In parallel to the decline of their strength in certain institutions of civil society, members of the former hegemonic group greatly increased their power in other institutions—market enterprises. Starting in the 1970s, members of the former hegemonic group created new and significant bases of power for themselves: from the state, the *Histadrut*, and the Jewish Agency they bought many of the public corporations that these institutions had formerly held; they developed many new businesses, some of global reach; they established new, private publishing houses; they founded private television and radio channels, and established private healthcare organizations. By these various means they vastly increased their wealth, both vis-à-vis their own situation in previous decades and vis-à-vis groups that had not been part of the hegemony (Jewish immigrants from Arab countries, Arab citizens). Moreover, members of the former hegemonic group succeeded in preserving their power in the press, the electronic media, the universities, and in artistic and cultural institutions.

The accumulation of wealth by members of the former hegemonic group was accompanied by their energetic advocacy of neo-liberalism (premised on a belief in the extension of the logic of the unregulated market to as many spheres of life as possible),[17] turning it into the dominant

---

[17] David Harvey, *A Brief History Of Neoliberalism* (Oxford, Oxford University Press, 2005).

socioeconomic ideology in Israel since the 1980s.[18] In 1951 Yaakov Hazan, the leader of the leftist party Mapam, said that Israel would have to make a choice between Jerusalem and Wall Street.[19] Some four decades later the former hegemonic group lost Jerusalem (the venue of Israel's political institutions) and chose Wall Street. 'The object of ambition, power, generally presents itself nowadays in the form of money alone,' wrote Oliver Wendell Holmes of American society of the late nineteenth century.[20] The same observation was true of the former liberal hegemons in Israel of the late twentieth century.[21]

Yagil Levy, a scholar of the IDF (Israel Defense Forces), writes that when new avenues of career and wealth opened up for members of the former hegemonic group in the rapidly expanding and globalizing Israeli business sector, they reversed their attitude toward the IDF: Whereas since the establishment of the state they had treated service in the IDF as a key to the accumulation of symbolic and material rewards, in recent decades they have come to view it as an obstacle to personal self-realization and success in the business sector. (Levy claims, therefore, that the central posts in the IDF, evacuated by members of the former hegemonic group, are being taken over by members of peripheral groups, such as religious-Zionist settlers and immigrants from the former Soviet Union and Ethiopia, who still view service in the IDF as a means of attaining upward mobility.)[22]

---

[18] Eisenstadt, above n 15, Chapter 8. Ariel Rubinstein, one of Israel's most prominent economic theoreticians, writes as follows on Israel of the last decades:

> Market culture has flooded us. It has represented the entire truth regarding the way society should be run…and regarding the way it will be run whether we like it or not. A self-assured, materialist culture, intolerable of doubt and hesitation, entirely premised on drives and power, which draws on the 'science' of economics.

Ariel Rubinstein, 'How the Jewish People Lost its Soul' in Ruvik Rosenthal (ed), *The Heart Of The Matter—Redefining Social And National Issues* (Jerusalem, Keter Publishing House, 2005) 185, 186 (Hebrew).

[19] Bareli, above n 8, at 466.

[20] Oliver Wendell Holmes, 'The Path of the Law' (1897) 10 Harv L Rev 457, 478.

[21] One need not go as far as Marx's *The German Ideology* to realize that the divide between the political realm and the economic realm is not that sharp: Economic power usually translates into political power. This is the case of the Israeli former liberal hegemons. Even though since the late 1970s they have lost much political power in election politics, they have managed to compensate themselves for this loss, and exert much power over the Israeli political system, by means of their control over the economic sector. Also, in a neo-liberal era, the logic of the market infiltrates into state action, while business leaders position themselves in charge of political responsibilities by adopting the ideology and practices of 'corporate social responsibility.' Ronen Shamir, 'The Age of Responsibilization: On Market-Embedded Morality' (2008) 37 Economy And Society 1. This makes it natural for business leaders to make claims on the decisions undertaken in the political sphere and to be appointed to political and public missions. A prominent case in point in Israel was the Dovrat Committee, appointed by the government in 2003 to suggest revisions of the state's public education system. The head of the committee, Shlomo Dovrat, is a prominent businessman.

[22] Yagil Levy, *From 'People's Army' To 'Army Of The Peripheries'* (Jerusalem, Carmel, 2007). See also: Amos Harel, *'While You Were Asleep'* (May 9 2010) Haaretz:

(iii) The culture

People are creative. Social and cultural life is ceaselessly in flux, though change is usually gradual rather than revolutionary. The hegemonic culture of the labor movement also changed over the years and two of these changes, particularly relevant to the present discussion, are pointed out below. The analysis of these changes draws on Raymond Williams' conceptualization of cultural elements and their mutual relationships.

Williams, who drew on Gramsci's concept of hegemony, argues that three elements are discernible in the culture of every society:[23]

The first, the *dominant* element, is the system of meanings, values, opinions, and assumptions effectively prevalent in the consciousness of a majority of the people living in the society at a particular time—the contents of that society's hegemonic culture.

The second, *residual* element is the system of meanings, values, behavioral practices, and so forth, which had formerly guided many people's lives, but subsequently was demoted by the culture's currently functioning dominant element. Certain parts of the residual element are always assimilated into the dominant culture and become part of it. Others, although they too become part of the active culture, are not so easily reconciled with its dominant contents and it is they that constitute the residual element.

The third element found in every culture, according to Williams, is the *emergent*, consisting of a new system of meanings, values, behavioral practices and so forth, differing from those of the dominant cultural element. According to Williams, emergent cultural elements can be either *alternative* or *oppositional*. Those of the first kind are endorsed by people who seek to live differently from people who live according to the dominant cultural element, but all they want is to be left alone: they want to be allowed to live as they wish, and have no intention of changing the dominant cultural element. The second kind of emergent cultural element, the *oppositional*, is endorsed by people who not only want to be left alone to live their lives as they choose, but also seek to change the dominant cultural element in accordance with their own views. Williams argues that the dominant culture reacts to these two types of emergent element with attempts at incorporation.

> In 1990 the share of religious cadets in the IDF's infantry officers training course, the spearhead of the IDF's combat units, was 2 percent. In 2007 their share surged to 30 percent.... Six out of seven lieutenant generals in the elite Golani infantry brigade are currently religious.... In some of the infantry brigades the share of religious company commanders is over 50 percent, more than three times the share of the religious-Zionist group in the population.... The ranks abandoned by the leftist secular group have been filled by others.

[23] Williams, above n 6; Raymond Williams, 'Base and Superstructure in Marxist Culture Theory' in *Problems Of Materialism And Culture* (London, Verso, 1980).

Relying on Williams' conceptualization, I argue that the contents of the hegemonic culture promulgated by the labor movement were the dominant cultural element in Israeli culture during the hegemonic period. They were fundamentally collectivistic and impregnated with the expectation that Jewish individuals would devote their lifetimes—and their lives as well, if necessary—to the realization of the central aims of the Jewish group in Eretz Israel: the creation of a Jewish state, its defense, and its development. However, an oppositional cultural element began to emerge as early as the 1950s, and particularly in the 1960s, in the context of the hegemonic culture, but based on values of individualism, self-realization, and hedonism—values diametrically opposed to those of the hegemonic culture in its original version. The emergence of this cultural element was accompanied by the rise of an approach that identified the market rather than the state as the key factor in the country's economic and social development, consequently advocating the transfer of many state roles to the market.

This cultural element became increasingly prominent in the consciousness and the day-to-day practices of the members of the hegemonic group, as it came to include a widening middle class. This class consisted of the elites of the public administration, the public economic sector, the business sector, the press, the cultural and arts establishments, the army, the security establishment, the legal community and academia. The members of these elites acted in close association with parallel elites in the United States in the professional, social, and cultural realms, reflecting the growing influence of American culture over Israeli culture. Indeed, since the 1960s, through massive processes of cultural borrowing,[24] all spheres of life in Israel have undergone profound processes of Americanization. 'America has become Israel's *alter ego* politically, economically and culturally,' writes Tom Segev. 'It has become the teacher; a huge father figure that casts a shadow over everything. It holds the keys to the Israeli way of life.'[25]

Besides the collectivistic component, another element of the hegemonic culture that declined significantly in the decades following the 1950s was the Hebrew element. As noted above, the hegemonic culture had promoted the creation of a new society in Eretz Israel resting on healthy and productive foundations, which would be the antithesis of Jewish society in the Diaspora and give rise to the 'new Jew'. Apparently, the Hebrew vision was already fading in the 1950s: the self-image of a society working to develop a new Hebrew culture began to ebb, as did the use of the adjective 'Hebrew,'

---

[24] On cultural borrowing, see chapter 1, n 38.
[25] Tom Segev, 'Facing Elvis' Statue' in *The New Zionists* (Jerusalem, Keter Publishing House, 2001) 42, 43 (Hebrew).

which had been widespread in the 1940s. In the decades that followed, more and more Israelis began to define themselves above all as Jews and Israelis, rather than as Hebrews (see Chapter 1, above).

The completion of Israeli culture's transition from its Hebrew to its Jewish phase was given symbolic expression by the definition of Israel as a 'Jewish and democratic state' in the Basic Law: Human Dignity and Liberty, and the Basic Law: Freedom of Occupation, enacted in 1992. Furthermore, this was not merely symbolic expression. The enactment of the 'Jewish and democratic state' formula evoked lively discussion concerning the Jewish content and the Jewish identity of Israeli law and Israeli culture in general. In Williams' terms, we could say that the vision of creating a Hebrew culture and a Hebrew identity, which had been part of the dominant element in Israeli culture, began to decline from the 1950s onward, whereas the self-perception of Jewishness in its exilic version, which had been part of the residual element of Israeli culture, began to emerge. Dan Laor, a scholar of Israeli literature and Israeli culture, has referred to this process as 'the return of the repressed.'[26]

In the brief course of one or two generations, then, the hegemonic group underwent a significant transformation in its perception of its identity and its constitutive cultural foundations: from faith in socialism and far-reaching state involvement in the economy to a neo-liberal belief in capitalism, the free market, and 'small' government; from cherishing the collectivist values of contribution and sacrifice to endorsing individualism, self-realization and hedonism; from seeing themselves as Hebrews estranged from the contents of exilic Jewish culture to seeing themselves as Jews seeking acquaintance with these very contents. In the 1980s and 1990s, as I will show below, the formerly hegemonic group found itself in a profound clash with the Jewish religious group over the future shape of Israeli culture. The transformations affecting it, however, brought the formerly hegemonic group to this struggle at a time when its own intellectual underpinnings were underdeveloped, its cultural endowment insufficient, lacking in depth and continuity. Its rival, by contrast, could rely on a rich and longstanding culture. Therefore members of the formerly hegemonic group were reduced to conducting their struggle with the Jewish religious group in conditions of insecurity and distress, while the adoption of more and more elements from the cultural world of the competing group added nothing to their self-confidence.

---

[26] Dan Laor, 'New Israeli Identity: Were We Borne from the Sea?' (2003) 9 New Directions 62 (Hebrew).

(d) The post-hegemonic situation

In the previous sections, I discussed two significant changes unfolding *within* the hegemonic culture, which began in the early 1950s and gathered momentum in the ensuing decades. The most significant change concerning the hegemonic culture, however, occurred in the 1980s and 1990s, the post-hegemonic period, and it concerned the *status* of the hegemonic culture. On the one hand, the hegemonic culture became one of several in a society that eventually began to be perceived, and also to behave, as a multicultural society. On the other hand, the hegemonic group found itself contending with another social group that strove to create a new hegemony and offered itself as a substitute.

(i) From hegemony to multiculturalism

As long as the hegemonic culture was in control, most Jews living in Israel accepted its principles and viewed the hegemonic group (the *Yishuv* members, their descendants and 1950s immigrants from Europe) as the personification of Israeli culture and identity. In the 1980s and 1990s, the hegemonic culture lost this status. Israeli society split into many subgroups, each one developing specific cultural features, its members' separate identity, its unique historical memory concerning the history of the Jewish people, the creation of the State of Israel and its place in these historical processes, and a separate vision concerning the future of the state. Once the group whose culture served as a yardstick for Israeli culture and identity in general, the hegemonic group became just one more group among many. Whereas various processes had formerly worked to create a relatively high level of cultural uniformity, molded after the culture of the hegemonic group (the situation at the time of the hegemony), Israel shifted to the opposite situation of multiculturalism, with its society split between separate cultural groups and no dominant group being able to impose a supra-culture over all or most of the others. (See Chapter 7, below.)

(ii) Shaping Israeli culture: The onset of the struggle

Besides the transition from a hegemony to multiculturalism, a second process was unfolding in Israeli society and culture in the 1980s and 1990s: another social and political group emerged that began to perceive itself and also began to be perceived by others as a comprehensive alternative to the previous hegemony with regard to the future shape of Israeli culture.

The struggle over the shaping of Israeli culture—which seemed to have been decided long before—was renewed, and the two main approaches that surfaced were the same that had battled each other since the dawn of Zionism. One still sought to make Israel a secular state, strongly connected to Western culture, while the other sought to found Israel on the Halakhah and on traditional Judaism. The first approach was promoted by the liberal former hegemons—the sons and daughters of the group that, until the late 1970s, had enjoyed hegemonic status in Israel's politics, society, and culture. The second was advanced by certain groups within religious-Zionism, and also by segments of the ultra-Orthodox Jewish group. Each of the two competing groups had a rich hoard of scholarly and spiritual materials at its disposal, each could rely on many institutions of civil society, and each offered a polarized vision of Israel's character in the ensuing decades.

1. *Religious Zionism*

Dating back to the earliest days of the Zionist movement, religious-Zionism was a significant element in Zionism. But although religious Zionists wanted the emergent culture in Eretz Israel to be founded on the Halakhah and the tradition of Judaism, the culture that actually evolved in Eretz Israel in the first half of the twentieth century was distinctly secular. Left with little choice, religious-Zionism became a partner in the hegemony led by the labor movement. (A hegemonic bloc, as noted, can include various competing groups vying with one another over the shaping of the hegemonic culture.)

Avi Sagi and Dov Schwartz of Bar Ilan University, who study religious-Zionism, write that for many long years, religious-Zionism was shunted to the margins of the Zionist endeavor in Eretz Israel, in politics and in the realm of pioneering and contribution to the endeavor. It was in those years that religious-Zionism

> developed the self-image of a peripheral group shunted to the political margins. It was perceived as responsible for religious services and for the religious image of the *Yishuv* and the state.[27]

Similarly, columnist Yair Sheleg, an expert on the religious Zionist group, writes that

> the fundamental trauma of religious-Zionism that largely affects the processes unfolding within it lies somewhere in the 1940s and 1950s, when religiosity was seen as an anachronistic remnant, something bound to disappear within a few years, and its stubborn supporters as 'exilic Jews' or as second-class citizens.

During those years, religious Zionist society was 'extremely marginal' in the public sphere, writes Sheleg, and its primary aspiration was 'to be like the secularists' in regard to Zionist realization.[28] Gideon Aran, a scholar

---

[27] Avi Sagi and Dov Schwartz, 'From Pioneering to Torah Study: Another Perspective' in Avi Sagi and Dov Schwartz (eds), *A Hundred Years Of Religious Zionism* (Ramat Gan, Bar Ilan University Press, 2003) vol 3, 73, 73–4 (Hebrew). See also: Gideon Aran, 'From Pioneering to Torah Study: Background to the Growth of Religious Zionism' id, at 31; Schwartz, above n 9, at 9.

[28] Yair Sheleg, *The New Religious Jews* (Jerusalem, Keter Publishing House, 2000) 29–30, 42 (Hebrew).

of religious-Zionism, writes that the ascendancy of secular over religious-Zionism reached its peak at the moment of Israel's birth:

The establishment of Israel denotes the superiority of secular modern nationalism in its struggle with traditional religion over precedence in Judaism.[29]

Aviezer Ravitzky, a scholar of Jewish philosophy at the Hebrew University of Jerusalem, vividly describes the sense of marginality he himself had experienced as a religious child and youth in Israel during the 1950s and 1960s:

Secularists were then perceived as generals, diplomats, pioneers, and builders, the 'engine' pulling ahead, while we remained in the back as *kashrut* inspectors of the dining-car.[30]

Radical changes in the self-image and practices of the religious-Zionist group took place, however, in the 1970s, in parallel to the decline of the labor hegemony. The instigator of the changes was *Gush Emumin* ('Bloc of the Faithful'). The hard core of this religious-Zionist group adopted fundamentalist theology and practices. This meant, among other things, treating religion as the exclusive source of normative authority in all spheres of life of the individual, the state and society;[31] unmitigated adherence to religious tradition in its minute details; an ambivalent attitude toward the authority of the state; denigration of the normative, spiritual and artistic heritage of the West; viewing the secular way of life as hollow, normatively impoverished, and deplete of meaning;[32] adoption of an expansionist stance toward the Halakhah that applies it to all spheres of life, including the political and the legal; interpretation of political developments through halakhic-theological lenses; adoption of national-political radicalism and activism; geographical separation and concentration; an emphasis on

---

[29] Aran, above n 27, at 39.

[30] Aviezer Ravitzky, 'Israeli Society in the Wake of the Rabin Assassination' in Neri Horowitz (ed), *Religion And Nationalism In Israel And The Middle East* (Tel Aviv, Am Oved Publishing, 2002) 254, 260 (Hebrew).

[31] One possible interpretation of the assassination of Prime Minister Yitzhak Rabin in November 1995 is that it was the offshoot of the rise of religious fundamentalism, which awarded the Halakhah precedence over the law of the state. See: Yoram Peri, *Brothers At War: Rabin's Assassination And The Cultural War In Israel* (Tel Aviv, Babel Publishers, 2005) (Hebrew). Indeed, in his trial, Yigal Amir, Rabin's assassin, justified his deed with halakhic arguments. See: Leora Bilsky, 'Law and Politics: The Trial of Rabin's Assassin' (1999) 8 Plilim 13 (Hebrew).

[32] Gideon Aran, 'Jewish Zionist Fundamentalism: The Bloc of the Faithful in Israel (Gush Emunim)' in Martin E. Marty and R. Scott Appelby (eds), *Fundamentalism Observed* (Chicago, University of Chicago Press, 1991) 265, 330, 331

> Fundamentalism is generally presented as a response to the crises of modernity rather than as reaction to modernity itself.... [T]he point of departure for comprehending GE and similar radical movements is their obsession with modernity.

family values; suspicion toward feminism; and the segregation of men and women.[33]

These far-reaching changes in theology and religious practices brought about far-reaching changes in the self-image of the religious-Zionist group. Prominent subgroups within religious-Zionism increasingly began to perceive themselves no longer as *partners* in the cultural and political ruling hegemony, but as potential *leaders* of a new hegemony that might evolve in Israel. Obviously, at the center of this religious Zionist vision concerning the future of Israel stands the notion of a halakhic state. Other elements of this vision, however, have been adopted after their 'abandonment' by the previous hegemonic culture, individualistic elements of self-realization having replaced the collectivist aspects that originally characterized the hegemony of the Labor movement.

At that time, as Sheleg notes,

> the desire of religious-Zionism to become part of Israeli society turned into a desire to assume a dominant role within it and lead it in light of new and improved values.

Many religious Zionists:

> came to believe that the secular State of Israel had indeed reached the end, at least normatively, and efforts should from now on be invested in building it on a renewed normative foundation, with Judaism as the dominant element.

Religious Zionists therefore began to see themselves as no longer interested in a partnership with the secular world in carrying the Zionist banner, but rather its replacement at the leadership. The widespread metaphor was that of a 'relay baton' in a race, which has been transferred from the labor movement to religious-Zionism.[34]

(Interestingly enough, in the same period that religious-Zionism came to interpret the transition of the hegemonic culture from collectivistic to individualistic ideals as manifesting the demise of that culture, voices at the very center of the hegemonic culture gave warning that this transition was breeding a sense of meaninglessness and hollowness among members

---

[33] Aran. id; Eliezer Don Yehiya, 'The Book and the Sword: Nationalist "Yeshivas" and Political Radicalism in Israel' in Avi Sagi and Dov Schwartz (eds), *A Hundred Years Of Religious Zionism* (Ramat Gan, Bar Ilan University Press, 2003) vol 3, 187; S.N. Eisenstadt, *Fundamentalism And Modernity* (Tel Aviv, Ministry of Defense, 2002) (Hebrew) chapters 2, 11; Eisenstadt, above n 15, chapter 10; Hanan Moses, 'From Religious Zionism To Post-Modern Religiosity' (PhD Dissertation, Department of Political Science, Bar Ilan University, 2009) (Hebrew); Aran, above n 27; Sheleg, above n 28, at 38–42, 46.

[34] Sheleg, above n 28, at 15, 16, 21, 44. See also: Gadi Taub, *The Settlers And The Struggle Over The Meaning Of Zionism* (Tel Aviv, Miskal-Yedioth Ahronoth Books, 2007) 26–7, 61, 62, 71, 98, 120 (Hebrew).

of the hegemonic group.³⁵ This discontent and discomfort with Israel's secular culture was exacerbated at the end of the twentieth century when neo-liberalism ascended to the fore as the dominant socioeconomic ideology in the country. Premised on the notion that the logic of the unregulated market should be extended to as many spheres as possible, neo-liberalism unavoidably breeds normative impoverishment.)

This reversal in the self-image of religious-Zionism found expression in many articles that appeared in the 1980s in *Nekudah*, the journal of the settlers in Judea, Samaria and Gaza. According to the analysis by Israel Harel, the founding chairman of the settlers' chief organization 'Association of the Jewish Communities in Judea, Samaria and the Gaza Strip' and the founding editor of *Nekudah*, for many years the religious Zionist group accepted the leadership of the labor movement and collaborated with it, but after the Six Day War of 1967 the powers of the 'senior and dominant partner in this collaboration', the labor movement, began to wane, whereas 'the junior partner', the religious Zionist group, discovered a hitherto unknown vigor within itself, making it demand that the 'relay baton' of Zionist leadership be transferred to it.³⁶

Sociologist Baruch Kimmerling sees the extensive settlement endeavor of *Gush Emunim* (Bloc of the Faithful) in the occupied Palestinian territories (OPT) of Judea, Samaria, and the Gaza Strip as the nucleus for turning the whole of Israel into a halakhic state. In his view, the aim of the *Gush* was not only to extend Israel's borders as far and as close as possible to those of the biblical Promised Land, but also to create a base for spreading the idea of the halakhic state.

'Eretz Israel' in the occupied territories, a kind of state within a state, was meant to expand and absorb within it the secular sections of the State of Israel, while providing a decisive response about the state's collective identity, which is Jewish-religious, ethnocentric, and far removed from any liberal and universal view.³⁷

writes Kimmerling.

These new trends within religious-Zionism are strikingly apparent in the report by author Amos Oz about a meeting with settlers from Judea and Samaria in Ofrah in 1982. Settler leader Israel Harel spoke about the clash between advocates of a connection with Jewish culture and supporters of

---

[35] The artistic depiction of this sense of meaninglessness and hollowness reached its peak in Yaakov Shabtai, *Past Continuous* (Dalya Bilu trans, Philadelphia, Jewish Publication Society of America, 1985).

[36] Israel Harel, 'Toward Post-Zionist Religious Nationalism' (October 3 1995) Haaretz.

[37] Kimmerling, above n 9, at 15, 201. See also: Idith Zertal And Akiva Eldar, *Lords Of The Land: The Settlers And The State Of Israel 1967–2004* (Or Yehuda, Dvir Publishing House, 2004) 273–4, 250, 279, 283, 430–1 (Hebrew).

a connection with Western culture, referring derisively to the latter and presenting them as materialistic and rootless:

> The major barricade is the one that divides the Jews from the Israelis. The Jews are those who want to live, to one degree or another, in accordance with the Bible. The Israelis pay lip service, maybe, to the heritage, but in essence they aspire to be a completely new people here, a satellite of Western culture. For many of those Israelis the Land of Israel is no more than a 'biographical accident.' As it happens, they make a decent living here, but if they were offered a better job somewhere else, abroad, they'd simply pack up and move. Eretz Yisrael means very little to them.[38]

Uri Elitzur, another settler leader, said:

> Western culture is all alien to the spirit of Judaism, and the current tryst with Western culture is a passing episode in our history, like earlier romances with foreign cultures.[39]

To which Oz responded: 'You threaten to boot Israel out of the union between Jewish tradition and Western humanism.'[40]

In parallel to the processes that were prompting segments of religious-Zionism to perceive themselves as a new hegemonic alternative, other processes also began to unfold in the 1980s and 1990s, leading to religious extremism and radicalism.

Signs of the radicalization of religiosity within religious-Zionism became increasingly manifest:[41] Rigorous halakhic observance; the adoption of the widespread practice among the ultra-Orthodox group to seek the rulings of rabbis in all areas of life, including in the realm of politics (*da'at Torah*); the adoption of ultra-Orthodox dress codes; the endorsement of severe segregation between boys and girls in both schools and extra-curricular activities, such as youth movements; the growing ascendance of ultra-Orthodox trends and practices in the *yeshivot* and educational institutions of religious-Zionism; the enrolment of children in private educational institutions that are not part of the state-religious system; the preference for living in a homogeneous environment; avoidance of recourse to the state judiciary and a preference for courts that rule according to the Halakhah; the adoption of a messianic attitude toward the state; and a growing hostility towards democracy.

Students of religious-Zionism agree that the far-reaching changes that the group underwent in the 1970s are another aspect of its painful

---

[38] Amos Oz, *In The Land Of Israel* (Maurie Goldberg-Bartura trans, San Diego, Harcour Brace Jovanovich, Publishers, 1983) 115. Years later, Harel said that these words of his provoked much anger against him, 'but I would not recant. On the contrary; I feel reaffirmed as to the justice of my remarks.' Taub, above n 34, at 30.

[39] Id, at 120–1.   [40] Id, at 139.   [41] Eisenstadt, above n 15, chapter 10.

ongoing contention with a series of pressing, unresolved issues related to its encounter with modernity, Zionism and Israel's secular statehood, eg, the place of modern Western cultural contents in the life of the group; the extent to which Jewish theology can provide meaning to the activities of religious Jews in contexts dominated by secular culture, such as the professions, art, science and politics; the gap between the utopian ideal of a halakhic state and the realities of a secular Jewish state; the extent to which the group should be loyal to and involved in the affairs of a secular Jewish state; the place of rabbis in the life of the group; the extent to which the group should insist on the enforcement of traditional Jewish values in Israel's public sphere; how to reconcile the Halakhah with democracy; the attitude toward the ultra-Orthodox group; and whether to prefer a strategy of long-term investment in education over immediate participation in state projects, such as service in the IDF.[42]

2. Ashkenazi Ultra-Orthodox

The ultra-Orthodox (*Haredim*)[43] are the second largest subgroup in the Jewish religious group. To understand their positions and behavior, it is necessary to return to the eighteenth century, particularly its latter half. At that time the Jewish Enlightenment movement [*Haskalah*] sought to bring elements from European culture into Jewish education and culture, namely, to establish Jewish identity on elements from both Jewish and European culture. The movement also challenged the status of rabbis who

---

[42] Avi Sagi and Dov Schwartz, 'The Religious Zionist Enterprise in the Face of the Modern World—Introductory Essay' in Avi Sagi and Dov Schwartz (eds), *A Hundred Years Of Religious Zionism* (Ramat Gan, Bar Ilan University Press, 2003) vol 1, 9 (Hebrew); Avi Sagi, 'From the Land of the Torah to the Land of Israel—From One Broken Dream to Another: Study of the Crisis in Religious Zionism' in Avi Sagi and Dov Schwartz (eds), *A Hundred Years Of Religious Zionism* (Ramat Gan, Bar Ilan University Press, 2003) vol 3, 457; Ehud Luz, 'The Failure of the Bridge' id, at 351; Yosef Shalmon, 'Tradition and Modernity in Early Religoius-Zionist Thought' in Ben-Zion Yehoshua and Ahron Kedar (eds), *Ideological And Political Zionism* (Jerusalem, Zalman Shazar Center, 1978) 21 (Hebrew).

[43] Menachem Friedman, *The Haredi (Ultra-Orthodox) Society—Sources, Trends And Processes* (Jerusalem, The Jerusalem Institute for Israel Studies, 1991) (Hebrew); Dan Miron, 'Between Rabbi Sach and the New Hebrew Literature' in *Essays On Literature And Society* (Tel Aviv, Zmora-Bitan Publishers, 1991) 9 (Hebrew); Aviezer Ravitzky, 'Exile in the Holly Land: The Ultra-Orthodox Dilemma' in *Messianism, Zionism And Jewish Religious Radicalism* (Tel Aviv, Am Oved Publishers, 1993) 201 (Hebrew); Jacob Katz, *A Time For Inquiry—A Time For Reflection—A Historical Essay On Israel Through The Ages* (Jerusalem, Zalman Shazar Center, 1999) (Hebrew); Ricky Tesler, *In The Name Of God—Shas And The Religious Revolution* (Jerusalem, Keter Publishing House, 2003) (Hebrew); Kimmy Caplan, 'Research of the Israeli Ultra-Orthodox Society' in Kimmy Caplan and Emmanuel Sivan (eds), *Israeli Haredim: Integration Without Assimilation?* (Tel Aviv, Hakibbutz Hameuchad Publishing House, 2003) 224 (Hebrew); Aharon Rose, 'The Haredim: A Defense,' (2006) 25 Azure; Kimmy Kaplan and Nurit Stadler (eds), *Leadership And Authority In Israeli Haredi Society* (Jerusalem, Van Leer Jerusalem Institute, 2009) (Hebrew); Eisenstadt, above n 15, chapter 10; Kimmerling, above n 9, chapter 5. The ultra-Orthodox operate an extensive network of welfare and educational institutions. A landmark decision in the development of ultra-Orthodox education was the recognition (even if indirectly) of its independent system as one of the country's educational streams in the Law of State Education 5713-1953, entitling it to state budgeting.

abide by the Halakhah as the spiritual leaders of the Jewish community (Chapter 1, above).

The rabbinic establishment counter-reacted with an uncompromising struggle against the Jewish Enlightenment movement, endorsing strategies of stricter segregation and greater religious stringency. However, even though the ultra-Orthodox reject the intellectual and spiritual heritage of the West in its entirety, they (unlike the Amish of North America) nonetheless have never objected to the use or consumption of Western technology. A century later, when Zionism emerged in the closing decades of the nineteenth century, the leaders of ultra-Orthodox Judaism in Eastern Europe were opposed to it too. Those ultra-Orthodox leaders who nevertheless did try to participate in the Zionist endeavor in its early days withdrew from it as soon as its secular character became apparent.

The ultra-Orthodox stance against modernity remained consistent throughout the twentieth century, as did their opposition to Zionism. Since the ultra-Orthodox consider the Jewish people to exist outside history, sheltered by Divine Providence, they reject the Zionist attempt to engage actively in the shaping of the people's destiny. They also object to the secular Jewish culture created by the Jewish society in Eretz Israel in the course of the twentieth century. Hence, they have never perceived the establishment of Israel as a significant turning point in Jewish history or one that requires a reconsideration of their stance. Given the character of the emergent secular culture, their approach in the pre-state *Yishuv* period and for many years after the establishment of the state was that their life in Eretz Israel is one of 'exile in the Holy Land.' Their recognition of the State of Israel has for the most part been pragmatic, an *ex post factum* acceptance of reality without any commitment to it, with no ideological identification with it, and absent any endorsement of its symbols (flag, national anthem, president). Similarly, the ultra-Orthodox group accepts Israeli laws de facto; the only laws it genuinely recognizes are halakhic laws, whose origin is divine. Consequently, the ultra-Orthodox have never subscribed to the religious Zionist vision concerning the transformation of Israel into a halakhic state.

At the time of the labor hegemony, the ultra-Orthodox, like the Arab citizens of Israel, had no part in it. The decline of the hegemony, however, marked a significant turning point in the political behavior of the ultra-Orthodox group and its connections to the state and society. Following the 1977 political turnabout, *Agudat Yisrael* (the main ultra-Orthodox political party) joined the government coalition for the first time since 1952, largely because the ultra-Orthodox needed to ensure state budgets to support the 'learners' society' they had created since the establishment of Israel. (During the years 1952–77, ultra-Orthodox parties provided political support to the government in exchange for financial support of the group's institutions. Since 1977, when ultra-Orthodox parties have joined government coalitions, their representatives have abstained from serving as ministers, serving instead as deputies of the prime minister, fully in charge, however, of the ministries entrusted to their control.)

Budgetary allocations to ultra-Orthodox religious institutions have indeed grown tremendously since 1977. More importantly, however, the ultra-Orthodox thereby entered the center of the political arena and the country's key institutions, extending their involvement far beyond their sectorial interests. They began participating in important political decisions and showing increasing interest in influencing the character of Israeli society, on the assumption that they would succeed where Zionism had failed—the creation of an ideal society. Since 1977, and despite their traditional rejection of Zionism, the ultra-Orthodox have in fact emerged as the most nationalistic Jewish group in Israel. These developments have led to considerable tension between the political behavior of the ultra-Orthodox group and its traditional positions vis-à-vis Zionism, the establishment of the State of Israel, and the perception of ultra-Orthodox life in Israel as exile in the Holy Land. Nevertheless, although ultra-Orthodox society has entered the political arena, it still preserves its social and geographic segregation.

3. Sephardic ultra-Orthodox

The early 1980s saw the emergence of a religious-political movement of the Sephardic ultra-Orthodox in Israel—Shas. The movement's activity is spearheaded by the Shas party, whose representatives first entered the Knesset in 1984.[44]

Shas' Sephardic version of ultra-Orthodoxy is essentially different from the Ashkenazi version. It is not hostile to Zionism, nor does it view the State of Israel as a fact to be accepted merely on pragmatic grounds. It accepts Israel as a positive event because it views Israel's existence as vital to the potential redemption of the Jewish people. It therefore offers to revivify

---

[44] Yoav Peled (ed), *Shas—The Challenge Of Israeliness* (Tel Aviv, Miskal-Yedioth Ahronoth Books, 2001) (Hebrew); Chaim Shine, *The Jewish State—Concluding Summary* (Tel Aviv, Peri Publishers, 2003) (Hebrew); Tesler, above n 43; Kimmerling, above n 9, chapter 6; Benjamin Lau, 'Changes in Sephardic Halakhic World: From Tradition to Literature' in Kimmy Caplan and Emmanuel Sivan (eds), *Israeli Haredim: Integration Without Assimilation?* (Tel Aviv, Hakibbutz Hameuchad Publishing House, 2003) 11 (Hebrew); Aviezer Ravitzky (ed), *Shas: Cultural And Ideological Perspectives* (Tel Aviv, Am Oved Publishers, 2006) (Hebrew); Eisenstadt, above n 33, chapters 2, 13. On the differences between Ashkenazi and Sephardic ultra-Orthodoxy, see: Eliezer Ben-Rafael and Nissim Leon, 'Communal Segregation, Religiosity and Politics: The Origins of the Haredi Movement Amongst the Mizrachim' in Uri Cohen et al (eds), *Israel And Modernity* (Beer Sheva, Ben Gurion University of the Negev, 2006) 285 (Hebrew).

Zionism and Israel's cultural character with new content. Like the Ashkenazi ultra-Orthodox, however, though Shas rejects the intellectual and spiritual heritage of modernity in its entirety, it has no objection to utilizing modern technology. It supports strict adherence to the religious character of Jewish life, and is therefore opposed to hegemonic Zionism because of its attempt to reformulate Jewish existence in new, secular terms.

In line with its positive attitude toward the State of Israel, Shas has not isolated itself from the state and its institutions. To the contrary, from the start it has participated in government coalitions and considered itself a partner to decisions on all subjects. Moreover, unlike the Ashkenazi ultra-Orthodox parties, Shas pitches its address to the entire public, not only its ultra-Orthodox Sephardic segment. The party's supporters have not chosen geographic segregation; they are dispersed throughout the entire population and include not only the ultra-Orthodox, but also religious and even secular individuals. The party's main constituency is nevertheless concentrated in development towns and in poor urban neighborhoods—needy Jews whose families arrived from Arab countries in the 1950s. (In the 1999 elections, Shas came out as the strongest party in Israel's development towns. In the elections held since 1999, it lost its primacy to Likud, but it still enjoys vast support among development town inhabitants.)

Shas offers an alternative narrative to the history of Zionism and to the place of Sephardic Jews within it. In their countries of origin, so goes the tale, Sephardic Jews had lived pure and upright lives in the light of religion. When secular Zionism moved them to Israel, it relegated them to the margins of society, violated their dignity, robbed them of their religious and cultural legacy, and devastated their lives: the outcome was broken families, poverty, use of alcohol and drugs, crime, and prostitution. The way for Sephardim to rectify the grave wrongs that Zionism inflicted upon them is to return to a life of Torah and religious observance and to restore the ancestral traditions. Only thus can Sephardim regain their self-dignity, repair their family and human relationships, restore themselves to a proper moral and spiritual level, and attain economic prosperity.

Early on, Shas took action mainly to correct the budgetary discrimination against the religious institutions of the ultra-Orthodox Sephardic group in comparison to those of the Ashkenazi ultra-Orthodox. From 1992 onward, however, an essential change in Shas' aims becomes discernible: to replace Israeli democracy with a theocracy—'restore the crown to its rightful place' [*le-hahazir atarah le-yoshna*]. In other words, Shas' aim is to establish a Sephardic version of a halakhic state, in reliance on the halakhic *oeuvre* of R. Joseph Caro and on that of the movement's spiritual leader, R. Ovadia Yosef. Sociologist Baruch Kimmerling writes that the version of Judaism promoted by Shas is:

> the most original populist-religious reform in Judaism since the appearance of Hasidism...and since the emergence of the Reform movement in Western Europe.[45]

Shas, then, is driven by a vision of the character of the entire State of Israel, regardless of any specific ethnic context, and a major component of its drive to attain its goal is an extensive undertaking to persuade Jews to 'return to Judaism.'

'Shas is the largest socio-political movement ever established in Israel' writes Chaim Shine.[46] Shas operates through the extensive institutional network it has established, which is funded mainly by state budgets. In the course of Shas' existence, budgetary support for these activities has ballooned.[47] In the early years of the twenty-first century, Shas was operating around a thousand institutions in more than a hundred local authorities. The party views every one of these institutions, which are staffed by its people, as one of its branches. Through its extensive institutional network, Shas has replaced the state in providing a range of religious, educational, cultural, welfare, healthcare, housing, and occupational services, in ways that create strong bonds with its clients and lead to their dependence. This institutional network—a mélange of party, community, synagogue, social movement, educational, cultural and welfare systems—creates among its beneficiaries a profound identification with the party that operates these services. Although the importance of the material support that this institutional system provides to its clients cannot be dismissed, what it provides above all is a cultural home, a system of meaning, a sense of community and belonging, and the restoration of its members' self-dignity and self-esteem. Thus, through this institutional network, Shas doesn't make contact with its supporters only once every four years, before the elections, but is materially and culturally present in their everyday lives.

(e) The change in the structure of the Knesset's religious representation

Shas' entry into the Knesset in 1984 marked a turning point in the political representation of the Jewish religious group in Israel. Until the 1980s, only one-third of the Knesset's religious members had belonged to ultra-Orthodox parties, whereas two-thirds had been members of the National Religious Party (NRP)—a Zionist party closely linked to Israel's secular

---

[45] Kimmerling, above n 9, at 17. [46] Shine, above n 44, at 26–7.
[47] For an extensive discussion, see: Tesler, above n 43.

mainstream. Since the 1980s, the internal balance of power in the religious camp has been reversed: following the political weakening of the NRP and the strengthening of Shas, the religious public is now represented in the Knesset mainly by ultra-Orthodox parties. The political behavior of the NRP has also changed during these years: the party began to concentrate more and more on political topics and on protecting the settlement endeavor, leaving concern with religious issues to the ultra-Orthodox parties. Since the 1980s, then, religious interests increasingly have been represented in the Knesset by religious radicals, non-Zionists, detached from Israel's secular mainstream. This process reached a peak in the 1999 elections, when Shas won seventeen out of the Knesset's 120 seats (raising the representation of the ultra-Orthodox camp from fourteen Knesset members to twenty-two), whereas the NRP dropped from nine seats to five.[48]

(f) The shift from 'consensual politics' to 'crisis politics'

The two subgroups that make up the religious Jewish group—religious-Zionism and the ultra-Orthodox (both Ashkenazi and Sephardic)—participated in government coalitions throughout the 1980s. They devoted vigorous efforts to broadening their hold on the state's public administration and enlisting more supporters. By contrast, the group of liberal former hegemons recurrently failed in its attempt to return to power and assume control of the state's central institutions and administration.

Following the 1977 political turnabout, the religious parties also came to represent the pivotal swing votes between the political bloc of the 'left' and the political bloc of the 'right.' Bernard Susser and Asher Cohen present this new situation as part of the far-reaching change in Israeli politics during the 1980s. In their view, from the time of the *Yishuv* and until the 1980s, the relationship between religion and state in Israel had followed the consociation model (politics of accommodation) of Arend Lijphart,[49] which is founded on pragmatic arrangements, mutual concessions, avoidance of confrontation, and restrained use of unilateral political power. What made this model possible was Mapai's uncontested control of Israeli politics. After the 1980s, however, this model was replaced by what Susser and Cohen call 'crisis politics.' Israeli politics became split between two

---

[48] Asher Cohen And Bernard Susser, *Israel And The Politics Of Jewish Identity* (Baltimore, Johns Hopkins University Press, 2000) chapters 3, 4; Asher Cohen And Bernard Susser, *From Accommodation To Escalation* (Tel Aviv, Schocken Publishing House, 2003) chapter 5 (Hebrew).

[49] Arend Lijphart, *The Politics Of Accommodation* (Berkeley and Los Angeles, University of California Press, 1968); Arend Lijphart, *Democracies* (New Haven and London, Yale University Press, 1984); Arend Lijphart, *Democracy In Plural Societies* (New Haven and London, Yale University Press, 1997).

more or less equally balanced political blocs. The religious parties thereby acquired the power to decide which of the large parties would form the government coalition, while imposing on the ruling party arrangements desirable to them. The shift to crisis politics, then, greatly empowered the religious parties and enabled them to considerably advance their goals. As a result

> secular-religious relations have gone from compromise to crisis, from mitigating arrangements to aggravated strife, from bad to worse. Consociationalism—that is, the adaptive, unity-preserving political style of the first decades of Israel's existence—has given way... to a crisis-dominated relationship between secular and religious Jews that becomes progressively more strident as the erstwhile common political language between them is lost. Rather than an accommodation of each other's needs in the interest of preserving national unity, a majoritarian, winner-take-all style has grown more and more dominant.[50]

C. ANXIETY

I will argue below that, following Israel's transition to the post-hegemonic phase, the group of liberal former hegemons (henceforth LFH) reacted with anxiety. I will further argue that this anxiety is the main explanation for the far-reaching changes that took place in the jurisprudence of the Supreme Court during the 1980s, and for the significant support for these changes among members of this group.

I am here adopting Heidegger's distinction between two concepts: fear and anxiety. *Fear* is a reaction to an identified and defined danger. To the contrary, *anxiety* is a 'general' mood, which cannot be explained as a reaction to an identified and defined danger: 'That in the face of which one is anxious is completely indefinite,' writes Heidegger.

> Anxiety 'does not know' what that in the face of which it is anxious is... That in the face of which anxiety is anxious is nothing ready-to-hand within-the-world.[51]

Psychologically, then, whereas fear usually passes after a short time, once the danger that inspired it has passed, anxiety, which is unconnected to an identified and defined source or has no source at all, may persist unbroken.

---

[50] Cohen and Susser, *Israel and the Politics of Jewish Identity*, above n 48, at xii–xiii. See also: Asher Cohen and Bernard Susser, 'From Accommodation to Decision: Transformations in Israel's Religio-Political Life' (1996) 38 J Church & State 817; Hofnung, above n 3.

[51] Martin Heidegger, *Being And Time* (John Macquarrie and Edward Robinson trans, San Francisco, Harper, 1962) 231. See also: Rollo May, *The Meaning Of Anxiety* (New York, Ronald Press Co, 1979) chapter 2; Reidar Thomte, 'Historical Introduction' in *Sorn Kierkegaard, The Concept Of Anxiety* (Reidar Thomte trans, Princeton, Princeton University Press, 1980) xv–xviii.

In the wake of this distinction between fear and anxiety, I argue that, from the late 1970s onward, the LFH went into a state of anxiety following the decline of the labor hegemony and the renewal of the cultural struggle over the future of Israel. This anxiety had two, mutually reinforcing sources. One is *external*, stemming from Israel's relations with its Arab neighbors. From the beginning of Zionist settlement in Eretz Israel and throughout Israel's existence, Jews living in Israel have had to deal with an element of existential anxiety—anxiety about the destruction of the *Yishuv*, afterwards the State of Israel, and about the physical extermination of the Jewish group living there.[52] The second source of anxiety is *internal* and has to do with the profound changes that have taken place in Israel's politics and culture since the latter half of the 1970s, and their effects on the LFH.[53]

(a) A new political leadership

On the night of May 17, 1977, the night of the political 'turnabout' when for the first time in Israel's twenty-nine years of statehood the labor movement had to cede power following the Likud's victory in the elections, the LFH underwent the traumatic experience of being abruptly and unexpectedly placed under a prime minister and leadership group largely unknown to them. Changes of this sort inevitably evoke insecurity and anxiety. Indeed, novelist A. B. Yehoshua inadvertently used the term 'death' to describe his feelings at the results of the 1977 elections—death, meaning the absolute collapse and termination of all that is, the ultimate source of anxiety in human consciousness.[54] And in kibbutz *Afikim*, one of the oldest and most prosperous kibbutzim in the country, on the night of the political turnabout and in the following months, people said to each other: 'Our state has been taken from us.'[55]

At first, the LFH held that the 1977 election results were a one-time 'accident.' In the years that followed, however, they saw their political rep-

---

[52] There are numerous expressions of the external anxiety of Israelis. For two striking examples, see: Amos Oz, 'Where the Jackals Howl' in *Where The Jackals Howl* (Tel Aviv, Am Oved Publishers, 1976) 9 (Hebrew); A. B. Yehoshua, 'Against the Forests' in *The Stories* (Tel Aviv, Hakibbutz Hameuchad Publishing House, 1993) 99 (Hebrew). In 1992 the renowned Israeli author Yizhar Smilansky said that Zionist pioneers lived in a 'continuous state of endless anxiety.' Ariana Melamed, '*The End of Silence*' (March 13 1992) Hadashot. Similar remarks were made by poet Haim Guri in 2000. Ari Shavit, 'Now It's Your Turn' (March 3 2000) Haaretz.

[53] My argument below relates to the consciousness of the LFH, that is, to their perception of the reality that began to unfold in Israel at the end of the 1970s and in the 1980s. This is not an argument about the *actual* situation in Israel at the time. Concerning this question, a number of interpretations could be suggested, some of which do not accord with the consciousness of the LFH.

[54] Levi-Yitzhak Ha-Yerushalmi, 'The Likud Year and Days of Disengagement—Interview with A. B. Yehoshua' (September 17 1982) Maariv.

[55] Assaf Inbari, *Home* (Tel Aviv, Miskal-Yedioth Ahronoth Books, 2009) 248, 254 (Hebrew). See also: Levy, above n 22, at 58.

resentatives fail three more times (1981, 1984, and 1988) in their attempt to regain control of the country's central institutions and state administration, while politicians representing a culture unknown and hence threatening to them repeatedly succeeded in winning political power and placing their people at the head of these bodies.

(b) A new culture

In the years after the 1977 turnabout, the LFH found themselves facing new social and cultural groups, unknown to them. With their own culture challenged and no longer self-evident, they experienced feelings of existential insecurity vis-à-vis the new groups, which were becoming increasingly significant in Israeli culture.[56] 'The 1977 political turnabout was also, and perhaps mainly, a cultural turnabout,' write historians Eyal Naveh and Esther Yogev.

New, 'other' forces, which had so far been perceived as the cultural margins of the society, entered the government and the political bureaucracy and attained legitimacy for their culture and for their aspiration to represent a new and different kind of Israeli identity.[57]

Likewise, sociologist S.N. Eisenstadt writes that following the political turnabout of 1977 Israel underwent processes in which the former, labor version of Zionism was challenged, leading to far-reaching changes in the country's collective identity and self-definition.[58]

---

[56] On the anxiety caused following an encounter with unfamiliar cultural groups, see: Walter G. Stephan and Cookie White Stephan, 'Intergroup Anxiety' (1985) 41 J Social Issues 157; Walter G. Stephan and Cookie White Stephan, 'Antecedents of Intergroup Anxiety in Asian-Americans and Hispanic-Americans' (1989) 13 Int'l J Intercultural Relations 203; Cookie White Stephan and Walter G. Stephan, 'Reducing Intercultural Anxiety Through Intercultural Contact' (1992) 16 Int'l J Intercultural Relations 89; Lauri L. Hyers and Janet K. Swim, 'A Comparison of the Experiences of Dominant and Minority Group Members During an Intergroup Encounter,' (1998) 1 Group Processes & Intergroup Relations 143; Irene V. Blair, Bernadette Park and Jonathan Bachelor, 'Understanding Intergroup Anxiety: Are Some People More Anxious Than Others?' (2003) 6 Group Processes & Intergroup Relations 151. Michael Walzer writes that

> In a number of ancient languages, Latin among them, strangers and enemies were named by a single word. We have come only slowly, through a long process of trial and error, to distinguish the two and to acknowledge that, in certain circumstances, strangers (but not enemies) might be entitled to our hospitality, assistance, and good will.

Michael Walzer, 'Membership' in Shlomo Avineri and Avner De-Shalit (eds), *Communitarianism And Individualism* (Oxford, Oxford University Press, 1992) 65, 67. Kimmerling writes that the decline of a hegemony is usually accompanied with apocalyptic feelings among those who identify with the hegemony. Kimmerling, above n 9, at 499.

[57] Eyal Naveh And Esther Yogev, *Histories—Towards A Dialogue With The Israeli Past* (Tel Aviv, Babel Publishers, 2002) 51.

[58] Eisenstadt, above n 15, at 11, chapter 6. Eisenstadt compares the changes that took place in Israel following the decline of the labor hegemony to the transformations that took place in the United States in the first half of the nineteenth century, following the presidency of Andrew Jackson. Id, at 49.

From the end of the 1970s and throughout the 1980s, the LFH experienced the 'collapse of their cultural home.'[59] This experience meant that a culture familiar to them, the culture that had been transparent to them, in which they had grown up and functioned successfully and naturally, obviously and unquestionably, was no longer the country's dominant, self-evident culture. It had begun to lose its ability to impose itself on most social groups, entering an accelerated process of change as new and unknown cultural elements began taking up an increasingly central role in the culture and politics of the post-hegemonic era. During the 1980s, Israel's cultural mainstream and political culture were swiftly and broadly infiltrated by nationalists, the religious, people of Sephardic extraction, residents of development towns and poor urban neighborhoods—in short, new cultural groups. The culture familiar to the LFH, the culture whose main bearers they had been and whose concepts of success and prestige they had represented, had broken down, challenged by the cultures of different rising social groups that were unknown, unintelligible, and even opposed to their own, and hence threatening. Confronted with the collapse of their cultural home, alienated from these new cultures, members of the LFH lost their self-confidence and stumbled into insecurity, anxiety and stress.

Doron Rosenblum is one of the most talented and influential writers that have emerged in the Israeli press. Perhaps more than any other journalist, he has conveyed the experience of young members of the LFH in the last two decades of the twentieth century, particularly their reactions to the political and cultural reality that unfolded swiftly after the political turnabout of 1977. In 1982, Rosenblum described Israel as being at the peak of a comprehensive cultural transformation, where fundamental values that recently held sway uncontested (the situation prevailing in a hegemonic era, in Gramsci's terms), are displaced by new and unknown values:

Many fundamental values obvious only yesterday, appear today in a dim and highly strange light, as a clumsy and brutal caricature of themselves.... The political turnabout that brought [Menachem] Begin to power seems to be nothing but an external appendix to an unfathomable mental turnabout related to a changing national temperament, in a transition from one sphere to another.... In peace and in war, inwards and outwards—all is stamped by a crass seal of railing

---

[59] On culture as 'home,' see: Heidegger, above n 51, at 233, 234; Peter Berger et al, *The Homeless Mind* (New York, Vintage Books, 1973) 77–8, 82, 92; Zygmunt Bauman, *Culture As Praxis* (London, Sage Publications, 1973, 1999) xxiii; Zygmunt Bauman, 'From Pilgrim to Tourist—or a Short History of Identity' in Stuart Hall and Paul du Gay (eds), *Cultural Identity* (London, Sage Publications, 1966) 18, 19.

primitiveness...in such outrageous contradiction to our national profile in the past.[60]

In March 1983, Rosenblum wrote:

It appears that only now is the genuine meaning of the 'turnabout' becoming clear....As when waking up, we can see how systematically Israel has changed over the last five-six years....Together with us, Israel has changed and is still changing increasingly faster.

Rosenblum describes his contemporaries as a

mute and confused generation that does not even understand what is happening to its homeland, which is being pulled out from under its feet.[61]

A month and a half later, Rosenblum wrote:

Half of the 'Israeli mentality' looks at itself...with increasing despair....Who is this people? How is it possible that it has entirely changed, all of it, in the course of six years?[62]

In 1983, Professor Eliezer Schweid of the Hebrew University, an Israel Prize recipient, said:

The 'second Eretz Israel' is going to become the 'first Eretz Israel' and nothing will stop that....A new elite is beginning to crystallize....If the current intellectual leadership will alienate itself from that, and to my great sorrow this seems to be the case, a hard struggle will take place. And there is no doubt in my mind which leadership will have the upper hand![63]

Dan Miron, a renowned scholar of Israeli literature and culture, described the changes in Israeli culture in 1985 as a shift of Israel's cultural leadership from Tel Aviv ('the first Hebrew city') to Jerusalem. Until the Likud came to power, Tel Aviv had represented the essence of Israel, the stronghold of Zionism's new Hebrew culture—Tel Aviv, 'a soft and indulgent city, almost a riviera,' a bourgeois and hedonistic metropolis whose people are engaged in 'the eternal struggle for property, status, success, advantage.' But Tel Aviv belongs to Zionism's past, wrote Miron; it has turned into a 'social historical preserve.' The future of Israel belongs to Jerusalem, the stronghold of nationalism and ultra-Orthodoxy, which are growing

---

[60] Doron Rosenblum, 'Ancient Voice' (December 15 1982) 3 Koteret Rashit. Amnon Runbistein wrote three months earlier:
  All the great assets of the *Yishuv*, that in the passing years have suffered corrosion and fracturing, have turned into scrap within a night and are being replaced by new notions.
Amnon Rubinstein, 'This was the Year' (September 17 1982) Haaretz.
[61] Doron Rosenblum, 'A High and Vicious Hand' (March 23 1983) 17 Koteret Rashit.
[62] Doron Rosenblum, 'A Tentative Portrait of Our People' (April 14 1983) 19 Koteret Rashit.
[63] Israel Segal, 'The Second Eretz Israel will Become the First Eretz Israel' (March 2 1983) 14 Koteret Rashit.

increasingly stronger and relegating the Hebrew culture represented by Tel Aviv to the margins. Jerusalem, 'a brutal and pretentious place,' had become 'a Middle-Eastern capital close to Amman and Damascus,' wrote Miron: 'Here, in Jerusalem, the fire of the civil war toward which we are gradually moving may break out,' concluded Miron. Here, in the city of the parliament and the government, the forces that will try to suppress or abolish Israeli democracy are gathering together; and here, in the city of the Supreme Court, the calls to suspend the rule of law in the country have already begun to resonate.[64]

(c) Status anxiety

Canadian sociologist Raymond Breton writes that state institutions everywhere are engaged in the dissemination of symbolic resources no less than in the allocation of material resources. Citizens everywhere wish to find in their state institutions people who resemble them and with whom they can identify, writes Breton: People with biographies similar to their own, whose cultural affiliation is close to theirs, who speak a language similar to their own, with the same diction, and so forth. Similarly, citizens everywhere wish to see their institutions promoting values approximate to those they live by, participating in rituals with which they can identify, and disseminating symbols for which they feel an affinity (anthem, flag, and so forth). In these senses, writes Breton, members of certain social groups can identify with the country's institutions more than those of other groups. When a country's institutions begin to behave in ways that make it harder for people belonging to certain groups to identify with them, but far easier for people belonging to other groups, the former are likely to experience 'status anxiety' or 'cultural anxiety' due to their sense of status devaluation.[65]

In the hegemony years, members of the hegemonic group could identify with Israel's state institutions, in the senses discussed by Breton, more than members of other groups (such as new immigrants from Arab countries who arrived after the establishment of Israel and were subjected to 'melting pot' processes, and obviously the Arabs and the ultra-Orthodox).

---

[64] Dan Miron, 'If There Is No Jerusalem' in *If There Is No Jerusalem* (Tel Aviv, Hakibbutz Hameuchad Publishing House, 1987) 227 (First published in Politics, 1985). For the same argument, see also: Dan Miron, 'Trying to Understand its Character' (May 1991) 38 Politics.

[65] Raymond Breton, 'The Production and Allocation of Symbolic Resources: An Analysis of the Linguistic and Ethnocultural Field in Canada' (1984) 21 Canadian Rev Soc & Anthrop 123; Raymond Breton, 'Multiculturalism and Canadian Nation-Building' in Alan Cairns and Cynthia Williams (eds), *The Politics Of Gender, Ethnicity And Language In Canada* (Toronto, University of Toronto Press,1986) 27.

Everywhere they went, members of the hegemony would have encountered people who looked and sounded just like them: in politics, on radio, on TV, in state ceremonials, etc. State ceremonials reflected their own personal experiences, first and foremost active participation in the 1948 War of Independence and Israel's subsequent wars. By contrast, those that did not belong to the hegemony time and time again felt alienated from what they encountered in these venues. Following the hegemony's decline, however, the LFH found themselves in the opposite situation—in politics, on radio and TV, at state ceremonials, they began to encounter people who did not speak and look like them, or resemble them in terms of their biographies and life experiences, etc. The ability of the LFH to identify with the state's institutions declined, and, in Breton's terms, they were stricken with status anxiety.

The social groups that came to control the political system and the public administration after 1977 also began to promote and disseminate a new historical memory concerning Israel's creation and the history of the state. This was a way to play down the contribution of the former hegemons to that history, highlighting instead the contribution of alternative social groups. The revised historical memory also presented in a negative light the actions of the former hegemons when they had ruled the country.[66]

(d) Anxiety about the strengthening of the religious group

The LFH succumbed to anxiety when faced with the growing power of the two elements comprising the Jewish religious group—religious-Zionism and ultra-Orthodox Judaism—in the political realm and in the state administration. In press reports, newspaper columns (particularly in the daily *Haaretz*, the newspaper most closely identified with the LFH),[67] and in the literature of the LFH group, ominous predictions repeatedly warned that Israel would soon be ruled by ayatollahs,[68]

---

[66] Levy, above n 22, at 63.

[67] 'Haaretz is the central arena in which the Israeli intelligentsia conducts its public discourse. It is the newspaper of the educated and affluent class in Israel.' Gadi Taub, 'The Israeliness is not Us' Eretz Acheret, May-June 2008, 31.

[68] 'El Al With God's Help?' (May 2 1982) Haaretz; Eliyahoo Salpeter, 'David's City in a Halakhic State' (September 17 1981) Haaretz; Joel Markus, 'Incremental Religious Coup' (April 2 1982) Haaretz.

khomeinism,[69] a theocracy,[70] zealotry,[71] superstition,[72] obscurantism,[73] ignorance,[74] irrationality,[75] or diehard reactionaries;[76] that Israel was about to return to the Middle Ages;[77] that Israel would soon resemble Iran or Saudi Arabia;[78] that the values of liberalism, humanism, enlightenment, modernity, the West, progress and freedom—all were in danger;[79] that Israel was about to turn from a country ruled by law into a halakhic state, from one under the rule of the Supreme Court to one under the rule of rabbis.[80] The moves of the religious group were

[69] Michael Handelsaltz, 'President between Humanism and Khomeinism' (February 6 1984) Haaretz; Joel Markus, 'Incremental Religious Coup' (April 2 1982) Haaretz; Amos Ben-Vered, 'Humanism v Khomeinism' (February 21 1983) Haaretz; Eliyahoo Salpeter, 'Religious Reign' (April 7 1986) Haaretz; Eliyahoo Salpeter, 'Back to the Middle Ages' (February 17 1987) Haaretz.

[70] 'Democratic, Not Theocratic State' (September 17 1981) Haaretz; 'Getting Rid of the Rabbis' Reign' (March 19 1982) Haaretz; 'El Al With God's Help?' (May 2 1982) Haaretz; 'Turning Israel into Saudi Arabia' (May 30 1984) Haaretz; Doron Rosenblum, 'Monologue of an Anxious Voice' (May 27 1977) Haaretz.

[71] 'The Digging in David's City Will Resume This Morning' (September 6 1981) Haaretz; 'Freedom of Science—A National Asset' (August 19 1981) Haaretz; 'Halakhic Ruling Against the Law' (August 21 1981) Haaretz; See also: 'A Test for the Rule of Law' (September 2 1981) Haaretz; Uzi Benziman, 'The Hamer Crisis' (September 2 1981) Haaretz; 'The Justices Expressed Astonishment Regarding the Minister of Education's Measure' (September 6 1981) Haaretz; 'Put a Dam to Block Reigning Rabbis' (September 6 1981) Haaretz; 'Democratic, Not Theocratic State' (September 17 1981) Haaretz; 'The Rule of Law, Not the Rule of Halakhah' (September 22 1981) Haaretz; Michael Handelsaltz, 'President between Humanism and Khomeinism' (February 6 1984) Haaretz; G. S., 'Overreaching Theology' (August 1 1985) Haaretz.

[72] 'Halakhic Ruling Against the Law' (August 21 1981) Haaretz. See also: 'A Test for the Rule of Law' (September 2 1981) Haaretz; Uzi Benziman, 'The Hamer Crisis' (September 2 1981) Haaretz; 'The Digging in David's City Will Resume This Morning' (September 6 1981) Haaretz; 'The Justices Expressed Astonishment Regarding the Minister of Education's Measure' (September 6 1981) Haaretz; 'Put a Dam to Block Reigning Rabbis' (September 6 1981) Haaretz; 'Democratic, Not Theocratic State' (September 17 1981) Haaretz; 'The Rule of Law, Not the Rule of Halakhah' (September 22 1981) Haaretz.

[73] 'Middle Ages Darkness 1981' (August 11 1981) Haaretz; 'Halakhic Ruling Against the Law' (August 21 1981) Haaretz. See also: 'A Test for the Rule of Law' (September 2 1981) Haaretz; Uzi Benziman, 'The Hamer Crisis' (September 2 1981) Haaretz; 'The Digging in David's City Will Resume This Morning' (September 6 1981) Haaretz; 'The Justices Expressed Astonishment Regarding the Minister of Education's Measure' (September 6 1981) Haaretz; 'Put a Dam to Block Reigning Rabbis' (September 6 1981) Haaretz; 'Democratic, Not Theocratic State' (September 17 1981) Haaretz; 'The Rule of Law, Not the Rule of Halakhah' (September 22 1981) Haaretz; 'Turning Israel into Saudi Arabia' (May 30 1984) Haaretz; G. S., 'Overreaching Theology' (August 1 1985) Haaretz; 'Ultra-Orthodox Terror Continues' (July 10 1985) Haaretz.

[74] 'Halakhic Ruling Against the Law' (August 21 1981) Haaretz.

[75] Eliyahoo Salpeter, 'David's City in a Halakhic State' (Sepember 17 1981) Haaretz.

[76] Id; Doron Rosenblum, 'Monologue of an Anxious Voice' (May 27 1977) Haaretz.

[77] 'Middle Ages Darkness 1981' (August 11 1981) Haaretz; Amos Elon, 'Challenging the Rule of Law' (September 27 1981) Haaretz; Eliyahoo Salpeter, 'David's City in a Halakhic State' (Sepember 17 1981) Haaretz; Joel Markus, 'Little Dictators' (March 19 1982) Haaretz; Eliyahoo Salpeter, 'Back to the Middle Ages' (February 17 1987) Haaretz.

[78] 'Turning Israel into Saudi Arabia' (May 30 1984) Haaretz.

[79] 'The Messiah Play in Haifa' (February 3 1984) Haaretz.

[80] 'The Rule of Law, Not the Rule of Halakhah' (September 22 1981) Haaretz; Amos Elon, 'Challenging the Rule of Law' (September 27 1981) Haaretz; 'Ultra-Orthodox Rabbis Against the High Court of Justice' (September 7 1982) Haaretz.

described using such terms as 'assault,'[81] 'takeover'[82] and 'coercion.'[83] The logic of the 'slippery slope' was recurrently applied: every achievement of the religious Jewish group was presented as a basis for its further achievements in the future.[84]

With the establishment of Menachem Begin's first government in 1977, a religious politician, Zebulon Hammer, the leader of the National Religious Party, was put in charge of the Ministry of Education. Thus, not only did the labor movement lose control over this highly sensitive ministry for the first time in twenty nine years of statehood, but it lost it to a religious politician. In 1981, Professor Zeev Sternhell of the Hebrew University in Jerusalem wrote:

secular education is gradually turning into a religious domain... Tenaciously and persistently skull-capped people are taking it over.[85]

A 1984 *Haaretz* editorial noted that:

bit by bit secular curriculum is turning religious... The Ministry of Education is amidst a bold plan to influence secular education from early age.[86]

A few weeks later leftist politician Shulamit Aloni claimed that the Ministry of Education was conducting a campaign against the humanistic values of secular education.[87]

With the establishment of Menachem Begin's second government in 1981, M.K. Abraham Shapira, the leader of the ultra-Orthodox party *Agudat Israel*, was elected chairman of the Knesset's highly influential Finance Committee. Shapira became one of the most powerful figures in the Israeli administration—the personification of the change in the relative power of the secular and religious groups in Israeli politics, as well

---

[81] 'Don't Talk; Enforce the Law' (June 17 1986) Haaretz; 'Poles, The Ultra-Orthodox Endanger the State' (June 20 1986) Haaretz.

[82] 'Put a Dam to Block Reigning Rabbis' (September 6 1981) Haaretz; Eliyahoo Salpeter, 'David's City in a Halakhic State' (September 17 1981) Haaretz; 'Getting Rid of the Rabbis' Reign' (March 19 1982) Haaretz; G. S., 'Overreaching Theology' (August 1 1985) Haaretz; Eliyahoo Salpeter, 'Religious Reign' (April 7 1986) Haaretz.

[83] 'Getting Rid of the Rabbis' Reign' (March 19 1982) Haaretz; 'El Al With God's Help?' (May 2 1982) Haaretz; 'The Campaign Against Religious Coercion' (March 18 1984) Haaretz; G. S., 'Overreaching Theology' (August 1 1985) Haaretz; Akiva Eldar, 'The Seculars' Red Line' (March 25 1981) Haaretz.

[84] 'Soccer in Shabbat in Ramat Gan—A Test of the Powers of Freedom' (September 13 1985) Haaretz; Gideon Samet, 'In Favor of Confrontation' (March 15 1984) Haaretz; 'Against Halakhic State' (May 7 1982) Haaretz.

[85] Zeev Sternhell, 'To Put an End to Religious Reign' (January 25 1981) Haaretz.

[86] 'Secular Education Turning Religious' (April 26 1984) Haaretz.

[87] Nili Mendler, 'Aloni Wants the Ministry of Education' (August 9 1984) Haaretz.

as of the ultra-Orthodox group's new and profound involvement in Israeli politics. In July 1983, columnist Israel Segal wrote that:

two years after the establishment of the current coalition Shapira has made himself the central figure in it.[88]

Two months later columnist Nahum Barnea called Shapira 'the regent of the state'.[89]

In 1984, Benjamin Tammuz, a renowned Israeli writer, published *Jeremiah's Inn*.[90] The plot of this futuristic story takes place in the closing decades of the twenty-first century. Zionist Israel has by then long become an ultra-Orthodox country, with a population comprised of several religious groups living in three separate strongholds—one in Jerusalem, the other in the center of the country, and the third in the north. Most of Israel's secular citizens have long fled, and those remaining, constituting a small part of the population, are persecuted by the secret services of these strongholds. To save their lives, secular Israelis conceal their identity and present themselves as living in strict compliance with halakhic commands, 'passing as' religious, though they occasionally perpetrate terror attacks against ultra-Orthodox institutions. The author narrates the history of Israel in the hundred years since 1980: the ultra-Orthodox, who wielded the power to tilt the scales in the prevailing political draw, forged an alliance with the nationalist groups and, in a gradual and incremental process, transformed Israel from a Zionist into an ultra-Orthodox state.

Writing about Tammuz, literary scholar Menuha Gilboa says:

Jeremiah's Inn is the story of an apocalypse that will come upon the State of Israel and destroy it because of its messianic-religious fanaticism. When one reads this novella, one senses that Israel has already been entirely annihilated.... This is a political nightmare.[91]

Reviewing the book, critic Benny Tsipper writes:

In *Jeremiah's Inn*, Tammuz was beguiled by the possibility of improvising... on the threat commonly brandished over the conscience of Israelis—the threat of Israel's de-humanization. Improvising on the theme of de-humanization, Tammuz succeeds beyond expectations, *inter alia*, because of a readership ripe to voraciously swallow any apocalyptic and sinister message, whatever it might be.[92]

---

[88] Israel Segal, 'The Coalitions' Master of the Seal' (July 6 1983) Koteret Rashit.
[89] Nahum Barnea, 'Aridor on the Right Way: Out' (October 12 1983) Koteret Rashit.
[90] Benjamin Tammuz, *Jeremiah's Inn* (Jerusalem, Keter Publishing House, 1984) (Hebrew).
[91] Menucha Gilboa, *The Golden Dreams And Their Shattering* (Tel Aviv, Hakibbutz Hameuchad Publishing House, 1995) (Hebrew).
[92] Benny Tsipper, 'Between Farce and Apocalypse' (September 21 1984) Haaretz.

A series of incidents conveyed the anxiety of the LFH over the growing power of the Jewish religious group. Four Knesset members representing the Shas party were elected for the first time in the 1984 elections (the third campaign since 1977), but on the night of the elections, Israeli TV failed to place any reporters at the Shas election headquarters. That decision, writes Arye Dayan,

> expresses the detachment of most Ashkenazi secularists, even those who follow political developments closely, from the moods prevailing in the ultra-Orthodox public and among the Sephardic group (Mizrahim).

Dayan goes on to quote journalist Amnon Abramowitz:

> The day after the elections I made a few phone calls to sources in the religious public to ask what this Shas is. I hadn't the faintest.... I had never ever seen a Shas candidate or a Shas voter.... It turns out you can be born in this country, go through all its settings, be a journalist, and still have no idea what is going on under your nose.

Shas, then, entered the consciousness of the secular-liberal group in Israel as something alien, unknown, and threatening.

Dayan also writes that when it became known that Shas was about to receive the interior portfolio in the new coalition, the newspapers filled with reports about the far-fetched plans that Shas was weaving to limit secular freedom, including the allocation of separate beaches for men and women and the prohibition of nudism. Many secularists felt panicky at the prospect of Shas entering the ministry of the interior. 'Shas is a new phenomenon in the Knesset. New and not fresh,' wrote, for instance, the leftist Mapam newspaper *Al Ha-Mishmar*, in an article bearing the title 'Dark Medieval Fanaticism.'

Several months later, in November 1984, the IDF headquarters in the Lebanese city of Tyre were targeted in two devastating attacks. Many dozens of soldiers and members of the security forces were killed. The Shas representative in the Knesset's Foreign Affairs and Defense Committee, Shimon Ben-Shlomo, remarked that the cause of the disaster was not the IDF's presence in Lebanon, but the promiscuity of its female soldiers. 'The storm erupted with the publication of these remarks,' writes Dayan. 'Politicians, journalists, women's organizations, and retired army officers reacted sharply, and again described Shas as a dark and fundamentalist movement, strange and alien to Israeli society.'

In June 1985, a train collided with a bus whose driver had attempted to cross a railway junction. The bus was carrying pupils from a Petah Tikvah school. Twenty-one were killed, including nineteen pupils. The magnitude of the tragedy and young age of most of the victims cast a pall over the country. Shas' political leader, Rabbi Yitzhak Peretz, claimed that the pupils had been killed due to the mass desecration of the Sabbath in the country in general, and in the city of Petah Tikvah in particular. The comment related to a controversy then raging in Israel: the decisions of the Petah Tikvah and Tel Aviv municipalities to open cinemas on the eve of the Sabbath. Peretz's exploiting the children's death to justify a political stance evoked a stormy reaction and enraged the secular public.[93]

In 1989, the monthly *Politics*, identified with the secular, liberal, leftwing Meretz party, declared on its front page: 'Religious war? The background, facts, analysis, risks and meanings of the rise of the religious camp.' The editor, Gideon Samet, wrote:

> The political strengthening of the ultra-Orthodox camp is not a temporary matter. To some extent we have been taken by surprise in the face of something that has deep roots.... Secular Israelis need to see themselves involved in an important struggle that is far from reaching its end.... The increasing ultra-Orthodox political power determined who formed the new government.... Here is the most important fact: groups with very different cultures and customs are currently in the midst of a tough confrontation over the future aspect of the State, as well as over the shaping of its current daily life.[94]

(e) Anxiety about the rise of Sephardim

Amos Oz's book *In the Land of Israel*, published in 1983, has been mentioned above. The book was extensively discussed in the press, particularly the chapter 'The Insult and the Fury,' a dialogue between the author and a group of residents meeting at a café in the development town of Bet Shemesh, which sharply and incisively conveys the deep-seated feelings of affront and rage against the Ashkenazi, hegemonic group harbored by immigrants who had come to Israel from Arab countries in the 1950s. The chapter traced the onset of the processes that had shifted power from the hegemonic group to one of the groups that had begun to take its place in Israel's politics and public administration—residents of development towns, largely consisting of such immigrants. It also reflected the collapse of the idealized Israeli image of the former hegemonic culture, and the shift from the relative uniformity that had prevailed in the hegemonic era to rift and separation between key groups in the population after the collapse of the hegemony and the transition to a post-hegemonic situation. Among other things, the Bet Shemesh residents told Oz:

> 'Power to [Menachem] Begin'? Sure, people still shout 'Power to Begin.' But to this day the real power is not in Begin's hands. You've got the *Histadrut* and you've

---

[93] Arye Dayan, *The Story Of Shas* (Jerusalem, Keter Publishing House, 1999) 135, 145, 146, 158–9, 162–3 (Hebrew).

[94] Gideon Samet, 'Beyond Calculating' (January 1989) 24 Politics.

got the newspapers and the big money, and you've also got the radio and the TV. You're still running the country.

...

When you were on top, you hid us away in holes, in *moshavim* [agricultural settlements] and in development towns, so the tourists wouldn't see us; so we wouldn't stain your image; so they'd think this was a white country. But that's all over now, because now we've come out of our holes. You still haven't figured out what hit you, have you? It's your arrogance that's hit you. As if you'd inherited this country from your father. What, the State of Israel comes from the papa of the Alignment? Not from the Bible? Not from our sweat? Not from our backbreaking work? Not from our blood?

...

You guys, your time is past. Even after Begin you won't make a comeback. You won't make a comeback in another hundred years.[95]

In a similar spirit, journalist Amnon Dankner describes the events at a political rally of Labor (Alignment) leader Shimon Peres in the development town of Kiryat Shmona in November 1982:

He stood like that for a long while and was silent, listening to the jeers, to the calls of 'Begin, Begin!' thundering from the first rows in front of him...

There was no violence in Kiryat Shmona's main square on Saturday night. There was a lot of shouting, many raised fists, many obscene gestures known in Hebrew as 'Mizrahi gestures'.

...

Shimon Peres, the Alignment—are hated in Kiryat Shmona. They stumble upon an impossible crossroads of feelings: the old hatred of the underdogs who claim discrimination and oppression by the kibbutzim of the area, which they see as estranged and arrogant, is one component. The ethnic hatred against all that the satiated Ashkenazi represents is the other.[96]

Indeed, the polarization between Ashkenazi and Sephardic Jews, which overlaps the polarization between the country's veteran residents—the LFH—and those in the development towns, was a key issue in the 1981 elections,[97] and was widely discussed in the press throughout the first half of the 1980s.[98]

---

[95] Oz, above n 38, at 36–7, 40–1, 41.
[96] Amnon Dankner, 'With Shimon Peres in Kiryat Shmona' (November 1 1982) Haaretz.
[97] Uzi Benziman, 'The Elections and Ethnic Drives' (May 28 1981) Haaretz; Yizhar Smilansky, 'The Defendants: The Ashkenazim' (June 14 1981) Haaretz; Amos Elon, 'Toward a New Society' (October 9 1981) Haaretz.
[98] Akiva Eldar, 'The Second Myth' (November 3 1981) Haaretz; Amnon Dankner, 'I Don't Have a Sister' (February 18 1982) Haaretz; Amnon Rubinstein, 'Political Violence and the Ethnic Question' (March 1 1983) Haaretz; Amnon Rubinstein, 'I Have Brothers' (March 2 1983) Haaretz; Arye Dayan, 'The Ashkenazim: A Disappearing World' (February 2 1983) 10 Koteret Rashit.

(f) Anxiety about the growth of nationalism and the future of democracy

The LFH were anxious about the rise of both secular and religious nationalist groups. They feared that Israel would become a state that, invoking collectivist interests, would breach democracy and violate its citizens' fundamental rights. They conveyed the impression that the political turnabout of 1977 had not been a routine political change, with one party replacing another in the country's leadership, but rather would lead to an essential change in Israel's political culture and hence to a cultural change, when an entire culture would move aside to make room for another entire culture.

Ten days after the 1977 elections, Doron Rosenblum published in *Haaretz* a fictitious monologue by an 'anxious voter,' describing his feelings after the proclamation of the 'turnabout':

> I have never been so shaken by a political event, including the wars. Why deny it? At that moment, I was overwhelmed by a terrible fear.... [Menachem] Begin at the helm! The first, instinctive, impulse was: Escape! The second impulse—Rebel! Until then, it had been irrevocably clear to me that the rise of the extreme right to the government means the beginning of the end for the State of Israel. At least—the State of Israel as known to us so far. I never slept a wink that night, or the next. I gave in to sorrow and loss.... Apocalyptic visions flashed before my eyes: crazy military and religious rituals....A twentieth-century theocratic state....I saw my personal freedom vanish....I saw all kinds of visions related to the frenzy of right-wing-religious reactionaries. I saw dark censors, black figures who knock on the door at night and drag citizens from their homes. I saw wild demonstrations and lynching of Arabs....Religious wars....I saw a minister of education with a skullcap....Above all, I waited for the siren. Only later did I understand that the war would not break out immediately but after a few hours, or a few days. In brief—to detail all the nightmarish visions in which I was submerged in the fever of shock is quite pointless.[99]

Several months after the 1977 turnabout, an issue of the leading literary journal, *Siman Kriy'ah*[100] featured several poems by Bertolt Brecht in its opening pages. The following lines represent the spirit of the poems:

In the dark ages,
   Will there be poetry?
   There will be.
   On the dark ages.

And also:

They want war.

---

[99] Doron Rosenblum, 'Monologue of an Anxious Voice' (May 27 1977) Haaretz.
[100] 7 Siman Kriy'ah (May 1977) (Hebrew).

> He who wrote it
> Has already fallen.

A short piece by Amos Oz also appeared in that issue, entitled 'From Now On':

> Evil days are now coming upon us. The petit-bourgeoisie...will from now on also be the official code of behavior...increasingly accompanied by the tam-tam drums of a blurry, ritual tribalism, blood and soil and instincts and heady slogans, Betar and Massada, 'the whole world is against us,' 'Israel trust in God,' with different versions of purity and impurity wars, zealotry with dark fears, the oppression of reason in the name of inflammatory visions....Hovering above all will be a cloud of self-pity, of self-righteousness, the pitiful wretchedness of exile dressed up as pride, with head held high and a strong, tough, and erect standing...
>
> If the Likud government begins to silence 'defeatists,' if they 'cleanse' the radio and the television and the newspapers of the 'inciters' and 'destroyers' of Israel—we will have to react *in the streets*. With our lives. (emphasis in the original)

Years later, Professor Ariel Rubinstein, of the Department of Economics at Tel Aviv University, said:

> We were sure that Begin's rise to power symbolizes the beginning of fascism in Israel and we were anxious and felt it was the end of the world.[101]

In February 1983, a Peace Now rally was held in Jerusalem to protest against the First Lebanon War and the then-Minister of Defense Ariel Sharon. A hand grenade was thrown at the demonstrators, and one of them, Emil Grintzweig, was killed. The next day, Professor Shlomo Ben-Ami, then chairman of the History Department at Tel Aviv University, analyzed the event in terms borrowed from the experience of Germany, Italy and Spain in the 1930s:

> The most relevant analogy for what is currently taking place in Israel is 1930s Europe. This is so mainly for the reason that in Germany or Italy of the 1930s, and also in Spain in certain periods, nationalization of patriotism took place: someone managed to monopolize patriotism and determine that his worldview is the one and exclusive worldview. According to this approach, it is absolutely impossible for your political rival to be just. Once such an approach becomes dominant, everything becomes permissible. Politics ceases to be the realm of the debatable; it becomes the province of apocalypse.... He who comes with a rational worldview that opposes the apocalyptic truth cannot be just and his blood is permissible.[102]

In 1984, Amos Kenan, a prominent journalist and writer, published a novel named *The Road to Ein Harod*. Its plot unfolds at the height of a military

---

[101] Dalya Karpel, 'A Beautiful Mind 2' (March 1 2002) Haaretz.
[102] Arye Dayan, 'Professor Ben Ami: Begin Made Bloodshed Permissible' (February 16 1983) 12 Koteret Rashit.

coup led by nationalist generals who have become tired of pointless political struggles. In the course of the rebellion, leftist supporters are persecuted and, when caught, summarily executed. Kibbutz Ein Harod is the leftists' last stronghold. The entire Arab population of Israel has been expelled to neighboring countries, and the conspirators are pushing Israel and the entire Middle East to the verge of destruction in a nuclear war.[103]

Amnon Dankner's review of *The Road to Ein Harod* resembles Gilboa's review of Tammuz's *Jeremiah's Inn*:[104]

Kenan chose the genre of a futuristic horror story to talk about our day-to-day horror... *The Road to Ein Harod* is a kind of apocalypse—the path that Amos Kenan goes through every day within the chilling, terrifying reality of our lives.[105]

In press reports, opinion columns and the literature of the LFH, the analogy between Israel in the 1980s and Germany, Italy, and Spain in the 1930s was indeed repeatedly invoked.[106] Warnings abounded about the imminent collapse of Israeli democracy,[107] Israel's transformation from a democratic into a 'totalitarian' or 'authoritarian' or 'fascist state'[108] and the public's yearning for a 'strong leader.'[109]

(g) The link between internal and external anxiety

As mentioned above, one component of the LFH's existential anxiety was the 'traditional,' external Israeli anxiety, which has accompanied the lives of Jews in Eretz Israel since the dawn of Zionism, over the long-term viability of the Zionist enterprise in the conditions prevailing in the Middle East. Among the former hegemons this anxiety intensified in the wake of the new, internal anxiety over the political, social, and cultural changes affecting Israel, which they perceived as weakening Israel's ability to

---

[103] Amos Kenan, *The Road To Ein Harod* (Tel Aviv, Am Oved Publishers, 1984) (Hebrew).
[104] Above n 91.
[105] Amnon Dankner, 'Everyday Apocalypse' (March 2 1984) Haaretz. Benny Tsifer writes that Jeremiah's Inn and The Road to Ein Harod are 'two futuristic books... that foresee a bleak future for Israel.' Benny Tsifer, 'A Week of Books' (August 3 1984) Haaretz.
[106] Arye Dayan, 'Professor Ben Ami: Begin Made Bloodshed Permissible' (February 16 1983) 12 Koteret Rashit; Amos Elon, 'Toward a New Society' (October 9 1981) Haaretz.
[107] Zeev Sterenhell, 'To Put an End to Domination' (January 25 1981) Haaretz; Amos Elon, Toward a New Society' (October 9 1981) Haaretz; Akiva Eldar, 'Black TV' (February 20 1981) Haaretz. See also: 'Freedom of Speech—Not at the Prime Minister's Mercy' (January 13 1982) Haaretz; 'Broken Fences' (September 15 1982) Haaretz.
[108] Doron Rosenblum, 'Monologue of an Anxious Voice' (May 27 1977) Haaretz; 'The Alignment Blames Likud for Fascism' (June 16 1981) Haaretz; 'Stop Political Violence' (June 16 1981) Haaretz; Zeev Yefet, 'Hoodlums Ltd.' (June 19 1981) Haaretz; Amnon Dankner, 'I Didn't Want to Write an Article; All I Wished Was to Get Home Safely' (June 19 1981) Haaretz; Eliyahoo Salpeter, 'The Democratic Road to Totalitarianism' (January 15 1982) Haaretz.
[109] Nahum Barnea, 'The Government that will Follow the Next Government' in *They Shoot And They Cry* (Tel Aviv, Zmora, Bitan, Modan Publishers, 1983) 203 (Hebrew) (originally published in October 12 1979). See also: Eisenstadt, above n 15, at 54.

stand up to its enemies. In other words, as if the internal anxiety were not enough by itself, it also fueled the external anxiety. Not only did the LFH find themselves in cultural and political decline, but they also perceived that decline and the rise of new cultural, social, and political groups as magnifying the external threat—the possible collapse of the State of Israel and the physical extermination of its inhabitants in a war between Israel and its neighbors.

D. THE JURISPRUDENCE OF THE SUPREME COURT IN THE 1980S AND 1990S IN LIGHT OF THE TRANSITION TO A POST-HEGEMONIC SITUATION

(a) The Supreme Court and the struggle over Israel's normative identity

In order to explain the developments in the jurisprudence of the Supreme Court during the 1980s and 1990s, it is necessary to place them in the context of the political, social, and cultural changes that overtook Israel in the 1980s and 1990s, after the decline of the labor hegemony and the shift to a post-hegemonic situation in which the struggle over the shaping of Israeli culture was rekindled.

During the 1980s, the LFH repeatedly failed to realize their aim of returning to power, that is, winning a majority in the Knesset and control of the main power positions in the government and in the state's public administration. Indeed, groups that the LFH perceived as a danger to their cultural values (the religious Jewish group above all, but also nationalist groups they viewed as a threat to the political system's liberal characteristics) broadened their hold in the Knesset, in the government, and in the public administration, using these institutions to disseminate the cultural values they considered important.

The LFH reacted to their failure in 'election politics' by displacing some of their political struggle to the Supreme Court. They did so by submitting petitions meant to disrupt the workings of the elected government and its subordinate public administration. In their attempt to turn the Supreme Court into an arena of political struggle, they were relying on the Court's tradition as the state institution most closely identified with secular, liberal values since Israel's foundation. In particular, since liberalism is 'the project of specifying universal limits to the authority of government,'[110] the

---

[110] John Grey, 'From Post-Liberalism to Pluralism' in *Enlightenment's Wake* (London and New York, Routledge, 1995) 196.

FLH could count on the Court to attempt to curb government and Knesset actions identified with the values of religious and nationalist groups that were inimical to the liberal values of the LFH.

The Supreme Court could have reacted to these petitions by continuing to adhere to the jurisprudence it had developed since the establishment of Israel. In other words, it could have clung to its self-image as an apolitical, professional institution. It could have gone on endorsing a non-activist approach, allowing other institutions to serve as the main venues for normative and distributive struggles, without its intervention. And it could have retained its mainly formalistic legal reasoning, thereby downplaying the clearly liberal contents of its opinions.

The Court chose the opposite course. In a spellbinding process of cultural change—in fact a 'political' process—some of the Court's judges, led by Aharon Barak, succeeded in changing its approach towards the 'division of labor' between itself and the other branches of government. Also, elements in the Court's customary mode of reasoning that formerly had been considered marginal took center stage in its professional culture, and the Court changed its perception of the role it is meant to play among the state's institutions.

The Court, then, joined the Jewish-secular-liberal group, which I have called the LFH, and cooperated with them closely and consistently to defend the values of Western liberalism they shared in common by making the Court a significant venue for promoting that group's values and positions. Needless to say, this is not in any way a 'conspiracy.' Rather, it is a classic case of 'culture-bound action': an unplanned and unintentional development set off by the behavior, not necessarily sufficiently conscious, of people who have similar reactions to changes that affect them because they share the same culture (habitus, to borrow a term from Pierre Bourdieu's sociology of culture).[111]

(b) *Judicial activism*

(i) Standing and justiciability

By introducing essential changes in the doctrine of standing, during the 1980s the Supreme Court significantly expanded the types of situations that allow for petitions. It also considerably multiplied the types of cases considered justiciable, granting itself extensive power to discuss petitions

---

[111] Pierre Bourdieu, *Outline Of A Theory Of Practice* (Richard Nice trans, Cambridge, Cambridge University Press, 1977) 72–95; Pierre Bourdieu, *The Logic Of Practice* (Richard Nice trans, Stanford, California, Stanford University Press, 1990) 52–79.

that require it to exercise judicial review of the actions of the government, the public administration, and the Knesset.

By redefining the doctrines on standing and justiciability, the Court not only assumed power vis-à-vis the other branches of government, but also granted power to the potential petitioners against these branches, which, in the present context, means the LFH. Pierre Bourdieu's writings on the transformation of a day-to-day conflict into a legal conflict are illuminating in this context.[112]

Bourdieu analyzes the changes in the relationship between parties to a dispute at the moment one of them initiates judicial proceedings. At that point, the dispute turns from a direct into an indirect conflict; it is 'translated' and rewritten into the law's language of rights; the parties submit themselves to the decision-making logic of the law: each of the parties is given equal opportunity to raise legal arguments before an impartial arbiter who is supposed to decide in favor of the party adducing the best legal arguments. Bourdieu's analysis implies that entering the legal field, ie, transforming a non-judicial into a judicial dispute, largely 'neutralizes' the discrepancies in the resources (in Bourdieu's terminology: 'Capital') available to the parties outside the legal field, where large inequalities might prevail concerning the kinds and quantities of resources at their disposal. As legal proceedings begin, the parties shift to a situation of relatively high equality (at least regarding the procedure of resolving the conflict, though not regarding their status according to the contents of the law that dictate how the conflict between them is supposed to be resolved). When legal proceedings begin, then, the party that owns large amounts of resources outside the legal field loses some of its power vis-à-vis the other party, whereas the party with limited resources acquires greater power vis-à-vis the other.

In any country, government institutions and the public administration obviously have relatively more power than anyone in dispute with them in their relationships. Bourdieu's analysis shows that they lose some of that power when the dispute is shifted to the judiciary. The broadening of the Supreme Court's jurisdiction in the 1980s through the expansion of the doctrines of standing and justiciability resulted in a transfer of power from government institutions and the public administration to social groups that sought to oppose the policies and decisions of the government and the administration by submitting petitions to the Court—above all, the LFH.

---

[112] Pierre Bourdieu, 'The Force of Law: Toward a Sociology of the Juridical Field' (1987) 38 Hastings L J 805.

Bourdieu's analysis also suggests that, once judicial proceedings begin, a conflict between parties undergoes 'juridicization,' ie, it is rewritten in the rights language of the law. The content of the law that has been created and implemented in Israeli courts since the country's foundation is fundamentally liberal. Therefore, expanding the jurisdiction of the Supreme Court in the 1980s and 1990s by expanding the doctrines of standing and justiciability enabled the LFH to subordinate the policies and decisions of government institutions and of the public administration to the liberal value-system they upheld, a system largely embodied in the law implemented by the Court.

(ii) Reasonableness and proportionality

The development of the reasonableness test in the course of the 1980s as the main tool used in the review of decisions made by government institutions and by the public administration carried similar implications. Whereas the Court's review of the government and the administration had formerly focused on whether their decisions had been within the purview of their legal authority, the Court now dealt with the *content* of those decisions. When applying the test of 'legal reasonableness', the Court subjected the decisions of the government and the administration to the liberal values embodied in the law that it applies, which are also central values in the culture of the LFH group. When applying the test of 'professional reasonableness', however, the Court examined the actual professional considerations underlying the decisions of the government and the state's public administration. By doing so, the Court subjected these decisions to the criteria of its own common sense. Supreme Court judges, however, are individuals who largely belong to the LFH group—they have internalized its culture. Consequently, applying the professional reasonableness test ultimately subjected the government's and the administration's decisions to the standards of that group's culture.[113]

The implications of the proportionality test are similar to those of the reasonableness test: the evaluation of decisions of the government and the state's public administration by the criteria of the liberal values and the commonsense understandings of the Court and the LFH.

---

[113] Legal sociologist Ronen Shamir writes that the Court's reasonableness doctrine embodies the values of a social group that distrusts, and even detests, the compromise-based, slow and clumsy machineries of parliamentary politics, and that glorifies instead professional expertise and managerial skills—some of the core values of the LFH. Ronen Shamir, 'The Politics of Reasonableness: Reasonableness and Judicial Power in Israel's Supreme Court' (1994) 5 Theory And Criticism 7 (Hebrew).

(iii) Annulling Knesset laws

By holding it has the authority to annul Knesset laws (according to the Basic Law: Human Dignity and Liberty, the Basic Law: Freedom of Occupation, and perhaps according to all the other Basic Laws enacted by the Knesset), the Court subjected the content of Knesset legislation to the test of the values that permeate the law created and applied by the courts. Since those contents are mainly liberal, that move clearly gave the LFH group the means to intervene in the contents of Knesset legislation, a power denied to it within the Knesset in the context of the new balance of power that took shape in Israel's politics after the late 1970s.

(c) The rise of the normative style of argumentation

The formalistic style of reasoning endorsed by the Supreme Court since the 1950s had served its needs in light of the Court's problematic status as a 'cultural alien,' operating as an agent of liberal values in a hegemonic collectivistic culture of nation-building. Formalism enabled the Court to downplay the normative dimension of its opinions and present judicial decision-making as mechanistic, leading to decisions that necessarily follow from the very essence of the process, rather than being the outcome of the Court's choice, as it were, of specific normative contents.

In the 1980s, the *Kulturkampf* that has accompanied the Jewish people in the last two-hundred and fifty years erupted in full force—a 'war' that had lain dormant during the first half of the twentieth century. By adopting a value-laden style of reasoning from the 1980s onward, the Supreme Court fully disclosed its normative identity as a state institution acting in close association with the LFH group—one of the two competing groups in the struggle over the shaping of Israeli culture. Furthermore, by issuing opinions that broadly and openly expose its liberal values, the Court gave this group a set of contemporary texts providing it with the intellectual underpinnings around which it could consolidate. A liberal philosophy formulated in Israel is hard to come by, and Supreme Court opinions are indeed *the* texts to which recourse is made to support Israeli liberalism.

(d) The change in the perception of the Supreme Court's role

With the rise of judicial activism and normative reasoning in the Supreme Court's opinions, both the Court itself and the country's citizens and institutions changed their perception of the Court's role: from a professional institution, whose main task is to resolve disputes, to an institution playing a political role beside the Knesset.

This change was also helpful to the struggle of the LFH group. It now became self-evident, part of the nature of things, that political decisions in Israel (decisions on normative and distributive questions) are made not only in the country's parliament, the Knesset, but also in the Supreme Court—an institution that operates in the context of liberal values, and is staffed by people largely belonging to the LFH group.[114]

(e) Petitions of Knesset members

(i) **The trend**

What the above analysis indicates is that the far-reaching changes in the jurisprudence of the Supreme Court during the 1980s gave the LFH group the power to subject the decisions of the government and the public administration, as well as decisions of the Knesset, to its values. Indeed, since the end of the 1970s, Knesset members that might be considered the group's political representatives have submitted many dozens of petitions to the Supreme Court against government institutions, the public administration and the Knesset. Finding themselves in the minority in the Knesset, cut off from state budgets and losing power in the state's public administration, they turned the Supreme Court into an important arena for their political struggles.[115] Former Knesset member Yossi Sarid, one of the most prominent LFH spokespersons and the MK who submitted more petitions to the High Court of Justice than any other, candidly described this process

---

[114] An explanation resembling the one suggested here concerning the developments in the Supreme Court's jurisprudence during the 1980s is suggested by Ran Hirschl regarding the circumstances surrounding the 1992 enactment of the Basic Law: Human Dignity and Liberty and the Basic Law: Freedom of Occupation. Hirschl argues that elites that sense a threat to their control of the legislature due to the rise of peripheral groups, but feel a cultural affinity with the judiciary, are inclined to initiate the enactment of a bill of rights and grant the courts powers of judicial review over legislation and over the administration. Elites whose power in the legislature is threatened, then, will seek to initiate a (partial) displacement of politics from the legislature to the courts. According to Hirschl, this explanation applies to constitutional developments that have taken place in Canada, New Zealand, South Africa, and Israel. Concerning Israel, Hirschl points out that, from the early 1980s until the end of the 1990s, the parties representing the elites lost a third of their power in the Knesset, whereas parties representing peripheral groups in Israeli society—Sephardim (Mizrahim), residents of deprived neighborhoods and development towns, new immigrants from the former Soviet Union—more than doubled their power. In response to these processes, argues Hirschl, the Israeli elite—the bourgeois, Ashkenazi, affluent group, supported by the industrialists and the big economic corporations to which I have referred as the LFH—initiated the enactment of Basic Laws in 1992. Ran Hirschl, *Toward Juristocracy—The Origins And Consequences Of The New Constitutionalism* (Cambridge and London, Harvard University Press, 2004). For a similar explanations of processes in Turkey of the early 1960s see: Ceren Belge, 'Friends of the Court: The Republican Alliance and Selective Activism of the Constitutional Court of Turkey' (2006) 40 Law & Soc Rev 653.

[115] For a discussion of this process, see Yoav Dotan and Menachem Hofnung, 'Legal Defeats-Political Wins: Why Elected Representatives Go to Courts?' 38 (2005) Comp Pol Stud 75. The authors point to the anomaly involved in Knesset members displacing their political action from the Knesset to the Supreme Court. In their view, an important reason for Knesset members submitting petitions is their desire for media exposure, as part of the transition of Israeli politics from the 'party' to the 'personal' model.

in an article significantly entitled 'We Took Everything to the High Court of Justice.'[116]

(ii) Data

I examined all the petitions submitted by Knesset members in the period 1977–2005. (In many cases, more than one Knesset member submitted the exact same petition. Note, then, that the following numbers refer not to the number of petitions submitted by Knesset members, but to the number of petitioners from among Knesset members). The survey turned up the following figures:

The total number of petitions submitted by Knesset members: 260.

The parties whose Knesset representatives submitted the largest number of petitions are the following:

Meretz:[117] 78 petitions of Knesset members = 30 percent
Labor: 38 petitions of Knesset members = 14.61 percent
Likud: 34 petitions of Knesset members = 13.07 percent
Shinui: 14 petitions of Knesset members = 5.38 percent

Meretz, Shinui and Labor can clearly be viewed as the political representatives of the LFH. Adding up the number of Knesset members from these three parties who submitted petitions, we reach the sum of 130 petitions of Knesset members = 50 percent. These numbers indicate that the Knesset members identified more than all others with the LFH group are the ones who submitted the largest number of petitions to the Supreme Court between 1977 and 2005.[118]

Furthermore, and no less important, an analysis of the data reveals that petitions submitted by Knesset members from Meretz, Shinui and Labor were directed, almost without exception, against decisions and policies adopted by the government, the state administration and the Knesset. The decisions, then, did not affect the petitioners personally. By contrast, petitions submitted by Knesset members from other parties, such as Shas, were by and large directed against decisions that influenced the petitioning Knesset members personally. In other words, the petitions submitted by Knesset members not representing the LFH group were not meant to disrupt government decisions and policies, but to protect the Knesset

---

[116] Yossi Sarid, 'We took everything to the High Court of Justice' (August 25 2004) Haaretz.

[117] Meretz was established in 1989 by three parties: Mapam, the Civil Rights Movement (Ratz) and Shinui. Together with the Labor party and Shinui, Meretz is the party most identified with the LFH.

[118] Detailed data is at the author's disposal. In the same vein, Ran Hirschl points out that a group of 32 Knesset members stood behind the legislation of the two basic laws of 1992. 18 of these members were from the Labor party, 8 from Likud and 6 from Meretz. Hirschl, above n 114, at 54–5.

members themselves from Knesset-inflicted or from government-inflicted wrongs.

(f) The Link between the Court and the liberal former hegemons: the Court's stance on social and economic issues

Following the hegemony's decline, many of the institutions of civil society that had been controlled by the LFH lost much of their power. The balance of power in civil society is, however, a complex issue. Whatever power the LFH lost in some institutions of civil society was counterbalanced by their great accumulation of power in its key institution: the marketplace.

The hegemons—Jews who had arrived from Eastern and Central Europe before and after the foundation of the state, and their descendants—had been the wealthiest and most highly educated group since Israel's establishment. (The link between education and wealth in the current era has been widely recognized, eg, in Pierre Bourdieu's discussion of the interrelationship between cultural capital and economic capital.[119] This link has become particularly evident in Israel since the 1990s when the Israeli economy began to be based on know-how and to reward highly educated and skilled employees, particularly in the hi-tech and financial sectors.) In that respect, the advantage they enjoyed over the other social groups only grew in the years after the hegemony's decline, during which the former hegemons accumulated vast fortunes in capital and assets. At the same time, the gap between rich and poor in Israel widened considerably. From one of the most egalitarian countries in the West until the 1970s, Israel turned into one of the least egalitarian countries since then.[120] The LFH thus compensated themselves for their loss of power in the institutions of the state and civil society by a vast expansion of their power in the marketplace.

In the course of these processes, and at the initiative of the LFH group, a new popular perception began to emerge in Israel of state institutions on the one hand, and of the marketplace on the other. It held that state institutions are wholly negative and unworthy, being ineffective, politically motivated and corrupt, whereas the market is wholly positive, a stronghold of efficiency, practicality and professionalism. That the new popular perception should have included these two (mutually complementary) elements was no accident: When the LFH lost their power in the state's institutions

---

[119] Pierre Bourdieu, *Distinction—A Social Critique Of The Judgment Of Taste* (Richard Nice trans, London, Routledge, 1984); Pierre Bourdieu in Randal Johnson (ed), *The Field Of Cultural Production* (New York, Columbia University Press, 1993); Bourdieu, 'The Logic of Practice' above n 111, at 112–121; Bourdieu, 'Outline of a Theory of Practice' above n 111, at 171–183.

[120] Dahan, above n 13; Cohen, above n 13.

and administration, it was only natural that they would paint the latter in a bad light and propagate their negative image on one hand, and champion the positive image of the marketplace—an institution where they enjoyed a clear advantage—on the other. (It is ironic that members of the LFH group have adopted this stance toward state institutions, for it was their parents and grandparents working in the framework of state and other public institutions that made Israel one of the greatest success stories of the twentieth century in many spheres of life.)

(i) The Supreme Court, negative rights and positive rights
During the years the Supreme Court displayed judicial activism, it showed 'judicial passivity' ('under-juridicization') in everything concerned with the development of social rights, and was even an 'obstructive hindrance' to their development.[121] Indeed, a study of the Supreme Court's jurisprudence from the early 1980s onward shows that the Court developed a series of doctrines meant to enable the undisturbed operation of the market on the one hand, while adopting a restrictive doctrine of social rights on the other.

Throughout its existence, including the years since the Basic Law: Human Dignity and Liberty and the Basic Law: Freedom of Occupation, the Supreme Court developed a rich jurisprudence protecting 'negative' rights, namely, rights requiring the state to refrain from interference in the lives of its citizens. These include such rights as the right to property, freedom of expression, freedom from detention, freedom of religion, freedom from religion, freedom of assembly, freedom of movement, right to privacy, and so forth. By contrast, the Court hardly developed any jurisprudence protecting 'positive' rights, the social rights requiring the state to grant its citizens services ensuring that they enjoy minimal conditions of wellbeing, in such areas as healthcare, education, and housing. From the establishment of Israel, then, the Supreme Court has defended groups able to take care of their own needs through the mechanism of the market, but not the groups who are injured by it.[122]

In this vein, in the mid-1990s the Court had occasion to discuss a positive right—the right to education. Justice Or, relying on Justice Barak in

---

[121] Yuval Elbashan, *Strangers In The Realm Of The Law* (Tel Aviv, Hakibbutz Hameuchad Publishing House, 2005) 128, 133 (Hebrew).
[122] Ran Hirschl argues that lack of protection of positive rights and widespread protection of negative rights characterizes the constitutional jurisprudence of the courts in Israel, Canada and New Zealand. Put differently, most constitutional cases in these countries involve negative rights. Moreover, the chances of winning a claim for the protection of a negative right are higher than those of winning a claim for the protection of a positive right. Ran Hirschl, '"Negative" Rights vs. "Positive" Entitlements: A Comparative Study of Judicial Interpretations of Rights in an Emerging Neo-Liberal Economic Order' (2000) 22 Human Rights Q 1060.

his book on constitutional interpretation,[123] stated that that right is not included within the concept of 'human dignity' in the Basic Law: Human Dignity and Liberty, and thus is not protected by it![124] Likewise, when in 2005 a petition was submitted to require the state to guarantee its citizens a decent living, the Court formulated the concept of 'dignified living' in narrow terms, and rejected the petition (by a majority of six to one) on grounds that no factual evidence had been presented attesting that anyone in Israel was unable to obtain a dignified living.[125]

(ii) Protecting property

Applying the Basic Law: Human Dignity and Liberty, the Court awarded extensive protection to the right to property. In an opinion written by Justice Barak, it held that the right to property is 'the cornerstone of the liberal regime' and 'guarantees the existence of other rights.' It proposed a broad view of property violations, stating that they occur any time 'the proprietary value of an interest diminishes' as a result of a state action.[126] The Court thereby adopted 'the proprietary conception of property', focusing on the protection of what a person 'has,' which hinders the redistribution of resources through the action of state institutions. This approach differs from 'the distributive conception of property', whereby the state must ensure everyone a minimal quantity of resources, if necessary through redistributive measures.[127] Interestingly enough, in some cases the Supreme Court stated that it might be the case that the right

---

[123] Aharon Barak, *Interpretation In Law* (vol 3 Constitutional Interpretation, Jerusalem, Nevo Publishing House, 1994) 423 (Hebrew).

[124] HCJ 1554/95 *Amotat Shocharei Gilat v Minister of Education, Culture and Sports*, 50(3) PD 2.

[125] HCJ 366/03 *Commitment to Peace and Social Justice v Minister of Finance*.

It could be argued that the Court is a reactive body that does not initiate the claims brought before it, but responds to judicial proceedings initiated by those seeking its involvement. According to this argument, then, the Court's limited jurisprudence protecting positive—social—rights is not necessarily due to the Court's preference for negative rights, but reflects a lack of petitions to the Court asking it to protect positive rights. The use of the law, however, requires knowledge of its content, a psychological affinity with the law's cultural values, and an ability to bear the costs of legal action. Hence, in all countries, only certain groups in society tend to turn to the Supreme Court and to other courts of law to promote their interests. The fact that the Israeli Supreme Court was asked to protect mainly negative but not positive rights points to the close link that prevails in Israel between the Court and affluent social groups interested in promoting negative rights, and the dissociation of the Court from weak social groups, which require the advancement of positive rights.

[126] CA 6821/93 *United Mizrahhi Bank Ltd. v Migdal*, 49(4) PD 221, 341, 431. See also: Aeyal Gross, 'Property as a Constitutional Right and Basic Law: Human Dignity and Liberty' (1998) 21 Tel Aviv U L Rev 405, 418–9 (Hebrew).

[127] Frank I. Michelman, 'Possession v Distribution in the Constitutional Idea of Property' 72 Ia L Rev (1987) 1319; Gross, id, at 410; Aeyal Gross, 'The Israeli Constitution—A Distributive Justice Instrument or Vice Versa?' in Menachem Maunter (ed), *Distributive Justice In Israel* (Tel Aviv, Ramot Publishing House, 2000) 79, 90 (Hebrew).

to property enjoys wider protection under Israeli law than it does under American law.[128]

(iii) Protecting freedom of occupation and competition

Since the establishment of the State of Israel, the Court has recognized the right to freedom of occupation. This protection has expanded considerably and gained centrality in the Court's jurisprudence since the enactment of the Basic Law: Freedom of Occupation in 1992. In a series of opinions,[129] the Court adopted the 'personality approach' towards freedom of occupation, which had prevailed in Israeli law from the outset,[130] and according to which individuals have a right to choose an occupation that enables them to make a living and express their personality. However, the Court also promoted the 'competition approach' towards freedom of occupation, which holds that freedom of occupation is intended 'to protect free trade and free competition in the economy and in the labor market.'[131] Hence, the Court stated that 'a subsidy given to one individual and denied to another violates freedom of competition, and thereby violates freedom of occupation.' The Court also stated that freedom of occupation in the sense of freedom of competition applies not only to individuals, but also to corporations.[132] Turning the right to free competition into a constitutional right, which extends to corporations as well, is an exceptional move in the context of the accepted perception of interests that are protected as human rights. The right of freedom of occupation is usually applied in the protection of human personality, not of competition in the marketplace.[133]

---

[128] CA 6821/93 *United Mizrahi Bank Ltd. v Migdal*, 49(4) PD 221, 432; CA 6581/98 *Zeevi v State of Israel, Department of Public Works*.

[129] HCJ 1452/93 *Igloo Construction Co. Ltd. v Minister of Commerce and Industry*, 47(5) PD 610; HCJ 726/94 *Clal Insurance Co. Ltd. v Minister of Treasury*, 48(5) PD 441; HCJ 1715/97 *Investment Managers Bureau in Israel v Minister of Treasury*, 51(4) PD 367; Aeyal M. Gross, 'How Did "Free Competition" Become a Constitutional Value? Changes in the Meaning of the Right to Freedom of Occupation' (2000) 23 Tel Aviv U L Rev 229, 230 (Hebrew).

[130] HCJ 1/49 *Bezerano v Minister of Police*, 2 PD 80.

[131] CA 2247/95 *Antitrust Commissioner v Tnuva*, 52(5) PD 213, 229–30; HCJ 1703/92 CAL *Cargo Airlines Ltd. v Prime Minister*, 52(4) PD 193, 216, 218, 227–8; HCJ 5936/97 *Lam v Director General of the Ministry of Education, Culture and Sports*, 53(4) PD 673, 693; HCJ 4915/00 *Reshet Communications and Productions (1992) Co. Ltd. v Government of Israel*, 54(5) PD 451, 464; HCJ 1089/01 *Arkia Israeli Airlines Ltd. v Minister of Transportation*, 58(4) PD 207, 214; Aeyal M. Gross, 'How Did "Free Competition" Become a Constitutional Value? Changes in the Meaning of the Right to Freedom of Occupation' (2000) 23 Tel Aviv U L Rev 229, 230 (Hebrew); Gross, above n 127, at 92.

[132] HCJ 726/94 *Clal Insurance Co. Ltd. v Minister of Treasury*, 48(5) PD 441.

[133] Gross, above n 127, at 93; Gross, above n 131, at 241. Andrei Marmor argued that the Supreme Court had always been the most liberal element in Israeli society. In the last two decades, however, the Court endorsed the most 'rightist' view in the current liberal discourse—the libertarian view. At the core of this conception lies the value of freedom, whereby individuals are perceived as the owners of their bodies and their talents, so that any interference with the results of a person's acts is perceived as a violation of a person's property. Andrei Marmor, 'Judicial Review in Israel' (1997) 4 Mishpat Umimshal 133 (Hebrew). See also: Eli M. Salzberger and Alexander (Sandy) Kedar, 'The Quiet Revolution: More on Judicial Review According to the New Basic Laws' 4 (1997) Mishpat

(g) Lack of criticism of the Supreme Court

Most of the far-reaching changes in the jurisprudence of the Supreme Court took place in the 1980s. In that decade, however, almost no critique was voiced of the Court's moves, either by leaders of the religious groups (the religious Zionists, the Ashkenazi ultra-Orthodox, and the Sephardic ultra-Orthodox) or by representatives of the LFH group.[134] Religious critiques of the Supreme Court began to resonate only in the mid-1990s, when in its *Danilovich* opinion[135] the Court stated that the partner of a homosexual employee is entitled to the same benefits that the employer grants an employee's spouse (in the specific case, a free plane ticket, once a year, for the partner of a flight attendant in El Al, then Israel's national carrier). The ruling prompted spiritual and political leaders of both the religious Zionist and ultra-Orthodox groups to launch a strong attack on the Court, which included the claim that its opinions represent the values of only a small group within Israeli society.[136] (Note that, according to biblical law, the punishment for homosexual relationships is death.)

In the early 1990s, criminal proceedings were instituted against Arye Deri, the political leader of the Sephardic ultra-Orthodox party Shas, on charges of financial corruption. Shas speakers, including the party's spiritual leader, R. Ovadia Yosef, consequently assumed a prominent

Umimshal 488, 502 (Hebrew) ('the conclusive characterization of the Court's entire jurisprudence as libertarian is questionable'); Guy Mundlak, 'Socio-Economic Rights in the New Constitutional Discourse' (1999) 7 Labor Law Annual 65 (Hebrew) ('the jurisprudence of the Supreme Court is neither libertarian nor neo-liberal. The dominant model in this jurisprudence is indeed the liberal model, which emphasizes the atomistic dimension of basic rights, but a parallel model is also developing, which relates positively to the social dimension of human rights').

[134] Hillel Sommer writes that in recent decades 'the media and the press...treated the Barak Court as if it were a precious gem.' Hillel Sommer, 'Richard Posner on Aharon Barak: The View from Abroad' (2007) 49 Hapraklit 523, 535 (Hebrew). Sommer cites the words of Tovah Zimuki, the senior legal correspondent of Israel's leading daily, *Yedioth Ahronoth*:

> For years the press granted the Courts free PR services as a matter of course. We have barely asked any questions; we have barely cast doubt or made any comments of our own.

Id, at 536.
[135] HCJ 721/94 *El Al Israel Airlines v Danilovich*, 48(5) PD 749.
[136] Shachar Ilan, 'The Religious National Party Intends to Launch a Campaign Against the Supreme Court and Particularly Against Aharon Barak' (December 5 1994) Haaretz; Gideon Alon, 'Law School Deans Denounce Attacks on Barak' (December 9 1994) Haaretz; Gideon Alon and Zvi Zerachia, 'Benizri in Knesset's Constitution Committee: We Won't Let the HCJ Go Wild' (December 13 1994) Haaretz; 'Libai: The Proposal to Limit Barak is Not Meant to Improve the Position of the Supreme Court' (December 14 1994) Haaretz; Gideon Alon, 'MK Hamer: The Supreme Court Promotes Leftist Agenda and does not Represent Israeli Society' (April 9 1996) Haaretz; Ran Kislev, 'The Campaign to Conquer the HCJ' (August 6 1996) Haaretz; Shachar Ilan, 'The Viznich Rabbi: I shall Personally Act to Pull the HCJ Down' (November 24 1996) Haaretz; Tova Zimuki, 'Heavy Pressure on Netanyahu to Appoint Two Religious Justices to the Supreme Court' (December 22 1996) Yedioth Ahronoth. See also: Cohen and Susser, 'Israel and the Politics of Jewish Identity' above n 48, chapter 4; Menachem Mautner, 'Appointment of Justices to the Supreme Court in a Multicultural Society' (2003) 19 Legal Research 423, 427–34 (Hebrew).

role in the attacks on the legal system, particularly against the Supreme Court.[137] In 1997, in the course of a demonstration in support of Deri, hundreds of Shas supporters almost burst into the Supreme Court building (they were driven back by the police at the last minute).[138] Shas' attacks on the Court reached a peak in the 1999 election campaign. Shortly before that, Deri had been convicted in the Jerusalem District Court and sentenced to four years in prison. Shas founded its entire 1999 election campaign on Deri's conviction, mounting an unrestrained attack against the legal system in general and the Supreme Court in particular.[139]

In February 1999, ultra-Orthodox leaders organized a demonstration against the Supreme Court, staged before the Court's premises. In the buildup towards it and during the demonstration, strong accusations were hurled against the Court. Knesset member Moshe Gafni, who represents the Ashkenazi ultra-Orthodox group, called Chief Justice Aharon Barak 'tsorer' [enemy], an epithet usually reserved for Haman, the villain in the biblical Book of Esther. R. Ovadia Yosef said that Supreme Court judges are evil and ignorant. Knesset member Menahem Porush, a political leader of the Ashkenazi ultra-Orthodox group, warned that a war would break out with the ultra-Orthodox group unless the Court changed its rulings. Estimates of the number of participants at the demonstration varied between 250,000 and 400,000. In the course of the demonstration, the police were afraid that the demonstrators would storm the Court building. (The religious Zionist leaders and public, however, showed only qualified support for this demonstration.)[140]

What explanation is there for the fact that, though extensive changes had taken place in the Supreme Court's jurisprudence since the late 1970s, they met with almost no criticism until the mid-1990s?

Human experience shows that whenever a person or an institution tries to operate in different ways than those of the past, they usually face broad and vigorous opposition. Machiavelli understood this well.

---

[137] Gideon Alon and Zvi Zerachia, 'Benizri in Knesset's Constitution Committee: We Won't Let the HCJ Go Wild' (December 13 1994) Haaretz; Moshe Swissa, 'The Justices Do not Deserve to Adjudicate for Jews' (October 28 1997) Yedioth Ahronoth; Shachar Ilan, 'Arye Deri in a Shas Festivity: Israel Should be a Halakhic State' (April 9 1999) Haaretz. See also: HCJ 3087/99 *The Movement for Quality of Government in Israel v Attorney General*, 54(1) PD 414 (discussing a petition against the decision of the Attorney General not to indict Shas' leader Rabbi Ovadia Yosef for derisive language used by him against the Supreme Court).

[138] Rami Hazut, 'The Night the Supreme Court was almost Conquered' (May 14 1997) Yedioth Ahronoth; 'Police Inquiry: Shas People Moved the Fences and Burst Toward the Supreme Court' (May 15 1997) Haaretz.

[139] Cohen and Susser, *Israel and the Politics of Jewish Identity*, above n 48, chapter 3, 4.

[140] Id.

[T]here is no more delicate matter to take in hand, nor more dangerous to conduct, nor more doubtful in its success, than to set up as a leader in the introduction of changes,

he wrote.

For he who innovates will have for his enemies all those who are well off under the existing order of things, and only lukewarm supporters in those who might be better off under the new. This lukewarm temper arises partly from the fear of adversaries who have the laws on their side, and partly from the incredulity of mankind, who will never admit the merit of anything new, until they have seen it proved by the event.[141]

In the same spirit, a contemporary expert on the theory of change notes that opposition to change is 'natural to all people in all contexts' and, therefore, those who seek to bring about change face 'forces that preserve continuity and stability, opposing and halting pressures to change.'[142]

Opposition to change might have been expected, particularly from jurists. Jurists operate within a tradition, a conservative professional culture based on preserving and accumulating legal materials and applying them to contend with current problems. Lawyers operate in a professional culture premised on piecemeal, incremental, step by step development of the law. And yet, the many and far-reaching changes in the Supreme Court's jurisprudence during the 1980s met with hardly any opposition from Israel's jurists for many years, insofar as can be gleaned from that community's professional literature.

Moreover, the changes in the Supreme Court's jurisprudence also had obvious political and cultural implications. What explanation is there, then, for the fact that the political and cultural groups that were purportedly the 'losers' as a result of these changes did not oppose or criticize them?

The vast majority of the country's jurists, including law teachers, belongs to the group I have called 'liberal former hegemons.' The explanation for the lack of criticism on their part is simply that the LFH had already turned to the Supreme Court as the state institution most clearly identified with their liberal values, whose activism might help them halt or disrupt the actions of rising religious and nationalist forces, both in the public administration and in the Knesset. Hence, not only did members of this group (including the jurists among them) fail to criticize the opinions issued by the Supreme Court in the 1980s, despite their significant

---

[141] Niccolo Machiavelli, in Charles W. Eliot (ed), *The Prince* (New York, Harvard Classics, P.F. Collier & Son) 21–2 (chapter VI).

[142] Shaul Fox, *The Psychology Of Resistance To Change* (Ramat Gan, Bar Ilan University Press, 1998) 11 (Hebrew).

innovations; they also protected the Court from any potential criticism that might have emerged from the other social groups and legitimated its endeavor. (Striking as this may sound, it took years after the rise of the Court's new jurisprudence until legal academics began to publish law review articles critical of the Court. If the expectation exists that academics will reflectively and critically scrutinize the deeds of state institutions, this certainly was not legal academia's finest moment.)

But what explanation is there for the prolonged lack of criticism of the Supreme Court on the part of the rising social groups (the religious, nationalists, Sephardim, and so forth) in the post-hegemonic 1980s, despite the far-reaching changes in the Court's jurisprudence during that period? That is a question I find hard to answer. The main clue may be that the law created and applied by the courts is less important than what jurists tend to think. The people in government control the state budget and the human resources in the state's public administration, and can use them to promote their aims and views. Only rarely can courts initiate social change. Usually, a court can (temporarily?) disrupt a government's moves. Throughout the 1980s and 1990s, Jewish settlement in the Occupied Palestinian Territories continued unhindered; huge budgets were transferred to the Ministry of Religious Affairs to fund religious-Zionist and ultra-Orthodox institutions; the divide between rich and poor kept widening; the appalling discrimination against the Israeli Arab population went on in all realms of life; a peace treaty was signed with Egypt in 1979; a war erupted in Lebanon in 1982; the First Intifada broke out in 1987; in 1993 the Oslo Accords were signed by Israel and the Palestine Liberation Organization (PLO); in the mid-1990s Israel's healthcare system was nationalized; since the 1990s hundred of thousands of guest workers have begun to live in Israel; Shas established an independent educational network in the 1980s and the 1990s. Possibly, then, the heart of the matter is that the Supreme Court's rulings during the 1980s hardly or never bothered the rising social groups, and as far as significant historical events and far-reaching processes affecting Israel are concerned, their value may have been marginal or merely symbolic.[143]

Additional explanations could be offered as to why the rising social groups did not criticize the Supreme Court in Israel's early post-hegemonic era. One is that these groups were busy assuming control of the Knesset, the government and the public administration of the state, and they had no

---

[143] For the argument that the rulings of the Supreme Court had little effect on the Israeli political system, see: Daphne Barak-Erez, 'Judicial Review of Politics: The Israeli Case' 29 J Law & Soc (2002) 611; Barak Medina, 'Four Myths of Judicial Review: A Response to Robert Bork's and Richard Posner's Criticism of Aharon Barak's Judicial Activism' (2007) 3 Din Udvarim 399, 410 (Hebrew).

intellectual energy to spare to deal with developments within the Supreme Court. Another explanation is that these social groups found themselves too weak to criticize the Supreme Court, particularly given the broad support that the Court received from the LFH, who to this very day continue to control much of the press, the media, the universities, and the business sector. Yet another explanation is that not many within these social groups read Supreme Court opinions. Another is that years passed until the actual picture and the implications of the Supreme Court's endeavor during the 1980s became clear. Still another explanation is that the religious groups refrained from attacking the Supreme Court because of their basic deference to the authority of jurists and tribunals. And, finally, representatives of the religious group may have refrained from attacking the Supreme Court for many long years due to their basic respect for the country's institutions.

CHAPTER 6

THE SUPREME COURT AND THE FUTURE OF LIBERALISM

In his enigmatic memorandum *Dictatus papae* (1075)... [Pope] Gregory [VII] gave a first indication of his challenge to sacred kingship, stating that it was licit for a pope to depose an emperor. He...put forward a theological argument that the clergy, headed by the pope, were superior to kings and other lay powers, whose roles was to carry out the clergy's directions.

[Emperor] Henry IV's active resistance to the pope's initiatives led Gregory to excommunicate Henry and depose him from his office as king (1076), declaring the nobles free from their feudal obligations toward Henry. With a Saxon rebellion on his hands, Henry, in desperation, went to Italy and appeared before the castle of Canossa in northern Tuscany, where Gregory was a guest...(January 1077). Henry's famous episode of allegedly performing penance by standing barefoot in the snow for three days earned him reconciliation with the church, but only temporarily. No sooner had he returned to Germany and extinguished the rebellion then he turned against the pope once more. A second excommunication of Henry IV in 1080—in complete contrast to that of 1076—prompted the majority of the German and Italian bishops to side with the king. Upon Henry's invasion of Italy, Gregory had no choice but to flee Rome for the south...In Salerno Gregory died an exile.[1]

In the previous chapters I discussed the three major changes that have taken place in the jurisprudence of Israel's Supreme Court in the past three decades. I have argued that these changes need to be understood in the context of the renewal of the struggle over the shape of Israeli culture in the post-hegemonic chapter of Israel's history that began in the latter half of the 1970s. I have depicted the Court as being identified with one of the two major social groups that are taking part in this struggle, the liberal former hegemons.

---

[1] Alex Novikoff, 'Licit and Illicit in the Rhetoric of the Investiture Conflict' in Ruth Mazo Karras, Joel Kaye and E. Ann Matter (eds), *Law And The Illicit In Medieval Europe* (Philadelphia, University of Pennsylvania Press, 2008) 183, 184.

In the present chapter, I wish to discuss the implications of the Court's conspicuous and activist involvement in Israel's cultural struggle. I shall show that, as might have been expected, the Court has lost much of its legitimacy among members of the other major group contending over the shape of Israel's culture—the religious group (including both subgroups of which it is comprised, namely the religious Zionists and the ultra-Orthodox). Even more striking, however, is the fact that in recent years the Court has also lost legitimacy among members of the social group that for a generation gave it their uncompromising support—the liberal former hegemons. I shall show that this last development has something to do with the widespread feeling among group members that the Court does not score well enough when the criterion of integrity is applied to its own conduct (namely, whether it practices what it preaches), particularly in the context of appointments to the Court's ranks. (I shall show that the Court's profound involvement in the appointment process has been nothing less than devastating to its public stature.)

The upshot of this analysis is that the Court is currently in the midst of the worst crisis it has faced since the establishment of the State of Israel over six decades ago: it is being fiercely attacked not only by its cultural adversaries, but also by the social group that identifies with its values. As the Court has played an indispensable and vital role in entrenching and in cultivating liberal-democratic values in Israel's political culture, it is a moment of crisis not only for the Court, but for Israel's liberal-democratic project in its entirety.

A. THE COURT'S TWO-FRONT STRUGGLE

Even though the far-reaching changes in the jurisprudence of the Supreme Court began to take place in the late 1970s, it was only in the mid-1990s, some fifteen years after the new era in the Court's jurisprudence had begun, that critiques of those changes began to resonate. The criticism of the mid-1990s came from the political and spiritual leadership of the ultra-Orthodox group (both the Ashkenazi and the Sephardic).

The first significant criticism of the Court was heard following the Court's ruling in the *Danilovich* case of 1994[2] that the partner of a homosexual employee is entitled to the same benefits that the employer grants to an employee's spouse. Further attacks on the Court came following the initiation of criminal proceedings against Arye Deri, the political leader

---

[2] HCJ 721/94 *El Al Israel Airlines v Danilovich*, 48(5) PD 749.

of the Sephardic ultra-Orthodox Shas movement, on charges of financial corruption. Finally, in February 1999, ultra-Orthodox leaders organized a demonstration against the Supreme Court, which was staged before the Supreme Court building and attended by 250,000 to 400,000 participants. (See Chapter 5, above.)

There is nothing surprising, of course, in the fact that it was these groups from which criticism of the Court emanated. The more striking development with regard to the Court's standing came in the early 2000s, when it became the target of harsh critiques by speakers belonging to the liberal former hegemonic group. Since then, articles and columns sharply critical of the Court have appeared in the press almost weekly, often worded in offensive, derisive, and contemptuous terms. A new and unprecedented situation has arisen: the Court's harshest critics come from the social group that, since the late 1970s, had given unqualified support to the Court's moves and treated the Court as its own stronghold in the struggle over the shaping of Israel's culture in the post-hegemonic era. Thus, the Court currently finds itself locked in an ideological struggle against the religious groups and exposed to their criticism, while at the same time it faces the harshest criticism from the very same social group whose values it represents and that had traditionally defended it in its struggle to defend and promote these values in the country. This change in the political behavior of the liberal former hegemons is *nothing less than dramatic* and demands an explanation. I will offer three.

(a) First explanation: Anxiety on the wane

A generation passed, and Israeli democracy proved that it could function successfully over a long period and had not suffered any damage due to the hegemony's decline and the transition to the post-hegemonic period. The realization sunk in that daily life had not changed at all for the secular group, despite the rise of a new self-perception of itself by the religious-Zionist group as the potential leader of a new hegemony in Israel and the increased strength of the ultra-Orthodox group in the Knesset. Quite to the contrary, in fact, during this period the secular group won unprecedented achievements, particularly in regard to the opening of theaters, cinemas, restaurants, and shops on the Sabbath and on Jewish holidays in many places in Israel, including Jerusalem! (Thirty years ago, anyone who had said that someday theatres and cinemas would operate in Jerusalem on the Saturday eve would have been regarded as a lunatic, but for a fact that has been the situation in Jerusalem for over two decades now.)[3] Moreover, the fear of religious coercion diminished considerably with the arrival of more than a million immigrants from the former Soviet Union in the early 1990s—most of them secular in worldview and lifestyle, and many of them non-Jews according to the Halakhah. Likewise, the quality of Israel's democracy has not diminished at all, even though for most of the time since 1977 the country has been governed by rightwing governments in coalition with ultra-Orthodox parties. Moreover, it was these rightwing governments that negotiated and signed the historic 1979 peace agreement with Egypt, and conducted the disengagement from Gaza and the northern Samaria in 2005. As the years passed, the LFH's feeling that they were facing rising religious-nationalist forces and that the Supreme Court was the last stronghold that would protect them from a takeover by these forces weakened, and the post-hegemonic situation became part of the country's normal, ongoing daily reality.

(b) Second explanation: Declining trust in the Court

People have many values they hold dear and to which they adhere. In the first generation after the decline of the hegemony, in their political behavior the LFH insistently emphasized the protection of liberal-democratic values against what they perceived as a threat on the part of rising religious and nationalist social groups. As the years passed and their anxiety over the harm to these values waned, the LFH could make room in their political behavior for other important values, such as integrity. Over the years, when that value was applied to the conduct of the Supreme Court, the Court did not appear to fully meet the test.

Every organization operates within two normative systems. One is the declared, '*official*' system. That is the organization's 'noble vision,' reflecting the ideal way in which it is supposed to function. The official system envisions and dictates action guided by considerations meant to lead to the optimal realization of the organization's aims. In every organization, however, another normative system is also invariably present, the '*political*' normative system, which often reflects the organization's actual functioning. This system dictates action guided by ulterior motives, which promote the personal aims of the organization's members and subvert the organization's ability to realize its officially declared aims and values.[4]

What has happened to the Supreme Court in recent years is that the political normative system that in part dictates its action has been publicly exposed. This exposure has proved highly destructive. First, a court

---

[3] S.N. Eisenstadt, *Changes In Israeli Society* (Tel Aviv, Ministry of Defense, 2004) 86 (Hebrew).
[4] Yitzhak Samuel, *The Political Game—Power And Influence In Organizations* (Haifa, Haifa University Press, 2002) 17–24, 82–107 (Hebrew).

is supposed to act without blemish, in conformance with lofty values of justice, honesty, fairness and integrity. As Francis Bacon wrote about judges, 'Above all things, integrity is their portion and proper virtue.'[5] Second, the Supreme Court's routine duty (when it sits as a High Court of Justice) is to supervise the conduct of the state's public administration so as to ensure that the first, official normative system takes precedence over the second, political normative system. Third, this exposure occurred during the very years in which the Court's action was characterized by a sweeping activism, that is, when the Court had considerably expanded the scope of its supervision over the government, the public administration and the Knesset in order to enforce worthy norms in their conduct.

In combination, these three elements shattered the public's trust in the Court and undermined its legitimacy even among many of its staunchest supporters. Gradually, various speakers began to express their sense that the Court was failing to live up to its own high ideals. They criticized the Court and proclaimed—initially without any empirical findings to support this—that public trust in the Court had declined, signaling the rise of what can be called 'the discourse about the decline of public trust in the Court.'[6] This impressionistic discourse has been corroborated by a

---

[5] Francis Bacon, 'Of Judicature' in John Pitcher (ed), *The Essays* (Harmondsworth, Middlesex, Penguin Books, 1985) 222, 222.

[6] In March 2001, Professor Yaakov Ne'eman, formerly Treasury Minister and currently Israel's Minister of Justice, stated that 'public trust in the judicial system has snapped.' Or Heller, 'Yakov Neeman Attacks: Trust of Judicial System Cracks' (March 21 2001) Maariv. In May 2005, Knesset member Michael Eitan, chairman of the Knesset's Constitution, Law, and Justice Committee, stated that Israel's judicial branch is in a situation similar to the sinking of the Titanic—'dancing on the upper deck, while public trust in the judges' integrity and standards is breaking.' Hadas Magen, 'Member of the Judges Appointments Committee: Most Opposition in the Committee Was to the Appointment of Rubinstein' (May 11 2004) Globes. In September 2005, Ben-Dror Yemini, a senior columnist for the high circulation daily Maariv, wrote that in the years he had served as Chief Justice,

> [Aharon] Barak grew and the Court went on eroding. For ten years Barak has been repeating the mantra about 'public trust' in the Supreme Court, but public trust is declining.

Ben-Dror Yemini, 'Little-Great Man' (September 9 2005) Maariv. In February 2007, Nahum Barnea, whom many consider Israel's leading columnist, wrote about 'the weakening of the Supreme Court' and its 'shrinking status.' Nahum Barnea, 'Confrontational Minister of Justice' (February 5 2007) Yedioth Ahronoth. In May 2007, Moriel Matalon, a partner-director in a leading Tel Aviv law firm, wrote that 'the image of the judicial system and the public trust in it have reached an all-time low...previously unknown.' Moriel Matalon, '*Bribe Your Judge*' (May 25 2007) Globes. In July 2007, Mordechai Kremnitzer, of the Faculty of Law at the Hebrew University, said: 'We are witnessing a phenomenon of devaluation of trust, affecting also the judicial system, including the Supreme Court.' Gidi Weitz, 'Mazuz, Mature!' (July 11 2007) Haaretz. In August 2008, Amnon Lord, the editor-in-chief of the rightwing daily Makor Rishon, referred to 'a dramatic decline in the status of the Supreme Court.' Amnon Lord, 'Violence with the Court's Permission' (December 5 2008) Makor Rishon. In June 2009, Nahum Barnea wrote that 'the Supreme Court has lost much of its status' and that 'it is accompanied by a cloud of debasement.' Nahum Barnea, 'Temporary Freeze' (June 26 2009) Yedioth Ahronoth. In a public lecture delivered in Jerusalem in July 2009, Justice Dorit Beinish, who succeeded Aharon Barak as Chief Justice of the Supreme Court, said that 'the justices are shocked to see the ease with which the public discourse descends to debasement of the Court.' Tomer Zarhin,

study conducted at Haifa University in 2000–7 by Arye Ratner, who heads the University's Center for the Study of Crime, Law, and Society. Ratner reported the study's findings as follows:

> In 2000, 56 percent of the Jewish public reported a high level of trust in Israeli courts. By contrast, in 2007, the rate of those expressing trust in Israeli courts is only 33 percent. A similar trend of erosion is also evident when we examine public trust in the Supreme Court. The data of the study indicate that, whereas in 2000 the Supreme Court enjoyed the trust of more than 74 percent of the Jewish public, trust levels have dropped today to 51 percent.... Whereas in 2000, 71 percent of all Jewish respondents agreed that the courts perform their task fairly, only 48 percent said so in 2007.... In 2000, 65 percent indicated that they agree that the courts treat all citizens equally. In 2007, only 46 percent thought so.... The general picture emerging from the data collected over the years indeed attests to a clear trend of erosion—both in the public's trust in the legal and judicial system and in their evaluation of the various indices related to its performance.... We face a gloomy picture, pointing to a profound crisis in the public's perception of the rule of law and the measure of legitimacy they grant or do not grant to the legal and judicial system.[7]

Yedioth Ahronoth, Israel's leading daily, reported the findings of the study in its headline story: 'Sharp Drop in Trust in the Judicial System.'[8] A few days later, Justice Dorit Beinish, who succeeded Aharon Barak as Chief Justice of the Supreme Court, announced a propaganda campaign to improve the Court's public image.[9] Similar findings by other studies have subsequently been reported, as well.[10]

Several significant reasons may be pointed out for the widespread feeling that a political normative system dictates the work of the Supreme Court, besides the official normative system, so that the Court fails to live up to its own high ideals. The most important reason would appear to concern the processes of appointing judges to the Court.

Under Israeli law, judges to all courts in the country are appointed by a nine-member appointment committee made up as follows: three justices of the Supreme Court; two representatives of the Israel Bar Association (IBA); two government ministers, one of whom is the Minister of Justice;

'The Supreme Court Launches a Propaganda Campaign; Chief Justice Beinish to "Haaretz": The Public Does Not Understand Us' (July 7 2009) Haaretz.

[7] Arye Ratner, 'Only 33% Trust the Judicial System' (July 3 2007) Haaretz.
[8] 'Sharp Drop in Trust in the Judicial System' (July 4 2007) Yedioth Ahronoth.
[9] Tomer Zarhin, 'The Supreme Court Launches a Propaganda Campaign; Chief Justice Beinish to "Haaretz": The Public Does Not Understand Us' (July 7 2009) Haaretz.
[10] Noam Sharvit, 'Multi-year Study: Public Trust in the Court System Reached its Lowest Point in Seven Years' (November 20 2007) Globes; Jonathan Haleli, '52% Distrust the Supreme Court' (April 8 2008) Maariv; Noam Sharvit, '90% of Israeli Public: Israel is a Corrupt Country; 64% Have no Confidence in the Attorney General' (June 11 2008) Globes.

and two members of the Knesset (usually, but not always, one from the coalition and one from the opposition).[11] When an appointment to the Supreme Court is being considered, the three Supreme Court justices who are members of the committee always vote *en bloc*, following prior internal consultation and a resolution undertaken by the forum of all the Court's justices. (As noted by some commentators, this practice runs counter to a basic principle of Israel's administrative law, according to which a legally authorized official must apply his or her own discretion and act independently). When appointments to other courts are being considered, almost without exception the three Supreme Court justices vote as one, as well. Add to this the fact that for many years the IBA representatives, as well as the Ministers of Justice, voted in concert with the justices of the Court, and that the Knesset representatives abided by the choices of the Court as well, and it is easy to see how for many years the Supreme Court actually controlled *all* appointments to its ranks, and much of the process with regard to appointment to all other courts of the country.

Unsurprisingly, for many years and on numerous occasions, the justices of the Supreme Court have claimed that Israel's appointment procedure, being 'professional' rather than 'political', is 'the best in the world'. But looking at the record of the Court's involvement in the appointment process in the past three decades, particularly when it has had to do with appointments to the ranks of the Court itself, one cannot but arrive at the sad conclusion that it has been this involvement, more than anything else, that has contributed to the exposure of the political normative system underlying the Court's conduct and to the deterioration in the Court's status and legitimacy.

For years, press reports and articles have contended that the appointments and/or promotions of spouses and other family members of Supreme Court justices to judicial offices have been tainted with nepotism. Similarly,

---

[11] In Australia, judges of the High Court are selected by the prime minister. In Canada, judges to the Supreme Court are selected by the prime minister. In India, judges of the Supreme Court are selected by the Chief Justice and the four most senior Supreme Court judges after considering a list submitted by the government. In Ireland, judges of the Supreme Court are appointed by the government acting on the nonbinding advice of a judicial advisory board. In New Zealand, judges of the Supreme Court are selected by the Attorney General, after consulting senior judges and lawyers. In South Africa, judges of the Constitutional Court are selected by the president after considering nominations by the Judicial Service Commission and consulting with the Chief Justice and party leaders. In the United States, judges of the Supreme Court are selected by the president, subject to confirmation by the Senate. In the United Kingdom, judges of the House of Lords were selected by the prime minister on the advice of the Lord Chancellor. Brice Dickson, 'Comparing Supreme Courts' in Brice Dickson (ed), *Judicial Activism In Common Law Supreme Courts* (Oxford, Oxford University Press, 2007) 1, 5. Judges to the Supreme Court, which on October 1, 2009 replaced the Appellate Committee of the House of Lords as the highest court in the United Kingdom, are appointed by the Lord Chancellor following a recommendation made by a 15-member, independent Judicial Appointments Commission. See: Constitutional Reform Act, 2005.

it has been claimed that the children of Supreme Court justices are selected to do their clerkship in the Court not necessarily due to relevant considerations of merit.[12] These reports have had a detrimental, if not devastating, effect on the Court's standing. Israel is a small country; if people were indeed chosen, appointed, or promoted on inappropriate grounds, concern with and discussion of such issues was bound to spread quickly.[13]

Likewise, in the late 1990s and at the start of the new millennium, of the Supreme Court's twelve permanent justices, four had formerly been members of the Faculty of Law at the Hebrew University. Each of these appointments was unquestionably worthy, but the fact that fully one-third(!) of the Court's justices came from such a small pool aroused an uncomfortable feeling in many that a crucial element in the process of appointment to the Court is a connection with sitting justices. Due to this troubling situation, numerous statements have been made in the press and the media to the effect that the Court appoints justices to its ranks on the basis of the 'one friend brings another' principle.[14] All of this has had stern implications in terms of the Court's standing, because the fundamental logic of the judicial process is that of impartiality, namely the neutralization of personal ties between judge and litigants. With four members of the Supreme Court having come from the same law faculty, however, the presence of such ties was all too obvious.

In the first decade of the twenty-first century it became clear to many observers of the Court that its involvement in (read: Domination of) the appointment of justices to its ranks is devastating to the Court's standing. Many observers came to realize that the appointment of worthy candidates is too often aborted by the justices, either for fear of being overshadowed by distinguished appointees, or out of concern that appointees not approved by the Court will challenge its prevailing jurisprudence.[15] The failed appointment of Ruth Gavison is a case in point. Gavison is a world-renowned professor of jurisprudence and one of the most outstanding intellectuals of

---

[12] See eg Einat Berkovitz, 'The Supreme Court as a Family Business' (December 19 1994) Ha'ir; Shabtai Azriel, 'Your Petition is Denied; Warm Regards to Mom' (October 14 1996) Haaretz.

[13] Amnon Abramowitz, the chief commentator of Israel's Channel 2 TV News, expressed a widespread feeling in October 2006 when he wrote the following: 'Before our very eyes, with permission and authority, judicial appointments have taken place that were more nepotistic and less esthetic than those political appointments for which people have faced criminal charges'. Amnon Abramowitz, 'Presidential Embrace' (October 16 2006) Globes.

[14] Hadas Magen, 'A Member of the Justices' Appointment Committee Talks on the Recent Appointments' (May 11 2004) Globes.

[15] Boaz Okon, the leading legal commentator in the Israeli press, wrote that the last four appointments to the United States Supreme Court made by Presidents George W. Bush and Barack Obama (Chief Justice John G. Roberts and Justices Samuel Aleto, Sonia Sotomayor and Elena Kagan) reflect a striving for excellence not particularly manifest in the appointments made to the Israeli Supreme Court. Boaz Okon, 'The Age of the Outsiders' (May 17 2010) Yedioth Ahronoth.

Israel. Since the 1990s she has persistently criticized the Court's activism. But when, in 2005, the then-Minister of Justice Tzipi Livni suggested her appointment to the Court, the idea triggered staunch opposition on the part of the Court, first and foremost by Aharon Barak.[16]

What proved most devastating to the Supreme Court's image was its involvement in the failed attempt to appoint Nili Cohen to its ranks. Cohen, a professor of contract law at the Faculty of Law of Tel Aviv University, who had served in the 1990s as the university's rector, is an outstanding jurist and a beloved teacher. But in a closed meeting of Supreme Court justices held in 2003—which, as noted above, is the Court's routine procedure when appointments to its ranks are being considered—the majority of the justices voted against Cohen's appointment. That in turn led to an unprecedented torrent of criticism in the press, contending that the Court's stance was driven by extraneous considerations, sacrificing the institution's interests for some of the justices' own personal benefit.

Subsequently, Cohen's friend and academic partner, Professor Daniel Friedmann, embarked on a scathing critique of the Court. Friedmann, an Israel Prize recipient who is also a professor of contract law at the Faculty of Law of Tel Aviv University, is one of Israel's most respected jurists. He published a series of articles in the weekend edition of Yedioth Ahronoth,[17] claiming that Supreme Court justices had for many years controlled the appointments to the Court uncontested; that the justices' considerations in regard to appointments had been driven in recent years by ulterior motives; and that in the very years the Court had granted itself unprecedented powers, it had been staffed by justices of low professional and intellectual capabilities. Consequently, claimed Friedmann, the Court had lost its moral standing.

It would hardly be an exaggeration to say that Friedmann's criticism of the Court was *one of the most important developments in the history of Israeli law*. Nothing like it had ever been said about the Court and its justices, or in such vitriolic language, and by so central a figure in the legal community. After Friedmann's articles, all the barriers came tumbling down. References to the Supreme Court in insulting and offensive terms, unimaginable in any Western country, began to appear as a matter of routine.[18]

---

[16] Shani Mizrahi, 'Barak: 'I Object to Gavison's Appointment; She has an Agenda' (November 11 2005) Ynet.

[17] Daniel Friedmann, 'No More Supreme' (June 10 2005) Yedioth Ahronoth; Daniel Friedmann, 'Politics in the High Court of Justice' (July 1 2005) Yedioth Ahronoth; Daniel Friedmann, 'For Your Care, Next Minister of Justice' (April 21 2006) Yedioth Ahronoth; Daniel Friedmann, 'The Supreme Court Stepped Down to the Street' (December 9 2007) Yedioth Ahronoth.

[18] Two more events should be noted in connection with the deterioration in the Court's standing. First was the publication in 2006 of journalist Nomi Levitsky's *The Supremes: Inside the Supreme Court* (Tel Aviv, Hakibbutz Hameuchad Publishing House, 2006) (Hebrew). The book, which quickly

Finally, in the first decade of the twenty-first century the Court has not only suffered a decline in the public's trust. It has faced another, related, problem: there are signs that other state branches are increasingly taking the liberty of disregarding the Court's rulings.[19] In one case[20] the Court defined the conduct of the Ministry of Education in implementing a previous Court ruling as 'standing in blatant contradiction to the holdings of the Court, in terms of both their language and spirit.' The Court added that the Ministry's conduct was particularly grave because it reflected a total lack of commitment to implementing the ruling in any way in the future. The Court therefore described the Ministry's attitude as undermining the rule of law. In another case,[21] following its ruling to overturn discriminatory funding of the Arab school system, the Court stated that the Office of the Prime Minister together with the Ministry of Education 'have taken the liberty to disregard the Court's ruling ... treating it as if it were merely a recommendation.' In a third case,[22] the Court ruled that discriminatory separation between Ashkenazi and Sephardic female students in an ultra-Orthodox school system be abolished. When eight months had passed without any change in the practices of the system, the Court imposed a heavy daily fine on it until it abides by the Court's ruling. In a lecture delivered at the Israel Democracy Institute's 2008 Israeli Democracy Index Conference, Chief Justice Dorit Beinish cautioned against 'a corrosive attitude of disrespect toward the Court's rulings' on the part of other state authorities. 'There is a growing concern that government's branches will delegitimize the Court's rulings,' said Beinish.

---

became a bestseller, sweepingly exposed the political normative system underlying the Court's conduct, particularly concerning appointments. Second, in 2005, the press reported that a judge in the Haifa magistrate court, Hillah Cohen, had been convicted in the judges' disciplinary court for fabricating court proceedings. The sentence issued in her case, however, did not order her dismissal as a judge. The presiding judge of the disciplinary tribunal was Justice Mishael Cheshin of the Supreme Court. Dozens of articles appeared in the press attacking the sentence. Merav Arlosoroff, the senior columnist of the leading economic daily TheMarker, wrote:

> The Israeli judiciary is the oracle of integrity and proper conduct in the country, until the issue is its own conduct.... The Cohen incident is not a random event. It represents the normative insensitiveness that has overtaken the Israeli judiciary in recent years, leading to the loss of its standing as the country's conscience.

Merav Arlosoroff, 'Judge Hillah Cohen is Right' (September 12 2005) TheMarker.

[19] '[T]here were cases in the early 1950s in which a government blatantly defied court orders.' Menachem Hofnung, 'The Unintended Consequences of Unplanned Constitutional Reform: Constitutional Politics in Israel' (1996) 44 Am J Comparative L 585, 597. Since then, however, and for many years, no problem of noncompliance with the Court's rulings has been noted.

[20] HCJ 4805/07 *Jewish Pluralism Center v Ministry of Education*.

[21] HCJ 11163/03 *Supreme Watch Committee of the Arabs in Israel v Prime Minister of Israel*.

[22] HCJ 1067/08 *Noar Ka-Halacha v Ministry of Education*. See also: Edna-Ullmann-Margalit, 'Teaching a Lesson' (April 14 2010) Haaretz; HCJ 6298/07 *Ressler v The Knesset* (declaring the Court's dissatisfaction with the implementation of its rulings on military service of ultra-Orthodox *Yeshiva* students).

In the past, abiding by the Court's rulings was self-evident. ... Today there is no assurance that we won't shortly face a slippery slope that may take the form of disregard of judicial writs.[23]

A report published in March 2010 by Yehudit Karpp, a former Deputy Attorney General, detailed a series of cases in which state authorities have disregarded the Court's rulings.[24] Thus, in addition to the rise of a discourse about 'the decline of public trust in the Court,' in recent years the Court has also faced the rise of a discourse about 'the non-enforcement of the Court's rulings.' Needless to say, each of these two discourses has been devastating to the standing of the Court. The combination of the two of them is particularly destructive.[25]

(c) Third explanation: The conservative right v the Court

A group of writers critical of the Supreme Court coalesced at the end of the 1990s around the journal Azure, published by the rightwing Shalem Center. They drew upon two sources of inspiration. The first was the conservative constitutionalism that has resonated in American law in recent decades (as part of the neo-Conservatism that emerged in the United States in the 1970s). In reliance upon it, the members of this group attacked the activism of the Court.[26] As David Hazony writes in the 'From the Editors' column:

Over the past few years, the pages of *Azure* have given voice to a broad critique of Israel's Supreme Court. Under the stewardship of President Aharon Barak, the court has strayed far beyond its proper bounds in a democracy, imposing its own worldview on the country's laws in the name of 'enlightenment,' and in so doing usurping the authority reserved for the elected representatives of the people.[27]

A second source of inspiration for the critique of the Supreme Court published in Azure was Zionist ideology. The writers attacked opinions they perceived as prejudicial to the country's Jewish character or constraining

---

[23] <http://www.idi.org.il/events1/Events_The_President's_Conference/2008/Pages/2008_main.aspx#p3 >.

[24] Tomer Zarhin and Or Kashti, 'How the State Systematically Disregards High Court of Justice Decisions' (March 5 2010) Haaretz; 'Enough with Deriding the High Court of Justice' (March 7 2010) Haaretz.

[25] See also: Tom R. Tyler, 'Promoting Employee Policy Adherence and Rule Following in Work Settings' (2005) 70 Brooklyn L Rev 1287, 1302 (arguing that studies have shown that 'people are more likely to comply with laws when they feel that legal authorities are legitimate and ought to be obeyed').

[26] Hillel Neuer, 'Aharon Barak's Revolution' (1998) 3 Azure; Evelyn Gordon, 'Is It Legitimate to Criticize the Supreme Court?' (1998) 3 Azure; Evelyn Gordon, 'How the Government's Attorney Became its General' (1998) 4 Azure; Evelyn Gordon, 'The Creeping Delegitimization of Peaceful Protest' (1999) 7 Azure; Evelyn Gordon, 'The Supreme Court in Loco Parentis' (2001) 10 Azure; Evelyn Gordon, 'Center Court' 13 (2002) Azure; Robert H. Bork, 'Barak's Rule' (2007) 27 Azure.

[27] David Hazony, 'What Do You Mean, "He's Innocent"?' (1988) 8 Azure 16.

the defense authorities. As David Hazony writes, again in his 'From the Editors' column:

[T]ime after time the gavel ends up falling the same way: Against the particular cultural traditions and unique needs of the Jewish state, and in favor of a universalist vision, built upon a conception of unbridled tolerance and equality.[28]

The ideas of these writers took shape in a legal document published in 2006— 'Constitution of the State of Israel Proposed by the Institute for Zionist Strategies.'[29] The proposal for the constitution includes a series of provisions meant to revoke changes that the Supreme Court had introduced in its jurisprudence in the last three decades, particularly in the context of the doctrine on standing, the justiciability doctrine, and the Court's power to annul Knesset legislation.

In 2007, Daniel Friedmann was appointed as Minister of Justice, and almost immediately launched various initiatives to reverse changes made in Israeli law by the Supreme Court in the past three decades, particularly with regard to the issue of justiciability. Interestingly, not a few of the changes instigated by Friedmann appear as items in the proposal for the constitution of the Institute for Zionist Strategies (see below).

B. RETHINKING THE COURT'S JUDICIAL ACTIVISM

Of the three changes that have taken place in the Court's jurisprudence, the one that has attracted the most scholarly, political and public discussion is the Court's activism. In what follows, I would like to make some observations on this issue that may, I think, shed some new light on it. My conclusion, indeed, is that some of the activist doctrines developed by the Supreme Court in the 1980s and 1990s need to be rethought.

Joint human action can follow one of two courses. It can take the path of the 'market,' which is based on impersonal exchange through contractual transactions, and involves parties interested in promoting what each construes as its own individual interests. Or it can appeal to 'culture,' relying on one group of people to internalize a shared system of values and goals and then act cooperatively, through division of labor, with the aim of realizing those values and goals.[30]

---

[28] David Hazony, 'The Year of Ruling Dangerously' (2001) 10 Azure 19.
[29] <http://www.izs.org.il/heb/default.asp?father_id=114&catid=169>.
[30] The line dividing these two types of action is not rigid. Whereas economists present the market as a site of impersonal exchange relations between self-regarding individuals, sociologists present market actors as involved in a rich tapestry/web of ongoing personal relations, and as acting in solidarity with each other, often against their immediate self-interest. Moreover, such presentations of the market lay great emphasis on the culture within which market actors operate. For the economic view of the market, see: Elizabeth Anderson, *Value In Ethics And Economics* (Cambridge, Harvard

The economic realm operates according to the logic of the market. A state's public administration, by contrast, operates according to the logic of culture. For a public administration to function successfully, its organizational culture must be fostered. This is where the Supreme Court comes into the picture as an administrative court. The principles of administrative law must serve as the 'skeleton' of the organizational culture of the country's public administration.

Since the foundation of the State of Israel, and particularly in recent decades, when the neo-liberal magic of the market has come to dominate Israeli consciousness, too little has been done to foster the organizational culture of Israeli public administration. A court that applies administrative law in an activist way may strengthen the legal skeleton of the organizational culture of the country's public administration, or at least prevent its corrosion.[31] In that sense, it can be said that a court that exhibits an activist spirit in the area of administrative law is engaging in an important pursuit.

However, some of the Court's activist doctrines are problematic.

(a) Standing

The first of these is the Court's almost limitless expansion of the doctrine on standing. Relying on this expansion, Knesset members have petitioned the Court hundreds of times since the late 1970s. A disproportionate number of these petitions were submitted by members of the Knesset identified with the liberal former hegemons (ie, members of the Meretz, Shinui and Labor parties). Moreover, petitions submitted by Knesset members identified with the LFH usually were not meant to protect those Knesset members from personal injury, but constituted part of their routine political activity. By contrast, petitions by Knesset members belonging to religious and rightwing parties usually were meant to protect these Knesset members from personal injury to them by the State's public administration and by the Knesset's administrative organs. (See Chapter 5, above.)

Moreover, petitions submitted by the political representatives of the LFH, usually dealing with burning political issues, have often enjoyed

---

University Press, 1993). For the sociological view of the market, see: Mark Granovetter, 'Economic Action and Social Structure: The Problem of Embeddedness' (1985) 91 Am J Soc 481; Neil Fligstein and Luke Dauter, 'The Sociology of Markets' 33 Ann Rev Soc (2007) 105; Pierre Bourdieu, *The Social Structures Of The Economy* (Chris Turner trans, Cambridge, Polity, 2005); Stewart Macaulay, 'Non-Contractual Relations in Business: A Preliminary Study' (1963) 28 Am Soc Rev 55; Ian Macneil, 'The Many Futures of Contract' (1974) 47 S Cal L Rev 691; Ian R. Macneil, *The New Social Contract: An Inquiry Into Modern Contractual Relations* (New Haven, Yale University Press, 1980).

[31] For an approach holding that legal rights must serve as the skeleton of richer interpersonal relations (such as marriage), see Jeremy Waldron, *Liberal Rights* (Cambridge, Cambridge University Press, 1993) chapter 15.

extensive media coverage (often initiated by the petitioning Knesset members themselves), particularly when the petitions have been accepted.[32] In the public mind this has created a clear overlap between the Court, on the one hand, and a defined group of Knesset members and the social group they represent (the LFH), on the other. References to the Court as 'the Jerusalem branch of Meretz' (the party most closely identified with the LFH group) have recurrently been made by religious and nationalist spokespersons.[33] All of this has had a devastating effect on the Court's public stature. Members of social groups not identified with the Court, such as the religious Zionists and the ultra-Orthodox, have become alienated from the Court and developed an intense hostility toward it. Clearly, the Court would do well to set limits to the standing of Knesset members: Knesset members not adducing grievances concerning personal injury should be prevented from submitting petitions to the Court, and their political activity limited to the traditional arenas for it (the Knesset, the media, and so forth).[34]

(b) Justiciability

A second problematic aspect of the Court's activism is the drastic expansion of the justiciability doctrine, and this on two counts.

First, there is the disruption to the division of authority between the various branches of government. Identifying a legal dimension in every political and administrative decision is certainly not difficult, particularly in a legal system that applies the criterion of 'reasonableness' as the main test for supervising the conduct of the state's public administration, and that is itself guided by a value-laden, as opposed to a formalistic, approach to the law. (Indeed, it is impossible to properly understand the Court's justiciability doctrine without thinking of it in tandem with the Court's open-ended, expansive reasonableness doctrine and the Court's non-formalistic approach.) It is therefore not really difficult to make a political or administrative decision justiciable. But when the Supreme Court is the branch deciding on a political or administrative question (usually by determining its 'reasonableness'), the outcome is that, of all the state's institutions, the Court is the one that has the 'last word' in the matter. Yet giving the Court the last word in *every* political or administrative decision is definitely inappropriate.

---

[32] Yoav Dotan and Menachem Hofnung, 'Legal Defeats-Political Wins—Why Elected Representatives Go to Courts?' (2005) 38 Comp Pol Stud 75.

[33] See eg Sophia Ron-Moriah, 'There is a Committee in Jerusalem' (June 12 2009) Makor Rishon (arguing that the Supreme Court is a stronghold of the Meretz party).

[34] According to Dotan and Hofnung, above n 32, under American law politicians are not allowed to petition the courts in matters having to do with their political activity.

A court is clearly most justified to intervene in an administrative decision when that decision violates a fundamental right of a citizen. The more fundamental the right, the more urgent the court's intervention, ie, the more justiciable the matter should be. The distinct mission of courts among all state branches is the protection of citizens' rights, in both the public and private spheres. But many political and administrative decisions do not involve the violation of a right, and their legal dimension is limited, so that their 'center of gravity' may lie in the area of expertise of another state authority, and considerations pertinent to such other authority should be given greatest weight. The doctrine of justiciability should be invoked in such instances by a court to prevent it from intervening when it shouldn't. That was the spirit of Justice Shamgar's remarks in the early 1980s, in the *Ressler* case,[35] when he opposed the then incipient trend to expand the Court's justiciability doctrine. But the restrictive approach of Justice Shamgar was defeated by the more expansive understanding of justiciability promoted by Justice Barak. Obviously, the Court would do well to reconsider its stance.[36]

For example, in HCJ 5973/92 *The Association for Civil Rights in Israel v Minister of Defense*,[37] the Court dealt with writs for the deportation to Lebanon of 415 residents of the OPT, members of the Hamas and the Islamic Jihad organizations. The writs were issued following the kidnapping and execution of an IDF soldier. The deportees had not been given the opportunity to voice their arguments prior to the execution of the deportation orders. This was in violation of one of the natural justice rules that are part of Israeli law, *audi alteram partem*, according to which a state authority cannot infringe upon an interest of an individual without first giving him or her the opportunity to voice his or her objection. Clearly, the government regarded the situation at the time as a state of emergency (the soldier had been kidnapped in the center of the country), and it was for this reason that it took these drastic measures. But the severe injury inflicted upon the deportees, who had been both deported and denied the right to be heard, rightly made the issue justiciable.[38]

---

[35] HCJ 910/86 *Ressler v Minister of Defense*, 42(2) PD 441. For a similar approach, see Justice Procaccia in HCJ 7712/05 *Polard v Government of Israel*.

[36] In the course of Professor Daniel Friedmann's term as Minister of Justice, the Ministry of Justice came out with a proposed bill on justiciability that was meant to adopt the 'center of gravity' test put forward by Justice Shamgar in *Ressler*. The proposed bill made non-justiciable, *inter alia*, decisions undertaken in the realms of foreign affairs and defense. See: Proposed Basic Law: Adjudication (Amendment—Justiciability) 2008.

[37] 47(1) PD 267.

[38] The seven-member panel of the Court unanimously rejected the petition. This is the only case in the history of the Court in which the names of the justices do not appear at the top of their opinion.

By contrast, in HCJ 3123/99 *Hilman v Minister of Internal Security* the Court dealt with a petition seeking to prevent Prime Minister Benjamin Netanyahu from deploying military forces in the 'Orient House' (the headquarters of the Palestinian Authority in East Jerusalem) and issued an interlocutory order against it. The petition did not point out the violation of any individual's right, but rather it stated in general terms that intervention by the government in the Orient House would cause severe damage to the 'public peace'. As no violation of any particular right was indicated, and since the 'center of gravity' of the matter was clearly the government's relations with the Palestinian Authority, the Court should have deemed the case non-justiciable.

Second, there are institutional considerations having to do with the Court itself that make the expansive justiciability doctrine problematic. The justiciability doctrine is highly important for preserving the institutional status of every Supreme Court. The Court is sometimes asked to rule on issues on which other institutions as well as public opinion hold particularly strong views (defense and foreign affairs are prominent examples). In such cases, the Court may find itself facing a dilemma. On the one hand, if it decides according to the legal imperatives, it may be forced into confrontation with powerful state institutions, as well as with public opinion, which may accuse it of applying the law in ways injurious to vital national interests. On the other hand, the Court may find itself powerless to protect what is demanded by the law, thereby damaging its own integrity as an institution and the integrity of the law as a normative system. The doctrine of justiciability gives the Court a way out in such situations: It enables the Court to decide not to decide, thus avoiding any such confrontation with powerful state institutions and with public opinion, avoiding injury to its own integrity and to the integrity of the law, as well.[39] Indeed, by expanding the justiciability doctrine since the 1980s to many national security issues, the Supreme Court has alienated and even agitated many in the religious-nationalist group and thus contributed to the decline of its standing. (One needs to bear in mind in this context that in recent decades the central posts in the IDF's fighting units have been evacuated by members of the LFH group and taken over by members of other groups, such as the religious-Zionist settlers.[40] The Court's extension of the jusiticiability doctrine to the defense sphere has therefore widened the rift between the Court and the nationalist religious-Zionist group.)

[39] cf Alexander M. Bickel, *The Least Dangerous Branch*, 2nd edn, (New Haven and London, Yale University Press, 1962, 1986) chapter 4 ('The Passive Virtues').

[40] Yagil Levy, *From 'People's Army' To 'Army Of The Peripheries'* (Jerusalem, Carmel, 2007) (Hebrew).

(c) Reasonableness

A third problematic of the Court's activism is its reliance on the reasonableness test as the main tool in its review of the public administration. In some cases, in this context the Court has applied what I have called 'professional reasonableness,' that is, it has resorted to examining administrative decisions on their merits, rather than according to legal criteria. This type of activism is indefensible.

(d) Judicial review of Knesset legislation

The most problematic aspect of the Court's activism, however, is its most activist move so far: Assuming authority, in the *United Mizrahi Bank*[41] decision, for the annulment of Knesset laws.

The decision authorizing the Court to annul Knesset laws took the Court's judicial review into an area where it is seldom needed. In Israel, the violation of citizens' basic rights has come mainly not from Knesset legislation but from the actions of the public administration. (The Knesset can indeed point to an impressive record of legislation in the 1950s, which granted a series of significant social rights to the country's citizens.) Instances of injury to basic rights are hardly to be found in the Knesset legislation through six decades of statehood and, to the extent that such cases do exist, they have been aimed against the country's Arab citizens (confiscation of Arab land for the purpose of Jewish settlement is a prime example). We can safely assume, however, that should such laws be enacted, the Court will not have the power to confront the Knesset (and the public opinion supporting such Knesset laws) to rescue Arab citizens from the laws' potential damage. The decision granting the Court power to annul Knesset laws is, therefore, to a large extent either unnecessary or irrelevant.

One important implication of the Supreme Court's having assumed the authority to annul Knesset laws could be an increasing shift of the Court toward *conservatism*, in terms of the protection it is able to afford to citizens' rights from violation by the state's public administration. From the establishment of Israel until the 1990s, the Court developed an impressive array of doctrines to protect basic constitutional rights. Despite the lack of a written constitution, and without granting itself the power to annul Knesset laws, the Court accomplished this by adjudicating petitions submitted against decisions of the *public administration*. Israel's constitutional law was largely developed by riding 'piggyback' on administrative law: When discussing petitions directed against the state administration, the

---

[41] CA 6821/93 *United Mizrahi Bank Ltd. v Migdal*, 49(4) PD 221.

Court delineated the lines dividing governmental action taken to promote the state's collective good, on the one hand, and the citizens' protected rights, on the other, and developed a rich constitutional jurisprudence of protected rights. The Court succeeded in this important endeavor because what it was asked to revoke, and often did, was not Knesset legislation, but rather decisions of the state's public administration.

The balance of power between the Supreme Court and the other branches of state changes entirely when the Court is asked to revoke not an administrative decision, but a law enacted by the country's legislature. No constitutional court is allowed to cancel too many decisions of the legislature; such annulments can only be acceptable in rare and exceptional cases. Contesting the decision of an administrative body is one thing, but contesting a law enacted by the country's legislative body is something else altogether.

Bringing judicial review to bear not only on administrative decisions, but on Knesset legislation as well, then, necessarily leads to the development of a restrictive jurisprudence in the area of protected constitutional rights. A Court that is asked to annul a Knesset law will be able to do so in far less cases and far less easily than a Court asked to revoke an administrative decision. Furthermore, a Court that is asked to annul Knesset legislation will become conservative not only at the level of the result. Since it will be required to support its restrictive decisions, it will also become conservative at the level of the reasoning adduced to justify its rulings. Consequently, such a Court will be bound to formulate a conservative legal doctrine.

The Court's decision on the issue of family unification may serve as an example.[42] In that case, a petition was submitted to annul a Knesset law that had resulted in the denial of Israeli Arabs' requests for 'family unification' in Israel if they had married a resident of the Occupied Palestinian Territories. The Court *rejected* the petition to annul the law. Had a petition been submitted against the Minister of Defense or the Minister of the Interior in order to enable family unification in a particular instance, the contrary result might have obtained (or at least it would have been far easier for the Court to come up with a contrary result) and the Court have protected the rights of the Arab citizen. The Court would have also been able to develop liberal reasoning to support the ruling it had issued. Moreover, in such a case, a precedent would also have been established, making it possible to resolve the problems of people whose circumstances resembled those of the petitioners. To the group of potential petitioners, then, the end

---

[42] HCJ 7052/03 *Adala, The Arab Minority's Legal Rights Center v Minister of Interior*.

result would have been more favorable than what was attained by filing a petition seeking to annul the Knesset law regulating this issue.

In the wake of the decision in the family unification case, Haaretz published an editorial entitled 'Badge of Shame for the Supreme Court.'[43] It stated that 'the ruling had been issued by the Supreme Court at one of its shameful moments.' Note the exceptional acerbity of the title and contents. Haaretz is the newspaper most closely identified with the liberal, secular group in Israel (the LFH) and with the Court's liberal values. During the 1980s and 1990s, the positions of the Supreme Court were remarkably akin to those expressed by the newspaper, particularly in its editorials. The editorial published after the ruling on family unification, then, supports the argument that lifting the Court's level of judicial review from the public administration to the Knesset will only make the Court more conservative, and undermine support for it among its traditional backers in Israeli society.

Moreover, following the decision in the family unification case various proposals have been made to strip the Supreme Court of the power to deal with citizenship issues, as well as proposals to the effect that the Court should be denied the power to rule that provisions of the Citizenship Law contradict the Basic Law: Human Dignity and Liberty. Interestingly enough, under the threat of one such legislative proposal, Haaretz published an editorial in which it stated that

requests for immigration, marriage and family unification need to be taken care of on a case-to-case basis and not in any sweeping manner.[44]

Thus, the newspaper recognized the shortcomings of action for the protection of human rights at the legislative level, given the existing constellation of power in the Knesset, and the advantage of doing so by tackling administrative decisions relating to specific cases.

The decision in the *United Mizrahi Bank* case, holding that the Supreme Court has the authority to annul Knesset laws, has had further negative consequences. Following that decision, proposals were put forward for the establishment of a constitutional court (most of whose judges would *not* be jurists, but public figures, and only a minority of them justices of the Supreme Court),[45] as well as proposals for increasing the number of politicians sitting on the judges appointment committee, so that the Supreme Court would lose its hold over the committee. If indeed the Supreme Court

---

[43] 'Badge of Shame for the Supreme Court' (May 15 2006) Haaretz.
[44] 'Racism in Constitutional Camouflage' (December 20 2009) Haaretz.
[45] Menachem Mautner, 'Appointment of Judges to the Supreme Court in a Multicultural Society' (2003) 19 Legal Research 423 (Hebrew).

has the power to annul Knesset laws, goes the argument, then the political element—in both the judicial review of the constitutionality of Knesset legislation and the appointment process of justices to the Court—should be strengthened. (This development may also be understood through Pierre Bourdieu's concept of the field: The Court's activist entry into the political field led to a counter-reaction suggesting the entry of political actors into the legal field.[46]) Should the proposal to establish a constitutional court be implemented, it will impair the Court's ability to protect the basic rights of the citizens. Furthermore, and no less significant, the very existence of the two aforementioned proposals (which, needless to say, entail taking powers away from the Supreme Court) constitutes a threat to the Court, and as an inevitable outcome the Court's ability to act through the annulment of Knesset laws will be diminished, forcing it to come up with conservative rulings and develop a conservative legal doctrine to support decisions in which it refrains from annulling legislation. From this perspective as well, then, the conservative implications of the *United Mizrahi Bank* ruling are unequivocal.[47]

And finally, it should be borne in mind that Israel does *not* have a written constitution.

A short while after the enactment of the two Basic Laws of 1992 (Basic Law: Human Dignity and Liberty and Basic Law: Freedom of Occupation) Aharon Barak declared that Israel had gone through 'a constitutional revolution': To Israeli law a constitutional layer had been added, on the basis of which the Supreme Court would henceforth review the legislation of the Knesset and the decisions of the state's public administration.[48] Barak subsequently reiterated this theme, saying: 'We presently have a constitution. Our extant current constitution is the basic laws.'[49] Barak

---

[46] Pierre Bourdieu, in Randal Johnson (ed), *The Field Of Cultural Production* (New York, Columbia University Press, 1993); Pierre Bourdieu, 'The Force of Law: Toward a Sociology of the Juridical Field' (1987) 38 Hastings L J 805.

[47] In the course of Professor Daniel Friedmann's term as Minister of Justice, the Ministry of Justice came out with a proposed bill to the effect that the Knesset, by a simple majority, would have the power to reenact a law annulled by the Supreme Court. Were the Knesset to make use of this power, the Court would have the power to annul the law again five years after its reenactment by the Knesset. See: Proposed Basic Law: Adjudication (Amendment—Judicial Review). An additional proposal that constituted a threat to the Court was the proposal to rewrite the Basic Law: Human Dignity and Liberty to the effect that Israel would not be defined as a 'Jewish and democratic state', but rather as a 'Jewish state with a democratic regime.' This proposal is meant to create a hierarchy between Israel's Jewishness and its democracy by according superiority to the former over the latter. See: Tzameret Parnet, 'An Initiative in the Knesset to Redefine the State' (December 8 2009) Calcalist.

[48] Aharon Barak, 'The Constitutional Revolution: Protected Basic Rights' (1992) 1 Mishpat Umimshal 9 (Hebrew).

[49] Aharon Barak, 'Israel's Constitution: Past, Present and Future' in *Selected Papers* (Jerusalem, Nevo, 2000) 355, 368; Aharon Barak, 'The Constitutional Revolution—12th Anniversary' (1994) 1 Law And Business 3.

admitted, however, that 'the public at large has not yet internalized the normative reality that we already have, now, at present, a constitution.'[50] But the advent of the 'constitutional revolution' discourse gives rise to two trenchant criticisms of the Court.

The first relates to the *procedure* whereby the two Basic Laws of 1992 were enacted. It has been argued that when the Knesset enacted these two Basic Laws, nobody meant to introduce a constitution into Israeli law: the Knesset debate accompanying their enactment contained no language that might indicate any such intention on the part of the Knesset, nor was there any public or professional debate that might indicate an understanding on the part of the public at large and the legal community that such a dramatic change in the country's law was meant to be effected. (For instance, it has been claimed that the passing of the two Basic Laws was barely mentioned in the press the next day). The rhetoric of 'a constitutional revolution', so goes the argument, is simply a ruse to provide the Court and its supporters with powers vis-à-vis the Knesset and the government that the Knesset never intended to grant.[51]

The second criticism is *substantive*. The two Basic Laws of 1992 are thin statutes that refer to only a few (and not necessarily the most important) of the basic constitutional rights that citizens in a liberal democracy enjoy. The rights mentioned in the Basic Law: Human Dignity and Liberty are the rights to life, bodily integrity and dignity, the right to property, the right to personal liberty, the right to exit from and entry into the country, and the right to privacy and personal confidentiality. Important liberal rights such as the right to equality, freedom of speech, freedom of religion and freedom from religion are not mentioned. The Basic Law: Freedom of Occupation protects only one right, namely the right to freedom of occupation. Likewise, all the other ten Basic Laws enacted by the Knesset since 1958 provide the state's citizens with hardly any constitutional rights at all, and they do not deal with fundamental constitutional questions, such as the state's official languages and the status of the Arab minority. Rather, these basic laws deal mainly with the institutional design of the various

---

[50] Barak, *The Constitutional Revolution*, id, at 23.

[51] See eg Moshe Landau, 'Reflections on the Constitutional Revolution' (1996) 26 Mishpatim 419, 420 ('the constitutional revolution came upon us inadvertently and accidentally') (Hebrew); Moshe Landau, 'Three Years After Bank Hamizrahi Decision' (2000) 10 Hamishpat 249, 254 ('this is the only constitution in the world that has been created by the mouth of a court') (Hebrew); Gideon Sapir, 'Between Liberalism and Multiculturalism' (2010) 26 Legal Research 311, 322 ('I am not familiar with any other state where there is a controversy regarding the question whether a constitution exists') (Hebrew). See also: Eli Salzberger, 'Judicial Activism in Israel' in Brice Dickson (ed), *Judicial Activism In Common Law Supreme Courts* (Oxford, Oxford University Press, 2007) 217, 232–33 ('Aharon Barak, already a veteran Supreme Court Justice at the time, was an active partner in these efforts [leading to the enactment of the two basic laws of 1992]. He appeared several times in front of the Knesset's Committee for Constitution, Law and Legal Affairs.').

state branches and their powers. If Israel wishes to have a constitution, no 'shortcuts' are available: Israelis will have to tackle all the fundamental questions that currently divide them, and in a long and painstaking process hammer out a document that embodies the compromises necessary for them to unite behind one shared credo.[52] Until that happens, if ever, the advent of the constitutional revolution discourse cannot but be interpreted as just one more measure initiated by an activist Court and the declining social group identified with it (the LFH) so as to preserve one of their last strongholds in the ongoing struggle over the shaping of Israel's culture.

---

[52] Ruth Gavison and Alan Shapira, 'Introduction' in *The Federalist* (Aharon Amir trans, Jerusalem, Shalem Center, 2001) 11 (Hebrew).

CHAPTER 7

ISRAEL AS A MULTICULTURAL STATE

The cultural struggle that is currently taking place in Israel between secular and religious Jews is the contemporary manifestation of a conflict which has riven the Jewish people throughout the modern era, the previous round of which took place in the last two decades of the nineteenth century—Zionism's formative years. In the period of the labor hegemony, the struggle appeared to have been decided in favor of the secular group, but with the decline of the hegemony it became apparent that this was an illusion. Moreover, since the establishment of the State of Israel the cultural schism in Israel has been exacerbated because about a fifth of Israel's population is composed of Arabs. Thus, Israeli society is divided by two cultural schisms: One internal to the Jewish group, the other between the Jewish and Arab groups.

The transition to a post-hegemonic situation in the latter half of the 1970s calls for fresh thinking as to the basic arrangements for Israel's governance and as to the interrelations of the major cultural groups that compose Israel's society. This kind of thinking should not be conducted in the abstract. Rather, it should draw on as intimate an understanding as possible of Israel's unique conditions and of the traits of the different groups that are contending over the shaping of the country's regime, political culture and law. In this chapter, I wish to point out some of the distinctive aspects of Israel's multicultural condition. In the next chapter I shall offer some basic principles for a political theory suited to a post-hegemonic, multicultural Israel.

A. ISRAEL'S MULTICULTURAL CONDITION

(a) *A new conceptualization of the Israeli situation*

Since the 1990s, Israeli scholars have been conceptualizing Israel's post-hegemonic situation as one of multiculturalism.[1]

---

[1] Eliezer Ben-Rafael and Nissim Leon argue that the rise of the Shas movement in the mid-1980s, see chapter 5 above, signaled the turning point after which the multicultural character of

Sociologist Baruch Kimmerling writes that following the decline of the labor hegemony Israel became 'a multicultural state'[2]; 'a state in which profound cultural differences exist'[3]; a state composed of 'several societies and cultures that are almost autonomous and separate from each other'.[4] Kimmerling adds that the boundaries dividing these groups 'are sharp and almost impassable, and the differences are greater than what is shared in common.' Moreover, 'each such culture has got its own distinct conceptions as to the country's "rules of the game" and as to what would be an appropriate distribution of resources in the country.' Therefore, 'it is at present impossible to discuss "Israeli society" as one society,' writes Kimmerling. Rather, 'the Israeli state serves as a shared framework for cultures and countercultures enjoying varying levels of autonomy and operating their own separate institutions.' Since 20 percent of Israel's citizens are Arabs, notes Kimmerling as well, 'Israel is not only a multicultural state, but demographically also a de facto bi-national state.'[5]

Historian Shlomo Ben-Ami portrays Israeli society as 'a multiethnic and multicultural society'[6]; a society that has ceased to have 'a collective ethos shared by all its members'; a society in which there is no longer any 'agreement over the basic rules of the game'[7]; a society 'broken into several cultures, dialects, and in particular into several adversarial positions as to the desirable image of the state'; and a society divided by profound disagreements 'on issues of culture, society, religion and identity.'[8]

Sociologist Gadi Yatziv describes Israeli society as a multicultural society broken up into various 'sectors', ie, communities whose members share a distinct historical memory and a distinct vision as to the political, ideological and cultural future of the state.[9]

Israeli society became widely acknowledged. Eliezer Ben-Rafael and Nissim Leon, 'Communal Segregation, Religiosity and Politics: The Origins of the Haredi Movement Amongst the Mizrachim', in Uri Cohen et al (eds), *Israel And Modernity* (Beer Sheva, Ben Gurion University of the Negev, 2006) 285, 309 (Hebrew).

[2] Baruch Kimmerling, *Immigrants, Settlers, Natives—The Israeli State And Society Between Cultural Pluralism And Cultural Wars* (Tel Aviv, Am Oved Publishers, 2004) 166 (Hebrew).

[3] Baruch Kimmerling, *The End Of Ashkenazi Hegemony* (Jerusalem, Keter Publishing House, 2001) 72 (Hebrew).

[4] Baruch Kimmerling, 'The New Israelis—Multiple Cultures Without Multiculturalism' (1998) 16 Alpaim 264, 264 (Hebrew).

[5] Kimmerling, above n 2, at 13, 21, 496, 498.

[6] Shlomo Ben-Ami, 'Israeli Identity as Immigrant Identity' in Neri Horowitz (ed), *Religion And Nationalism In Israel And The Middle East* (Tel Aviv, Am Oved Publishers, 2002) 225, 227–8 (Hebrew).

[7] Shlomo Ben-Ami, 'Introduction; Israel as a Multicultural Society' in Yoav Peled and Adi Ophir (eds), *Israel: From Mobilized To Civil Society?* (Tel Aviv, Hakibbutz Hameuchad Publishing House, 2001) 18, 20 (Hebrew).

[8] Ben-Ami, above n 6, at 230.

[9] Gadi Yatziv, *The Sectorial Society* (Jerusalem, Bialik Institute, 1999) 11–2, 164 (Hebrew).

Social Scientist Elazar Leshem writes that in recent years :

Israel has crystallized as a multi-communal, sectarian society in which loyalty to the various peripheral communities competes with loyalty to the shared sovereign center.

The various sectors differ from each other not only in culture, writes Leshem, but in language as well; they are concentrated in distinct geographical locations; they have defined class identities; they maintain distinct political machineries that make sectarian claims on behalf of the sectors they represent.[10]

In a book entitled 'Multiculturalism in a Democratic and Jewish State', Menachem Mautner, Avi Sagi and Ronen Shamir write that following the decline of the labor hegemony, Israeli society broke up into different cultural groups, each with its own basic beliefs, myths and ethos, as well as its distinct cultural practices. The processes whereby these groups constitute their self-identity often involve negation of the profound convictions of other groups, write the authors. Moreover, in some cases the different groups have their distinct political parties, so that they are constantly competing with each other over the control of the political, cultural, economic, and media institutions of the state.[11]

Historian Anita Shapira writes that in recent years Israel has turned into a society that lacks 'a single focus of identity'; a society 'that no longer recognizes a single ethos accepted by all'; a society 'whose political, social and cultural schisms are so profound it finds it impossible to create one, agreed upon ideal image and normative world that is acceptable to everybody.'[12]

Sociologist Eva Etzioni-Halevy discusses the schism between secular and religious Jews in a book entitled *The Divided People*.[13]

Sociologist S.N. Eisenstadt admits there are centrifugal processes at work in Israel's society and culture, but points out some opposite developments: 'Even a superficial observation of various cities in the country would identify ongoing encounters between people belonging to different sectors,' writes Eisenstadt.

They meet in streets, in small and big stores, in entertainment sites, and somehow they learn to live with each other, to accept each other, albeit not necessarily to agree with each other's way.

---

[10] Elazar Leshem, 'Israel as a Multicultural State at the Turn of the Twenty-First Century' in Elazar Leshem and Dorit Roer-Strier (eds), *Cultural Diversity—A Challenge To Human Services* (Jerusalem, Magnes Press, Hebrew University, 2003) 13, 14, 92 (Hebrew).

[11] Menachem Mautner, Avi Sagi and Ronen Shamir, 'Thoughts on Multiculturalism in Israel' in Menachem Mautner, Avi Sagi and Ronen Shamir (eds), *Multiculturalism In A Democratic And Jewish State* (Tel Aviv, Ramot Publishing House, 1998) 67, 67–8 (Hebrew).

[12] Anita Shapira, 'Introduction' in *New Jews, Old Jews* (Tel Aviv, Am Oved Publishers, 1997) 9, 15.

[13] Eva Etzioni-Halevy, *The Divided People* (Kfar Sava, Arye Nir Publishing House, 2000) (Hebrew).

Eisenstadt discerns similar trends in the country's intellectual and pubic discourses, particularly in the joint efforts to constitute a shared Jewish identity in the country.[14]

(b) War of cultures

Moreover, while the various cultural groups that compose Israeli society cultivate their different visions regarding the overall cultural identity of the country, many scholars present Israel as a country in which a 'war of cultures' is being waged. Consequently, the term *kulturkampf*, which was in use in the decades following the rise of the Jewish Enlightenment in the latter half of the eighteenth century (Chapter 1, above), resurfaced in Israel's academic and public discourses in the closing decades of the twentieth century.

Kimmerling, for instance, writes that:

> the Israeli state is currently in the midst of a multidimensional war of cultures that may have many manifestations, including varying degrees of civil war in which force and violence may be employed.[15]

Shlomo Ben-Ami writes about 'the war of cultures that is currently taking place in Israel'[16] and says that the schisms that exist in Israel 'seriously hold the potential for an eruption of violence.'[17]

Political scientists Asher Cohen and Bernard Susser write that:

> [f]rom a struggle over specific and, hence, resolvable religion-state issues, Israel at the turn of the millennium appears to be moving toward a principled and first-order struggle over the very nature of the Jewish state.

At its heart, write Cohen and Susser, the struggle revolves around the question

> [w]hat kind of a political community Israel will be—one whose central loyalty is to the Jewish nation, to its separate, enclave integrality, its halakhic and religious traditions, or one whose Jewish national character is mediated through the prism of modern, Western, and democratic values? These are, by their nature, ultimate and nonnegotiable (or at least irresolvable) issues,

conclude Cohen and Susser, 'a fortiori, when the contending sides perceive compromise as both irrelevant and insufferable.'[18]

Poet Hava Pinhas-Cohen writes that 'an internal cultural war is currently taking place in Israeli society between great spiritual forces over

---

[14] S.N. Eisenstadt, *Changes In Israeli Society* (Tel Aviv, Ministry of Defense, 2004) 91–2 (Hebrew).
[15] Kimmerling, above n 3, at 14, 15; Kimmerling, above n 1, at 499. See also: Id at 354, 503, 505 n 8.
[16] Ben-Ami, above n 6, at 225, 228.   [17] Ben-Ami, above n 7, at 20.
[18] Asher Cohen and Bernard Susser, *Israel And The Politics Of Jewish Identity* (Baltimore, Johns Hopkins University Press, 2005) 65.

Israel's identity in the twenty-first century.'[19] Sociologist Uri Ram describes Israel as a country in which 'a struggle over the shaping of the new regime is taking place, with a tendency to spill over into civil war.'[20]

(c) On the verge of civil war

Indeed, twice in the first decade of the twenty-first century Israel has found itself on the verge of civil war.

(i) The disengagement

In 1993, Israel signed the 'Oslo Accords' with the PLO and began taking measures to evacuate areas and military installations in Judea and Samaria (the West Bank). Subsequently, certain rabbis, mostly residents of Judea and Samaria, including senior figures such as Rabbi Shlomo Goren, formerly the IDF's Chief Military Rabbi and Chief Rabbi of Israel, began calling upon their followers serving in the military to disobey the IDF's commands and not cooperate in carrying out the government's policy.[21] These calls were justified by the rabbis based on their interpretation of the Halakhah as prohibiting any cession of lands within the bounds of Eretz Israel to non-Jews. It was not a *political* disagreement that the rabbis had with the government. Rather, they objected to the government's measures because they found them to be contrary to the dictates of the Halakhah, the alternative normative system by which the rabbis abide and which they deem superior to the law of the state. Their calling on their followers to disobey the government and the IDF therefore strikingly illustrates the cultural divide and polarization in Israel between the Jewish religious group, some of whose members regard themselves as subject first and foremost to the Halakhah, and the Jewish secular group, whose members see themselves as subject to the laws of a state that are premised on liberal-democratic Western values.

Such calls by rabbis upon their followers to disobey the government proliferated in 2004 after the government adopted the 'disengagement plan', which meant the evacuation of all twenty Israeli settlements in the Gaza Strip and four settlements in northern Samaria (the decision was approved

---

[19] Hava Pinhas-Cohen, 'From The Editor' (Autumn, 1996) 10 Dimuye (Hebrew).
[20] Uri Ram, *The Globalization Of Israel* (Tel Aviv, Resling, 2005) 7 (Hebrew). See also: Eisenstadt, above n 14, at chapter 11; Yoram Peri, *Brothers At War: Rabin's Assassination And The Cultural War In Israel* (Tel Aviv, Babel Publishers, 2005) (Hebrew).
[21] For a review, see: Menachem Mautner, *Law And Culture In Israel At The Threshold Of The Twenty-First Century* (Tel Aviv, Am Oved Publishers, 2008) 278–82 (Hebrew). See also: Eliezer Don Yehiya, 'The Book and the Sword: Nationalist 'Yeshivas' and Political Radicalism in Israel' in Avi Sagi and Dov Schwartz (eds), *A Hundred Years Of Religious Zionism* (Ramat Gan, Bar Ilan University Press, 2003) vol 3, 187 (Hebrew); Yagil Levy, *From 'People's Army' To 'Army Of The Peripheries'* (Jerusalem, Carmel, 2007) chapter 6 (Hebrew).

by both the Knesset and the Supreme Court). On dozens of occasions, rabbis, some of them senior rabbis, issued rulings to the effect that taking part in the execution of the plan was forbidden under the Torah's prohibition (as interpreted by the rabbis) to cede parts of Eretz Israel to non-Jews.[22] On one occasion, a group of rabbis headed by Rabbi Abraham Shapira, formerly Chief Rabbi of Israel, called upon their followers to defect from military service in order to obstruct the government's plan.[23]

In July 2005, a month before the disengagement was to begin, tens of thousands of opponents of the plan gathered in *Kfar Meimon*, on the border of the Gaza Strip, intent on joining the Gaza settlers and helping them resist the evacuation. About 20,000 policemen and soldiers surrounded them. For several tense hours, it seemed as if the besieged crowd would break into the Gaza Strip and clash with the policemen and soldiers. Eventually, responsibility and sobriety prevailed, the gathered protestors retreated without any violence, and the confrontation died out peacefully.

(ii) The October 2000 events

Israel had reached the verge of civil war a first time even earlier, between the 1st and 8th of October 2000. After Ariel Sharon's ascent to the Temple Mount, a wave of riots broke out in Judea, Samaria and the Gaza Strip. In parallel, Israeli Arabs, particularly those residing in the northern sector of the country, mounted a series of violent demonstrations. In clashes between the rioters and the police, 12 Arab citizens of Israel and one resident of Gaza were killed. Many Israeli Arabs were injured. One Jewish citizen was also killed when his car was struck by a stone thrown from a nearby Arab village. In retaliation, Israeli Jews in many parts of the country took to harassing Arabs, desecrating their holy sites, and damaging their property.[24]

(d) *Republicanism in crisis*

The republican ideal envisages the citizens of a state as participating equally in a free, deliberative political process for the determination of their common good. Republicanism aims therefore at eliminating citizens' subordination to particularistic interests (Chapter 8, below).

For many years, under the umbrella of the labor-led hegemony, there was a strong republican tradition in the *Yishuv* and in the State of Israel.

---

[22] For a review, see: Mautner, id.
[23] Nadav Shragai, 'The Attorney General will Check Rabbis' Calls to Defect from the IDF' (April 1 2005) Haaretz.
[24] 'Official Committee Of Inquiry In The Matter Of The Clashes Between Security Forces And Israeli Citizens In October 2000' (Jerusalem, 2003) ('The Or Committee') (Hebrew).

There was a widespread belief in a common good for all Jews living in the country, to which all individuals were supposed to contribute—the establishment of a state and execution of its collective projects in the spheres of defense, development, settlement and the absorption of immigration.[25] Needless to say, this republican understanding of the common good excluded the state's Arab citizens.[26]

The republican element in Israel's political culture has substantially dwindled in the post-hegemonic era: With the renewal of the struggle over the future shape of the country's regime, political culture and law, the Israelis, both Jews and Arabs, have failed to cultivate a shared perception of the common good. In fact, one could say that Israel at the beginning of the twenty-first century is experiencing a 'crisis of republicanism'. This crisis has several hallmarks:

First, Israel is among the few countries in the world that do not have a written constitution. The Declaration of Independence of 1948 anticipated the adoption of a constitution by the new state. By 1950, however, it became evident that that was not to be the case.[27] In recent years, three attempts have been made to advance the adoption of a constitution.[28] They all failed. The chances that a constitution will be adopted in the coming years are slim. A written constitution, though, is a prime republican institution that consolidates a state's citizens around a shared normative credo. The fact that Israel lacks a written constitution means that it cannot enjoy the republican benefits of this institution.

Jurgen Habermas writes that in the multicultural, post-nation-state era constitutional patriotism, namely loyalty to the country's political culture, should replace the former loyalty to the national group as the focus of

---

[25] Avi Bareli, *Mapai In Israel's Early Independence 1948-1953* (Jerusalem, Yad Ben Zvi, 2007) chapters 8, 9 (Hebrew); Nir Kedar, *Mamlakhtiyut—David Ben-Gurion's Civic Thought* (Jerusalem, Yad Ben Zvi, 2009) (Hebrew).

[26] On this aspect of traditional Israeli republicanism, see: Yoav Peled, 'Ethnic Democracy and the Legal Construction of Citizenship: Arab Citizens of the Jewish State' (1992) 86 Am Pol Sci Rev 432; Yoav Peled And Gershon Shafir, *Being Israeli—The Dynamics Of Multiple Citizenship* (Cambridge, Cambridge University Press, 2002).

[27] Several reasons are often listed in the literature for this failure: The reluctance of David Ben-Gurion, the founder and first prime minister of Israel, to transfer power from the executive to the judicial branch; Ben-Gurion's aversion to a constitutional court following the confrontation between President Roosevelt and the United States Supreme Court in the early years of the New Deal; Ben-Gurion's admiration of the British legal system which functions without a written constitution; the disagreement between the secular and religious Jewish groups over the nature of the country's culture; and the force of the argument that it would not be appropriate for an immigration country such as Israel to constitutionally bind itself at that early stage (Kedar, above n 25, at 154–9).

[28] The Proposed Constitution of the Knesset's Committee of Constitution, Law and Legal Affairs; The Israel Democracy Institute's Proposal for a Constitution by Consensus; The Proposed Constitution of the Institute for Zionist Strategies.

citizens' common identification.²⁹ Israel suffers from the centrifugal drawbacks of its multicultural condition, without the offsetting benefits of a standing constitution.

Second, unlike dozens of other countries in the world, Israel does not have a constitutional court. Rather, the Supreme Court serves as the country's constitutional court (Chapter 2). The Jewish religious group (both the religious-Zionist and the ultra-Orthodox subgroups), however, widely perceive the Court as a partisan institution that serves as a cultural and political agent of the liberal former hegemons and therefore fails to appropriately express the religious groups' worldview. The fact that Israel does not have a written constitution does not mean, of course, that it does not have a constitutional law. But if Israel had a constitutional court, that would enable all major cultural groups to join forces in developing a shared body of constitutional law.³⁰

Third, Israel's cultural divides are reflected in the country's highly fragmented educational system. There are five different educational streams: statist-secular, religious-Zionist, Ashkenazi ultra-Orthodox, Sephardic ultra-Orthodox, and Arab. Moreover, there are very few culturally mixed schools, and the state does not insist on all children's studying a common core curriculum aimed at preparing them to cooperate with each other as adults in the same political and economic systems. In addition, the state does not insist that children learn about the cultural heritage of other groups, or that children meet with children belonging to other cultural groups.

Fourth, in every country the army, controlled by the state's central political authorities, is the most republican, ie, nonpartisan and nonparticularistic, institution. Indeed, with the establishment of Israel, David Ben-Gurion took some bold measures to integrate the various pre-state paramilitary organizations into the newly established IDF.³¹ In recent decades, however, the cultural division between secular and religious Jews is reflected in the functioning of the IDF: More and more religious military

---

²⁹ Jurgen Habermas, 'Citizenship and National identity: Some Reflections on the Future of Europe' (1992) 12 Praxis Int'l 17. See also: Jurgen Habermas, 'Pre-Political Foundations of the Democratic Constitutional State?' in Florian Schuller (ed), *Dialectics Of Secularization* (San Francisco, Ignatius Press, 2005) 19, 33; Jan-Werner Muller, *Constitutional Patriotism* (Princeton, Princeton University Press, 2007). Charles Taylor objects to the constitutional patriotism project. See: Charles Taylor, 'The Dynamics of Democratic Exclusion' (1998) 9 J Democracy 143; Charles Taylor, 'Cross-Purposes: The Liberal-Communitarian Debate' in *Philosophical Arguments* (Cambridge, Harvard University Press, 1995) 181.

³⁰ cf Ran Hirschl, 'The Theocratic Challenge to Constitution Drafting in Post-Conflict States' (2008) 49 Wm & Mary L Rev 1179, 1200 ('A common strategy for addressing some of the difficulties presented in the ongoing friction between traditional religious outlooks and principles of modern constitutionalism is the construction of constitutional courts armed with judicial review powers.').

³¹ Kedar, above n 25, at 121.

men serve in separate, culturally homogeneous units. Moreover, the army allows ongoing involvement by these military men's rabbis in the lives of their disciples in the course of their service, and the latter in turn view themselves as practically under the authority of both their military commanders and their rabbis.[32] As if that were not enough, in recent years the Chief Military Rabbi has overtly challenged the authority of the Chief Education Officer as the supreme authority regarding education and indoctrination in the IDF. In many cases, the messages propagated by these two IDF institutions have conflicted. In addition, the mandatory draft is only partially applied: all Arab women, most Arab men, all ultra-Orthodox women, most ultra-Orthodox men, and many religious-Zionist women are exempt from military service on national and cultural grounds. As a result, only about 50 percent of Israel's eighteen-year-olds are actually enlisted each year.

Fifth, about a fifth of Israel's population lives in development towns in the southern and northern sections of the country. The majority of these people are Jews who immigrated in the 1950s from Arab countries and their descendants. However, the integration of this population into the mainstream of Israeli society has thus far been only partially successful: By all socioeconomic indicia, people living in the development towns are significantly inferior to the mainstream of Israel's society (composed mainly of Ashkenazi Jews living in the center of the country).

Sixth, about a fifth of Israel's population consists of Arabs. As I shall show below, the Arab citizens largely form a separate civil society and their ratings are significantly inferior to those of the Jewish group by all socioeconomic indicia.

Seventh, since the 1980s Israel has become one of the most inegalitarian countries in the West. The republican ideal entails narrow gaps in the incomes of citizens, the idea being that a wide disparity of income breeds disparity in the lifestyles and life-experiences of citizens, which, in turn, undermines their ability to develop a shared conception of the common good.

Eighth, in recent years the religious-Zionist group has made an effort to establish a network of arbitration tribunals, with the intention that these tribunals, adjudicating in accordance with the Halakhah, should compete with the state courts in resolving private law disputes. In addition to the establishment of this network, the state's rabbinical courts have been conducting a campaign to position themselves as possessing jurisdiction not only over family matters, but also in the provision of arbitration services

---

[32] Levy, above n 21, at 86–8, 262–5.

in private law matters.³³ (Thus, even private law has become a site for waging the war of cultures!) If these initiatives succeed, there will be two or three competing systems for the resolution of private law disputes in the country.³⁴

B. THE UNIQUE TRAITS OF ISRAEL'S MULTICULTURALISM

The concept of multiculturalism has been applied in the context of many Western countries, such as Canada, Australia, Britain, Germany, France and the United States. (Although over the past four decades a vast literature has grown on the topic in all disciplines of the social sciences and the humanities, as well as in the law, there is still no single, clear-cut, agreed-upon meaning of the term.³⁵) But looked at from the perspective of Western countries, Israel's multicultural condition is unique. Usually, at least in Western countries, cultural diversity raises problems that have to do with the relationship between the liberal center of the state (the state's regime, political culture and law) and non-liberal, peripheral cultural groups living in the country. Those problems largely relate to the extent to which the liberal center should tolerate the illiberal cultural practices of such peripheral groups. Indeed, since the 1990s liberal political theorists have devoted much of their thinking to addressing this issue (so much so that Jacob T. Levy has written about 'the multicultural turn in liberal theory').³⁶

---

[33] In HCJ 8638/03 *Amir v Great Rabbinic Court in Jerusalem*, the Supreme Court held that the rabbinical courts have no jurisdiction beyond what has been explicitly granted to them under state law, namely jurisdiction in matters of marriage and divorce. Subsequently, it has been suggested that the rabbinical courts should be explicitly granted jurisdiction in private law matters through Knesset legislation.

[34] Adam Hofri-Winogradow, 'Increased Legal Pluralism in Israel: The Rise of Halakhic Civil Tribunals in the Religious Zionist Sector' (2010) Tel Aviv U L Rev (Hebrew); Amichai Radziner, 'Between the High Court of Justice and the Rabbinic Court: On the Meaning of Private Law Adjudication in the Official Tribunal' (unpublished paper) (Hebrew). About this development, Yedidia Stern writes: 'From an all-Israeli perspective this is a recipe for disaster… It will exert an immensely disintegrating, centrifugal power on Israel's social tissue. It will echo deep currents in Israeli society that aim at increased sectorial tribalism at the expense of social cohesion.' Yedidia Stern, 'Judicial Autonomy to the Religious Group?' (February 2 2010) Yedioth Ahronoth.

[35] Charles Taylor, Book Review: *Multicultural Citizenship*, by Will Kymlicka, (1996) 90 Am Pol Sci Rev 408; Michel Wieviorka, 'Is Multiculturalism the Solution?' (1998) 21 Ethnic & Racial Stud 881; David Bennett, 'Introduction' in David Bennett (ed), *Multicultural States* (New York, Routledge, 1998) 1; C. Joppke and S. Lukes, 'Introduction: Multicultural Questions' in Christian Joppke and Steven Lukes (eds), *Multicultural Questions* (New York, Oxford University Press, 1999) 1; Charles Lemert, 'Multiculturalism' in George Ritzer and Barry Smart (eds), *Handbook Of Social Theory* (London, Sage Publications, 2001) 297.

[36] Jacob T. Levy, 'Liberal Jacobinism' (2004) 114 Ethics 318, 322. James Bohman writes that '[t]he political problems of pluralism have moved to the center of much liberal political thought, including Rawls's recent account of a well-ordered democratic society.' James Bohman, *Public Deliberation* (Cambridge, MIT Press, 1996) 72.

Such problems arise in the context of Israel's multicultural condition as well, eg, the widespread discrimination against women in the ultra-Orthodox and Arab groups, or the prevalence of polygamy and honor killings among the Arab group. The more pressing problems in the context of Israel's multicultural condition, however, have to do with the constitution of the Israeli center, ie, the character of the regime, political culture and law of the country. In that respect, the problems of Israel's multicultural condition are more similar to those of such countries as Turkey, Algeria, Egypt, Malaysia, Pakistan and the Palestinian Authority.[37]

Israel's multicultural condition is unique in another respect as well: As the struggle over the shaping of Israel's culture has never been resolved, Israel, despite being a liberal democracy, provides massive funding to institutions of the ultra-Orthodox and religious-Zionist groups that do not accept the state's current regime, and in some instances even actively undermine it. This became readily apparent in the months that preceded the disengagement from the Gaza Strip and Northern Samaria in August 2005. Rabbis teaching at institutions that receive much of their funding from the state, including some that operate in close collaboration with the IDF, called on their students and followers to disobey the IDF's orders and not cooperate in carrying out the government's decisions.[38]

In order to understand this aspect of Israel's multicultural condition, it may be useful to discuss the American case of *Bob Jones University*.

Bob Jones is a Christian fundamentalist university in South Carolina. Based on its reading of religious doctrine, it adopted a disciplinary rule that prohibits interracial dating and marriage. When the rule was brought to the attention of the IRS, it revoked the university's status as a tax-exempt institution. The Supreme Court affirmed this measure by the IRS. Chief Justice Warren Burger wrote:

> [O]ver the past quarter of a century, every pronouncement of this Court and myriad Acts of Congress and Executive Orders attest a firm national policy to prohibit racial segregation and discrimination in public education.
> ...[39]
>
> [I]t would be anomalous for the Executive, Legislative, and Judicial Branches to reach conclusions that add up to a firm public policy on racial discrimination, and at the same time have the IRS blissfully ignore what all three branches of the Federal Government had declared.[40]

---

[37] Sami Zubaida, 'Trajectories of Political Islam: Egypt, Iran and Turkey' in David Marquand and Ronald L. Nettle (eds), *Religion And Democracy* (Oxford, Blackwell Publishers, 2000) 60; Seyla Benhabib, 'Turkey's Constitutional Zigzag' (Winter 2009) Dissent.

[38] Mautner, above n 21, at 279–82.

[39] *Bob Jones University v United States*, 461 US 574, 593.

[40] Id, at 598.

William Galston, a political theorist who holds that illiberal cultural groups should enjoy widespread toleration of their practices, nevertheless justifies the Court's decision:

> associations conducting their internal affairs in a manner contrary to core public purposes can legitimately be burdened.... In such cases, a policy of what might be called 'reverse exception'—that is, the removal of all forms of otherwise applicable public encouragement and favor—may well be the most appropriate course.[41]

Because of the indeterminacy regarding the nature of Israeli culture, the Israeli state provides massive funding to institutions that openly preach against the country's liberal-democratic regime. Clearly, then, the Israeli Supreme Court would never have been able to issue a decision such as *Bob Jones University*. Were the Court ever to rule in the manner of its American counterpart, it would stir up an earthquake in the relations between the Israeli state and the Jewish religious group.

Following Thomas Kuhn's distinction between 'normal' and 'revolutionary' science,[42] Richard Rorty defines a 'normal discourse' as one which is 'conducted within an agreed-upon set of conventions' about what the participants are involved in, and an 'abnormal discourse' as what takes place 'when someone joins in the discourse who is ignorant of these conventions or who sets them aside.'[43] Borrowing from Rorty, we could say that Israel is an 'abnormal country': There is disagreement between the major cultural groups as to the basic rules of the country's regime, political culture and law.

Likewise, John Rawls writes that agreement among the citizens of a state about the principles governing the fundamentals of their political system is 'a very great public good, part of society's political capital,' that 'removes from the political agenda the most divisive issues, serious contention about which must undermine the bases of social cooperation.'[44] Israel does not enjoy the benefits of this 'public good'.

Israel's abnormal condition is something that goes far beyond the area of state funding; it is a legally institutionalized matter. The rabbinical courts system is part of the state's court system. Almost without exception, though, Knesset legislation and precedents of the Supreme Court are not cited in the opinions of the rabbinical courts.[45] Interestingly, this conduct

---

[41] William A. Galston, 'Two Concepts of Liberalism' (1995) 105 Ethics 516, 532.

[42] Thomas S. Kuhn, *The Structure Of Scientific Revolutions* (Chicago, University of Chicago Press, 1962).

[43] Richard Rorty, *Philosophy And The Mirror Of Nature* (Princeton, New Jersey, Princeton University Press, 1979) 320.

[44] John Rawls, *Political Liberalism* (New York, Columbia University Press, 1993) 157.

[45] AD 23/69 *Yosef v Yosef*, 24(1) PD 792, 809; Yitzhak Cahan, 'Rabbinical Adjudication and Secular Adjudication' (1976) 7 Dinei Israel 205, 210. See also Chapter 2, above.

is sanctioned, to some extent, by the oath of allegiance of the rabbinical courts judges. According to section 10 of the Dayanim [Rabbinical Courts Judges] Act of 1955, the text of the oath of a rabbinical court judge reads:

I hereby undertake to be loyal to the State of Israel, to justly adjudicate among the people, to remain impartial, and not to unjustly prefer one side over the other.

What is missing is the judge's undertaking to be loyal to the 'laws of the State', a statement included in the oath of all other high-ranking state officials, such as the Prime Minister, cabinet ministers, members of the Knesset, the state comptroller and judges of all other state tribunals.

C. THE SCHISM BETWEEN JEWS AND ARABS

I have pointed out two characteristic elements of Israel's multicultural condition. First, there is a profound disagreement between the two major Jewish groups—the secular and the religious—over the basic principles of the regime, political culture and law of the state. Second, as a corollary to this disagreement, the Israeli state provides massive funding to religious institutions that do not accept the basic principles of the current regime and are often openly subversive of them. However, in addition to the divide between secular and religious Jews, there is another divide between the Jewish group and the Arab group over the definition and national character of the state.[46]

There is at least one clear-cut connection between the two divides; together they create what could be called 'the zero-sum game of the Israeli multicultural condition': The more Israel accentuates traditional Jewish beliefs and practices in its public culture, the more appealing it would be to Jewish religious Israelis, but the more repugnant to Israel's Arab citizens. And vice versa, ie, the more Israel downplays the role of traditional Jewish beliefs or practices in its public culture (eg, by defining itself as a bi-national state, or as what is known in Israeli discourse as 'a state of all its citizens', to take two extreme scenarios), the more appealing it would be to Israel's Arab citizens, but by the same token the more appalling to Jewish religious Israelis. Israel is trapped between a rock and a hard place.

The common view among Israeli Jews is that Israel is and should remain 'a Jewish and democratic state', ie, the nation-state of the Jewish people

---

[46] On the eve of the establishment of the state of Israel, about 940,000 Arabs lived in the territory that became the State of Israel at the end of the Independence War of 1948. In the course of the war, about 780,000 Arabs fled or were expelled, leaving 160,000 Arabs in the territory of the state of Israel at the end of the war. As'ad Ghanem and Sarah Ozacky-Lazar, 'The Status of the Palestinians in Israel in the Age of Peace: Part of the Problem but not Part of the Solution' in Uri Cohen et al (eds), *Israel And Modernity* (Beer Sheva, Ben Gurion University of the Negev, 2006) 211 (Hebrew).

in which the Jews exercise their right to self-determination. The Jewish group, which controls the central institutions of the state, has ceaselessly tried to reinforce and disseminate this perception of Israel. That effort was given legal expression by the two Basic Laws of 1992, which define Israel as 'a Jewish and democratic state' (Chapter 2).

However, some 20 percent of Israel's citizens are Arabs,[47] and it is estimated that by the year 2020 their share of the state's population will have risen to 23 percent.[48] Clearly, then, from a demographic standpoint Israel is already a bi-national state.[49] However, the common view among Israeli Jews, which is also embodied in many sites of Israeli law, is that while the Jewish people is entitled to use the state as a means of exercising its right to national self-determination, the Arabs are entitled to their rights on an individual basis only, ie, as citizens of the state, but not in any way as a collective entity.[50] (The state's Arab citizens currently enjoy some rights that are of a collective nature, nonetheless).[51]

---

[47] The sum total of Israel's population on its sixty-second independence day (April 2010) was 7,587,000, out of which 5,726,000 (75.5 percent) were Jews, 1,548,000 (20.4 percent) were Arabs and 313,000 (4.1 percent) were from other ethnic groups. Among the Arabs, on December 31 2008, 83.36 percent were Muslims, 8.45 percent Christians, and 8.19 percent Druze. Israel's Central Bureau of Statistics <http://www.cbs.gov.il>

[48] Yaakov Kop And Robert E. Litan, *Sticking Together—The Israeli Experiment In Pluralism* (Washington DC, Brookings Institution Press, 2002) chapter 3.

[49] Kimmerling, above n 1, at 404; Gad Barzilai, *Communities And Law* (Ann Arbor, The University of Michigan Press, 2003) 9.

[50] Yoav Peled And Gershon Shafir, *Being Israeli—The Dynamics Of Multiple Citizenship* (Cambridge, Cambridge University Press, 2002); Kimmerling, above n 1, at 376.

[51] First, under Article 82 of the Palestine Order-in-Council, 1922, which is still part of Israeli law, Arabic is an 'official language' in Israel in the sense that

[a]ll Ordinances, official notices and official forms of the Government and municipalities in areas to be prescribed...shall be published in...Arabic and Hebrew.

Second, the Arabs run a separate (though highly supervised and far from autonomous) educational system. Third, Israel preserves the Ottoman *millet* system which allows its Arab citizens (and its Jewish citizens as well) autonomy in the sphere of family law, ie, under Israeli law it is religious law that governs the family sphere. Fourth, in both the jurisprudence of the Supreme Court and in Knesset legislation, one can find the seeds of an evolving 'affirmative action' doctrine in favor of the Arab citizens, in areas such as appointment to the state administration, as well as in matters having to do with the allocation of state budgets and resources. Fifth, under Israeli law the Arabs are entitled to maintain their religious sabbaticals and holidays.

By contrast, however, Israeli law prohibits Israel's Arab citizens from taking action aimed at changing Israel's current identity as the Jewish people's nation-state. First, section 7a(a)(1) of the Basic Law: The Knesset provides that no party will be allowed to participate in elections to the Knesset if its platform or actions amount to a 'denial of Israel's existence as a Jewish and democratic state.' Second, section 5 of the Parties Law, 1992 provides that no party will be registered if its goals or actions amount to a 'denial of Israel's existence as a Jewish and democratic state.' Third, section 134(c) of the Knesset Bylaws provides that the Knesset speaker or his deputies will not approve the submission of any draft legislation which 'denies the existence of the state of Israel as the Jewish people's state.' See: Gad Barzilai, 'Fantasies of Liberalism and Liberal Jurisprudence: State Law, Politics, and the Israeli Arab-Palestinian Community' (2000) 34 Israel L Rev 425; Ilan Saban, 'The Minority Rights of the Palestinian-Arabs in Israel: What is, What Isn't and What is Taboo' (2002) 26 Tel Aviv U L Rev 241 (Hebrew); Ilan Saban and Muhammad Amara, 'The Status of Arabic in Israel: Reflections on the Power of Law to Produce Social Change' (2002) 36 Israel L Rev 5; Ilan

Every now and then, Israeli Arab (and some Jewish) spokespersons voice their objection to Israel's definition as the nation-state of the Jewish people, while suggesting alternative definitions, such as Israel as a bi-national state,[52] or Israel as 'a state of all its citizens', ie, a state that lacks any defined national identity and serves as a means for providing its citizens with basic individual rights and services.[53] Other Arab spokespersons sometime make the claim that the Arab citizens should be granted cultural autonomy[54] and recognized as a national minority with some collective rights.[55]

Once Israel embarked on 'the definition game' in the two basic laws of 1992 (in which Israel was defined as a 'Jewish and democratic state'), it was only a matter of time until the country's Arab citizens came out with their own ideas as to how the state should be defined.[56] Indeed, in

---

Saban, 'Minority Rights in Deeply Divided Societies: A Framework for Analysis and the Case of the Arab-Palestinian Minority in Israel' (2004) 36 NYU J Int'l L & Pol 885.

[52] See eg, A. Ghanem, 'State and Minority in Israel: The Case of the Ethnic State and the Predicament of its Minority' (1998) 21 Ethnic & Racial Stud 444.

[53] According to a study conducted by Gad Barzilai, the vast majority of Israeli Arabs supports the option of defining Israel as 'the state of all its citizens.' Barzilai, above n 49, at 118. A study conducted by As'ad Ghanem elicited similar findings. See: Ghanem and Ozacky-Lazar, above n 46, at 233, 234. See also: Azmi Bishara, 'On the Question of the Palestinian Minority in Israel' (1993) 3 Theory & Criticism 7 (Hebrew) (arguing that Israel should be made a state of all its citizens in which the Arab citizens are regarded as a national minority and enjoy cultural autonomy); Sammy Samooha, 'Ethnic Democracy: Israel as a Proto-Type' in Pinhas Ginossar and Avi Bareli (eds), *Zionism: A Contemporary Controversy* (Sede Boqer Campus, Ben Gurion Research Center, 1996) 277 (Hebrew) (discussing the positions of the Arab citizens over the issue of turning Israel into a state of all its citizens); Yoav Peled, 'Will Israel be a State of Its Citizens on its 100th Anniversary?' (2001) 17 Legal Research 73 (Hebrew); Yossi Yonah And Yehuda Shenhav, *What Is Multiculturalism?* (Tel Aviv, Babel Publishers, 2005) 173–6 (Hebrew) (arguing that Israel should define itself as a state of all its citizens); Peled and Shafir, above n 50, chapter 3 (discussing the positions of Arab parties on the issue of Israel's definition).

[54] Sammy Smooha, *Autonomy For Arabs In Israel?* (Raanana, Institute for Israeli Arab Studies, 1999) (Hebrew); Ilan Saban, 'The Zionist Paradigm Edge Option' in Sarah Ozacky-Lazar, As'ad Ghanem and Ilan Pappe (eds), *Seven Roads: Theoretical Options For The Status Of The Arabs In Israel* (Givat Haviva, The Institute for Peace Research, 1999) 79 (Hebrew); Yossi Yonah, 'A State of all its Citizens, a Nation-State or a Multicultural Democracy?' (1998) 16 Alpaim 238 (Hebrew). See also the findings reported by Ghanem and Ozacky-Lazar, above n 46, at 235.

[55] See eg, Hassan Gabareen, 'The Future of Arab Citizenship' (2001) 6 Mishpat Umimshal 53 (Hebrew); Amal Jamal, 'We Demand Full Partnership in the Shaping of the Public, Cultural and Political Spheres in which We Live' (2003) 16 Eretz Acheret 20 (Hebrew); Muhammad Dakhla, 'The Claim for Collective Rights to the Arab Minority in Israel' in Elie Rekhess and Sara Ozacky-Lazar (eds), *The Status Of The Arab Minority In The Jewish State* (Tel Aviv, Tel Aviv University, 2005) 84 (Hebrew).

[56] On the 'Jewish and democratic state' definition, political scientist Shlomo Avineri has written: 'Reformers, beware your words…Sometime it is better to maintain ambiguity that allows for conflicting interpretations.' Shlomo Avineri, 'On Israel as a Jewish and Democratic State' in Ron Margolin (ed), *Israel As A Jewish And Democratic State* (Jerusalem, World Union of Jewish Studies, 1999) 79 (Hebrew). Zeev Jabotinsky said in 1937 that a state's national identity should not be defined by its constitution, but rather should be determined by the demography of the state and by the ways of life of the citizens living in it. Zeev Jabotinsky, 'Fulfill Your Promise or Get Out of the Mandate!' in *Writings And Speeches* (Jerusalem, Eri Jabotinsky Publishing House, 1948) 221, 224 (Hebrew). I sympathize with Avineri's and Jabotinsky's pragmatic approaches. Israel should be the nation-state of the Jewish people, where it exercises its right of self-determination. Without discounting

2006–7 four groups of Arab intellectuals issued four different policy papers, collectively termed 'The Arab Vision Documents'.[57] These documents strikingly express the Arab citizens' opposition to the definition of Israel as a Jewish state. Common to all four of them is the claim that Israel should give up its current definition as a Jewish state and define itself instead as a bi-national, bilingual, Lijphart-type consociational state run jointly by the elites of the two national groups that compose its population,[58] with extensive cultural autonomy enjoyed by its Arab citizens.

Likewise, between 1998 and 2000 a group of Jewish intellectuals and a group of Arab intellectuals met under the auspices of the Israel Democracy Institute with the aim of signing an agreed-upon document ('treaty') on the status of the Arab citizens and their relation with the state.[59] The majority of the Jewish participants preconditioned their assent to the (almost completed) document on the Arab participants' explicit recognition of the state's Jewishness (ie, its being the nation-state of the Jewish people). The Arab participants refused, claiming that de facto acceptance of the state and peaceful cooperation with it on their part sufficed. Thus, the parties found themselves trapped in 'the definition game'. The initiative ground to a halt and died out. To paraphrase Rawls,[60] the participants failed to reach an overlapping consensus on Israel's being the nation-state of the Jewish people; all they could agree to was a modus vivendi regarding the country's current status.

---

the importance of cultural categories, however, at the end of the day it is always preferable to act pragmatically and to accommodate the reality on the ground.

[57] 'The Future Vision For Palestinian Arabs In Israel' (National Committee of Heads of Arab Municipalities in Israel, 2006) <http://www.7th-day.co.il/medina/mismah-hahazon.htm> (Hebrew); Adalah's 'Bill Of Rights' (2007) <http://www.adalah.org/eng/democratic_constitution-e.pdf> (Hebrew); 'Equal Constitution For All?' (Haifa, Mossawa Center, 2006) <http://mossawacenter.org/files/files/File/constitution_paper_heb.pdf>; 'The Haifa Declaration' (Mada al-Carmel, 2007) <http://www.mada-research.org/UserFiles/file/haifaenglish.pdf>. For a discussion, see: Amal Jamal, 'The Political Ethos of Palestinian Citizens in Israel: Critical Reading in the Future Vision Documents' (2008) 23 Israel Stud Forum 3; Sarah Ozacky-Lazar and Mustafa Kabha (eds), 'Between Vision And Reality: The Vision Papers Of The Arabs In Israel, 2006–7' (Jerusalem, Citizens' Accord Forum, 2008) (Hebrew).

[58] Examples of this kind of regime are Canada, Belgium, Switzerland, Macedonia, and at certain periods also Lebanon and Cyprus.

[59] Uzi Benziman (ed), *Whose Land Is It? A Quest For A Jewish-Arab Compact In Israel* (Jerusalem, Israel Democracy Institute, 2006) (Hebrew). This initiative was preceded by a series of attempts made since the 1990s to reach agreement between groups of secular and religious Jewish intellectuals and public figures. What characterized these initiatives, therefore, was that none of them encompassed the three fundamental cultural groups living in Israel, namely secular Jews, religious Jews and Arabs. Rather, secular Jews convened with religious Jews, and then Jews convened separately with Arabs. All these initiatives formed part of the massive process of legalization that Israel has gone through since the late 1970s. See Chapter 3.

[60] Rawls, above n 44, chapter 4.

Two of the Arab Vision Documents[61] define the Arabs in Israel as an 'indigenous people'. This is clearly an attempt to channel into the discourse on the status of Arabs in Israel the vocabulary of the rights of indigenous peoples under international law. On 12 September 2007 the UN General Assembly accepted the United Nations Declaration on the Rights of Indigenous Peoples, which states that indigenous peoples are the bearers of a series of important rights, such as the right to self-determination; the right to have their own political representatives; the right to maintain their distinct political, legal, economic, social and cultural institutions; the right to establish and control their educational systems; and the right to their lands. It may be assumed that in the coming years Israeli Arabs will increasingly draw on this emergent discourse to better their situation.[62]

In recent years, there has also been a growing tendency among the younger generation of Israeli Arabs to identify with the Palestinian nationalist movement and view themselves as Palestinian, in spite of living in Israel and being Israeli citizens.[63] By contrast, there are also many signs that Israel's Arab citizens have gone though profound processes of Israelization, ie, the internalization of large portions of Israeli culture (the liberal democratic political culture, the business culture, feminism, Western technology, etc.) and the endorsement and cultivation of a self-identity as Israeli citizens who wish to be active in both Israel's politics and civil society.[64]

---

[61] 'Adalah's Bill Of Rights' (2007) (Hebrew); 'The Haifa Declaration' (Mada al-Carmel, 2007) (Hebrew).

[62] Will Kymlicka writes about the 'internationalizing' of minority rights issues, and adds that '[t]oday, virtually all Western states that contain indigenous peoples...have become "multination" states.' Will Kymlicka, 'Multiculturalism and Minority Rights: West and East' (2002) 4 J Ethnopolitics & Minority Issues In Europe. See also: Will Kymlicka, *Multicultural Odysseys* (Oxford, Oxford University Press, 2007) 66–8, 147–54. In HCJ 4112/99 *Adala v Tel Aviv-Jaffa Municipality*, 56(5) PD 393, 418, Chief Justice Barak said that 'the Arabs are the largest minority in Israel' and defined them as 'a minority that has been living in Israel from time immemorial.'

[63] Dan Rabinowitz And Khawla Abu Baker, *The Stand Tall Generation—The Palestinian Citizens Of Israel Today* (Jerusalem, Keter Publishing House, 2002) (Hebrew).

[64] Samooha, above n 53; Peled and Shafir, above n 50, chapter 3; Azmi Bishara, 'The Arab in Israel: A Study in a Split Political Debate' in Pinhas Ginossar and Avi Bareli (eds), *Zionism: A Contemporary Controversy* (Sede Boqer Campus, Ben Gurion Research Center, 1996) 312; Sammy Samooha, 'The Relations of Jews and Arabs in Israel as a Jewish and Democratic State' in Ephraim Ya'ar and Ze'ev Shavit (eds), *Trends In Israeli Society* (Tel Aviv, Open University, 2003) 231 (Hebrew). Ghanem and Ozacky-Lazar sum up studies conducted among Israeli Arabs, as follows:

> Israeli Palestinians see their future as Israeli citizens. They are not interested in living in a Palestinian state in the West Bank or Gaza. They do not view Palestinian national institutions as representing them. They see their place, future and representative institutions as distinct from those of the Palestinians living in the West Bank, Gaza and the Palestinian Diaspora. The self-perception of the Israeli Palestinians as to their situation, place and future is very clear: they see themselves as Israeli citizens that will continue to live in Israel; they are not interested in moving to any other place, not even to a Palestinian state established in the West Bank and Gaza.

Ghanem and Ozacky-Lazar, above n 46, at 228.

The schism between Jews and Arabs in Israel relates not only to the issue of the definition of the state. The Arab citizens suffer severe discrimination in the allocation of the state's resources—budgets, lands, positions in the state's public administration—as well as in their representation in the media.[65] As noted in the report of the 'Official Committee of Inquiry in the Matter of the Clashes between Security Forces and Israeli Citizens in October 2000', headed by Supreme Court Justice Theodor Or,

the Arab citizens live in a reality in which they are discriminated against. This has been documented in a large number of professional researches and studies; it was confirmed in court opinions and government decisions; and it is reflected in State Comptroller reports, as well as in other official documents.[66]

The Arab citizens are also excluded from participation in significant political decisions, most notably those having to do with Israel's defense and foreign relations—talk about the need for 'a Jewish majority' as a precondition for the legitimacy of such decisions is often heard in Israel.[67]

Moreover, the state does not recognize even a single holiday of its Arab citizens as an official national holiday. The Jewish and Arab civil societies are very much separate: Over 70 percent of the Arabs live in homogeneous Arab settlements, and in the case of mixed cities, Jews and Arabs usually live in separate neighborhoods. The Jewish and the Arab labor markets are almost entirely separate.[68] Jews and Arabs maintain separate institutions

---

[65] 'Official Committee of Inquiry in the Matter of the Clashes between Security Forces and Israeli Citizens in October 2000' above n 24, vol 1, at 33-60; Menachem Mautner, 'Distributive Justice in Israel' in Menachem Mautner (ed), *Distributive Justice In Israel* (Tel Aviv, Ramot Publishers, 2000) 9; Oren Yiftachel, '"Ethnocracy", Geography and Democracy' (2000) 19 Alpaim 78 (Hebrew); Daphna Golan-Agnon, 'Why are Arab Students being Discriminated Against?' in Daphna Golan-Agnon (ed), *Inequality In Education* (Tel Aviv, Babel Publishers, 2004) 70 (Hebrew); Peled and Shafir, above n 50, chapter 3. See also: Ilan Saban 'The Impact of the Supreme Court on the Status of the Arabs in Israel' (1996) 3 Mishpat Umimshal 541 (Hebrew); Ilan Saban and Scott Strainer, 'On Two Types of "Appropriate Representation"' (2005) 11 Labor, Society And Law 247 (Hebrew).

[66] 'Official Committee of Inquiry in the Matter of the Clashes between Security Forces and Israeli Citizens in October 2000' above n 24, vol 1, at 33. See also: id, at 54; id, vol 2, at 766.

[67] Kymlicka writes about the 'securitization' of ethnic relations that takes place in many countries where minorities are seen as 'allies or collaborators with external powers'. Kymlicka, Multiculturalism and Minority Rights, above n 62. See also: Kymlicka, Multicultural Odysseys, above n 62, at 118–21, 180–86. Studies conducted among Israeli Arabs show that 'the vast majority of them are dissatisfied with their situation as a collectivity with respect to their conditions, achievements, ability to influence their future, their integration at the national level and their collective status.' Ghanem and Ozacky-Lazar, above n 46, at 231.

[68] Kop and Litan, above n 48, chapters 1, 4; Jose Bruner and Yoav Peled, 'On Autonomy, Capabilities and Democracy: Critique of Liberal Multiculturalism' in Menachem Mautner, Avi Sagi and Ronen Shamir (eds), *Multiculturalism In A Democratic And Jewish State* (Tel Aviv, Ramot Publishers, 1998) 107 (Hebrew); Majd Alhaj, 'Multicultural Education in Israel in Light of the Peace Process' id, at 703. For a similar situation in Canada, Belgium and Switzerland, see Kymlicka, Multiculturalism and Minority Rights, above n 62.

in areas such as the press, the radio, television, culture, art, music, cinema, etc.; Jews and Arabs maintain school systems that are almost entirely separate; the Arabs' rate of income, standard of living, life expectancy, standards of housing, level of education, level of participation in the labor market, and level of infrastructure development are all substantially lower than those of the Jewish group.[69] Israel is manifestly bi-national, then, not only in its demography, but also in the almost complete separation between members of the Jewish and Arab groups in the conduct of their daily lives.

The Arab citizens' substantial demographic presence and exclusion from important political decisions, the severe discrimination against them in the allocation of state resources, their segregated civil society, their belief that the establishment and continued existence of the State of Israel are based on the use of violence against them, and the ongoing state of war between Israel and the Palestinian people in the Occupied Territories—all of these make for a potent and highly explosive mixture. Many writers have pointed out that a combination of just a few of these elements in the relations between a majority and a minority may ultimately lead to a violent struggle between the two groups.[70]

However, in contrast to the struggle between the secular and religious Jewish groups, which enjoys a high degree of visibility in many sites of Israeli life, Israeli Arabs' opposition to the definition of Israel as the nation-state of the Jewish people, their exclusion from important political decisions, the discrimination they suffer and their absence from the mainstream civil society are all seldom discussed in Israel's political and public discourses. Most Israeli prime ministers have prudently refrained from openly dealing with the problem of the Arab citizens and avoided making the fate of the Arab citizens an important item on the public agenda.[71] However, given the size of Israel's Arab population (which, as noted

---

[69] Mautner, above n 65; Kop and Litan, above n 48, chapters 1, 2; Peled and Shafir, above n 50, chapter 3; Bruner and Peled, id; Rassem Khamaissi, 'The Disengagement Option: Irredentism or Transfer for Israeli Arabs and their Meanings' in Sarah Ozacky-Lazar, As'ad Ghanem and Ilan Pappe (eds), *Seven Roads: Theoretical Options For The Status Of The Arabs In Israel* (Givat Haviva, The Institute for Peace Research, 1999) 155 (Hebrew).

[70] Arend Lijphart, *Patterns Of Democracy* (New Haven, Yale University Press, 1999); Ann Phillips, *The Politics Of Presence* (New York, Oxford University Press, 1995) chapter 1; Jeff Spinner-Halev, 'Cultural Pluralism and Partial Citizenship' in Christian Joppke and Steven Lukes (eds), *Multicultural Questions* (New York, Oxford University Press, 1999) 65; Andrew Mason, 'Political Community, Liberal-Nationalism, and the Ethics of Assimilation' (1999) 109 Ethics 261, 277; Margaret Moore, *The Ethics Of Nationalism* (New York, Oxford University Press, 2001) chapters 3, 4; Joseph Eliot Magnet, *Modern Constitutionalism* (Markham, Butterworths, 2004) 16–7, 21, 23.

[71] A striking example was the Second Lebanon War (July–August 2006), in which about half of the civilian casualties were Arabs. An opportunity therefore arose to promote a discourse that unifies the Arab and Jewish citizens of the state. Yet no state official seized the opportunity to do that. The political leadership behaved as if the casualties were all Jewish.

earlier, may increase in the coming years), it is only a question of time until the Arab citizens' demands to change the definition of the state and their status in it will echo loudly through the public discourse. Needless to say, such claims are bound to encounter stiff opposition from the Jewish group in Israel.[72] At best, the struggle between the two groups will be conducted peacefully. At some point in time, however, it may quite possibly descend into violence, with unthinkable results.

---

[72] cf the reaction of British Canadians to the adoption of multicultural policies by the government in the late 1960s: Raymond Breton, 'The Production and Allocation of Symbolic Resources: An Analysis of the Linguistic and Ethnocultural Field in Canada' (1984) 21 Canadian Rev Soc & Anthrop 123; Raymond Breton, 'Multiculturalism and Canadian Nation-Building' in Alan Cairns and Cynthia Williams (eds), *The Politics Of Gender, Ethnicity And Language In Canada* (Toronto, University of Toronto Press, 1986) 27.

CHAPTER 8

LAW AND CULTURE IN THE COMING DECADES

Israel's multicultural condition—the cultural divide within the Jewish group and between the Jewish and Arab groups—necessitates fresh, new thinking as to the basic principles of Israel's regime and political culture. In this Chapter, I would like to outline some preliminary thoughts.

A. POLITICAL LIBERALISM

Israeli liberals need to actively pursue the preservation and cultivation of Israel's liberal democratic regime. Not only does such a regime embody central, highly important humanistic values and constitute the most appropriate regime in itself, but liberalism also guarantees both individuals and groups the utmost freedom to live by their own choices and cultures. In addition, liberalism emphasizes the importance of the values of pluralism and toleration. All of this makes liberalism the political theory and regime most appropriate for multicultural states such as Israel.[1]

In its over six decades of statehood, Israel has managed to develop and maintain an impressive liberal-democratic regime, political culture and law. True, Israel's democracy is not perfect. Jews are treated differently than Arabs. Important cultural groups have only partly internalized the

---

[1] Susan Moller Okin, 'Humanist Liberalism' in Nancy L. Rosenblum (ed), *Liberalism And The Moral Life* (Cambridge, Harvard University Press, 1989) 39; Chantal Mouffe, 'Democratic Citizenship and the Political Community' in Chantal Mouffe (ed), *Dimensions Of Radical Democracy* (New York, Verso, 1992) 225, 232–3; Jurgen Habermas, 'Citizenship and National Identity: Some Reflections on the Future of Europe' (1992) 12 Praxis Int'l 1, 17 rep in: Jurgen Habermas, 'Citizenship and National Identity: Some Reflections on the Future of Europe' in Ronald Beiner, (ed), *Theorizing Citizenship* (Albany, State University of New York Press, 1995); Jeff Spinner, *The Boundaries Of Citizenship* (Baltimore, Johns Hopkins University Press, 1994) chapter 1; James Ceaser, 'Multiculturalism and American Liberal Democracy' in Arthur M. Melzer, Jerry Weinberger and M. Richard Zinman (eds), *Multiculturalism And American Democracy* (Lawrence, Kansas, University Press of Kansas, 1998) 139; Chandran Kukathas, 'Liberalism and Multiculturalism—The Politics of Indifference' (1998) 26 Pol Theory 686, 695.

essentials of the country's regime and political culture, and some groups are even subversive of them. Still, Israel is a liberal democracy and most of its citizens (Jews, Arabs, secular and religious) support the preservation and cultivation of its current regime and political culture and view them as one of the state's great accomplishments.

The question is: What kind of liberalism is most appropriate to the Israeli multicultural condition?

Traditional liberalism is a comprehensive theory about the good life that takes human reason as its point of departure. One major variant of comprehensive liberalism, identified with Kant, places the value of autonomy at the center of the concept of the good life. Another, identified with Mill, places the values of authenticity and individualism in that position. These two comprehensive theories derive from their visions of the good life particular political conceptions of the state as an instrument for the enhancement of the values that underpin the theories.

In the past generation we have witnessed the rise of a new variant of liberalism—political liberalism, identified with the later writings of John Rawls.[2] As its point of departure, political liberalism takes it that there are profound disagreements among the citizens of a state: Different people adhere to different 'comprehensive doctrines', as Rawls calls them, namely different philosophical, moral and religious doctrines regarding the good life. Rawls claims, however, that citizens living in liberal democracies can unite behind a shared political conception of the principles governing the functioning of the central institutions of their states, even though they may profoundly disagree with each other over the meaning of the good life.

This may happen because people who grow up in a liberal democracy internalize the 'shared fundamental ideas' which are 'implicit in the public

---

[2] John Rawls, *Political Liberalism* (New York, Columbia University Press, 1993). On Rawls' political liberalism see: Joseph Raz, 'Facing Diversity: The Case for Epistemic Abstinence' (1990) 19 Phil & Pub Aff 8; Michael J. Sandel, 'Political Liberalism (1993)' (1994) 107 Harv L Rev 1765; Lief Wenar, 'Political Liberalism, An Internal Critique' (1995) 106 Ethics 32; Brian Barry, 'John Rawls and the Search for Stability' (1995) 105 Ethics 874; Heidi Hurd, 'Political Liberalism' (1995) 105 Yale L J 795; David Estlund, 'The Insularity of the Reasonable: Why Political Liberalism Must Admit the Truth' (1998) 108 Ethics 252; Joshua Cohen, 'Moral Pluralism and Political Consensus' in Henry S. Richardson and Paul J. Weithman (eds), *The Philosophy Of Rawls* (New York, Routledge, 1999) 56; Jeremy Waldron, 'Disagreements About Justice' id, at 78; Samuel Scheffler, 'The Appeal of Political Liberalism' id, at 94; Paul Weithman, 'Liberalism and the Political Character of Political Philosophy' id, at 223; Jeremy Waldron, *Law And Disagreement* (Oxford, Oxford University Press, 1999) chapter 7; Victoria Davion and Clark Wolf (eds), *The Idea Of Political Liberalism* (Lanham, Rowman & Littlefield Publishers, Inc., 2000); Anthony Simon Laden, 'The House That Jack Built: Thirty Years of Reading Rawls' (2003) 113 Ethics 367. For a political view of liberalism, see also: Charles E. Larmore, *Patterns Of Moral Complexity* (Cambridge, Cambridge University Press, 1987); Charles Larmore, 'Political Liberalism' (1990) 18 Pol Theory 339; Charles Larmore, 'The Moral Basis of Political Liberalism' (1999) 96 J Phil 599; Mouffe, above n 1; Chantal Mouffe, 'Democratic Politics and the Question of Identity' in John Rajchman (ed), *The Identity Question* (New York, Routledge, 1995) 33; Chantal Mouffe, 'Democracy, Power, and the "Political"' in Seyla Benhabib (ed), *Democracy And Difference* (Princeton, Princeton University Press, 1996) 245.

political culture' of their country.[3] This 'public political culture' is manifest in the 'regime', the 'political institutions', and the 'public traditions of the interpretation' of the country's political culture and the functioning of its political institutions, including interpretations by courts. The 'public political culture' that the citizens internalize is also manifest in 'historic texts and documents that are common knowledge.'[4]

Citizens of a liberal democracy may also unite behind a shared political conception because the comprehensive doctrines to which they adhere may allow the creation of an 'overlapping consensus' regarding the nature of the country's political culture and the principles governing its political institutions. The overlapping consensus does not derive from any particular comprehensive doctrine, nor is it a compromise between various comprehensive doctrines.[5] Rather, it is 'a freestanding view',[6] 'a module' that 'fits into and can be supported by various reasonable comprehensive doctrines.'[7] Citizens who adhere to the prevalent comprehensive doctrines in a liberal democracy may be able to create an overlapping consensus that reflects the fundamentals of their public political culture. That is because the values embedded in their various comprehensive doctrines 'can be understood so as to be either congruent with, or supportive of, or else not in conflict with' the political values embedded in the overlapping consensus.[8] In addition, the overlapping consensus is not a 'modus vivendi' founded on 'a convergence of self- or group interests.'[9] Those who endorse it do so because it is a moral doctrine affirmed by their comprehensive doctrines, 'regardless of shifts in the distribution of political power.'[10]

Since so many Israelis (both Jews and Arabs) are religious, of the two variants of liberal political theory, namely comprehensive and political liberalism, Israel should opt for the political rather than the comprehensive. Israel may count on the possibility of collaboration between secular liberals (both Jewish and Arab) and religious Zionists in establishing a Rawlsian overlapping consensus in favor of the preservation and further cultivation of the country's liberal-democratic regime, political culture and law.

Indeed, the circumstances that made Rawls develop the notion of political liberalism, after his earlier formulation of a universalist version of liberal political theory in his great book *A Theory of Justice*, are similar to those in which Israeli secular liberals currently find themselves. In the years following the publication of *A Theory of Justice*, a large-scale

---

[3] Rawls, 'Political Liberalism' id, at 100.
[4] Id, at 13–14. See also at 141, 142. For a similar approach, see: Chantal Mouffe, *The Democratic Paradox* (London, Verso, 2000) chapter 4.
[5] Rawls, above n 2, at 170–1.
[6] Id, at 144.   [7] Id, at 145.   [8] Id, at 140.   [9] Id, at 147.   [10] Id, at 148.

Christian conservative revival began to take shape in the United States.[11] Rawls realized that it was futile to expect American religious citizens to endorse a political theory that rests on thick liberal assumptions regarding the good life. Rather, such citizens' cooperation in the preservation and cultivation of a liberal regime (making it 'stable', to use Rawls' phrase) would be made possible only if it drew on the internalization by these citizens of America's liberal political culture and constitutional tradition. It is this internalization and actual participation in America's liberal-democratic political processes, together with the fact that the religious doctrines to which these people adhere do not oppose the essentials of liberal democracy, or may even support them, that creates religious citizens' commitment to the preservation of a liberal regime. Likewise, Israeli secular liberals cannot expect religious citizens to endorse the fundamentals of liberalism as a theory. Rather, the latter's cooperation in making Israel's liberal democracy 'stable' will have to draw on religious citizens' having internalized the country's liberal-democratic political culture. Furthermore, support for liberal democracy can be found in Jewish tradition, with its vast intellectual resources, or at least there is no contradiction between the two, which already allows the ongoing participation of religious Jews in Israel's liberal-democratic political processes.

(a) Religious Zionism

It is no utopian[12] pipedream to expect collaboration between Israeli secular liberals and some religious citizens for the preservation and cultivation of Israel's liberal-democratic regime and political culture. In that context, it may be useful to draw a distinction between the ultra-Orthodox group and religious-Zionism.

The ultra-Orthodox willingly utilize all of Western technology (in which aspect they differ from such groups as the North American Amish), but their 'comprehensive doctrine' is 'fully comprehensive'.[13] They utterly reject and deny any value to the West's entire intellectual and spiritual heritage, including the political theories (and practices) of liberalism and democracy.[14] Therefore, the principles of liberalism and democracy are incorporated in neither the convictions of the

---

[11] James Rudin, *The Baptizing Of America* (New York, Thunder's Mouth Press, 2006).
[12] cf Rawls, above n 2, at 158: 'The last difficulty I consider is that an overlapping consensus is utopian: That is, there are not sufficient political, social, or psychological forces either to bring an overlapping consensus...or to render one stable.'
[13] Rawls, above n 2, at 168.
[14] cf John Grey, 'Enlightenment's Wake' in *Enlightenment's Wake* (London, Routledge, 1995) 215, 252 ('we have no reason to suppose that modernity and secularization are aspects, inseparably connected, of a single historical transformation').

ultra-Orthodox nor, largely, their political conduct. Rather, the political theory of the ultra-Orthodox is theocracy, and they run their political institutions in theocratic fashion, which means, among other things, that women are completely excluded from the political process (except for voting in Knesset elections).

That is not the case with regard to the religious-Zionist group. In Chapter 5, I discussed the rise of religious fundamentalism in religious-Zionism in the 1970s and its various manifestations: the extension of the Halakhah to all spheres of life of the individual, civil society and the state; the denigration of the normative, spiritual and artistic heritage of the West (but not Western science and its technological fruits); and religious radicalization in the daily practices of the individual. This fundamentalist strand has therefore brought some significant subgroups in contemporary religious-Zionism closer to ultra-Orthodoxy in terms of both theology and practice.

In parallel, however, opposite developments are discernible in the religious-Zionism of recent decades, as well. To some extent, these developments may be viewed as a reaction to the rise of fundamentalism within the group. A significant subgroup in religious-Zionism, composed mainly of religious academics and members of religious kibbutzim, has persistently and consciously emphasized its commitment to both the Jewish and Western heritage, including the political theory of liberal-democracy,[15] and it has even attempted to devise a synthesis of these elements in its comprehensive theologies and conduct of daily life.[16] This subgroup, often referred to as Modern Orthodoxy, may be viewed as a contemporary continuation of a theology persistently advanced in Judaism throughout the nineteenth and twentieth centuries by a diverse group of thinkers.[17]

One of the most far-reaching developments in religious-Zionism in recent decades is the rise of a vibrant and highly influential religious feminism.[18] Even though this development is identified mainly with Modern Orthodoxy, it is affecting other religious groups as well, such as the religious-Zionist fundamentalists and the ultra-Orthodox groups. The

---

[15] See eg Benny Porat (ed), *Reflections On Jewish Democracy* (Jerusalem, Israel Democracy Institute, 2010) (Hebrew).

[16] For a discussion, see: Menachem Mautner, 'The 1990s: Years of Reconciliation?' (2002) 26 Tel Aviv U L Rev 887 (Hebrew).

[17] The most prominent names in the group are Rabbi Azriel Hildesheimer, Rabbi Shimshon Raphael Hirsch, Rabbi Abraham Isaac Kook, Rabbi Yosef Dov Soloveitchik, Yeshayahu Leibowitz, Eliezer Goldman and David Hartman.

[18] The rise of religious feminism has been discernible since the 1970s in Christianity, Judaism and Islam. See: Merav Shmueli, 'The Power To Define Tradition: Feminist Challenges To Religion And The Israel Supreme Court' (PhD Dissertation, University of Toronto, 2005).

feminist revolution in religious-Zionism is manifest first and foremost in the establishment of educational institutions aimed at teaching the Talmud to women. The intention is to provide women with rabbinical knowledge that will enable them to fulfill rabbinical functions, ie, provide rabbinical guidance to other women. There are many other manifestations of this emergent religious feminism: Rabbis' rulings and conduct (eg, sexual harassment) are being scrutinized from a feminist perspective, new theologies devised that integrate traditional Jewish elements with feminist insights, and new interpretations of traditional texts offered by reading feminist insights into them, emphasizing the autonomy and personal self-realization of women. Work is being done to eradicate discrimination in women's daily lives. Since the early 1990s, women have been serving as rabbinical advocates in rabbinical courts,[19] and as members of municipal bodies in charge of providing religious services. Synagogues are being designed in ways that diminish the separation between men and women, and that do not convey the inferiority of women (eg, seating women in parallel to men, as opposed to seating them in the rear of synagogues); and women have begun actively participating in religious rituals. Thus, women are serving as agents of a social transformation that is channeling Western elements of democratization and equality into religious-Zionism, bringing the group closer to the secular liberal group in terms of both worldview and practices.[20]

In addition to the rise of feminism in religious-Zionism, another notable recent development is the open discussion of homosexuality within the group, made manifest by internet discussion groups[21] and press articles[22] in which rabbis have openly addressed the issue. In February 2010 a group of 70 religious-Zionist rabbis issued a statement calling for greater tolerance toward homosexuals.[23]

---

[19] Ronen Shamir, Michal Shitrai and Nelly Elias, 'Religion, Feminism, and Professionalism: The Case and Cause of Women Rabbinical Advocates' (1997) 38 Megamot 313 (Hebrew).

[20] Tamar Ross, 'The "Holy Rebellion" of Religious Zionist Women as a Bridge Between Halakhah and Democracy' in Avi Sagi and Dov Schwartz (eds), *A Hundred Years Of Religious Zionism* (Ramat Gan, Bar Ilan University Press, 2003) vol 3, 447 (Hebrew); Hanan Moses, 'From Religious Zionism To Post-Modern Religiosity' PhD Dissertation, Department of Political Science, Bar Ilan University, 2009 (Hebrew); Lior Ben-Haim, 'Haredut, National Religiousness and Secularization in Higher Education: A Multi-Modern Perspective' in Uri Cohen et al (eds), *Israel And Modernity* (Beer Sheva, Ben Gurion University of the Negev, 2006) 395 (Hebrew); Noa Shehar Eton, 'A New Revelation of Divine Will'—The Influence of Feminism on Religious-Zionism' in David Yoel Ariel et al (eds), *Blessed Be He Who Made Me A Woman* (Tel Aviv, Miskal Publishing House, 2009) 207 (Hebrew).

[21] <http://www.hod.org.il/> ('The Hod website is the first independent site for religious homosexual Jews, providing a platform for open-minded discussion in order to facilitate understanding.')

[22] See eg Yaacov Medan, 'Setting Boundaries to Gayness' (September 4 2009) Makor Rishon.

[23] Nisan Strauchler, 'Gay and Believing' (February 12 2010) Yedioth Ahronoth.

Furthermore, in the past two decades members of the religious-Zionist group have registered an impressive presence in the literary and artistic fields, as well as in cinema, television, and rock music.[24]

I have discussed two opposing subgroups within religious-Zionism: religious fundamentalism and Modern Orthodoxy. The polarization between these two subgroups has prompted some scholars to assert that religious-Zionism is on the verge of a schism, or, even worse, that it has already lost its former unity and is currently composed of two distinct groups.[25] It is widely accepted, however, that the majority of religious-Zionists in Israel adhere neither to religious fundamentalism nor to Modern Orthodoxy, but rather belong to a third group ('the silent majority'), often referred to as 'religious bourgeoisie' or as 'the new middle class'.[26] This group is composed mainly of professionals (lawyers, accountants, doctors, etc) who incorporate into their lives cultural elements and practices borrowed both from the Halakhah and religious Jewish tradition, and from the Western heritage. These people send their children to universities; they read Israeli and world literature; they attend the theatre, cinema and opera.

Importantly, the religious-Zionist group, unlike the ultra-Orthodox group, runs its political institutions in a highly democratic fashion.

What all of this means is that it is not unfounded to expect that some significant subgroups within religious-Zionism will object to Israel's becoming a theocracy and rather take action to preserve Israel's liberal-democratic regime and political culture. It also means that in many ways the religious-Zionist group holds the key to Israel's future cultural character. Put differently, the struggle between religious fundamentalism and Modern Orthodoxy is not just an internal struggle over the soul of religious-Zionism, but also a struggle over Israel's soul. If a majority of members of the religious-Zionist group insists on preserving Israel's current regime and political culture, Israel's liberal democracy will continue to exist and may even flourish. However, if the religious-Zionist group endorses more and more ultra-Orthodox, fundamentalist cultural elements and practices, Israel's liberal democracy is bound to find itself in great jeopardy.

---

[24] Mautner, above n 16.
[25] Yair Sheleg, 'The Division in Religious Zionism: Past, Present and Future' (2010) 46 Deot 6 (Hebrew).
[26] Moses, above n 20; Nissim Leon, 'The Transformation of Israel's Religious-Zionist Middle Class' (2010) 29 J Israeli History 61.

(b) Traditionalists

Thus far, in this book I have discussed three major Jewish groups living in Israel: Seculars, religious-Zionists, and ultra-Orthodox. In recent years, researchers have come to the realization that an additional group, hitherto mostly disregarded, needs to be taken into account in conceptualizing Israeli society: The traditionalists.[27] This group has been estimated to comprise about a third of Israel's Jewish population. It has also been asserted that about half of Israel's Sephardim and a fifth of Ashkenazim are traditionalists.

Traditionalists view the Halakhah as a binding source of authority in their lives. Their lives, however, are governed by custom rather than text. No social institutions (schools, newspapers, cultural institutions, etc.) exist that express and cultivate the traditionalist identity, nor is there any conscious traditionalist theology. Rather, the religious conduct of traditionalists is premised on the perpetuation of practices that have been internalized, mainly in the family domain. They abide by some religious commandments, namely those they regard as the core commandments of Judaism. They admit that a fully religious life is superior to theirs, but they self-consciously choose to assimilate only parts of the Halakhah into their lives.

The traditionalists are an intermediate group between the seculars and the religious. They make room in their lives for both the Halakhah and Western culture. The traditionalist option may prove to be the one that best solves the constant tension that lies at the basis of the Jewish nation-state project: the tension between (national-liberal) modernity and (ethnic, religious, national) tradition; between universal and particular identities; between a 'democratic' and 'Jewish' state.[28]

It may be expected therefore that many traditionalists will take the side of those committed to the preservation of Israel's liberal democracy in the context of the struggle over the country's future cultural identity.

B. DEFINING THE STATE'S IDENTITY: 'A JEWISH STATE'

In the two Basic Laws of 1992, Israel adopted an 'official' definition of itself as a 'Jewish and democratic state'. One of the features of the current debate

---

[27] Yaacov Yadgar, *Masortim In Israel* (Jerusalem, Shalom Hartman Institute, 2010) (Hebrew); Yaacov Yadgar and Charles S. Liebman, 'Beyond the "Religious-Secular" Dichotomy: Traditional Judaism in Israel' in Uri Cohen et al (eds), *Israel And Modernity* (Beer Sheva, Ben Gurion University of the Negev, 2006) 337 (Hebrew); Eliezer Ben-Rafael and Nissim Leon, 'Communal Segregation, Religiosity and Politics: The Origins of the Haredi Movement Amongst the Mizrachim' in Uri Cohen et. al. (eds), *Israel And Modernity* (Beer Sheva, Ben Gurion University of the Negev, 2006) 285 (Hebrew).

[28] Yadgar and Liebman, id, at 366.

over what it means to be a Jewish state is that parties to the debate tend to perceive Jewishness in essentialist terms: They swoop upon one element or aspect of the rich Jewish heritage, claiming that it expresses the essence of Judaism. That is always the case with ultra-Orthodox spokespersons, who identify Jewishness with the observance of halakhic commandments, to the exclusion of all other manifestations of Jewish life and heritage.

Yet such an approach is unacceptable. Israel should not be considered a Jewish state simply for adopting and validating only *one* component out of so many that make up the entire Jewish cultural heritage. Rather, Israel should be viewed as a Jewish state in the sense of enabling different groups of Jews to develop their unique Jewish cultures. In other words, Israel should be seen as 'the state of the Jews' rather than a 'Jewish state,' ie, as the state meant to enable various groups of Jews to develop to the fullest their different Jewish cultures—each group with its own cultural components, each group with its own unique mix of cultural elements. As Amnon Rubinstein writes:

Israel is sometimes defined as a Jewish state, but this definition misses the point.... It would be better to return to Herzl's original definition: Israel is the state of the Jews. It is the state of different Jews, who hold different and even conflicting outlooks regarding their Judaism.[29]

This view of the Jewish state rests on the history of the Jewish people during the last two-hundred and fifty years, a period characterized by the loss of uniformity in Jewish culture, a uniformity that had existed—at a high albeit far from perfect level—for as long as the Halakhah was dominant in the lives of all Jews.[30] The recent centuries have seen an extensive pluralism flourish in Jewish culture. In the course of the eighteenth century, secularization spread among Jews living in the urban centers of western and central Europe. From the end of the eighteenth century, the Jewish Enlightenment (*haskalah*), which sought to integrate traditional Jewish culture with Western culture, sparked the emergence of new Jewish ways of life and cultures, some of them wholly secular. From the end of the nineteenth century, various Jewish groups have been active within the framework of the Zionist movement, each with a culture premised on its own

---

[29] Amnon Rubinstein, *Being A Free People* (Tel Aviv, Schocken Publishing House, 1977) 196 (Hebrew). See also: Amnon Rubinstein, *From Herzl To Rabin—The Changing Image Of Zionism* (New York, Holmes & Meier, 2000); Alexander Yakobson And Amnon Rubinstein, *Israel And The Family Of Nations* (London, Routledge, 2009) 97–104; Ruth Gavison, 'On Israel as a Jewish and Democratic State' in Ron Margolin (ed), *Israel As A Jewish And Democratic State* (Jerusalem, World Union of Jewish Studies, 1999) 55.

[30] Avi Sagi, 'A Critique of Jewish Identity Discourse' in Avi Sagi and Nahem Ilan (eds), *Jewish Culture In The Eye Of The Storm* (Tel Aviv, Hakibbutz Hameuchad Publishing House, 2002) 248 (Hebrew).

unique mix of a wide range of cultural elements. Israel, then, should not be viewed as a Jewish state in the sense of being identified with one specific Jewish cultural element (eg, the Halakhah). Rather, it should be seen as a Jewish state because the various groups of Jews living in it are simultaneously developing different versions of Jewish culture using different cultural components.

Moreover, the attempt to think of Israel as a 'Jewish state', taking only one component out of the many in Jewish culture as the 'correct,' 'genuine,' and 'authentic' expression of Judaism, reflects an old-fashioned perception of culture as a homogeneous and consensual entity. According to the current understanding of the concept of culture, however, every culture is composed of a vast number of categories and practices, some widely shared and others partaken of by only a small number of individuals, some developed in the context of the culture itself and others borrowed from other cultures. Culture is also the site of endless disputes over the status of various cultural elements in the life of a cultural group and over their interpretation.[31]

The approach proposed here towards the meaning of the concept of a 'Jewish state' is in the spirit of the statement by the great Kabala scholar Gershom Scholem:

> It is impossible to define Judaism by a principle because it is not premised on one single principle. For that reason, it is also impossible to view it as a discrete historical phenomenon whose essence and development may be summed up in a number of historical, philosophical, doctrinal or dogmatic sayings...Judaism is a living substance that has been shaped and reshaped in the course of different historical stages...Just as it is impossible to define Judaism in any dogmatic way, we also cannot assume that it contains any a-priori essences that may emerge. The truth of the matter is that Judaism, being an ongoing, growing historical power, goes through transformations along all of its historical stations.
>
> ...
>
> Truly, as a historical phenomenon the Halakhah is an important and impressive aspect of Judaism. However, it is not identical with Judaism as a phenomenon in itself. Judaism has had various shapes. The tendency to contract it to mere

---

[31] Ulf Hannerz, *Cultural Complexity* (New York, Columbia University Press, 1992) 68, 69; Neil J. Smelser, 'Culture: Coherent or Incoherent' in Richard Munch and Neil J. Smelser (eds), *Theory Of Culture* (Berkeley, University of California Press, 1992) 3; William H. Sewell Jr., 'The Concept(s) of Culture' in *Beyond The Cultural Turn—New Directions* in Victoria E. Bonnell and Lynn Hunt (eds), *The Study Of Society And Culture* (Berkeley, University of California Press, 1999) 35, 39; Madhavi Sunder, 'Cultural Dissent' (2001) 54 Stan L Rev 49; Madhavi Sunder, 'Piercing the Veil' (2003) 112 Yale L J 1399.

legislated commandments seems to me, as a historian and as a historian of ideas, sheer nonsense.[32]

In the same vein, Moshe Halbertal, a scholar of Jewish philosophy, argues that Judaism is a 'surname.' 'Do I have an answer to the question who is a Jew?' asks Halbertal.

Certainly not...Jewishness, like nationality in general, is an expansion of the category of family, and, as Wittgenstein claims, between family members there is only a family resemblance, not one essence of which they are only different manifestations.[33]

C. DEFINING THE STATE'S IDENTITY: MAKING ROOM FOR THE ARAB CITIZENS

One of the major lessons to be drawn from the politics of identity that has emerged in many Western countries in recent decades is the connection between cultural categories and the material conditions of identity groups: if a culture perceives people of color, women, homosexuals, persons with disabilities, etc. in demeaning ways, those belonging to these identity groups will be adversely affected in terms of the life options available to them.[34]

'Israel as a Jewish state' is an exclusionary category. It excludes the state's Arab citizens from the state's definition of its identity. It could be said, applying the insights from the politics of identity to the Israeli context, that this has had two adverse consequences. First, the state's Jewish citizens have internalized a view of the state as being populated only by Jews, or that it so ought to be; that the state should promote mainly, or even exclusively, the interests of its Jewish citizens; and that the non-Jewish citizens living in the state are second-class citizens. Second, the state's Arab citizens have internalized the conviction that the state is not their state;

---

[32] Gershom Scholem, in Avraham Shapira (ed), *Explications And Implications—Writings On Jewish Heritage And Renaissance* (Tel Aviv, Am Oved, vol 2, 1986) 119, 120 (Hebrew). See also: Avraham Shapira (ed), *Continuity And Rebellion—Gershom Scholem In Speech And Dialogue* (Tel Aviv, Am Oved Publishers, 1987) (Hebrew) 36, 41, 50; Gershom Scholem, 'Who is a Jew' (1971) 60 Central Conference Of American Rabbis 135, 135.

[33] Moshe Halbertal, 'Who is a Jew' in Avi Sagi and Nahem Ilan (eds), *Jewish Culture In The Eye Of The Storm* (Tel Aviv, Hakibbutz Hameuchad Publishing House, 2002) 233, 246–7. Bernard Susser and Charles Liebman also adopt the term 'family' in speaking about Jewish culture. See: Bernard Susser And Charles S. Liebmen, *Choosing Survival—Strategies For A Jewish Future* (Tel Aviv, Hakibbutz Hameuchad Publishing House, 2004) 166 (Hebrew).

[34] Iris Marion Young, *Justice And The Politics Of Difference* (Princeton, New Jersey, Princeton University Press, 1990); Cornel West, 'The New Cultural Politics of Difference' in John Rajchman (ed), *The Identity Question* (New York, Routledge, 1995) 147; J. Nancy Fraser, 'From Redistribution to Recognition? Dilemmas of Justice in a 'Post-Socialist' Age' in Cynthia Willett (ed), *Theorizing Multiculturalism* (Cambridge, Blackwell Publishers, 1998) 19.

that it is impossible for them to develop their own self-identity within the category of the state's identity (Arabs cannot be Jewish); and that they are second-class citizens who cannot make claims on the state equal to those made by Jewish citizens. These consequences translate from the symbolic to the material realm. They greatly contribute to the unequal allocation of material public resources to the Arab citizens, to their exclusion from important political decisions, to their under-representation in the state's public administration, etc.[35]

Israel should take the following two measures to remedy the unfortunate consequences that follow from its exclusionary definition as a 'Jewish state'.

First, Israel should cultivate and emphasize *Israeliness* as an inclusive super-category that encompasses *all* its citizens, both Jewish and Arab. That would enable the state's Jewish citizens to define themselves as Jewish-Israelis and the Arab citizens as Arab-Israelis. Thus, Israel would perceive itself not only as the nation-state of the Jewish people, but also as the state of all its citizens, both Jews and Arabs.[36]

Pronouncements in this spirit have been incorporated in certain opinions of the Supreme Court.[37] Indeed, a liberal state needs to define itself first and foremost as the state of all its citizens, ie, a state whose function is to serve as an instrument in the hands of its citizens for the promotion of their vital human interests, such as personal security, healthcare, education, housing, and cultural accomplishment. From this perspective, preserving and cultivating the national culture of the people to which the citizens belong is just *one* human interest that a liberal state may promote, but which should not enjoy any priority over other essential human

---

[35] Chaim Gans argues that since most states in the world are populated by more than one people, allowing just one people in a state to exercise its right to self-determination in the state is unjust and discriminatory towards the other people(s) living in the state. It gives rise to a situation in the world in which some peoples enjoy the realization of their right to self-determination, while others are denied it. Gans recommends therefore that the right to self-determination be exercised at the sub-state level. Chaim Gans, *The Limits Of Nationalism* (Cambridge, Cambridge University Press, 2003).

[36] See also: Ruth Gavison, 'Both Israeli and Jewish' (March 16 2010) Haaretz ('Israel is Jewish and democratic...and also Israeli—a state in which all the citizens, and only the citizens, take part in democratic decisions for the state'). Studies conducted among Israeli Arabs show that the majority of them define themselves, both individually and collectively, using the term 'Israeli'. See: As'ad Ghanem and Sarah Ozacky-Lazar, 'The Status of the Palestinians in Israel in the Age of Peace: Part of the Problem but not Part of the Solution' in Uri Cohen et al (eds), *Israel And Modernity* (Beer Sheva, Ben Gurion University of the Negev, 2006) 211, 225 (Hebrew).

[37] In CAR 2316/96 *Izackson v Parties Registrar*, 50(2) PD 529, 549, Justice Cheshin stated as follows: 'Saying that Israel is "the state of all its citizens" does not negate its existence as a Jewish state.... Saying that the state is "the state of all its citizens" does not derogate from its being a Jewish state, the state of the Jewish people.' See also: EC 11280/02 *Central Elections Committee v Tibi*, 57(4) PD 1, 22; Aharon Barak, 'The Constitutional Revolution—12th Anniversary' (1994) 1 Law And Business 3 (Hebrew).

interests. Indeed, there is nothing to prevent a liberal state, a state of all its citizens, from being also the nation-state of its citizens or of the majority of them, namely a state concerned with the preservation and cultivation of the national heritage of all its citizens or a majority of them. As Michael Walzer has pointed out, the vast majority of liberal states in the world are at the same time also nation-states involved in the promotion of the national project of a people.[38]

Second, Israel should add to its current definition as a 'Jewish and democratic state' a third element of identity, that of a 'multicultural state'. Multiculturalism as an identity trait will serve as a constant reminder to Israelis that not only is the state's Jewish group not culturally homogenous, but the state's population is composed of another national group as well, the Arab. More importantly, the category of multiculturalism will allow for the inculcation in both schoolchildren and the state's population in its entirety of the 'multicultural virtues': understanding of the constitutive role that culture plays in the lives of human beings (in addition to genetics); understanding that respect for people necessitates respect for their cultures (at least prima facie); toleration of cultural practices and identities; the need to neutralize the anxiety and even tendency towards violence that may erupt whenever people encounter people belonging to a culture not their own; the understanding that every culture is partial; and the great cultural enrichment that may ensue as a result of cultural diversity and cross-cultural contacts. This last point may draw on a particular Jewish experience—the 'Golden Age' of the Jews in Spain of the tenth and eleventh centuries. Maria Rosa Menocal discusses this in the context of the great cultural flourishing that Spain enjoyed for a full seven centuries between the eighth and fifteenth centuries. Menocal's main argument is reflected in the title of her book: *The Ornament of the World—How Muslims, Jews and Christians Created a Culture of Tolerance in Medieval Spain.*[39]

There is nothing unusual in a state defining itself as having an identity composed of several elements, as Israel's current definition as a 'Jewish and democratic state' already does. There is nothing problematic therefore in adding to Israel's current definition a third element. Each and every one of us has many identities. The same person may be at the same time American, female, young, heterosexual, married, a parent, doctor, or person with disabilities, etc. A plurality of identities may also obtain in the

---

[38] Michael Walzer, 'Comment' in *Multiculturalism And The 'Politics Of Recognition'* (Princeton, Princeton University Press, 1992) 99. See also: Charles Taylor, 'Multiculturalism and the "Politics of Recognition"' id, at 51–61; Charles Taylor, 'Cross-Purposes: The Liberal-Communitarian Debate' in *Philosophical Arguments* (Cambridge, Harvard University Press, 1995) 181, 203.

[39] Maria Rosa Menocal, *The Ornament of the World—How Muslims, Jews And Christians Created a Culture of Tolerance in Medieval Spain* (Boston, Little, Brown and Company, 2002).

case of states. True, in the past two centuries, partly due to the dominance of the nation-state paradigm, we have become accustomed to thinking of states as having a single, dominant identity, namely the national identity. But as I have noted, by the same token that individuals perceive themselves and are perceived by others as having a plurality of identities, so too states can perceive themselves and be perceived as having a plurality of identities. (And by the same token that individuals need to constantly reconcile their various identities, eg, 'doctor' and 'parent', so also a state such as Israel needs to reconcile and maintain an equilibrium between its various identities, eg, as a Jewish state and as a democratic state, as a Jewish state and a state whose population includes an Arab national minority, etc.)

Third, in the alternative, Israel should find a way to add to the current definition of its identity an element that will express the existence in the country of an Arab national minority, eg, by adding to the 'Jewish and democratic state' definition the phrase 'with an Arab national minority'. As Alexander Yakobson and Amnon Rubinstein have written:

> [A]lthough the official recognition of a national minority is not required under the international norms on the protection of minorities...in the Israeli context there are good reasons for doing so. It is appropriate that a country that officially defines itself, in its Basic Laws, as a Jewish state, should also officially recognize the existence, within its citizen body, of a large community with a distinct national identity of its own. The authors of Israel's Declaration of Independence showed the way... [T]hey addressed themselves to the Arab population directly, referring to it as a national group ('members of the Arab people'), and guaranteed them full and equal citizenship. The country's Basic Laws and its future constitution should therefore include an explicit recognition of Israel's Arab community as a national minority.[40]

In the same vein, Israel needs to give expression to the fact that part of its population is Arab in its state symbols. It should add some Arabic text to its national anthem; it should add some signs expressive of the cultural heritage of its Arab citizens to its national flag and national emblem. Israel should also elevate the status of Arabic from its current 'semi-official' status to the same status as Hebrew, as one of the country's two official languages.

D. A NEW EQUILIBRIUM BETWEEN UNIFORMITY AND DIVERSITY

The Zionist project has been one of unification from several aspects. Cultural unification of the Jewish people was pursued by creating a new culture in Eretz Israel; geographical unification, by eliminating the scattered

---

[40] Yakobson and Rubinstein, above n 29, at 123.

existence of Jews in dozens of Diaspora countries and concentrating them in one place; organizational unification, by creating a single set of statist institutions for the Jewish people; and, of course, linguistic unification, by reviving Hebrew as a spoken language.

Israel was established as a nation-state and its state institutions, like those of all other nation-states, were involved in processes of cultural unification and assimilation aimed at achieving cultural uniformity. In Israel this has been known as 'nation-building', 'melting pot' and *mamlakhtiut*—processes that took place under the institutional and cultural umbrella of the labor-led hegemony.

However, as things currently stand, with the decline of the hegemony and the transition to a post-hegemonic situation that is conceptualized by many scholars as one of multiculturalism, or even as a war of cultures, in the coming years Israel needs to establish a new equilibrium between uniformity and diversity in the lives of its citizens. (In this Israel is not alone. With the decline of the nation-state paradigm and the growing awareness that almost all countries of the world are in fact multicultural, many Western countries are going through similar processes.)

(a) Decentralization

To disagree is part of the human condition. Although a person may be in disagreement with himself/herself,[41] when we think of disagreement, what we usually have in mind is disagreement between different individuals.

A distinction should be drawn between disagreement that involves people of the same cultural group and disagreement that involves people who belong to more than one cultural group. The first kind of disagreement arises when people differ as to the understanding of a situation or the action called for by a situation. This routinely happens in our lives: We are constantly surrounded by people who interpret situations differently than us; who evaluate the normative meaning of situations differently than us; and who assess the implications of possible alternative interventions in situations differently than us. At times, this kind of disagreement may cause stress, but it does not threaten anyone's entire personal identity.

It is another matter altogether when the disagreement is rooted in the fact that the parties involved belong to different cultural groups. In situations of this type, it is often not only the case that the parties lack any common

---

[41] Bernard Williams, 'Conflicts of Values' in *Moral Luck* (Cambridge, Cambridge University Press, 1981) 71. See also Brutus' remarks in Shakespeare's *Julius Caesar*:

> Between the acting of a dreadful thing and the first motion, all the interim is like a phantasma or a hideous dream: the genius and the mortal instruments are then in council; and the state of man, like to a little kingdom, suffers then the nature of an insurrection. William Shakespeare, *Julius Caesar*, Act II, Scene I.

ground for reaching agreement (they find themselves in an 'abnormal discourse', to borrow a term from Rorty)[42]; rather, because of the crucial role played by culture in constituting the personalities of human beings (ie, the mental categories through which human beings ascribe meaning to whatever transpires in their lives; Chapter 1, above), this kind of disagreement may be perceived as a threat to the very personalities of the parties involved. (Think of a religious Jew confronted by the claim that circumcising an eight-day old male infant is an act of brutal violence.)

Some cases of disagreement are tragic[43]—the circumstances allow for the endorsement of only one course of action at the expense of all other suggested courses of action (whether or not to go to war, adopt a certain economic measure, live in this or that town, get married to a particular person, etc.). There may be non-tragic disagreements, however, whenever it is possible to simultaneously implement more than one course of action: each party may not only uphold his or her position, but also implement it, in parallel to the implementation of the positions of all other parties to the disagreement.

Decentralization is an important means for resolving non-tragic disagreements, particularly those that involve parties who belong to different cultural groups. The great virtue of decentralization in situations of this kind is that it allows all parties to go on adhering to their cherished cultural convictions and practices. A well known version of decentralization as a means for addressing disagreement is federalism—a normative division on the basis of geographical separation (into states, cantons, provinces, etc).

Decentralization should be an important principle in the life of any multicultural state. The citizens of such a state need to understand that it would be unrealistic of them to expect their state to embody *all* of their normative convictions in its laws. Rather, they should expect to fully implement their normative convictions at the sub-state level, ie, in their municipalities, cultural communities or associations, and in their federal units (if they live in a federal state). Put differently, the citizens of a multicultural state must accept that while most of the law of their state will be uniform, some of it will remain differential, ie, it may be the case that the lives of different groups of citizens will be governed by different laws. The notion that the law of the state uniformly and equally applies to all the citizens of the state is an important element of the liberal concept of 'the rule of law', and in that

---

[42] Richard Rorty, *Philosophy And The Mirror Of Nature* (Princeton, Princeton University Press, New Jersey, 1979) 320.

[43] I use the term 'tragic' in the sense employed by Calabresi and Bobbitt in Guido Calabresi and Philip Bobbitt, *Tragic Choices* (New York, Norton & Co Inc, 1978).

context it should be preserved. The notion itself, however, belongs to the post-French Revolution era of the unifying and assimilating nation-state, and it requires qualification in light of the contemporary understanding that all states are multicultural, ie, sometimes the law of the state should retreat and give way to the particular normative convictions and cultural practices of the various cultural groups that live in the country.

Interestingly, Israeli law already applies the decentralization principle in various important contexts. For instance, there are five different educational streams in the country. In fact, this decentralization is too far-reaching, for there are very few culturally mixed schools in the country, and the state does not insist that all children study a common core curriculum aimed at preparing them to cooperate with each other as adults operating in the same political and economic systems. Nor does the state insist that children learn about the cultural heritage of other groups, or that children meet with children of other cultural groups (Chapter 7, above).

There is no uniform law of marriage and divorce in Israel. Rather, each religious group applies the religious law of the group to its members. That is part of the *millet* system that Israel inherited from the Ottoman Empire. In this context, the argument could be made that there is too little differentiation, for religious law applies to both religious and secular Jews and Arabs, in matters that are most personal and intimate. There is no uniform law to govern the observance of the Jewish Sabbath and other religious holidays. Rather, different norms, and thus different practices, apply in different settlements. There is no uniform law to govern the growing of pigs and the sale of pork. Rather, different norms apply in different settlements (sometimes different norms govern the sale of pork in different neighborhoods in the same town). There are different cemeteries for religious and secular Jews. Finally, there is a great deal of normative and cultural diversity in Israel in the country's hundreds of municipalities in the spheres of education, religion, welfare, licensure of businesses, public commercial advertising, etc.[44]

(b) Uniformity—a common good

In the second half of the twentieth century, the dominant model of politics in Western democracies has been interest-group liberalism ('the aggregative model'). The political sphere has been viewed as functioning according to the logic of the market (as perceived by economists), namely as an

---

[44] cf Nancy Fraser, 'Rethinking the Public Sphere: A Contribution to the Critique of Actually Existing Democracy' in Craig Calhoun (ed), *Habermas And The Public Sphere* (Cambridge, MIT Press, 1996) 109; Nancy Fraser, 'Transnationalizing the Public Sphere', <http://www.republicart.net>.

arena in which various groups, with their preferences and interests formed in civil society, ie, prior to the political process, compete with each other over the distribution of material and symbolic resources, in conditions of a zero-sum game. Politics, on this understanding, is primarily a procedure, rather than an arena for normative deliberation and for the constitution of a nation's normative tenets.[45]

If the liberal state is multicultural then, given the constitutive role played by culture in the lives of human beings, there is a danger that this market-type view of the political sphere will be accentuated and come to apply to cultural groups. Each of the major cultural groups that compose the state's population will engage in political action only for the promotion of the distinct interests and worldview of its members, and the political discourse will be lacking any discussion of the common good.

A multicultural state has to invest great effort in making the common good an important ideal in its political culture. It needs to remind its citizens that beyond their cultural diversity, there are some interests they all share. Put differently, a multicultural state has to cultivate the republican components in its political culture.

Republicanism is a longstanding Western tradition (identified with such varied thinkers, among others, as Machiavelli, Montesquieu and Rousseau) with many complex elements.[46] At the center of the republican worldview stands the perception of liberty as extant when the citizens of a state are not subordinated to particularistic interests, but rather to a common good that is determined in a free political process in which all citizens participate on an equal footing. Put differently, under republicanism all the citizens of a state are expected to deliberate over their common good, with none of them excluded from the process.[47]

At first sight, the association of multiculturalism and republicanism seems odd. Is not France, the country with the strongest republican

---

[45] The 'republican revival' in American jurisprudence in the 1980s, as well as the rise of the discourse of deliberative democracy in recent decades, has been motivated by a profound dissatisfaction with the impoverished view of politics propagated by interest-group liberalism. G. Edward White, 'Reflections on the 'Republican Revival': Interdisciplinary Scholarship in the Legal Academy' (1994) 6 Yale J L & Hum 1; Richard H. Fallon, 'What is Republicanism, and is it Worth Reviving?' (1989) 102 Harv L Rev 169; Mouffe, above n 4.

[46] Cynthia V. Ward, 'The Limits of "Liberal Republicanism": Why Group-Based Remedies and Republican Citizenship Don't Mix' (1991) 91 Columbia L Rev 581, 584 ('Republican theories have varied so widely that discussing republicanism in the contemporary context, without multiple qualifications, is a serious problem.').

[47] Maurizio Viroli, *Republicanism* (Antony Shugaar trans, New York, Hill and Wang, 1999); Philip Pettit, *Republicanism—A Theory Of Freedom And Government* (New York, Oxford University Press, 1997); Knud Haakonssen, 'Republicanism' in Robert E. Goodin and Philip Pettit (eds), *A Companion to Contemporary Political Philosophy* (Oxford, Basil Blackwell, 1993) 568; Morton J. Horwitz, 'Republicanism and Liberalism in American Constitutional Thought' (1987) 29 Wm & Mary L Rev 57; Taylor, 'Cross-Purposes' above n 38.

tradition in Europe, also the one that has faced the greatest difficulties in instilling multicultural notions into its public discourse? Moreover, is republicanism not usually associated with small, culturally homogeneous city-states? Yet the republican notion of the common good, important in itself in the setting of any liberal state, is particularly important in the context of multicultural states.[48]

For many years, under the umbrella of the labor-led hegemony, there was a strong republican tradition in the pre-state *Yishuv* and in the State of Israel. This republican understanding of the common good excluded the state's Arab citizens. The republican element in Israel's political culture dwindled substantially in the post-hegemonic era with the renewal of the struggle over the future shape of Israel's regime, political culture and law. The growing commitment of the former liberal hegemons to individualistic liberalism and to neo-liberal economic ideology has also contributed to the dilution of republican thinking in the country. Israel's most urgent task is to develop an updated, inclusive notion of the common good, a good that is indeed common to all its citizens, both Jews and Arabs.

Can any meaningful content, however, be assigned to the republican ideal of the common good in the context of Israel's multicultural condition? The answer is a qualified yes. I wish to outline briefly and tentatively the major planks of this argument.

First, let us assume the existence of a culturally homogeneous country, a pure nation-state (Case I). In such a case, common good republicanism is a morally higher ideal than that embodied in the aggregative model of interest-group liberalism. That is because thinking about the common good together with one's fellow citizens is to be involved in an other-regarding project (taking care of one's fellow citizens' good), something that is wholly missing from the self-regarding model of interest-group liberalism. The republican ideal of the common good lies somewhere in-between the poles of self-regarding and altruistic attitudes (it is no accident that praise of individual contributions to the welfare of the collectivity is often part of the republican discourse).

Furthermore, to think of the relations between fellow citizens within the frame of the (economic) concept of the market is almost a 'category mistake', to borrow a term from philosopher Gilbert Ryle. Fellow citizens are not strangers who every now and then enter into exchange transactions and

---

[48] cf Viroli, id, at 103 ('Republicanism should propose itself in democratic multicultural countries as a new political vision of civic ethos'); Ward, above n 46, at 585 (noting the importance of republicanism to contemporary diversified societies).

then retreat into their privacy.⁴⁹ Rather, they are people interdependently tied together, on an ongoing, broad basis, by the same destiny, the same culture, and the same historical memory. If the market metaphor is to be used at all, it can be said that fellow citizens are more like market actors as perceived by sociologists of markets (Chapter 6), namely actors whose conduct is governed by a rich shared culture and who are involved in ongoing relations, in the course of which they often demonstrate solidarity with and concern for each other. Fellow citizens much more resemble an extended family or a group of friends than they do alienated market actors.

Second, let us assume not a culturally homogeneous nation-state, but a multicultural state, such as Switzerland, Canada or Australia (Case II). To some extent, what I have said about a Case I state is also relevant to a multicultural state, although in the case of a multicultural state two additional considerations are relevant.

The first consideration is that citizens of all states share varied human interests. For example, they have an interest in their state being able to provide them with robust social services, such as high-standard healthcare services, education and housing. The provision of these services is an important common good of the citizens of all states (whether Case II or I).⁵⁰ Likewise, all citizens have an interest in high-standard personal security, economic development, cultural accomplishment and cross-cultural enrichment, protection of the environment, and the elimination of public corruption, crime and road accidents, etc. That the state should protect and foster these interests is an additional common good of all citizens of all states (whether Case II or I).

Secondly, from an even broader perspective, as made manifest by the vast post-World War II human rights jurisprudence, citizens of all states have certain common interests that all human beings share because of their humanity.⁵¹ Citizens of a state (whether Case II or I) may therefore define their common good in terms of this universalistic notion of humanity.⁵²

---

⁴⁹ Alasdair Macintyre analogizes viewing the citizens of a state as "a collection of strangers" to treating them as though they "had been shipwrecked on an uninhabited island with a group of other individuals, each of whom is a stranger to me and to all the others." Alasdair Macintyre, *After Virtue* (Notre Dame, University of Notre Dame Press, 1981) 233.

⁵⁰ Moreover, regardless of whether the provision of social services be regarded as the citizens' common good, a republican state, which expects its citizens to actively participate in politics and to deliberate over their common good, must provide its citizens with high-standard social services. That is so for at least two reasons. First, 'below a certain level of material and social well-being, and of training and education, people simply cannot take part in society as citizens, much less as equal citizens.' Rawls, above n 2, at 166. Second, wide gaps in income and wide disparities of life-style are repugnant to the republican ideal of shared deliberation toward a common good. See also: Viroli, above n 47, at 66, 67.

⁵¹ Menachem Mautner, 'From "Honor" to "Dignity": How Should a Liberal State Treat Non-Liberal Cultural Groups?' (2008) 9 Theoretical Inq L 609.

⁵² See also: Patrick Riley, 'Rousseau's General Will' in Patrick Riley (ed), *The Cambridge Companion to Rousseau* (Cambridge, Cambridge University Press, 2001) 124, 141–5 (offering universal definitions of the common good).

Third, let us assume a nation-state with a national minority living in it (Case III), as is the case with Israel. In such a case, difficult problems arise because the national minority cannot join forces with the national majority in the project of promoting the majority's national common good. Specifically, Israel's Arab citizens cannot be expected to subscribe to the Zionist common good.

Yet, what has been said about Case I is also relevant to some extent to Case III states, and everything said about Case II is fully relevant to Case III states (the fact that the Arab citizens cannot share in the national common good of the Jewish citizens does not mean that they cannot share with them in a wide spectrum of other types of common good). In addition, introducing some adaptations may make the common good ideal even more relevant to a Case III country, such as Israel.

The core of the nation-state project is the preservation and cultivation of a people's national culture. It could be maintained, invoking this ideal at a higher level of abstractness, that one of the state's functions is to promote the flourishing of its citizens' various cultures. In a Case III state such as Israel, that would entail the state's involvement in the preservation and cultivation not only of the cultures of the country's citizens belonging to the majority group, but also of the various cultures of the minority citizens, as well. In regard to the Israeli case, this idea may be put in different terms: since Israel's Arab citizens are perforce excluded from the state's project of preserving and cultivating the various Jewish cultures of its citizens, they should enjoy a cultural autonomy and be allowed within that framework to preserve and cultivate their own distinct cultures (with the state's help).[53] The fact that a state is a nation-state does not mean that it cannot protect and foster the cultural interests of its minority citizens (in addition to many other varied interests of all its citizens). It can and it should do so, and the citizens need to educate themselves that cultural prosperity, together with cross-cultural contacts between their flourishing cultures, are part of their common good.

I would therefore make the argument that the republican ideal of the common good, a noble ideal in itself, may be of relevance to multicultural states, and even to bi-national and multinational states that serve as the nation-states of their majority national groups.

Republicanism emphasizes the importance of equal participation by all citizens in politics. This point is of particular importance with regard to the integration of Israel's Arab citizens in the state's political process. In

---

[53] It may be argued that in any event the Arab citizens are entitled to that under various doctrines of contemporary international law. cf, Avihay Dorfman, 'Freedom of Religion' (2008) 21 Can J L & Jurisprudence 279 (positing freedom of religion as a compensatory principle in seeking to redress the exclusion of religious arguments from Rawlsian public reason democratic discourse).

Chapter 7, I noted that Israel's Arab citizens are excluded from much of the state's political process and from much of the state's administration. The infusion of republican elements into Israel's political culture will underline this problem and the need to take issue with it.

Finally, infusing Israel's political culture with republican notions may be viewed as the equivalent of according more space to the category of Israeliness in Israel's public discourse and in the way Israelis perceive their identities (see id).

CONCLUSION

To disagree is part of the human condition. Which factual elements of a case need to be taken into account in devising a normative solution for it? Which normative considerations need to be taken into account? What weight should be assigned to these values? What are the implications of adopting this or that possible solution? People disagree over these issues whenever they need to come up with a solution to a problem.

It is one thing when people of the same culture disagree, but another thing altogether when the disagreement is between people belonging to different cultures. The latter kind of disagreement raises particularly thorny questions. When people of different cultures need to reach agreement, it is not only the case that they may lack a shared normative platform on the basis of which to deliberate, but opting for a solution borrowed from one culture might even be interpreted by those of another as a threat to their personality and identity.

The law of the modern state is premised on uniformity, and this has served as an important instrument for creating homogeneity in culturally heterogeneous societies. But despite years of cultural homogenization, most of the states of the world are multicultural: Their populations are composed of more than one national group and/or more than one religious group, and of many ethnic groups. Each of these groups in itself is composed of many identity groups, ie, groups of people that share such identity marks as gender, sexual orientation, race, class, age, profession, etc. There is an unbridgeable gap between the uniformity of modern law and the prevalence of disagreement among human beings, as also between the uniformity of modern law and the diversity and complexity of the societies to which it applies.

Liberalism copes well with disagreement and cultural diversity. It is premised on equilibrium between a hard core of shared normative arrangements and the decentralization of other arrangements to civil society and the private realm. Since the 1990s, liberal thinking has arrived at the realization that civil society is composed not only of associations, but also of cultural groups, to whom liberal decentralization has therefore been extended as well.

Like all other modern states, Israel set in motion processes of cultural homogenization, employing such concepts as 'nation-building', 'melting pot' and *mamlakhtiyut*, all within the context of the reign of a political and cultural hegemony. But these processes came to a halt early on, and in the second half of the 1970s it became clear that the divide between secular Jews and religious Jews—which has been a central feature of the modern history of the Jewish people, and which threatened to tear early Zionism apart—has also become a central feature of the life of Israel in the waning decades of the twentieth century and early years of the twenty-first century. As if that weren't enough, with the publication of the 'Arab Vision Documents' in 2006 and 2007 it has become impossible not to realize that demographically Israel is a bi-national state.

Israel needs to find a new equilibrium between uniformity and decentralization. Most of its laws need to apply to all its citizens. But some normative arrangements need be decentralized to cultural groups, so that each will be able to live by its own distinct norms. Of this there are already some important manifestations in Israeli law.

But the major problems of the Israeli multicultural condition have to do not with decentralization, but with uniformity, or the lack thereof. There is profound disagreement within the Jewish group over the principles of the political culture, the contents of the law, and in some cases even over the nature of the country's regime in its entirety. It is no accident that to this very day, after more than sixty years of statehood, Israel is among the very few countries in the world that lacks a written constitution. Additionally, there is an even profounder disagreement between the Jewish group and the Arab group over the definition of the state and the nature of the mechanisms by means of which the country should be run. Moreover, these two disagreements are interrelated. This is the 'zero-sum game' of Israel's multicultural condition: The more Israel accentuates the Jewish elements in its public life, the more it alienates its Arab citizens; and the more Israel dilutes these elements, the more it agitates its Jewish religious citizens.

What Israel urgently needs is the creation and cultivation of new categories of thought and practice to strengthen the element of uniformity in its uniformity-decentralization equilibrium. It should cultivate the category of Israeliness to denote an overarching Israeli national identity common to all the state's citizens. (Israel could do that and still preserve its current definition as a 'Jewish state'; it is not unusual for states (and people) to have multiple identities which need to be reconciled). This should be complemented by the cultivation of the republican notion of the common good. In the years of the hegemony, republican thinking and discourse was vibrant in Israel. The hegemony disseminated the idea that Israeli Jews were involved in a great historical endeavor, the creation of a new society and state, necessitating personal contribution and sacrifice. Needless to say, this notion of the common good was confined to Jews only. But even before the decline of the hegemony, republican discourse in Israel had very much faded away: The liberal former hegemons adopted a market-oriented approach holding that private, rather than collective, initiative should be the motor for social and economic development, whereby the public good is promoted only as a byproduct of the promotion of private interests. This new approach gained substantial ground when the liberal former hegemons lost their control over the political system and the state administration and shifted much of their creative energy to the business sector.

Israelis need to understand that despite all the diversity among them, in certain matters they all share the same fate and are substantially dependent on one another: They all suffer in war, and they will all benefit if peace is established in the region; they all benefit from economic development; they all benefit from high-quality healthcare and education; they all flourish in times of economic prosperity; they all benefit from cultural flourishing; they all suffer if the country's politics, political culture and public administration deteriorate; they all suffer if crime and road accidents are on the rise; they all suffer if they fail to protect the environment.

The move from collectivism and republicanism to a market-oriented approach (which can also be phrased in terms of a move from collectivism to individualism and from collectivism to personal self-determination) is not the only change that the Israeli secular group has gone through within a time span of one or two generations. They have also gone from defining themselves as 'Hebrews' to defining themselves as Jews. What that means is that when the secular group takes part in the struggle over the shaping of the country's future culture, it is standing on an incoherent and shallow cultural platform. This is particularly noteworthy because in defining itself as Jewish, the secular group is borrowing cultural elements from the culture of its adversary, the religious group, which on its part can draw on an immensely rich culture that, in contemporary Israel, enjoys an exceptionally high degree of institutionalization (in the shape of myriad *yeshivot* (religious academies) and other educational institutions).

From the outset of Zionism, statements were made to the effect that the abandonment of traditional Jewish culture would breed cultural 'thinness' in the newly created secular Hebrew culture. One group of secular Israelis, however, certainly overcame the problem of cultural 'thinness'. These were the jurists who, through Israel's Anglicized law, enjoyed direct access not only to Anglo-American liberalism, but also to the Western heritage in its entirety. Moreover, this group too enjoyed the benefits of institutionalization, in the country's legal system, the apex of which, the Supreme Court, was regarded by the group not only as its professional leader, but first and foremost as its normative beacon.

Recent years, though, have been ones of great disillusionment regarding the integrity of the Court, which, as a result, has lost much stature not only among the Jewish religious group, but also among its own traditional supporters, who for many years uncompromisingly defended it. This deterioration in the Court's standing has far-reaching implications. It means that the Court's ability to continue playing its traditional role as a stronghold of Israel's liberalism is very much in jeopardy. It also means that the Israeli legal community is currently bewildered and at a loss for direction. Add to that the transitions that the Israeli secular group has gone through from collectivism (republicanism) to individualism and from Hebrewness to Jewishness, and the enormity of the crisis becomes even more apparent.

Yet having said all that, Israel's most threatening internal problem is the schism between Jews and Arabs. After sixty years of statehood, the Arabs still live in a separate civil society; they are excluded from the state's definition and ignored by its national symbols; they are excluded from important political decisions; they are badly discriminated against in the allocation of state resources; and they have a collective memory that stands in stark contrast to both that of the Jewish group and the official historic narrative disseminated by the state. All of this is taking place amidst continuous hostilities between Israel and the Palestinian people in the Occupied Territories and while Israel's demographic balance is steadily changing in favor of the Arab group. Israel will need much luck, goodwill, reason and toleration in the coming years to avoid a major upheaval in the context of the relations between the two peoples that compose its population. These have never been ubiquitous virtues, however, and history teaches us that usually they are adopted only after a heavy price has been paid.

BIBLIOGRAPHY

Ackerman, Bruce, *Property Law And The Constitution* (New Haven, Yale University Press, 1977).

Adalah's Bill Of Rights (2007) (Hebrew).

Adiv, Zvi, 'Zeev Jabotinsky's Zionist Thought' in Ben-Zion Yehoshua and Ahron Kedar (eds), *Ideological And Political Zionism* (Jerusalem, Zalman Shazar Center, 1978) 115 (Hebrew).

Ahad Ha-Am, 'Ahad Ha-Am, *Essays, Letters, Memoirs*' (Leon Simon trans, (ed), Oxford, 1946).
The Collected Writings Of Ahad Ha-Am (Tel Aviv, Dvir, 1954) (Hebrew).
Nationalism And The Jewish Ethic: Basic Writings Of Ahad Ha'am (Edited and introduced by Hans Kohn, New York, Schocken Books, 1962).
Selected Essays Of Ahad Ha'am (Leon Simon (ed) Trans, New York, Atheneum, 1970).

Aharoni, Yair, 'The Changing Political Economy in Israel' (1998) 555 Annals Of The American Academy Of Political Science 127.

Aktzin, Benjamin, *Regimes Theory* (Jerusalem, Academon, 1967) (Hebrew).

Aleinikoff, Alexander, 'Constitutional Law in the Age of Balancing' (1987) 96 Yale L J 943.

Alexander, Larry, '"With Me, It's All or Nothing": Formalism in Law and Morality' (1999) 66 U Chi L Rev 530.

Alhaj, Majd, 'Multicultural Education in Israel in Light of the Peace Process' in Menachem Mautner, Avi Sagi and Ronen Shamir (eds), *Multiculturalism In A Democratic And Jewish State* (Tel Aviv, Ramot Publishers, 1998) 703.

Almog, Oz, *The Sabra—A Profile* (Tel Aviv, Am Oved Publishers, 1997) (Hebrew).
'From "Our Right to Eretz Israel" to "Civil Rights" and from "a Jewish State" to "the Rule of Law": The Legal Revolution in Israel and its Cultural Meanings' (1999) 18 Alpaim 77 (Hebrew).

Almog, Shmuel, 'The Relation of Seculars to Religion in Early Zionism' in Anita Shapira (ed), *The Religious Trend In Zionism* (Tel Aviv, Am Oved Publishers, 1983) 31 (Hebrew).
'The Metaphoric Pioneer v. the Exilic Old Women' in Anita Shapira, Jehuda Reinharz and Jacob Harris (eds), *The Zionist Age* (Jerusalem, Zalman Shazar Center, 2000) 91 (Hebrew).

Amichai, Yehuda, *The Selected Poems Of Yehuda Amichai* (Chana Bloch and Stephen Mitchell trans, Harmondsworth, Viking, 1986).

Anderson, Elizabeth, *Value In Ethics And Economics* (Cambridge, Harvard University Press, 1993).

Appadurai, Arjun, 'Global Ethnoscapes—Notes and Queries for a Transnational Anthropology' in Richard G. Fox (ed), *Recapturing Anthropology—Working The Present* (Santa Fe, School of American Research Press, 1991).

Aran, Gideon, 'Jewish Zionist Fundamentalism: The Bloc of the Faithful in Israel (Gush Emunim)' in Martin E. Marty and R. Scott Appleby (eds), *Fundamentalism Observed* (Chicago, University of Chicago Press, 1991) 265.
'From Pioneering to Torah Study: Background to the Growth of Religious-Zionism' in Avi Sagi and Dov Schwartz (eds), *A Hundred Years Of Religious Zionism* (Ramat Gan, Bar Ilan University Press, 2003) vol 3, 31 (Hebrew).

Atiyah, P. S., *The Rise And Fall Of Freedom Of Contract* (Oxford, Clarendon Press, 1979).

Atiyah, Patrick S. and Robert M. Summers, *Form And Substance In Anglo-American Law* (Oxford, Clarendon Press, 1987).

Avinveri, Shlomo, *The Making Of Modern Zionism: The Intellectual Origins Of The Jewish State* (London, Weidenfeld and Nicolson, 1981).
'On Israel as a Jewish and Democratic State' in Ron Margolin (ed), *Israel As A Jewish And Democratic State* (Jerusalem, World Union of Jewish Studies, 1999) 79 (Hebrew).
Herzl (Jerusalem, Zalman Shazar Center, 2007) (Hebrew).

Avnon, Dan, '"The Enlightened Public": Jewish and Democratic or Liberal and Democratic?' 3 (1996) Mishpat Umimshal 417 (Hebrew).

Ayalon, Hanna, 'Higher Education' in Uri Ram and Nitza Berkovitch (eds), *In/Equality* (Beer Sheva, Ben-Gurion University of the Negev Press, 2006) 148 (Hebrew).

Bacon, Francis, 'Of Judicature' in John Pitcher (ed), *The Essays* (Harmondsworth, Middlesex, Penguin Books, 1985) 222.

Barak, Aharon, *Judicial Discretion* (Tel Aviv, Papyrus Publishing House, 1987) (Hebrew).
'The Foundation of Law Act and the Heritage of Israel' (1987) 13 Hebrew Law Annual 265 (Hebrew).
'Judicial Creativity: Interpretation, the Filling of Gaps (Lacunae) and the Development of Law' (1990) 39 Hapraklit 267 (Hebrew).
'Judicial Philosophy and Judicial Activism' (1993) 17 Tel Aviv U L Rev 475 (Hebrew).
'The Constitutional Revolution—12th Anniversary' (1994) 1 Law And Business 3 (Hebrew).
'Gaps in the Law and Israeli Experience' (1991) 20 Mishpatim 282 (Hebrew).
'The Constitutional Revolution: Protected Basic Rights' (1992) 1 Mishpat Umimshal 9 (Hebrew).
'Basic Law: Freedom of Occupation' (1994) 2 Mishpat Umimshal 195 (Hebrew).

Interpretation In Law (vol 3 Constitutional Interpretation, Jerusalem, Nevo, 1994) (Hebrew).
'The Enlightened Public' in Aharon Barak and Elinor Mazuz (eds), *Landau Book* (1995) 677 (Hebrew).
'On Israel as a Jewish and Democratic State' in Ron Margolin (ed), *Israel As A Jewish And Democratic State* (Jerusalem, World Union of Jewish Studies, 1999) 8 (Hebrew).
'Israel's Constitution: Past, Present and Future' in *Selected Papers* (Jerusalem, Nevo, 2000) 355 (Hebrew).
'The Limits of Law and the Limits of Adjudication' (2002) 2 Kiryat Hamishpat 5 (Hebrew).

Barak-Erez, Daphne, 'Judicial Review of Politics: The Israeli Case' (2002) 29 J Law & Soc 611.

Bareli, Avi, *Mapai In Israel's Early Independence 1948-1953* (Jerusalem, Yad Ben Zvi, 2007) (Hebrew).

Barnai, Yaacov, 'On the Beginning of Zionism' in Yechiam Weitz (ed), *From Vision To Revision: A Hundred Years Of Historiography Of Zionism* (Jerusalem, Zalman Shazar Center, 1997) 135 (Hebrew).

Barnea, Nahum, 'The Government that will Follow the Next Government' in *They Shoot And They Cry* (Tel Aviv, Zmora, Bitan, Modan Publishers, 1983) 203 (Hebrew).

Barry, Brian, 'John Rawls and the Search for Stability' (1995)105 Ethics 874.

Barzilai, Gad, 'Who is Afraid of the Supreme Court' (January 1997) 1 Panim 36 (Hebrew).
'Judicial Hegemony, Party Polarization and Social Change' (1998) 2 Politics 31 (Hebrew).
'Fantasies of Liberalism and Liberal Jurisprudence: State Law, Politics, and the Israeli Arab-Palestinian Community' (2000) 34 Israel L Rev 425.
Communities And Law (Ann Arbor, University of Michigan Press, 2003).
'The Ambivalent Language of Lawyers in Israel: Liberal Politics, Economic Liberalism, Silence and Dissent' in Terence C. Halliday, Lucian Karpik and Malcolm Feeley (eds), *Fighting For Political Freedom* (Oxford, Hart Publishing, 2007) 247.

Bauman, Zygmunt, 'From Pilgrim to Tourist—or a Short History of Identity' in Stuart Hall and Paul du Gay (eds), *Cultural Identity* (Miron, London, Sage Publications, 1996).
Culture As Praxis (London, Sage Publications, 1973, 1999).

Belge, Ceren, 'Friends of the Court: The Republican Alliance and Selective Activism of the Constitutional Court of Turkey' (2006) 40 Law & Soc Rev 653.

Ben, Israel Hedva, Book Review: *Religion and Zionism: First Encounters* by Yosef Shalmon, 2 (2002) Israel 189 (Hebrew).

Ben-Ami, Shlomo, 'Introduction; Israel as a Multicultural Society' in Yoav Peled and Adi Ophir (eds), *Israel: From Mobilized To Civil Society?* (Tel Aviv, Hakibbutz Hameuchad Publishing House, 2001) 18 (Hebrew).
'Israeli Identity as Immigrant Identity' in Neri Horowitz (ed), *Religion And Nationalism In Israel And The Middle East* (Tel Aviv, Am Oved Publishers, 2002) 225 (Hebrew).

Benhabib, Seyla, 'Turkey's Constitutional Zigzag' Dissent (Winter 2009).

Ben-Haim, Lior, 'Harediut, National Religiousness and Secularization in Higher Education: A Multi-Modern Perspective' in Uri Cohen et al (eds), *Israel And Modernity* (Beer Sheva, Ben Gurion University of the Negev, 2006) 395 (Hebrew).

Bennett, David, 'Introduction' in David Bennett (ed), *Multicultural States* (New York, Routledge, 1998) 1.

Bennett, Tony, Introduction: '"Popular Culture and 'The Turn to Gramsci"' in Tony Bennett, Colin Mercer and Janet Woollacott (eds), *Popular Culture And Social Relations* (Philadelphia, Open University Press, 1986) xi.
Culture—A Reformer's Science (London, Sage Publications, 1998).

Ben-Porat, Amir, *The Bourgeoisie—The History Of The Israeli Bourgeoisies* (Jerusalem, Magnes Press, The Hebrew University (1999) (Hebrew).

Ben-Rafael, Eliezer and Nissim Leon, 'Communal Segregation, Religiosity and Politics: The Origins of the Haredi Movement Amongst the Mizrachim' in Uri Cohen et al (eds), *Israel And Modernity* (Beer Sheva, Ben Gurion University of the Negev, 2006) 285 (Hebrew).

Benziman, Uzi (ed), *Whose land is it? A Quest For A Jewish-Arab Compact In Israel* (Jerusalem, Israel Democracy Institute, 2006) (Hebrew).

Berdyczewski, Micha Yosef, *The Writings Of Micha Yosef Berdyczewski* (Tel Aviv, Dvir, 1960) (Hebrew).

Berger, Peter et al, *The Homeless Mind* (New York, Vintage Books, 1973).

Berkowitz, Roger, *The Gift Of Science* (Cambridge, Harvard University Press, 2005).

Bickel, Alexander M., *The Least Dangerous Branch*, 2nd ed, (New Haven, Yale University Press, 1962, 1986).

Bilski Ben-Hur, Raphaela, *Every Individual Is A King—The Social And Political Thought Of Ze'ev (Vladimir) Jabotinsky* (Tel Aviv, Dvir, 1988) (Hebrew).

Bilski Cohen, Raphaela, *The Essence Of Democracy In The Liberal-Democratic Philosophy Of Ze'ev Jabotinsky* (Tel Aviv, Zeev Jabotinsky Institute, 2001) (Hebrew).

Bilsky, Leora, 'Law and Politics: The Trial of Rabin's Assassin' (1999) 8 Plilim 13 (Hebrew).

Bishara, Azmi, 'On the Question of the Palestinian Minority in Israel' (1993) 3 Theory & Criticism 7 (Hebrew).

'The Arab in Israel: A Study in a Splitted Political Debate' in Pinhas Ginossar and Avi Bareli (eds), *Zionism: A Contemporary Controversy* (Sede Boqer Campus, Ben Gurion Research Center, 1996) 312 (Hebrew).

Blair, Irene V., Bernadette Park and Jonathan Bachelor, 'Understanding Intergroup Anxiety: Are Some People More Anxious Than Others?' (2003) 6 Group Processes & Intergroup Relations 151.

Bodenheimer, Edgar, *Jurisprudence* (revised edition, Cambridge, Harvard University Press, 1974).

Bohman, James, *Public Deliberation* (Cambridge, MIT Press, 1996).

Bork, Robert H., 'Barak's Rule' (Winter 2007) Azure 146.

Bourdieu, Pierre, *Outline Of A Theory Of Practice* (Richard Nice trans, Cambridge, Cambridge University Press, 1977).
Distinction—A Social Critique Of The Judgment Of Taste (Richard Nice trans, Routledge, London, 1984).
'The Force of Law: Toward a Sociology of the Juridical Field' (1987) 38 Hastings L J 805.
The Logic Of Practice (Richard Nice trans, Stanford, Stanford University Press, California, 1990).
The Field Of Cultural Production (Randal Johnson (ed), New York, Columbia University Press, 1993).
'Rethinking the State: Genesis and Structure of the Bureaucratic Field' in George Steinmetz, (ed), *State/Culture—State Formation After The Cultural Turn* (Ithaca, Cornell University Press, 1999) 53.
Firing Back—Against The Tyranny Of The Market 2 (Loic Wacquant trans, London, Verso, 2003).
The Social Structure Of The Economy (Chris Turner trans, Cambridge, Polity Press, 2005).

Bracha, Baruch, *Administrative Law* (Tel Aviv, Schocken Publishing House, 1986) (Hebrew).

Breton, Raymond, 'The Production and Allocation of Symbolic Resources: An Analysis of the Linguistic and Ethnocultural Field in Canada' (1984) 21 Canadian Rev Soc & Anthrop 123.
'Multiculturalism and Canadian Nation-Building' in Alan Cairns and Cynthia Williams (eds), *The Politics Of Gender, Ethnicity And Language In Canada* (Toronto, University of Toronto Press, 1986) 27.

Brightman, Robert, 'Forget Culture: Replacement, Transcendence, Relexification' (1995) 10 Cultural Anthropology 509.

Brubaker, R., *The Limits Of Rationality* (London, Routledge, 1984).

Brubaker, Roger and Frederick Cooper, '"Beyond Identity"' (2000) 29 Theory And Society 1.

Bruner, Jose and Yoav Peled, 'On Autonomy, Capabilities and Democracy: Critique of Liberal Multiculturalism' in Menachem Mautner, Avi Sagi and

Ronen Shamir (eds), *Multiculturalism In A Democratic And Jewish State* (Tel Aviv, Ramot Publishers, 1998) 107 (Hebrew).

Burke, Edmund, *Reflections On The Revolution In France* (J.C.D. Clark (ed), Stanford, Stanford University Press, 2001).

Calabresi, Guido And Philip Bobbitt, *Tragic Choices* (New York, Norton & Co Inc, 1978).

Caplan, Kimmy, 'Research of the Israeli Ultra-Orthodox Society' in Kimmy Caplan and Emmanuel Sivan (eds), *Israeli Haredim: Integration Without Assimilation?* (Tel Aviv, Hakibbutz Hameuchad Publishing House, 2003) 224 (Hebrew).

Casanova, Jose, *Public Religions In The Modern World* (Chicago, University of Chicago Press, 1994).

Ceaser, James, 'Multiculturalism and American Liberal Democracy' in Arthur M. Melzer, Jerry Weinberger and M. Richard Zinman (eds), *Multiculturalism and American Democracy* (Lawrence, Kansas, University Press of Kansas, 1998) 139.

Cheshin, Mishael, 'Jewish Heritage and the Law of the State' in Ruth Gavison (ed), *Civil Rights In Israel—Essays In Honor Of Haim H. Cohen* (Jerusalem, The Association for Civil Rights in Israel, 1982) 47 (Hebrew).

Cincotta, Richard and Eric Kaufmann, 'The Changing Face of Israel' Foreign Policy Website (Summer 2009).

Cohen, Asher, *The Talit And The Flag—Religious Zionism And The Concept Of A Torah State 1947-1953* (Jerusalem, Yad Ben Zvi, 1998) (Hebrew).

Cohen, Asher and Bernard Susser, 'From Accommodation to Decision: Transformations in Israel's Religio-Political Life' (1996) 38 J Church & State 817.
Israel And The Politics Of Jewish Identity (Baltimore, Johns Hopkins University Press, 2000).
From Accommodation To Escalation (Tel Aviv, Schocken Publishing House, 2003) (Hebrew).

Cohen, Chaim, 'The Jewishness of the State of Israel' (1998) 16 Alpaim 9 (Hebrew).

Cohen, Joshua, 'Moral Pluralism and Political Consensus' in Henry S. Richardson and Paul J. Eeithman (eds), *The Philosophy Of Rawls* (New York, Routledge, 1999) 56.

Cohen Yinon, 'National, Gender and Ethnic Income Gaps' in Uri Ram and Nitza Berkovitch (eds), *In/Equality* (Beer Sheva, Ben-Gurion University of the Negev Press, 2006) 339 (Hebrew).

Comaroff, Jean and John Comaroff, *Of Revelation And Revolution* vol 1 (Chicago, University of Chicago Press, 1991).

Cooter, Robert D. and Tom Ginsburg, 'Comparative Judicial Discretion: An Empirical Test of Economic Models' (1996) 16 Int'l Rev L & Econ 295.

Curtis, Dennis and Judith Resnik, 'Images of Justice' (1987) 96 Yale L J 1727.

Dahan, Momi, 'Income Distribution' in Uri Ram and Nitza Berkovitch (eds), *In/Equality* (Beer Sheva, Ben-Gurion University of the Negev Press, 2006) 189 (Hebrew).

Dakhla, Muhammad, 'The Claim for Collective Rights to the Arab Minority in Israel' in Elie Rekhess and Sara Ozacky-Lazar (eds), *The Status Of The Arab Minority In The Jewish State* (Tel Aviv, Tel Aviv University, 2005) 84 (Hebrew).

Dan-Cohen, Meir, 'Decision Rules and Conduct Rules: On Acoustic Separation in Criminal Law' in *Harmful Thoughts* (Princeton, Princeton University Press, 2002) 37.

Dane, Perry, 'Constitutional Law and Religion' in Dennis Patterson (ed), *A Companion To Philosophy Of Law And Legal Theory*, 2nd edn (Chichester, UK, Wiley-Blackwell, 2010) 119.

Davion, Victoria and Clark Wolf (eds), *The Idea Of Political Liberalism* (Lanham, Rowman & Littlefield Publishers, Inc., 2000).

Dayan, Arye, *The Story Of Shas* (Jerusalem, Keter Publishing House, 1999) (Hebrew).

Deutch, Sinai, 'Jewish Law in Israeli Courts' (1988) 6 Legal Research 7 (Hebrew).

Dikshtein, Paltiel, 'Political Independence and Legal Independence' (1948) 5 Hapraklit 107 (Hebrew).

Dickson, Brice, 'Comparing Supreme Courts' in Brice Dickson (ed), *Judicial Activism In Common Law Supreme Courts* (Oxford, Oxford University Press, 2007) 1.

DiMaggio, Paul, 'Culture and Cognition' (1997) 23 Ann Rev Sociol 263.

Don-Yehiya, Eliezer, 'Ideology and Policy in Religious Zionism—Rabbi Yitzhak Ya'akov Reines' Conception of Zionism and the Policy of the Mizrahi Under his Leadership' (1983) 8 Zionism 103 (Hebrew).
'The Book and the Sword: Nationalist "Yeshivas" and Political Radicalism in Israel', in Avi Sagi and Dov Schwartz (eds), *A Hundred Years Of Religious Zionism* (Ramat Gan, Bar Ilan University Press, 2003) vol 3, 187 (Hebrew).

Dorfman, Avihay, 'Freedom of Religion' (2008) 21 Can J L & Jurisprudence 279.

Dotan, Yoav, 'Ripeness and Politics in the High Court of Justice' (1996) 20 Tel Aviv U L Rev 93 (Hebrew).
'Judicial Activism at the High Court of Justice' in Ruth Gavison, Mordechai Kremnitzer And Yoav Dotan (eds), *Judicial Activism—For And Against* (Jerusalem, Magnes Press, Hebrew University, 2000) 5 (Hebrew).

Dotan, Yoav and Menachem Hofnung, 'Legal Defeats-Political Wins—Why Elected Representatives Go to Courts?' (2005) 38 Comp Pol Stud 75.

Dworkin, Ronald, *Taking Rights Seriously* (Cambridge, Harvard University Press, 1977).

Eagleton, Terry, *Ideology* (Verso, London, 1991).

Edelman, Martin, 'Israel' in C. Neal Tate and Torbjorn Vallinder (eds), *The Judicialization Of Politics* (New York, New York University Press, 1995) 403.

Edrei, Arye, 'Why Teach Jewish Law' (2001) 25 Tel Aviv U L Rev 467 (Hebrew).

Eisenberg, Arthur N., 'Accommodation and Coherence: In Search of a General Theory for Adjudicating Claims of Faith, Conscience, and Culture' in Richard A. Shweder, Martha Minow and Hazel Rose Markus, (eds), *Engaging Cultural Differences—The Multicultural Challenge In Liberal Democracies* (New York, Russell Sage Foundation Publications, 2002) 147.

Eisenstadt, Samuel, 'The State and the Law' (1948) 5 Hapraklit 113 (Hebrew).
Zion In Justice (1967) (Hebrew).

Eisenstadt, Samuel. and P. Dikshtein (eds), *Hebrew Law* (Tel Aviv, Hebrew Law Society, 1918) (Hebrew).

Eisenstadt, S. N., 'The Struggle Over the Symbols of Collective Identity and its Boundaries in the Post-Revolutionary Israeli Society' in Pinhas Ginossar and Avi Bareli (eds), *Zionism—A Contemporary Controversy* (Sede Boqer, Ben-Gurion Research Center, 1996) 1 (Hebrew).
Fundamentalism And Modernity (Tel Aviv, Ministry of Defense, 2002) (Hebrew).
Changes In Israeli Society (Tel Aviv, Ministry of Defense, 2004) (Hebrew).

Elbashan, Yuval, *Strangers In The Realm Of The Law* (Tel Aviv, Hakibbutz Hameuchad Publishing House, 2005) (Hebrew).

Eliash, M. and P. Dikstein (eds), *Hebrew Law* (Tel Aviv, Hebrew Law Society, 1926) (Hebrew).

Elon, Menachem, 'Hebrew Law in the Law of the State' (1969) 25 Hapraklit 27 (Hebrew).
'More About the Foundations of Law Act' (1987) 13 Hebrew Law Annual 227 (Hebrew).
Jewish Law, History, Sources, Principles (1988) vol 3, 1329–37 (Jerusalem, Magnes Press, Hebrew University, Hebrew).
'Constitution by Legislation: The Values of a Jewish and Democratic State in Light of the Basic Law: Human Dignity and Liberty' (1993) 17 Tel Aviv U L Rev 659 (Hebrew).
'The Basic Laws: Their Enactment, Interpretation and Expectations' (1995) 12 Legal Research 253 (Hebrew).
'On Israel as a Jewish and Democratic State' in Ron Margolin (ed), *Israel As A Jewish And Democratic State* (Jerusalem, World Union of Jewish Studies, 1999) 18 (Hebrew).

Englard, Yitzhak, 'The Role of Court in the Recent Developments of Tort Law—Self Image and Reality' (1985) 11 Tel Aviv U L Rev 67 (Hebrew).

'Law and Religion in Israel' (1987) 35 Am J Comp L 185.

Equal Constitution For All? (Mossawa Center, Haifa, 2006) (Hebrew).

Eriksen, T. H., 'Anthropology, History of' (2001) 1 Int'l Encyclopedia Of The Social And Behavioral Sciences.

Estlund, David, 'The Insularity of the Reasonable: Why Political Liberalism Must Admit the Truth' (1998) 108 Ethics 252.

Etkes, Immanuel (ed), *The East European Jewish Enlightenment* (Jerusalem, Zalman Shazar Center, 1993) (Hebrew).

Ettinger, Shmuel, 'The Uniqueness of the Jewish National Movement' in Ben-Zion Yehoshua and Ahron Kedar (eds), *Ideological And Political Zionism* (Jerusalem, Zalman Shazar Center, 1978) 9 (Hebrew).

Etzioni-Halevy, Eva, *The Divided People* (Kfar Sava, Arye Nir Publishing House, 2000) (Hebrew).

Even, Zohar Itamar, 'The Emergence and Crystallization of Local Native Hebrew Culture in Eretz Israel 1882-1948' (1980) 16 Cathedra For The History Of Eretz Israel And Its Yishuv 165 (Hebrew).
'Introduction' (1980) 11 Poetics Today 1.
'Who is Afraid of Hebrew Culture' in Aharon Amir, Guy Ma'ayan and Amir Or (eds), *Ah'eret (Otherwise)—Miscellaneous Essays* (Jerusalem, Carmel, 2002) 38 (Hebrew).

Ezrahi, Yaron, *Rubber Bullets* (Berkeley, University of California Press, 1997).

Fallon, Richard H., 'What is Republicanism, and is it Worth Reviving?' (1989) 102 Harv L Rev 1695.

Feiner, Shmuel, 'Out of Berlin: The Second Phase of the Haskalah Movement (1797-1824)' in Ezra Fleischer, Gerald Blidstein, Carmi Horowitz, Bernard Septimus (eds), *Me'ah She'arim—Studies In Medieval Jewish Spiritual Life* (Jerusalem, Magnes Press, Hebrew University, 1991) 403 (Hebrew).
The Jewish Enlightenment In The Eighteenth-Century (Jerusalem, Zalman Shazar Center, 2002) (Hebrew).
Haskalah And History: The Emergence Of A Modern Jewish Historical Consciousness (Chaya Naor and Sondra Silverston trans, Oxford, Littman Library of Jewish Civilization, 2002).
'"They Look Like Jews But They Dress Like Cossacks": Pre-Zionist Origins of the Jewish Cultural Conflict' in Avi Sagi and Dov Schwartz (eds), *A Hundred Years Of Religious Zionism* (Ramat Gan, Bar Ilan University Press, 2003) vol 3, 375 (Hebrew).
Moses Mendelssohn (Jerusalem, Zalman Shazar Center, 2005) (Hebrew).
'Jewish Secular Society and Culture in Herzl's Vision' in Avi Sagi and Yedidia Z. Stern (eds), *Herzl Then And Now: An Old Jew Or A New Person?* (Jerusalem, Shalom Hartman Institute, 2008) 171 (Hebrew).
The Origins Of Jewish Secularization In 18th Century Europe (Jerusalem, Zalman Shazar Center, 2010) (Hebrew).

Feller, S. Z., 'The Application of the Foundations of Law Act in Criminal Law' in Aharon Barak et al (eds), *Sussman Book* (Jerusalem, 1984) 345 (Hebrew).

Fitzpatrick, Peter, *The Mythology Of Modern Law* (Routledge, London, 1992).

Fligstein, Neil and Luke Dauter, 'The Sociology of Markets' (2007) 33 Ann Rev Soc 105.

Fox, Shaul, *The Psychology Of Resistance To Change* (Ramat Gan, Bar Ilan University Press, 1998) (Hebrew).

Fraser, Nancy, 'Rethinking the Public Sphere: A Contribution to the Critique of Actually Existing Democracy' in Craig Calhoun (ed), *Habermas And The Public Sphere* (Cambridge, MIT Press, 1996) 109.
'From Redistribution to Recognition? Dilemmas of Justice in a "Post-Socialist" Age' in Cynthia Willett (ed), *Theorizing Multiculturalism* (Cambridge, Blackwell Publishers, 1998) 19.
'Transnationalizing the Public Sphere' http://www.republicart.net

Friedman Goldstein, Leslie, 'From Democracy to Juristocracy' (2004) 38 Law & Soc Rev 611.

Friedman, Menachem, 'Religious-Secular Relations' in Anita Shapira (ed), *The Religious Trend In Zionism* (Tel Aviv, Am Oved Publishers, 1983) 69.
The Haredi (Ultra-Orthodox) Society—Sources, Trends And Processes (Jerusalem, Jerusalem Institute for Israel Studies, 1991) (Hebrew).

Friedmann, Daniel, 'The Effect of Foreign Law on the Law of Israel' (1975) 10 Israel L Rev 192.

Fruman, Ram, 'What Do Secular Jews Do in the Holidays? Secular Jews and Jewish Holidays' in Aviad Kleinberg (ed), *Hard To Believe: Rethinking Religion And Secularism In Israel* (Tel Aviv, Tel Aviv University Press, 2004) (Hebrew).

Gabareen, Hassan, 'The Future of Arab Citizenship' (2001) 6 Mishpat Umimshal 53 (Hebrew).

Galnoor, Itzhak, 'The Judicialization of the Public Domain in Israel' (2004) 7 Mishpat Umimshal 355 (Hebrew).

Galston, William A., 'Two Concepts of Liberalism' (1995) 105 Ethics 516.

Gans, Chaim, *The Limits Of Nationalism* (Cambridge, Cambridge University Press, 2003).

Gardos, Yehuda, 'Geography of Center and Periphery' in Uri Ram and Nitza Berkovitch (eds), *In/Equality* (Beer Sheva, Ben-Gurion University of the Negev Press, 2006) 73 (Hebrew).

Garth, Bryant G. and Austin Sarat (eds), *Justice And Power In Sociolegal Studies* (Evanston, Northwestern University Press, 1998).

Gavison, Ruth, 'Introduction' in Ruth Gavison (ed), *Civil Rights In Israel—Essays In Honor Of Haim H. Cohen* (Jerusalem, The Association for Civil Rights in Israel, 1982) 9 (Hebrew).

'Constitutional Law' (1990) 19 Mishpatim 617 (Hebrew).

'A Jewish and Democratic State - Political Identity, Ideology and Law' (1995) 19 Tel Aviv U L Rev 631 (Hebrew).

The Constitutional Revolution—Depiction Of Reality Or A Self-Fulfilling Prophecy (Jerusalem, Israel Democracy Institute, 1998) (Hebrew).

Can Israel Be Both Jewish And Democratic—Tensions And Prospects (Tel Aviv, Hakibbutz Hameuchad Publishing House, 1999) (Hebrew).

'On Israel as a Jewish and Democratic State' in Ron Margolin (ed), *Israel As A Jewish And Democratic State* (Jerusalem, World Union of Jewish Studies, 1999) 55 (Hebrew).

'Public Involvement of the High Court of Justice: A Critical View' in Gavison Ruth, Mordechai Kremnitzer And Yoav Dotan (eds), *Judicial Activism—For And Against* (Jerusalem, Magnes Press, Hebrew University, 2000) 69 (Hebrew).

Gavison, Ruth and Alan Shapira, 'Introduction' in *The Federalist* (Aharon Amir trans, Jerusalem, Shalem Center, 2001) 11 (Hebrew).

Geertz, Clifford, *The Interpretation Of Cultures* (New York, Basic Books, Inc., Publishers, 1973).

Local Knowledge (New York, Basic Books, Inc., Publishers, 1983).

After The Fact (Cambridge, Harvard University Press, 1995).

Available Light—Anthropological Reflections On Philosophical Topics (Princeton, New Jersey, Princeton University Press, 2000).

Gertz, Nurith, Generation Shift In Literary History—Hebrew Narrative Fiction In The Sixties (The Porter Institute for Poetics and Semiotics, Tel Aviv University, 1983) (Hebrew).

Ghanem, A., 'State and Minority in Israel: The Case of the Ethnic State and the Predicament of its Minority' (1998) 21 Ethnic & Racial Stud 444.

Ghanem, As'Ad and Sarah Ozacky-Lazar, 'The Status of the Palestinians in Israel in the Age of Peace: Part of the Problem but not Part of the Solution' in Uri Cohen et al (eds), *Israel And Modernity* (Beer Sheva, Ben Gurion University of the Negev, 2006) 211 (Hebrew).

Gilboa, Menucha, *The Golden Dreams And Their Shattering* (Tel Aviv, Hakibbutz Hameuchad Publishing House, 1995) (Hebrew).

Gilmore, Grant, *The Ages Of American Law* (New Haven, Yale University Press, 1977).

Glendon, Mary Ann, *Rights Talk—The Impoverishment Of Political Discourse* (New York, Free Press, 1991).

Glenn, Patrick H., *Legal Traditions Of The World: Sustainable Diversity In Law* (Oxford, Oxford University Press, 2000).

Globus, Elazar L., *The Jewish Court*, (1947) 4 Hapraklit 111 (Hebrew).

Golan-Agnon, Daphna, 'Why are Arab Students being Discriminated?' in Daphna Golan-Agnon (ed), *Inequality In Education* (Tel Aviv, Babel Publishers, 2004) 70 (Hebrew).

Gordon, Evelyn, 'Is It Legitimate to Criticize the Supreme Court?' (1998) 3 Azure.
'How the Government's Attorney Became its General' (1998) 4 Azure.
'The Creeping Delegitimization of Peaceful Protest' (1999) 7 Azure.
'The Supreme Court in Loco Parentis' (2001) 10 Azure.
'Center Court' (2002) 13 Azure.

Gordon, Robert W., 'Critical Legal Histories' (1984) 36 Stan L Rev 57.

Gramsci, Antonio, *Selections From The Prison Notebook* (Quintin Hoare and Geoffrey Nowell Smith trans (eds), London, Lawrence and Wishart, 1971).

Granovetter, Mark, 'Economic Action and Social Structure: The Problem of Embeddedness' (1985) 91 Am J Soc 481.

Grey, John, 'From Post-Liberalism to Pluralism', in *Enlightenment's Wake* (London and New York, Routledge, 1995) 196.

Gross, Aeyal, 'Property as a Constitutional Right and Basic Law: Human Dignity and Liberty' (1998) 21 Tel Aviv U L Rev 405 (Hebrew).
'How Did "Free Competition" Become a Constitutional Value? Changes in the Meaning of the Right to Freedom of Occupation' (2000) 23 Tel Aviv U L Rev 229 (Hebrew).
'The Israeli Constitution—A Distributive Justice Instrument or Vice Versa?' in Menachem Maunter (ed), *Distributive Justice In Israel* (Tel Aviv, Ramot Publishing House, 2000) 79 (Hebrew).

Guarnieri, Carlo And Patrizia Pederzoli, *The Power Of Judges* (Oxford, Oxford University Press, 2002).

Gulak, Asher, 'On Our Legal Life in Our Country' in Jacob Bazak (ed), *The Jewish Law And The State Of Israel* (Jerusalem, Mosad Harav Kook 1969) 28 (first published in 'Ha-Toren', 1921) (Hebrew).

Gutwein, Daniel, 'Left and Right Post-Zionism and the Privatization of Israeli Collective Memory' (2001) 20 J Israeli History 9.

Haakonssen, Knud, Republicanism, in *A Companion To Contemporary Political Philosophy* (Robert E. Goodin and Philip Pettit (eds), Oxford, Basil Blackwell, 1993) 568.

Habermas, Jurgen, 'Citizenship and National Identity: Some Reflections on the Future of Europe' (1992) 12 Praxis Int'l 1, 17 rep in: Jurgen Habermas, 'Citizenship and National Identity: Some Reflections on the Future of Europe' in Ronald Beiner, (ed), *Theorizing Citizenship* (Albany, State University of New York Press, 1995).
'Pre-Political Foundations of the Democratic Constitutional State?' in Florian Schuller (ed), *Dialectics Of Secularization* (San Francisco, Ignatius Press, 2005) 19.
'Religion in the Public Sphere' (2006) 14 European J Phil 1.

Hadari, Yona, *Messiah Rides A Tank—Public Thought Between The Sinai Campaign And The You Kippur War 1955-1975* (Jerusalem, Shalom Hartman Institute, 2002) (Hebrew).

Halbertal, Moshe, 'Who is a Jew' in Avi Sagi and Nahem Ilan (eds), *Jewish Culture In The Eye Of The Storm* (Tel Aviv, Hakibbutz Hameuchad Publishing House, 2002) 233 (Hebrew).

Halpern, Stephen C. and Charles M. Lamb (eds), *Supreme Court Activism And Restraint* (Lexington, Lexington Books, 1982).

Hannerz, Ulf, *Cultural Complexity* (New York, Columbia University Press, 1992).

Hannerz, U., 'Anthropology' (2001) 1 Int'l Encyclopedia Of The Social And Behavioral Sciences.

Harris, Ron, 'Absent-Minded Misses and Historical Opportunities: Jewish Law, Israeli Law, and the Establishment of the State of Israel' in Mordechai Bar On and Zvi Zameret (eds), *On Both Sides Of The Bridge—Religion And State In The Early Years Of Israel* (Jerusalem, Yad Ben Zvi, 2002) 21 (Hebrew).
'Judicialization of the Public Sphere in the Third Decade' in Zvi Zameret and Hanna Yablonka (eds), *The Third Decade* (Jerusalem, Yad Ben Zvi, 2008) 251 (Hebrew).

Harshav, Benjamin, 'The Revival of Eretz Israel and the Modern Jewish Revolution: Reflection on the Situation' in Nurith Gertz (ed), *Perspectives On Culture And Society In Eretz Israel* (Tel Aviv, Open University Press, 1988) 7 (Hebrew).

Harvey, David, *A Brief History Of Neoliberalism* (Oxford, Oxford University Press, 2005).

Hazony, David, 'What Do You Mean, "He's Innocent"?' (1988) 8 Azure 16.
'The Year of Ruling Dangerously' (2001) 10 Azure 19.

Hebdige, Dick, 'From Culture to Hegemony' in Simon During (ed), *The Cultural Studies Reader* (London, Routledge, 1993) 357.

Heidegger, Martin, *Being And Time* (John Macquarrie and Edward Robinson trans, San Francisco, Harper, 1962).

Herget, James E. and Stephen Wallace, 'The German Free Law Movement as the Source of American Legal Realism' (1987) 73 Va L Rev 399.

Herzig, Hanna, *The Voice Saying I—Trends In Israeli Prose Fiction Of The 1980s* (Tel Aviv, Open University Press, 1998) (Hebrew).

Herzl, Theodor, *The Jewish State: An Attempt At A Modern Solution Of The Jewish Question*, 4th edn, (Sylvie D'Avigdor, trans, London, R Searl, 1946).
Altneuland—Old-New Land, 3rd edn, (Paula Arnold trans, Haifa, Israel, Haifa Pub. Co. 1964).

Hever, Hanan, 'An Imagined Native Community: Canaanite Literature in Israeli Culture' 2 Israeli Sociology (1999) 147 (Hebrew).
Literature Written From Here (Tel Aviv, Miskal-Yedioth Ahronoth Books, 1999) (Hebrew).

Hirschl, Ran, '"Negative" Rights vs. "Positive" Entitlements: A Comparative Study of Judicial Interpretations of Rights in an Emerging Neo-Liberal Economic Order' (2000) 22 Human Rights Q 1060.

'Beyond the American Experience: The Global Expansion of Judicial Review' in Mark A. Graber and Michael Perhac (eds), *Marbury Versus Madison—Documents And Commentary* (Washington DC, CQ Press, 2002) 147.

'Resituating the Judicialization of Politics: Bush v. Gore as a Global Trend' (2002) 15 Canadian J Law & Jurisprudence 191.

Toward Juristocracy—The Origins And Consequences Of The New Constitutionalism (Cambridge and London, Harvard University Press, 2004).

'The Theocratic Challenge to Constitution Drafting in Post-Conflict States' (2008) 49 Wm & Mary L Rev 1179.

Hofnung, Menachem, 'The Unintended Consequences of Unplanned Constitutional Reform: Constitutional Politics in Israel' (1996) 44 Am J Comparative L 585.

Hofri-Winogradow, Adam, 'Increased Legal Pluralism in Israel: The Rise of Halakhic Civil Tribunals in the Religious Zionist Sector' (2010) Tel Aviv U L Rev (Hebrew).

Hohfeld, Wesley Newcomb, 'Some Fundamental Legal Conceptions as Applied in Judicial Reasoning' (1913) 23 Yale L J 28.

Holland, Dorothy And Naomi Quinn (eds), *Language And Thought* (Cambridge, Cambridge University Press, 1987).

Holland, Kenneth M. (ed), *Judicial Activism In Comparative Perspective* (Macmillan, Houndmills, 1991).

Holmes, Oliver Wendell, 'The Path of the Law' (1897) 10 Harv L Rev 457.

Holtzman, Avner, *Essays On Micha Josef Berdyczewski (Bin Gurion)* (Tel Aviv, Reshafim, 1993) (Hebrew).

'The Literature of the "In Land Generation"' in Zvi Tzameret and Hanna Yablonka (eds), *The First Decade, 1948-1958* (Jerusalem, Yad Ben Zvi, 1997) 263 (Hebrew).

'Hebrew Literature and the "Cultural Controversy" in the Zionist Movement, 1897-1902' in Anita Shapira, Jehuda Reinharz and Jay Harris (eds), *The Age Of Zionism* (Jerusalem, Zalman Shazar Center, 2000) 145 (Hebrew).

Literature And Life—Essays On M. J. Berdyczewski (Jerusalem, Carmel, 2003) (Hebrew).

Horowitz, Dan And Moshe Lissak, *Trouble In Utopia* (Tel Aviv, Am Oved Publishers, 1990) (Hebrew).

Horwitz, Morton, 'The Rise of Legal Formalism' (1975) 19 Am J Leg History 251.

'Republicanism and Liberalism in American Constitutional Thought' (1987) 29 Wm & Mary L Rev 57.

The Transformation Of American Law 1870-1960 (Oxford, Oxford University Press, 1992).

Hurd, Heidi, 'Political Liberalism' (1995) 105 Yale L J 795.

Hyers, Lauri L. and Janet K. Swim, 'A Comparison of the Experiences of Dominant and Minority Group Members During an Intergroup Encounter' (1998) 1 Group Processes & Intergroup Relations 143.

Inbari, Assaf, *Home* (Tel Aviv, Miskal—Yedioth Ahronoth Books, 2009) (Hebrew).

Inglis, Fred, *Cultural Studies* (Oxford, Blackwell, 1993).

Jabotinsky, Ze'ev, *The Story Of My Life* (Jerusalem, Eri Jabotinsky Publishing House, 1947) 34 (Hebrew).
Selected Writings (Tel Aviv, S. Zaltzman, 1946) (Hebrew).
'Fulfill Your Promise or Get Out of the Mandate!' in *Writings And Speeches* (Jerusalem, Eri Jabotinsky Publishing House, 1948) 221 (Hebrew).
The Road To A State (Jerusalem, Eri Jabotinsky Publishing House, 1953) (Hebrew).
The Political And Social Philosophy Of Ze'ev Jabotinsky: Selected Writings (Mordechai Sarig (ed), Shimshon Feder, trans, Portland Ore: Vallentine Mitchell, 1999).

Jamal, Amal, 'We Demand Full Partnership in the Shaping of the Public, Cultural and Political Spheres in which We Live' (2003) 16 Eretz Acheret 20 (Hebrew).
'The Political Ethos of Palestinian Citizens in Israel: Critical Reading in the Future Vision Documents' (2008) 23 Israel Stud Forum 3.

Joppke, Christian and Steven Lukes, 'Introduction: Multicultural Questions' in Christian Joppke and Steven Lukes (eds), *Multicultural Questions* (New York, Oxford University Press, 1999) 1.

Kahan, Itzhak, 'Rabbinic and Secular Courts in Israel' (1976) 7 Dine Israel 205 (Hebrew).

Kalberg, Stephen, 'Max Weber's Types of Rationality: Cornerstones for the Analysis of Rationalization Processes in History' (1980) 85 Am J Soc 1145.

Kaplan, Kimmy and Nurit Stadler (eds), *Leadership And Authority In Israeli Haredi Society* (Jerusalem, Van Leer Jerusalem Institute, 2009) (Hebrew).

Katz, Jacob, 'Zionism and Jewish Identity' in *Jewish Nationalism—Essays And Studies* (Jerusalem, Zionist Library, 1979) 73 (Hebrew).
Out Of The Ghetto—The Social Background Of Jewish Emancipation 1770-1870 (Tel Aviv, Am Oved Publishers, 1985) (Hebrew).
A Time For Inquiry—A Time For Reflection—A Historical Essay On Israel Through The Ages (Jerusalem, Zalman Shazar Center, 1999) (Hebrew).

Katzenelson, Gideon, *The Literary War Between The Ultra-Orthodox And The Enlightened* (Tel Aviv, Dvir, 1954) (Hebrew).

Kedar, Nir, 'Interpretive Revolution: The Rise of Purposive Interpretation in Israeli Law' (2002) 26 Tel Aviv U L Rev 737 (Hebrew).
Mamlakhtiyut—David Ben-Gurion's Civic Thought (Jerusalem, Yad Ben Zvi, 2009) (Hebrew).

Kenan, Amos, *The Road To Ein Harod* (Tel Aviv, Am Oved Publishers, 1984) (Hebrew).

Kennedy, Duncan, 'Legal Formality' (1973) 2 J Leg Stud 351.

Khamaissi, Rassem, 'The Disengagement Option: Irredentism or Transfer for Israeli Arabs and their Meanings' in Sarah Ozacky-Lazar, As'ad Ghanem and Ilan Pappe (eds), *Seven Roads: Theoretical Options For The Status Of The Arabs In Israel* (Givat Haviva, Institute for Peace Research, 1999) 155 (Hebrew).

Kim, S., 'Hegemony: Cultural' (2001) 10 Int'l Encyclopedia Of The Social And Behavioral Sciences.

Kimmerling, Baruch, 'The New Israelis—Multiple Cultures Without Multiculturalism' (1998) 16 Alpaim 264 (Hebrew).
The End Of Ashkenazi Hegemony (Jerusalem, Keter Publishing House, 2001) (Hebrew).
The Invention And Decline Of Israeliness (Berkeley, University of California Press, 2001).
Immigrants, Settlers, Natives—The Israeli State And Society Between Cultural Pluralism And Cultural Wars (Tel Aviv, Am Oved Publishers, 2004) (Hebrew).

Kirschenbaum, Ahron, 'The Legal Foundation Law—Today and Tomorrow' 11 Tel Aviv U L Rev (1985) 117 (Hebrew).

Klein, Claude, 'The Exemption of Yeshivot Students' in David Cheshin et al (eds), *The Court Of Law—Fifty Years Of Adjudication In Israel* (Tel Aviv, Ministry of Defense, 1999) 152 (Hebrew).

Klenner, Hermann, 'Savigny's Research Program of the Historical School of Law and its Intellectual Impact in 19th Century Berlin' 37 (1989) Am J Comp L 67.

Kmiec, Keenan D., 'The Origin and Current Meanings of "Judicial Activism"' 92 Ca L Rev (2004) 1441.

Kolat, Israel, 'Religion, Society and State in the Era of Nationalism' in Shmuel Almog, Jehuda Reinharz and Anita Shapira (eds), *Zionism And Religion* (Jerusalem, Zalman Shazar Center, 1994) 329 (Hebrew).

Kop, Yaakov And Robert E. Litan, *Sticking Together—The Israeli Experiment In Pluralism* (Washington DC, Brookings Institution Press, 2002).

Kretzmer, David, 'The New Basic Laws on Human Rights: A Mini-Revolution in Israeli Constitutional Law?' (1992) 26 Israel L Rev 238.

Kronman, Anthony T., *Max Weber* (Stanford, Stanford University Press, 1983).
The Lost Lawyer—Failing Ideals Of The Legal Profession (Cambridge, Harvard University Press, 1993).

Kuhn, Thomas S., *The Structure Of Scientific Revolutions*, 2nd edn, (Chicago, University of Chicago Press, 1962).

Kukathas, Chandran, 'Liberalism and Multiculturalism—The Politics of Indifference' (1998) 26 Pol Theory 686.

Kuper, Adam, *Culture—The Anthropologist's Account* (Cambridge, Harvard University Press, 1999).

Kurland, Phillip B., 'Toward a Political Supreme Court' (1969) 37 U Chi L Rev 19.

Kurtz D.V., 'Hegemony: Anthropological Aspects' (2001) 10 Int'l Encyclopedia Of The Social And Behavioral Sciences.

Kurtzweil, Baruch, *Our New Literature—Continuation Or Turn*, 2nd edn, (Tel Aviv, Schocken Publishing House, 1965) (Hebrew).
The Struggle Over The Values Of Judaism (Tel Aviv, Schocken Publishing House, 1969) (Hebrew).
Facing The Spiritual Perplexity Of Our Time (Tel Aviv, Schocken Publishing House, 1976) (Hebrew).

Kymlicka, Will, 'Multiculturalism and Minority Rights: West and East' (2002) 4 J Ethnopolitics & Minority Issues In Europe.
Multicultural Odysseys (Oxford, Oxford University Press, 2007).

Laden, Anthony Simon, 'The House That Jack Built: Thirty Years of Reading Rawls' (2003) 113 Ethics 367.

Lahav, Pnina, 'Traits in Justice Agranat's Legal Worldview' in A. Barak et al (eds), *Essays In Honor Of Shimon Agranat* (Jerusalem, 1988) 9 (Hebrew).
Judgment In Jerusalem—Chief Justice Simon Agranat And The Zionist Century (Berkeley, University of California Press, 1997).

Landau, Moshe, 'Trends in the Decisions of the Supreme Court' (1982) 8 Tel Aviv U L Rev 500 (Hebrew).
'On Justice and Reasonableness in Administrative Law' (1989) 14 Tel Aviv U L Rev 5 (Hebrew).
'The Supreme Court as Constitution Maker for Israel' (1996) 3 Mishpat Umimshal 697 (Hebrew).
'Reflections on the Constitutional Revolution' (1996) 26 Mishpatim 419 (Hebrew).
'Three Years After Bank Hamizrachi Decision' Hamishpat (2000) 249 (Hebrew).
'On Judicial Activism' (2001) 12 Hamishpat 83 (Hebrew).

Laor, Dan, 'New Israeli Identity: Were We Borne from the Sea?' 9 New Directions (2003) 62 (Hebrew).
'"I am Hearing America Singing!"—On One Aspect in the Canaanite Worldview' 11 New Keshet (2005) 148 (Hebrew).

Larmore, Charles E., *Patterns Of Moral Complexity* (Cambridge, Cambridge University Press, 1987).
'Political Liberalism' (1990) 18 Pol Theory 339.
'The Moral Basis of Political Liberalism' (1999) 96 J Phil 599.

Lau, Benjamin, 'Changes in Sephardic Halakhic World: From Tradition to Literature' in Kimmy Caplan and Emmanuel Sivan (eds), *Israeli Haredim:*

Integration Without Assimilation? (Tel Aviv, Hakibbutz Hameuchad Publishing House, 2003) 11 (Hebrew).

Leiter, Brian, 'Positivism, Formalism, Realism' (1999) 99 Colum L Rev 1138.

Lemert, Charles, 'Multiculturalism' in George Ritzer and Barry Smart (eds), *Handbook Of Social Theory* (London, Sage Publications, 2001) 297.

Leon, Nissim, 'The Transformation of Israel's Religious-Zionist Middle Class' (2010) 29 J Israeli History 61.

Leshem, Elazar, 'Israel as a Multicultural State at the Turn of the Twenty-First Century' in Elazar Leshem and Dorit Roer-Strier (eds), *Cultural Diversity—A Challenge To Human Services* (Jerusalem, Magnes Press, The Hebrew University, 2003) 13 (Hebrew).

Levin, Donald N., 'Rationality and Freedom: Weber and Beyond' (1981) 51 Soc Inq 5.

Levin-Epstein, Noah, 'Mobility' in Uri Ram and Nitza Berkovitch (eds), *In/Equality* (Beer Sheva, Ben-Gurion University of the Negev Press, 2006) 291 (Hebrew).

Levitsky, Nomi, *The Supremes: Inside The Supreme Court* (Tel Aviv, Hakibbutz Hameuchad Publishing House, 2006) (Hebrew).

Levy, Gal, 'Education' in Uri Ram and Nitza Berkovitch (eds), *In/Equality* (Beer Sheva, Ben-Gurion University of the Negev Press, 2006) 181 (Hebrew).

Levy, Jacob T., 'Liberal Jacobinism' 114 (2004) Ethics 318.

Levy, Yagil, *'From "People's Army" To "Army Of The Peripheries"'* (Jerusalem, Carmel, 2007) (Hebrew).

Lewis, Jeff, *Cultural Studies* (Sage Publications, London, 2002).

Liebman, Charles S. And Eliezer Don-Yehiha, *Civil Religion In Israel* (Berkeley, University of California Press, 1983).

Lijphart, Arend, *The Politics Of Accommodation* (Berkeley, University of California Press, 1968).
Democracies (New Haven and London, Yale University Press, 1984).
Democracy In Plural Societies (New Haven and London, Yale University Press, 1997).
Patterns Of Democracy (New Haven, Yale University Press, 1999).

Likhovski, Assaf, 'Hebrew Law and Zionist Ideology in Mandatory Palestine' in Menachem Mautner, Avi Sagi and Ronen Shamir (eds), *Multiculturalism In A Democratic And Jewish State* (Tel Aviv, Ramot Publishing House, 1998) 633 (Hebrew).
'The Invention of "Hebrew Law" in Mandatory Palestine' (1998) 46 Am J Comp L 339.
'Legal Education in Mandatory Palestine' (2001) 25 Tel Aviv U L Rev 291 (Hebrew).

'Colonialism, Nationalism and Legal Education: The case of Mandatory Palestine' in Ron Harris, Alexander (Sandy) Kedar, Pnina Lahav and Assaf Likhovski (eds), *The History Of Law In A Multi-Cultural Society* (Aldershot, Ashgate, 2002) 75.

'Between Two Worlds: The Legacy of the Mandatory Judicial System in the Early Years of the State of Israel' in Yehoshua Ben-Arieh (ed), *Jerusalem And The British Mandate* (Jerusalem, Yad Ben Zvi, 2003) (Hebrew).

Law and Identity in Mandate Palestine (Chapel Hill, University of North Carolina Press, 2006).

Luz, Ehud, *Parallels Meet: Religion And Nationalism In The Early Zionist Movement (1882-1904)* (Lenn J. Schramm trans, Philadelphia, Jewish Publication Society, 1988).

'The Limits of Toleration—On the Problem of the Partnership Between Ultra-Orthodox and Secular Jews in the Hibat Zion Era (1882-1895)' in Shmuel Almog, Jehuda Reinharz and Anita Shapira (eds), *Zionism And Religion* (Jerusalem, Zalman Shazar Center, 1994) 55 (Hebrew).

'The Failure of the Bridge' in Avi Sagi and Dov Schwartz (eds), *A Hundred Years Of Religious Zionism* (Ramat Gan, Bar Ilan University Press, 2003) vol 3, (Hebrew).

Macaulay, Stewart, 'Non-Contractual Relations in Business: A Preliminary Study' (1963) 28 Am Soc Rev 55.

Machiavelli, Niccolo, *The Prince* (Charles W. Eliot (ed), New York, Harvard Classics, P. F. Collier & Son 1909–14).

Macintyre, Alasdair, *After Virtue* (Notre Dame, University of Notre Dame Press, 1981).

Macneil, Ian, 'The Many Futures of Contract' (1974) 47 S Cal L Rev 691.

Macneil, Ian R., *The New Social Contract: An Inquiry Into Modern Contractual Relations* (New Haven, Yale University Press, 1980).

Magnet, Joseph Eliot, *Modern Constitutionalism* (Markham, Butterworths, 2004).

Maletz, David, *Ma'agalot* (Tel Aviv, Am Oved Publishers, 1945).

Maoz, Asher, 'The Values of a Jewish and Democratic State' (1995) 19 Tel Aviv U L Rev 547, 629 (Hebrew).

Marmor, Andrei, 'Judicial Review in Israel' (1997) 4 Mishpat Umimshal 133 (Hebrew).

Martinez, 'Cultural Contact: Archeological Approaches' 5 Int'l Encyclopedia Of The Social & Behavioral Sciences (2001).

Mason, Andrew, 'Political Community, Liberal-Nationalism, and the Ethics of Assimilation' (1999) 109 Ethics 261.

Mautner, Menachem, *The Decline Of Formalism And The Rise Of Values In Israeli Law* (Tel Aviv, Maagalai Daat, 1993) (Hebrew).

'Invisible Law' (1998) 16 Alpaim 45 (Hebrew).

'The 1980s: The Fourth Decade' in David Cheshin et al (eds), *The Courts Of Law: Fifty Years Of Adjudication In Israel* (Tel Aviv, Ministry of Defense, 1999) 132 (Hebrew).

'Distributive Justice in Israel' in Menachem Mautner (ed), *Distributive Justice In Israel* (Tel Aviv, Ramot Publishers, 2000) 9 (Hebrew).

'Beyond Toleration and Pluralism: The Law School as a Multicultural Institution' (2002) 7 Int'l J Legal Profession 55.

'The 1990s: Years of Reconciliation?' (2002) 26 Tel Aviv U L Rev 887 (Hebrew).

'Law and Culture in Israel: The 1950s and the 1980s' in Ron Harris, Alexander Kedar, Pnina Lahav and Assaf Likhovski (eds), *The History Of Law In A Multi-Cultural Society: Israel 1917-1967* (Aldershot, Ashgate, 2002) 175.

Legal Education (Tel Aviv, Ramot Publishing House, 2002) (Hebrew).

'Appointment of Justices to the Supreme Court in a Multicultural Society' (2003) 19 Legal Research 423 (Hebrew).

'Good Faith and Implied Warranties' in Daniel Friedmann and Nili Cohen (eds), *Contracts* (Volume 3, Tel Aviv, Aviram, 2003) 313 (Hebrew).

'The 1980s—Years of Anxiety' (2003) 26 Tel Aviv U L Rev 645 (Hebrew).

'Judicial Intervention in the Contents of Contracts and the Question of the Future Development of Israeli Contract Law' (2005) 29 Tel Aviv U L Rev 17 (Hebrew).

'From "Honor" to "Dignity": How Should a Liberal State Treat Non-Liberal Cultural Groups?' (2008) 9 Theoretical Inq L 609.

Law And Culture In Israel At The Threshold Of The Twenty-First Century (Tel Aviv, Am Oved Publishers, 2008) (Hebrew).

Mautner, Menachem, Avi Sagi and Ronen Shamir, 'Thoughts on Multiculturalism in Israel' in Menachem Mautner, Avi Sagi and Ronen Shamir (eds), *Multiculturalism In A Democratic And Jewish State* (Tel Aviv, Ramot Publishing House, 1998) 67 (Hebrew).

May Rollo, *The Meaning Of Anxiety* (New York, Ronald Press Co, 1979).

McFadden, Patrick M., 'The Balancing Test' (1988) 29 Bc L Rev 641.

Medina, Barak, 'Four Myths of Judicial Review: A Response to Robert Bork's and Richard Posner's Criticism of Aharon Barak's Judicial Activism', (2007) 3 Din Udvarim 399 (Hebrew).

Meisler, Yoash, 'The Constitutional Revolution' Just Over a Decade Later—Law and Disorder' (2003) 7 Democratic Culture 131 (Hebrew).

Menocal, Maria Rosa, *The Ornament Of The World—How Muslims, Jews And Christians Created A Culture Of Tolerance In Medieval Spain* (Boston, Little, Brown and Company, 2002).

Mezey, Naomi, 'Law as Culture' (2001) 13 Yale J L & Human 35.

Michelman, Frank I., 'Possession v Distribution in the Constitutional Idea of Property' (1987) 72 Ia L Rev 1319.

Minda, Gary, *Postmodern Legal Movements* (New York, New York University Press, 1995).

Miron, Dan, 'If There Is No Jerusalem' in *If There Is No Jerusalem* (Tel Aviv, Hakibbutz Hameuchad Publishing House, 1987) 227.
'From Creators and Builders to Homeless' in *If There Is No Jerusalem* (Tel Aviv, Hakibbutz Hameuchad Publishing House, 1987) 9 (Hebrew).
'Between Rabbi Sach and the New Hebrew Literature' in *Essays On Literature And Society* (Tel Aviv, Zmora-Bitan Publishers, 1991) 9 (Hebrew).

Mollnau, Karl A., 'The Contributions of Savigny to the Theory of Legislation' (1989) 37 Am J Comp L 81.

Moore, Margaret, *The Ethics Of Nationalism* (New York, Oxford University Press, 2001).

Moses, Hanan, 'From Religious Zionism To Post-Modern Religiosity' PhD Dissertation, Department of Political Science, Bar Ilan University, 2009 (Hebrew).

Mouffe, Chantal, 'Hegemony and Ideology in Gramsci' in Chantal Mouffe (ed), *Gramsci And Marxist Theory* (London, Routledge & Kegan Paul, 1979).
'Democratic Citizenship and the Political Community' in Chantal Mouffe (ed), *Dimensions Of Radical Democracy* (New York, Verso, 1992) 225.
'Democratic Politics and the Question of Identity' in John Rajchman (ed), *The Identity Question* (New York, Routledge, 1995) 33.
'Democracy, Power, and the "Political"' in Seyla Benhabib (ed), *Democracy And Difference* (Princeton, Princeton University Press, 1996) 245.
The Democratic Paradox (London, Verso, 2000).

Muller, Jan-Werner, *Constitutional Patriotism* (Princeton, Princeton University Press, 2007).

Mundlak, Guy, 'Socio-Economic Rights in the New Constitutional Discourse' (1999) 7 Labor Law Annual 65 (Hebrew).
'The New Labor Law as a Social Text: Reflections on Social Values in Flux' (2005) 3 Israel Studies 119.

Naor, Arye, Jabotinsky's 'Constitutional Guidelines for Israel' in Avi Bareli and Pinhas Ginossar (eds), *The Eye Of The Storm—Essays On Ze'ev Jabotinsky* (Beer Sheva, Ben Gurion University, 2004) 49 (Hebrew).

Naveh, Eyal And Esther Yogev, *Histories—Towards A Dialogue With The Israeli Past* (Tel Aviv, Babel Publishers, 2002).

Neuer, Hillel, 'Aharon Barak's Revolution' (1998) 3 Azure.

Novikoff, Alex, 'Licit and Illicit in the Rhetoric of the Investiture Conflict' in Ruth Mazo Karras, Joel Kaye and E. Ann Matter (eds), *Law And The Illicit In Medieval Europe* (Philadelphia, University of Pennsylvania Press, 2008) 183.

Official Committee of Inquiry in the Matter of the Clashes between Security Forces and Israeli Citizens in October 2000 (Jerusalem, 2003) ('The Orr Committee').

Okere, Obinna, 'Judicial Activism or Passivity in Interpreting the Nigerian Constitution' (1987) 36 Int'l & Comp L Q 78.

Okin, Susan Moller, 'Humanist Liberalism' in Nancy L. Rosenblum (ed), *Liberalism And The Moral Life* (Cambridge, Harvard University Press, 1989) 39.

Oz, Amos, *Under This Blazing Light* (Nicholas de Lange trans, Cambridge University Press, 1979).
'Where the Jackals Howl' in *Where The Jackals Howl* (Tel Aviv, Am Oved Publishers, Tel Aviv, 1976) 9 (Hebrew).
In The Land Of Israel (Maurie Goldberg-Bartura trans, San Diego, Harcour Brace Jovanovich, Publishers, 1983).
'A Struggle of Seduction: The War of Cultures on the Heart of Judaism' in Ruvik Rosenthal (ed), *The Heart Of The Matter—Redefining Social And National Issues* (Jerusalem, Keter Publishing House, 2005) 15 (Hebrew).

Ozacky-Lazar, Sarah and Mustafa Kabha (eds), *Between Vision And Reality: The Vision Papers Of The Arabs In Israel, 2006-2007* (Jerusalem, The Citizens' Accord Forum, 2008) (Hebrew).

Oz-Salzberger, Fania, 'The Non-Israeli Herzl' in Avi Sagi and Yedidia Z. Stern (eds), *Herzl Then And Now: An Old Jew Or A New Person?* (Jerusalem, Shalom Hartman Institute, 2008) 125 (Hebrew).

Paris, Michael, 'The Politics of Rights: Then and Now' (2006) 31 Law & Soc Inq 999.

Peled, Yoav, 'Ethnic Democracy and the Legal Construction of Citizenship: Arab Citizens of the Jewish State' (1992) 86 Am Pol Sci Rev 432.
'Will Israel be a State of Its Citizens on its 100th Anniversary?' (2001) 17 Legal Research 73 (Hebrew).

Peled, Yoav (ed), *Shas—The Challenge Of Israeliness* (Tel Aviv, Miskal—Yedioth Ahronoth Books, 2001) (Hebrew).

Peled, Yoav And Gershon Shafir, *Being Israeli—The Dynamics Of Multiple Citizenship* (Cambridge, Cambridge University Press, 2002).

Peri, Yoram, *Brothers At War: Rabin's Assassination And The Cultural War In Israel* (Tel Aviv, Babel Publishers, 2005) (Hebrew).

Pettit, Philip, *Republicanism—A Theory Of Freedom And Government* (New York, Oxford University Press, 1997).

Phillips, Ann, *The Politics Of Presence* (New York, Oxford University Press, 1995).

Pinhas-Cohen, Hava, 'From the Editor' (Autumn, 1996) 10 Dimuye (Hebrew).

Porat, Benny (ed), *Reflections On Jewish Democracy* (Jerusalem, Israel Democracy Institute, 2010).

Posner, Richard, 'Enlightened Despot', The New Republic, April 23, 2007 (review of *The Judge in a Democracy* by Aharon Barak, Princeton University Press, 2006).

Pound, Roscoe, 'Mechanical Jurisprudence' (1908) 8 Colum L Rev 605.

Procaccia, G., 'The Foundation of Law Act 1980' (1984) 10 Tel Aviv U L Rev 145 (Hebrew).

Rabinowitz, Dan And Khawla Abu Baker, *The Stand Tall Generation—The Palestinian Citizens Of Israel Today* (Jerusalem, Keter Publishing House, 2002) (Hebrew).

Radziner, Amichai, 'Between the High Court of Justice and the Rabbinic Court: On the Meaning of Private Law Adjudication in the Official Tribunal' (unpublished paper) (Hebrew).

Ram, Uri, *The Changing Agenda Of Israeli Sociology* (Albany, State University of New York Press, 1995).
The Globalization Of Israel (Tel Aviv, Resling, 2005) (Hebrew).

Ratzabi, Shalom, 'Jabotinsky and Religion' (2004) 5 Israel 1 (Hebrew).

Ravitzky, Aviezer, 'Exile in the Holy Land: The Ultra-Orthodox Dilemma' in *Messianism, Zionism And Jewish Religious Radicalism* (Tel Aviv, Am Oved Publishers, 1993) 201 (Hebrew).
'On Israel as a Jewish and Democratic State' in Ron Margolin (ed), *Israel As A Jewish And Democratic State* (Jerusalem, World Union of Jewish Studies, 1999) 50 (Hebrew).
'Israeli Society in the Wake of the Rabin Assassination' in Neri Horowitz (ed), *Religion And Nationalism In Israel And The Middle East* (Tel Aviv, Am Oved Publishers, 2002) 254 (Hebrew).

Ravitzky, Aviezer (ed), *Shas: Cultural And Ideological Perspectives* (Tel Aviv, Am Oved Publishers, 2006) (Hebrew).

Rawls, John, *Political Liberalism* (New York, Columbia University Press, 1993).

Raz, Joseph, 'Facing Diversity: The Case for Epistemic Abstinence' (1990) 19 Phil & Pub Aff 8.

Refael, Geula, 'The Culture Question in the First Congresses' in Anita Shapira (ed), *The Religious Trend In Zionism* (Tel Aviv, Am Oved Publishers, 1983) 39 (Hebrew).

Reimann, Mathias, 'The Historical School Against Codification: Savigny, Carter, and the Defeat of the New York Civil Code' (1989) 37 Am J Comp L 95.
'Nineteenth Century German Legal Science' (1990) 31 BC L Rev 837.

Reiss, H. S., 'The Political Thought of the German Romantics' in H. S. Reiss (ed), *The Political Thought Of The German Romantics, 1793-1815* (Oxford, B. Blackwell,1955) 1.

Riley, Patrick, Rousseau's General Will, in Patrick Riley (ed), *The Cambridge Companion To Rousseau* (Cambridge, Cambridge University Press, 2001).

Roesler, Shannon, 'Permutations of Judicial Power: The New Constitutionalism and the Expansion of Judicial Authority' (2007) 32 Law & Soc Inq 545.

Rorty, Richard, *Philosophy And The Mirror Of Nature* (Princeton, New Jersey, Princeton University Press, 1979).

Rose, Aharon, 'The Haredim: A Defense' (2006) 25 Azure.

Rosen-Zvi, Issachar, 'Constructing Professionalism: The Professional Project of the Israeli Judiciary' (2001) 31 Seton Hall L Rev 760.

Ross, Tamar, 'The "Holy Rebellion" of Religious Zionist Women as a Bridge Between Halakhah and Democracy' in Avi Sagi and Dov Schwartz (eds), *A Hundred Years Of Religious Zionism* (Ramat Gan, Bar Ilan University Press, 2003) vol 3 (Hebrew).

Rozen-Zvi, Ariel, '"A Jewish and Democratic State": Spiritual Parenthood, Alienation and Symbiosis—Can We Square the Circle?' (1995) 19 Tel Aviv U L Rev 479 (Hebrew).

Rozin, Orit, *Duty And Love—Individualism And Collectivism In 1950s Israel* (Tel Aviv, Am Oved Publishers, 2008) (Hebrew).

Rubinstein, Amnon, *Being A Free People* (Tel Aviv, Schocken Publishing House, 1977) (Hebrew).
From Herzl To Rabin—The Changing Image Of Zionism (New York, Holmes & Meier, 2000).

Rubinstein, Ariel, 'How the Jewish People Lost its Soul' in Ruvik Rosenthal (ed), *The Heart Of The Matter—Redefining Social And National Issues* (Jerusalem, Keter Publishing House, 2005) 185 (Hebrew).

Rudin, James, *The Baptizing Of America* (New York, Thunder's Mouth Press, 2006).

Saban, Ilan, 'The Impact of the Supreme Court on the Status of the Arabs in Israel' (1996) 3 Mishpat Umimshal 541 (Hebrew).
'The Zionist Paradigm Edge Option' in Sarah Ozacky-Lazar, As'ad Ghanem and Ilan Pappe (eds), *Seven Roads: Theoretical Options For The Status Of The Arabs In Israel* (Givat Haviva, Institute for Peace Research, 1999) 79 (Hebrew).
'The Minority Rights of the Palestinian-Arabs in Israel: What is, What Isn't and What is Taboo' (2002) 26 Tel Aviv U L Rev 241.
'Minority Rights in Deeply Divided Societies: A Framework for Analysis and the Case of the Arab-Palestinian Minority in Israel' (2004) 36 NYU J Int'l L & Pol 885.

Saban, Ilan and Muhammad Amara, 'The Status of Arabic in Israel: Reflections on the Power of Law to Produce Social Change' (2002) 36 Israel L Rev 5.

Saban, Ilan and Scott Strainer, 'On Two Types of "Appropriate Representation"' (2005) 11 Labor, Society And Law 247 (Hebrew).

Sagi, Avi, 'A Critique of Jewish Identity Discourse' in Avi Sagi and Nahem Ilan (eds), *Jewish Culture In The Eye Of The Storm* (Tel Aviv, Hakibbutz Hameuchad Publishing House, 2002) 248 (Hebrew).

'From the Land of the Torah to the Land of Israel—From One Broken Dream to Another: Study of the Crisis in Religious-Zionism' in Avi Sagi and Dov Schwartz (eds), *A Hundred Years Of Religious Zionism* (Ramat Gan, Bar Ilan University Press, 2003) vol 3 (Hebrew).

Sagi, Avi and Dov Schwartz, 'The Religious Zionist Enterprise in the Face of the Modern World—Introductory Essay' in Avi Sagi and Dov Schwartz (eds), *A Hundred Years Of Religious Zionism* (Ramat Gan, Bar Ilan University Press, 2003) vol 1 (Hebrew).
'From Pioneering to Torah Study: Another Perspective' in Avi Sagi and Dov Schwartz (eds), *A Hundred Years Of Religious Zionism* (Ramat Gan, Bar Ilan University Press, 2003) vol 3, (Hebrew).

Sagi, Avi and Yedidia Z. Stern, 'Expulsion of Identity: Altneuland in the State of the Jews' in Avi Sagi and Yedidia Z. Stern (eds), *Herzl Then And Now: An Old Jew Or A New Person?* (Jerusalem, Shalom Hartman Institute, 2008) 257 (Hebrew).

Salzberger, Eli, 'Judicial Activism in Israel' in Brice Dickson (ed), *Judicial Activism In Common Law Supreme Courts* (Oxford, Oxford University Press, 2007) 217.

Salzberger, Eli M. and Alexander (Sandy) Kedar, 'The Quiet Revolution: More on Judicial Review According to the New Basic Laws' (1997) 4 Mishpat Umimshal 488 (Hebrew).

Salzberger, Eli and Fania Oz-Salzberger, 'The Hidden German Origin of the Israeli Supreme Court' in Daniel Gutwein and Menachem Mautner (eds), *Law And History* (Jerusalem, Zalman Shazar Center, 1999) 357 (Hebrew).

Samooha, Sammy, Ethnic Democracy: 'Israel as a Proto-Type' in Pinhas Ginossar and Avi Bareli (eds), *Zionism: A Contemporary Controversy* (Sede Boqer Campus, Ben Gurion Research Center, 1996) 277 (Hebrew).
Autonomy For Arabs In Israel? (Raanana, Institute for Israeli Arab Studies, 1999) (Hebrew).
'The Relations of Jews and Arabs in Israel as a Jewish and Democratic State' in Ephraim Ya'ar and Ze'ev Shavit (eds), *Trends In Israeli Society* (Tel Aviv, Open University, 2003) 231 (Hebrew).

Samuel, Yitzhak, *The Political Game—Power And Influence In Organizations* (Haifa, Haifa University Press, 2002) (Hebrew).

Sandel, Michael J., 'Political Liberalism' (1993), (1994) 107 Harv L Rev 1765.

Sapir, Gideon, 'Between Liberalism and Multiculturalism' (2010) 26 Legal Research 311 (Hebrew).

Sarat, Austin, '"… The Law is All Over": Power, Resistance and the Legal Consciousness of the Welfare Poor' (1990) 2 Yale L & Human 343.

Sarat, Austin and Thomas R. Kearns, (eds), *Law In Everyday Life* (Ann Arbor, University of Michigan Press, 1993).

Sarat, Austin and Thomas R. Kearns (eds), *Law In The Domains Of Culture* (Ann Arbor, University of Michigan Press, 1998).

Savigny, Carl von, 'On the Vocation of Our Age for Legislation and Jurisprudence' in H. S. Reiss (ed), *The Political Thought Of The German Romantics, 1793-1815* (Oxford, B. Blackwell,1955) 203.

Schatzki, Theodor R., Karin Knorr Cetina and Eike von Savigny (eds), *The Practice Turn In Contemporary Theory* (London, Routledge, 2001).

Schauer, Fredrick, Formalism, (1988) 97 Yale L J 509.

Scheffler, Samuel, 'The Appeal of Political Liberalism' in Henry S. Richardson and Paul J. Eeithman (eds), *The Philosophy Of Rawls* (New York, Routledge, 1999) 94.

Schluchter, Wolfgang, *The Rise Of Western Rationalism* (G. Roth trans, Berkeley, University of California Press, 1981, 1985).

Scholem, Gershom, 'Who is a Jew' (1971) 60 Central Conference Of American Rabbis 135.
Explications And Implications—Writings On Jewish Heritage And Renaissance (Avraham Shapira (ed), Tel Aviv, Am Oved, vol 2, 1986) (Hebrew).

Schneider, David M., 'Notes Toward a Theory of Culture' in Keith H. Basso and Henry A. Selby (eds), *Meaning In Anthropology* (Albuquerque, University of New Mexico Press, 1976) 197.

Schwartz, Dov, *Religious Zionism: History And Ideology* (Tel Aviv, Ministry of Defense, 2003) (Hebrew).

Schweid, Eliezer, *Toward A Modern Jewish Culture* (Tel Aviv, Am Oved Publishers, 1995) (Hebrew).

Segal, Zeev, 'The Supreme Court (Sitting as a High Court of Justice) Within the Framework of the Israeli Society—After 50 Years' (2000) 5 Mishpat Umimshal 235 (Hebrew).
'The Supreme Court as a Social Constructor' in Hanna Herzog (ed), *Reflection Of A Society* (Tel Aviv, Ramot Publishing House, 2000) 297 (Hebrew).

Segev, Tom, *1949—The First Israelis* (Jerusalem, Domino Publishing, 1984) (Hebrew).
'Facing Elvis' Statue' in *The New Zionists* (Jerusalem, Keter Publishing House, 2001) 42 (Hebrew).

Sewell, Jr., William H., 'The Concept(s) of Culture' in Victoria E. Bonnell and Lynn Hunt (eds), *Beyond The Cultural Turn—New Directions In The Study Of Society And Culture* (Berkeley, University of California Press, 1999) 35.

Shabtai, Yaakov, *Past Continuous* (Dalya Bilu trans, Philadelphia, Jewish Publication Society of America, 1985).

Shachar, Yoram, Ron Harris, and Meron Gross, 'Citation Practices of Israel's Supreme Court: Quantitative Analysis' (1996) 27 Mishpatim 119 (Hebrew).

Shachar, Yoram, Miron Gross and Chanan Goldsmidt, '100 Leading Precedents of the Supreme Court—Quantitative Analysis' (2004) 7 Mishpat Umimshal 267 (Hebrew).

Shaked, Gershon, 'Introduction' in G. Shaked and J. Yaron (eds), *Life On The Razor's Edge* (Tel Aviv, Hakibbutz Hameuchad Publishing House, 1979) 9 (Hebrew).

Shalmon, Yosef, 'Tradition and Modernity in Early Religious-Zionist Thought' in Ben-Zion Yehoshua and Ahron Kedar (eds), *Ideological And Political Zionism* (Jerusalem, Zalman Shazar Center, 1978) 21 (Hebrew).
Religion And Zionism: First Encounters—Essays (Jerusalem, Zionist Library, 1990) (Hebrew).
'Zionism and Anti-Zionism in Traditional Jewry of East Europe' in Shmuel Almog, Jehuda Reinharz and Anita Shapira (eds), *Zionism And Religion* (Jerusalem, Zalman Shazar Center, 1994) 33 (Hebrew).

Shamir, Ronen, 'Formal and Substantive Rationality in American Law: A Weberian Perspective' (1993) 2 Soc & Leg Stud 45.
'The Politics of Reasonableness: Reasonableness and Judicial Power at Israel's Supreme Court' (1994) 5 Theory And Criticism 7 (Hebrew).
'Lex Moriandi: On the Death of Israeli Law' in Menachem Mautner, Avi Sagi and Ronen Shamir (eds), *Multiculturalism In A Democratic And Jewish State* (Tel Aviv, Ramot Publishing House, 1998) 589 (Hebrew).
The Colonies Of Law—Colonialism, Zionism And Law In Early Mandate Palestine (Cambridge, Cambridge University Press, 2000).
'The Age of Responsibilization: On Market-Embedded Morality' (2008) 37 Economy And Society 1.

Shamir, Ronen, Michal Shitrai and Nelly Elias, 'Religion, Feminism, and Professionalism: The Case and Cause of Women Rabbinical Advocates' (1997) 38 Megamot 313 (Hebrew).

Shapira, Anita, 'The Religious Motives of the Labor Movement' in Shmuel Almog, Jehuda Reinharz and Anita Shapira (eds), *Zionism And Religion* (Jerusalem, Zalman Shazar Center, 1994) 301 (Hebrew).
'Elements of the National Ethos in the Transition to Statehood' in Jehuda Reinharz, Gideon Shimoni and Yosef Salmon (eds), *Jewish Nationalism And Politics—New Perspectives* (Jerusalem, Zalman Shazar Center, 1996) 253 (Hebrew).
New Jews Old Jews (Tel Aviv, Am Oved Publishers, 1997) 9 (Hebrew).
'Where has Negation of Exile Gone to?' (2003) 25 Alpaim 9 (Hebrew).
The Bible And Israeli Identity (Jerusalem, Magnes Press, Hebrew University, 2005) (Hebrew).

Shapira, Avraham, 'The 1948 Generation and the Legacy of Jewish Culture' in Mordechai Bar-On (ed), *The Challenge Of Independence—Ideological And Cultural Aspects Of Israel's First Decade* (Jerusalem, Yad Ben Zvi, 1999) 167 (Hebrew).

Shapira, Avraham (ed), *Continuity And Rebellion—Gershom Scholem In Speech And Dialogue* (Tel Aviv, Am Oved Publishers, 1987) (Hebrew).

Shapiro, Yonathan, *An Elite Without Successors* (Tel Aviv, Sifriat Poalim Publishing House, 1984) (Hebrew).

'The Historical Origins of Israeli Democracy' in Ehud Sprinzak and Larry Diamond (eds), *Israeli Democracy Under Stress* (Boulder, Lynne Rienner Publishers, 1993) 66.

Shavit, Yaacov, 'Hebrew Culture and Culture in Hebrew' (1980) 16 Cathedra For The History Of Eretz Israel And Its Yishuv 190 (Hebrew).

From Hebrew To Canaanite (Tel Aviv, Domino, 1984) (Hebrew).

'National Society and National Culture in Hebrew—Two Perspectives' (1984) 9 Ha-Tzionut 111 (Hebrew).

'*Judaism In The Greek Mirror And The Emergence Of The Modern Hellenized Jew*' (Tel Aviv, Am Oved Publishers, 1992) (Hebrew).

'Supplying a Missing System—Between Official and Unofficial Popular Culture in the Hebrew National Culture in Eretz-Israel' in Benjamin Z. Kedar (ed), *Studies In The History Of Popular Culture* (Jerusalem, Zalman Shazar Center, 1996) 327 (Hebrew).

'Culture and Cultural Status: Basic Developments in Hebrew Culture During the Second Aliya Period' in Israel Bartal (ed), *The Second Aliya—Studies* (Jerusalem, Yad Ben Zvi, 1997) 343 (Hebrew).

'The Yishuv Between National Regeneration of Culture and Cultural Generation of the Nation' in Jehuda Reinharz, Gideon Shimoni, Yosef Salmon (eds), *Jewish Nationalism And Politics—New Perspectives* (Jerusalem, Zalman Shazar Center, 1997) 141 (Hebrew).

'The Status of Culture in the Process of Creating a National Society in Eretz-Israel: Basic Attitudes and Concepts' in Zohar Shavit (ed), *The History Of The Jewish Community In Eretz-Israel Since 1882* (Jerusalem, Israeli Academy for Sciences and Humanities, 1998) vol 1 (Hebrew).

Shavit, Zohar, 'The Entrance of a New Model into the System' in Karl Eimermacher et al (eds), *Issues In Slavic Literary And Cultural Theory* (Bochum, Universitatsverlag Dr. N. Brockmeyer, 1989) 593.

'Introduction' in Zohar Shavit (ed), *The History Of The Jewish Community In Eretz-Israel Since 1882* (Jerusalem, Israeli Academy for Sciences and Humanities, 1998) vol 1, (Hebrew).

Shehar, Eton Noa, '"A New Revelation of Divine Will"—The Influence of Feminism on Religious- Zionism' in David Yoel Ariel et al (eds), *Blessed Be He Who Made Me A Woman* (Tel Aviv, Miskal Publishing House, 2009) 207 (Hebrew).

Sheleg, Yair, *The New Religious Jews* (Jerusalem, Keter Publishing House, 2000) (Hebrew).

'The Division in Religious-Zionism: Past, Present and Future' (2010) 46 Deot 6 (Hebrew).

Shilo, Shmuel, 'Comments and Some new Light on the Foundation of Law Act' 13 Hebrew Law Annual (1987) 351 (Hebrew).

Shimoni, Gideon, *The Zionist Ideology* (Hanover, NH, University Press of New England, 1995.
'The Theory and Practice of Shlilat Hagalut Reconsidered' in Anita Shapira, Jehuda Reinharz and Jay Harris (eds), *The Age Of Zionism* (Jerusalem, Zalman Shazar Center, 2000) 45 (Hebrew).

Shine, Chaim, *The Jewish State—Concluding Summary* (Tel Aviv, Peri Publishers, 2003) (Hebrew).

Shmueli, Merav, 'The Power To Define Tradition: Feminist Challenges To Religion And The Israel Supreme Court' (PhD Dissertation, University of Toronto, 2005).

Shochetman, Eliav, 'Israeli Law and Jewish Law: Affiliation and Alienation' (1990) 19 Mishpatim 871 (Hebrew).

Shweder, R. A., 'Culture: Contemporary Views' in (2001) 5 Int'l Encyclopedia Of The Social And Behavioral Sciences.

Shweder, Richard A. and Robert A. LeVine (eds), *Culture Theory* (Cambridge, Cambridge University Press, 1984).

Silberg, Moshe, 'The Law of the Hebrew State' in *The Writings Of Moshe Silberg* (Jerusalem, Magnes Press, Hebrew University, 1998) 180 (Hebrew).

Smelser, Neil J., 'Culture: Coherent or Incoherent' in Richard Munch and Neil J. Smelser (eds), *Theory Of Culture* (Berkeley, University of California Press, 1992) 3.

Smithey, Shannon Ishiyama and John Ishiyama, 'Judicial Activism in Post-Communist Politics' 36 (2002) Law & Soc Rev 719.

Smoira, Moshe, 'The Address of the President of the Supreme Court at the Opening Ceremony' 5 (1949) Hapraklit 187 (Hebrew).

Sommer, Hillel, 'Richard Posner on Aharon Barak: The View from Abroad' (2007) 49 Hapraklit 523 (Hebrew).

Spinner, Jeff, *The Boundaries Of Citizenship* (Baltimore, Johns Hopkins University Press, 1994).
'Cultural Pluralism and Partial Citizenship' in Christian Joppke and Steven Lukes (eds), *Multicultural Questions* (New York, Oxford University Press, 1999) 65.

Stanislawski, Michael, *Zionism And The Fin De Siecle—Cosmopolitanism And Nationalism From Nordau To Jabotinsky* (Berkeley, University of California Press, 2001).

Stephan, Walter G. and Cookie White Stephan, 'Intergroup Anxiety' (1985) 41 J Social Issues 157.
'Antecedents of Intergroup Anxiety in Asian-Americans and Hispanic-Americans' (1989) 13 Int'l J Intercultural Relations 203.

'Reducing Intercultural Anxiety Through Intercultural Contact' (1992) 16 Int'l J Intercultural Relations 89.

Sternhell, Zeev, *Nation-Building Or A New Society?* (Tel Aviv, Am Oved Publishers, 1995) (Hebrew).

Stigler, James W., Richard A. Shweder and Gilbert Herdt (eds), *Cultural Psychology—Essays On Comparative Human Development* (Cambridge, Cambridge University Press, 1990).

Stone Sweet, Alec, *Governing With Judges: Constitutional Politics In Europe* (Oxford, Oxford University Press, 2000).

Summers, Robert S., *Instrumentalism And American Legal Theory* (Ithaca, Cornell University Press, 1982).

Sunder Madhavi, 'Cultural Dissent' (2001) 54 Stan L Rev 49.
Piercing the Veil, (2003) 112 Yale L J 1399.

Sunstein, Cass R., *Legal Reasoning And Political Conflict* (Oxford, Oxford University Press, 1996).

Susser, Bernard And Charels S. Liebmen, *Choosing Survival—Strategies For A Jewish Future* (Tel Aviv, Hakibbutz Hameuchad Publishing House, 2004) (Hebrew).

Svirsky, Barbara, Health, in Uri Ram and Nitza Berkovitch (eds), *In/Equality* (Beer Sheva, Ben-Gurion University of the Negev Press, 2006) 64 (Hebrew).

Swidler, Ann, 'Culture in Action: Symbols and Strategies' (1986) 51 Am Soc Rev 273.
Talk Of Love—How Culture Matters (2001).

Tammuz, Benjamin, *Jeremiah's Inn* (Jerusalem, Keter Publishing House, 1984) (Hebrew).

Tate, C. Neal and Torbjorn Vallinder (eds), *The Judicialization Of Politics* (Oxford, Butterworth-Heinemann, 1995).

Taub, Gadi, *The Settlers And The Struggle Over The Meaning Of Zionism* (Tel Aviv, Miskal—Yedioth Ahronoth Books, 2007) (Hebrew).

Taylor, Charles, *Multiculturalism And 'The Politics Of Recognition'* (Princeton, Princeton University Press, 1992).
'Cross-Purposes: The Liberal-Communitarian Debate' in *Philosophical Arguments* (Cambridge, Harvard University Press, 1995) 181.
Book Review: *Multicultural Citizenship*, by Will Kymlicka, (1996) 90 Am Pol Sci Rev 408.
'The Dynamics of Democratic Exclusion' (1998) 9 J Democracy 143.

Tedeschi, Guido, 'The Law of Laws' 14 (1979) Israel L Rev 145.

Tesler, Ricky, *In The Name Of God—Shas And The Religious Revolution* (Jerusalem, Keter Publishing House, 2003) (Hebrew).

The Future Vision For Palestinian Arabs In Israel (National Committee of Heads of Arab Municipalities in Israel, 2006) (Hebrew).

The Haifa Declaration (Mada al-Carmel, 2007) (Hebrew).

Thomte, Reidar, 'Historical Introduction' in *Sorn Kierkegaard, The Concept Of Anxiety* (Reidar Thomte trans, Princeton, Princeton University Press, 1980).

Triandis, Harry C., 'The Self and Social Behavior in Differing Cultural Contexts' (1989) 96 Psych Rev 506.

Triandis, Harry C. et al, 'Individualism and Collectivism: Cross-Cultural Perspectives on Self-Ingroup Relationships' (1988) 54 J Personality & Soc Psych 323.

Triandis, Harry C. et al, 'Multimethod Probes of Individualism and Collectivism' (1990) 59 J Personality & Soc Psych 1006.

Tyler, Tom R., 'Promoting Employee Policy Adherence and Rule Following in Work Settings' (2005) 70 Brooklyn L Rev 1287.

Viroli, Maurizio, *Republicanism* (Antony Shugaar trans, New York, Hill and Wang, 1999).

Vital, David, *Zionism: The Formative Years* (Oxford, Oxford University Press, 1982).

Waldron, Jeremy, *Liberal Rights* (Cambridge, Cambridge University Press, 1993).
'Disagreements About Justice' in Henry S. Richardson and Paul J. Eeithman (eds), *The Philosophy Of Rawls* (New York, Routledge, 1999) 78.
Law And Disagreement (Oxford, Oxford University Press, 1999).

Wallace, Clifford J., 'The Jurisprudence of Judicial Restraint: A Return to Moorings' (1981) 50 Geo Wash L Rev 1.

Walzer, Michael, 'Membership' in Shlomo Avineri and Avner De-Shalit (eds), *Communitarianism And Individualism* (Oxford, Oxford University Press, 1992) 65.
'Comment' in Charles Taylor, *Multiculturalism And The Politics Of Recognition* (Princeton, Princeton University Press, 1992) 99.

Ward, Cynthia V., 'The Limits of "Liberal Republicanism": Why Group-Based Remedies and Republican Citizenship Don't Mix' (1991) 91 Columbia L Rev 581.

Weber, Max, *Economy And Society* (Guenther Roth and Claus Wittich (eds), Berkeley, University of California Press, 1978).

Weinrib, Ernest, 'Legal Formalism: On the Imminent Rationality of the Law' (1988) 97 Yale L J 951.

Weithman, Paul, 'Liberalism and the Political Character of Political Philosophy' in Henry S. Richardson and Paul J. Eeithman (eds), *The Philosophy Of Rawls* (New York, Routledge, 1999) 223.

Wenar, Lief, 'Political Liberalism, An Internal Critique' (1995) 106 Ethics 32.

West, Cornel, 'The New Cultural Politics of Difference' in John Rajchman (ed), *The Identity Question* (New York, Routledge, 1995) 147.

Wheeler, Ladd, Harry T. Reis and Michael Harris Bond, 'Collectivism—Individualism in Everyday Social Life: The Middle Kingdom and the Melting Pot' (1989) 57 J Personality & Soc Psych 79.

White, G. Edward, 'Reflections on the "Republican Revival": Interdisciplinary Scholarship in the Legal Academy' (1994) 6 Yale J L & Human 1.

Wieviorka, Michel, 'Is Multiculturalism the Solution?' (1998) 21 Ethnic & Racial Stud 881.

Williams, Bernard, 'Conflicts of Values' in *Moral Luck* (Cambridge, Cambridge University Press, 1981) 71.

Williams, Raymond, *Marxism And Literature* (Oxford, Oxford University Press, 1977).
'Base and Superstructure in Marxist Culture Theory' in *Problems Of Materialism And Culture* (London, Verso, 1980).

Witkon, Alfred, 'The Law in a Developing Land' in *Justice And The Judiciary* (Jerusalem and Tel Aviv, Schocken Publishing House, 1988) 39 (Hebrew).

Wright, J. Skelly, 'The Role of the Supreme Court in a Democratic Society—Judicial Activism or Restraint?' (1968) 54 Cornell L Rev 1.

Wuthnow, Robert, *Communities Of Discourse* (Cambridge, Harvard University Press, 1989).

Yadgar, Yaacov, *Masortim In Israel* (Jerusalem, Shalom Hartman Institute, 2010) (Hebrew).

Yadgar, Yaacov and Charles S. Liebman, 'Beyond the "Religious-Secular" Dichotomy: Traditional Judaism in Israel' in Uri Cohen et al (eds), *Israel And Modernity* (Beer Sheva, Ben Gurion University of the Negev, 2006) 337 (Hebrew).

Yakobson, Alexander And Amnon Rubinstein, *Israel And The Family Of Nations* (London, Routledge, 2009).

Yatziv, Gadi, *The Sectorial Society* (Jerusalem, Bialik Institute, 1999) (Hebrew).

Yehoshua, A. B., 'Against the Forests' in *The Stories* (Tel Aviv, Hakibbutz Hameuchad Publishing House, 1993) 99 (Hebrew).
'A Revolution, Nonetheless' in Ruvik Rosenthal (ed), *The Heart Of The Matter—Redefining Social And National Issues* (Jerusalem, Keter Publishing House, 2005) 58 (Hebrew).

Yiftachel, Oren, '"Ethnocracy", Geography and Democracy' 19 Alpaim (2000) 78 (Hebrew).

Yonah, Yossi, 'A State of all its Citizens, a Nation-State or a Multicultural Democracy?' (1998) 16 Alpaim 238 (Hebrew).

Yonah, Yossi And Yehuda Shenhav, *What Is Multiculturalism* (Tel Aviv, Babel Publishers, 2005) (Hebrew).

Young, Iris Marion, *Justice And The Politics Of Difference* (Princeton, Princeton University Press, New Jersey, 1990).

Zalkin, Mordechai, *A New Dawn—The Jewish Enlightenment In The Russian Empire—Social Aspects* (Jerusalem, Magnes Press, Hebrew University, 1990) (Hebrew).

Zamir, Itzhak, 'Public Law' 19 Mishpatim (1990) 563 (Hebrew).

Law and Politics, in Itzhak Zamir (ed), *Klinghoffer Book On Public Law* (Jerusalem, Institute for Legislative Research and Comparative Law, 1993) 209 (Hebrew).

Zeira, Moti, *Rural Collective Settlements And Jewish Culture In Eretz Israel During The 1920s* (Jerusalem, Yad Ben Zvi, 2002) (Hebrew).

Zertal, Idith And Akiva Eldar, *Lords Of The Land: The Settlers And The State Of Israel 1967-2004* (Or Yehuda, Dvir Publishing House, 2004) (Hebrew).

Zerubavel, Yael, *Recovered Roots* (Chicago, University of Chicago Press, 1995).

Zipperstein, Steven J., *Elusive Prophet—Ahad Ha'am And The Origins Of Zionism* (Berkeley, University of California Press, 1993).

Zubaida, Sami, 'Trajectories of Political Islam: Egypt, Iran and Turkey' in David Marquand and Ronald L. Nettle (eds), *Religion And Democracy* (Oxford, Blackwell Publishers, 2000) 60.

INDEX

Abramowitz, Amnon, 137, 166 n 113
Agranat, Shimon, Chief Justice, Supreme Court
— formalism of Israeli law, 81
— *Kol Ha-Am* opinion, 85–6, 92 n 42
Ahad Ha-Am
— controversy with Berdyczewski over issue of culture, 21
— criticism of Herzl's approach on culture, 19
— influence on Movement for Revival of Hebrew Law, 33
— Kurtzweil's criticism of, 29
— revival of Jewish culture in Eretz Israel, 15–16
— Zionist culture in Eretz Israel, 25
Aktzin, Benjamin, 96–7
Alignment-Labor (party), *see also* Mapai
— defeat in 1977 elections, 101, 106, 109, 171
— petitions to Court, 149
Aloni, Shulamit
— changes in education in post-hegemonic era, 135
Americanization of Israeli law, 37 n 10
Amichai, Yehuda
— legalization, 6
Anglicization of Israeli Law, 31, 34, 35–8, 81
— Jerusalem Law Classes, 36
Anxiety
— encounter with unfamiliar groups, 129 n 56
— Heidegger, 127
Arab citizens of Israel
— Arab Vision Documents, 196–7, 224
— demography, 9, 10, 182
— indigenous people, 197
— Israel as bi-national state, 9
— Israel as Jewish state, 211–13
— Israel as 'state of all its citizens', 9
— October 2000 events, 186, 198
— 'principles of Israel's heritage', 43
— republicanism, 189, 217–22
— schism between Jewish and Arab citizens, 181, 193–200, 226
Aran, Gideon
— religious-Zionism, 116–17
Arlosoroff, Merav, 168 n 18
Article 46 of the Palestine Order-in-Council, 36–7, 41
Avineri, Shlomo
— 'Jewish and democratic state' definition, 195 n 56

Avnon, Dan
— 'Jewish and democratic state', 44 n 30
Azure
— criticism of Court, 169–70
Bacon, Francis
— courts' integrity, 163
Barak, Aharon, Chief Justice, Supreme Court
— Arab citizens, 197 n 62
— Bork, Robert, activism of, 56
— 'constitutional revolution', 47, 178–9
— influence on changes in Court's jurisprudence, 102 n 5, 144
— involvement in enactment of basic laws, 179 n 51
— 'Jewish and democratic state', 45 n 33, 46–52
— justiciability, 3, 58–61
— Posner, Richard, activism of, 55–6
— 'principles of Israel's heritage', 42
— 'principles of Israel's heritage' and Arab citizens, 49, 51
— reasonableness doctrine, 69
— right to education, 151–2
— rights talk, 5
— Salzberger, Eli, activism of, 56
Barak, Ehud, Minister of Defense
— legalization of military operations, 5
Barnea, Nahum, 136
— decline in trust of Court, 163 n 6
Barzilai, Gad
— legalization of Israel, 4 n 13
— preferences of Arab citizens, 195 n 53
Basic Law
— Human Dignity and Liberty, Basic Law: Freedom of Occupation, 44–52, 114, 148 n 114, 149 n 118, 151, 152, 177–9, 194, 195, 208
Begin, Menachem, Prime Minister, 109 n 16, 135
Beinish, Dorit, Chief Justice, Supreme Court
— decline in trust of Court, 163 n 6, 164
— non-enforcement of Court's rulings, 168–9
Ben-Ami, Shlomo
— comparison of 1980s Israel to 1930s Europe, 141
— Israel's multiculturalism, 182, 184
Ben-Gurion, David, Prime Minister, 187 n 27, 188

INDEX

Berdyczewski, Micha Yosef
— controversy with Ahad Ha-Am on issue of culture, 21
— new Jewish culture in Eretz Israel, 21
Bi-national state, 193–6
Bohman, James
— multicultural turn in liberal theory, 190 n 35
Bork, Robert
— Court's activism, 56
Bourdieu, Pierre
— education and wealth, 150
— field, 178
— habitus, 144
— legal disputes, 145–6
Breton, Raymond
— status anxiety, 132–3
Burke, Edmund, 1

Cheshin, Mishael, Supreme Court Justice
— Anglicization of law, 37
— rabbinic courts, 45 n 31
Civil war, 184–6, see also War of cultures
Cohen, Asher
— 'crisis politics', 126–7
— war of cultures, 184
Cohen, Haim, Supreme Court Justice
— rabbinic courts, 45 n 31
Cohen, Hillah, 168 n 18
Cohen, Nili, 167
Consociationalism, 126–7, 196
'Constitutional revolution', 178–80
Culture, see also Bourdieu, Pierre; Gramsci, Antonio; Williams, Raymond
— collectivist and individualistic, 86 n 26
— concept of, 12 n 2, 27 n 44
— contradictions in, 85, 87, 104–5
— cultural borrowing, 25 n 38, 35–6, 39, 113
— culture-bound action, 144
— habitus, 144
— hegemonic, 103–6
— home, 130 n 59
— law and culture, constitutive approach, 101 n 4
— of public administration, 171
Culture, Israel, see also Zionism and culture
Americanization of, 27, 113
— Hebrewness v. Jewishness, 22–30, 48, 113–14
— hegemonic, 112–14
— literature (1950s), 89–90
— nation-building collectivism (1950s), 86–7
— secular, crisis of, 2–3, 6, 7, 27–30, 114, 118–19, 225–6
— secular, transformations of, 2–3, 29, 112–14

Dankner, Amnon, 139, 142
Dayan, Arye, 137–8
Decentralization, 215–17, 223
Deri, Arye, 155, 156
Disagreement, 215–16, 223–4
Dotan, Yoav
— petitions of Knesset members, 148 n 115
Dworkin, Ronald
— formalism of English law, 80

Eisenstadt S.N.
— Israel's multiculturalism, 183–4
— legalization of Israel, 4
— 1977 political turnabout, 109, 129, 129 n 58
Eitan, Michael, MK, 163 n 6
Elitzur, Uri, 120
Elon, Menachem, Supreme Court Justice
— Anglicization of Israeli law, 38
— Court's entrenchment of constitutional rights, 39–40
— 'Jewish and democratic state', 46–52
— justiciability, 59
— 'principles of Israel's heritage', 42–4
Englard, Yitzhak, Supreme Court Justice
— balancing jurisprudence, 93
Etzioni-Halevy, Eva, 183

Foundations of Law Statute (1980), 41–4
— Barak-Elon controversy on 'principles of Israel's heritage', 41–4, 49
Friedmann, Daniel
— criticism of Court, 167
— Minister of Justice, proposal on judicial review, 178 n 47
— Minister of Justice, proposal on justiciability, 173 n 36
— Minister of Justice, proposals on Court's new jurisprudence, 170

Gafni, Moshe, MK, 155
Galston, William
— funding associations undermining core constitutional values, 192
Gans, Chaim
— justice and multiculturalism of states, 212 n 35
Gavison Ruth
— Court's contribution to entrenchment of constitutional values, 39
— failed appointment of, to Court, 166–7
— 'principles of Israel's heritage' and Arab citizens, 43
Gilboa, Menuha, on Benjamin Tammuz's, *Jeremiah's Inn*, 137, 142
Gilmore, Grant
— legalization, 6
Glendon, Mary Ann
— rights talk, 5–6
Gramsci, Antonio
— hegemony, 103–6, 112, 130
Gregory VII, Pope, 160
Gush Emunim (Bloc of the Faithful), 117, 119

Haaretz
— affiliation with former liberal hegemons, 133, 177
Habermas, Jurgen
— constitutional patriotism, 187–8
Halbertal, Moshe
— Judaism, 211
Hammer Zebulon, Minister of Education, 135
Harel, Israel, 119, 120 n 38
Harris, Ron
— judicialization of public sphere, 74 n 99
— status of Jewish law in Israeli law, 40–1
Hazan, Yaakov, MK, 111
Hazony, David
— criticism of Court, 169–70
Hegemony, 103–6, *see also* Gramsci, Antonio
Hegemony, Labor movement, 106–9, 214–15, 224
— changes in culture of, 112–14
— 'crisis politics' in Knesset following decline of, 127–8
— decline of, 29, 109–16
— decline of, and Court, 1, 101–3
Heidegger, Martin
— anxiety, 127
Henry IV, Emperor, 159
Herzl, Theodor
— culture of Jewish society in Eretz Israel, 17–19
— Israeli law, 40
Higher School of Law and Economics, 34, 36
Hirschl, Ran
— courts and social rights, 151 n 122
— enactment of 1992 basic laws, 148 n 114, 149 n 118
Hofnung, Menachem
— petitions of Knesset members to Court, 148 n 115
Holmes, Oliver Wendell
— greed, 111
Holtzman, Avner
— 1950s literature, 89

Identity
— mind categories, 12 n 3
— personality traits, 12 n 3
— politics of, 12 n 3
Institute for Zionist Strategies
— proposed constitution, 170
Israeliness, 197, 222, 224

Jabotinsky, Zeev
— culture of new Jewish society in Eretz Israel, 19–20
— Israeli law, 40
— relation between definition and demography of states, 195 n 56
Jerusalem Law Classes, 36
'Jewish and democratic state', 44–52, 114, 178 n 47, 193–6, 211, 213, 224

— Arab citizens, 211–13
— Jewish state, 208–11
Jewish Enlightenment Movement, 12–13, 40, 209
Judicial activism
— Bork, Robert, Court's activism, 56
— definition of, 54
— evaluations of Court's activism, 55–6
— explanations for rise in Court's jurisprudence, 99–103
— Posner, Richard, Court's activism, 55–6
— Rubinstein, Amnon, Court's activism, 56
Judicial review, 73–4
— conservatism, 175–80
Justiciability, 3–4, 58–68
— appointments, 66–7
— Attorney General, 67
— 'center of gravity' test, 173, 174
— criticism of Court's doctrine, 172–4
— defense, 62–4
— foreign affairs, 64–5
— government agenda, 67
— institutional, 58–9
— Knesset administrative decisions, 61–2
— normative, 58, 59
— pardons, 67
— political agreements, 66
— reasonableness doctrine, 172
— separation of powers, 61
— socio-economic policies, 65–6

Kahan, Itzhak, Chief Justice, Supreme Court
— rabbinic courts, 45 n 31
Karp, Yehudit, 169
Kenan, Amos, *The Road to Ein Harod*, 141–2
Kimmerling, Baruch
— decline of hegemonies, 129 n 56
— *Gush Emunim* (Bloc of the Faithful), 119
— Israel's multiculturalism, 182, 184
— Shas, 125
Kremnitzer, Mordechai
— decline in trust of Court, 163 n 6
Kuhn, Thomas, 79 n 7, 192
Kurtzweil, Baruch
— criticism of Ahad Ha-Am, 28
— cultural thinness, 28
Kymlicka, Will
— internationalization of minority rights, 197 n 62
— securitization of ethnic relations, 198 n 67

Lahav, Pnina
— formalism of Israeli law, 81, 81 n 13
— *Kol Ha-Am* opinion, 86
Landau, Moshe
— formalism of Israeli law, 84–5
— rise of value-laden jurisprudence, 95 n 53
Laor, Dan
— Hebrewness v. Jewishness, 114

Legal formalism
— concept of, 75–8
— Court's formalism and 1950s Israeli literature, 89–90
— decline in 1980s and 1990s, 90–5
— English law, 80
— gap between legal culture and general culture, 87–9
— influence of English formalism on Israeli law, 80–1
— influence of German formalism on Israeli law, 81–2
— Israeli law, 78–86
— non-formalism in Court's 1950s jurisprudence, 85–6
Legal fundamentalism, 3
Legalization of Israel, 3–7, 196 n 59
Leshem, Elazar
— Israel's multiculturalism, 183
Levitsky Nomi, *The Supremes: Inside the Supreme Court*, 167 n 18
Levy, Jacob T.
— multicultural turn in liberal theory, 190
Levy, Yagil
— changes in attitudes toward IDF, 111
Liberal former hegemons (LFH)
— accumulation of wealth by, 110–11, 225
— anxiety of, 127–43
— attitude toward IDF, 111, 174
— Court, 1–2, 7–8, 101–3, 110, 143–53, 188
— decline in trust of Court, 8, 160–1, 162–9, 225–6
— power in press, media, universities, art and culture, 110
Liberalism
— disagreement, 223
— multicultural states, 201
— political, 201–4
Liberalism, Israel, 201–8
— Court's contribution to entrenchment of, 9, 38–41, 80, 160
Lijphart, Arend, consociationalism, 126–7
Likud (party)
— petitions to Court, 149
— Shas, 124
— victory in 1977 elections, 101, 106, 109
Livni, Tzipi, Minister of Justice, 167
Lord, Amnon
— decline in trust of Court, 163 n 6
Luz, Ehud
— Micha Yosef Berdyczewski, 21

Machiavelli, Niccolo
— change, 155–6
MacIntyre, Alasdair, 220 n 49
Maletz, David, *Ma'agalot*, 28
Mapai (party), *see also* Alignment-Labor (party)
— hegemony of, 100, 106–9, 126

Market, economic and sociological views of, 170 n 30, 220
Marmor, Andrei
— Court as libertarian, 153 n 133
Matalon, Moriel
— decline in trust of Court, 163 n 6
Menocal, Maria Rosa
— 'golden age' of Jews in Spain, 213
Meretz (party)
— affiliation with Court, 149, 171–2
Miron, Dan
— cultural changes in post-hegemonic era, 131–2
Movement for Revival of Hebrew Law, 31–6, 41, 43, 51
— Ahad Ha-Am's influence on, 33
— cultural revival approach, 35
— Higher School of Law and Economics, 34, 36
— opposition to Anglicization of law, 34
— Savigny's influence on, 33
Multiculturalism, Israel, 181–4, 215, *see also* War of cultures
— definition of Israel as multicultural state, 213
— hegemony to multiculturalism, 115–16
— 'multicultural virtues', 213
— traits of, 190–200
— zero-sum game of, 43–4, 193, 224
Mundlak, Guy
— decline of formalism in Labor Courts' jurisprudence, 95 n 54

Natural law 34
Naveh, Eyal
— 1977 political turnabout as cultural turnabout, 129
Ne'eman, Yaakov, Minister of Justice
— decline in trust of Court, 163 n 6
Neo-liberalism
— general, 6–7
— Israel, 2–3, 29, 30, 110, 114, 119, 171, 219

Okon, Boaz
— appointment of justices to Court, 166 n 15
Organizations
— official and political normative systems, 162, 164
Oz, Amos
— meeting with Judea and Samaria settlers, 119–20
— reaction to 1977 political turnabout, 141
— war of cultures, 8
Oz-Salzberger, Fania
— influence of German formalism on Israeli law, 81–2

Peres, Shimon, 109 n 16, 139
Pinhas-Cohen, Hava
— war of cultures, 184
Political turnabout (1977), 109, 128
Porush, Menahem, MK, 155
Posner, Richard
— Court's activism, 55–6
Proportionality, 71–2, 146

Rabbinic courts
— campaign to gain arbitration authority, 53
— disregard of Knesset legislation and Court's rulings, 45, 192–3
Ram, Uri
— war of cultures, 185
Ratner, Arye
— decline in trust of Court, 164
Ravitzky, Aviezer
— religious-Zionism in hegemonic era, 117
Rawls, John
— citizens' agreement on fundamentals of political system, 192
— 'overlapping consensus', 51 n 52, 196, 202–4
Reasonableness, 60–1, 68–71
— justiciability, 172
— legal, 69–70
— professional, 70–1, 175
Religious fundamentalism
— general, 2, 3
— Israel, 2, 3, 7, 29, 30, 53, 117–18, 205–7
Religious-Zionism
— attitude toward IDF, 111, 174
— criticism of Court, 154–8, 160–1, 172, 188
— culture of Zionism, 16–17
— halakhic arbitration tribunals, 53, 189–90
— hegemonic era, 116–17
— liberalism, 203–7
— Modern Orthodoxy, 205–7
— post-hegemonic era, 117–21
— radicalization of religiosity, 120
— religious bourgeoisie, 207
— religious feminism, 205–6
— representation in Knesset, 125–7
Republicanism
— crisis of, 186–90
— Israeli situation, 217–25
Rights talk, 5–6
Rivlin, Ruvi, Knesset Speaker
— legalization of Israel, 4
Roosevelt, Theodore, 'The Man in the Arena', 5
Rorty, Richard
— normal discourse, 192
Rosenblum, Doron

— cultural changes in post-hegemonic era, 130, 131
— monologue by anxious voter, 140
Rubinstein, Amnon
— changes in post-hegemonic era, 131 n 60
— Court's activism, 56
— inclusion of Arab citizens in definition of state, 214
— Jewish state, 209
— legalization of Israel, 4
Rubinstein, Ariel
— neo-liberalism in Israel, 111 n 18
— reaction to 1977 political turnabout, 141

Sagi, Avi
— Israel's multiculturalism, 183
— religious-Zionism in hegemonic era, 116
Salzberger, Eli
— Court's activism, 56
— influence of German formalism on Israeli law, 81–2
Samet, Gideon
— war of cultures, 138
Sarid, Yossi
— petitions of LFH Knesset members to Court, 148
Savigny, Friedrich Carl von
— influence on Movement for Revival of Hebrew Law, 33, 34 n 4
Scholem, Gershom
— Judaism, 210–11
Schwartz, Dov
— religious-Zionism in hegemonic era, 116
Schweid, Eliezer
— changes in post-hegemonic era, 131
— 'cultural thinness', 27–8
Segal, Israel, 136
Segev, Tom
— Americanization of Israeli culture, 113
Shabtai, Yaakov, *Past Continuous*, 29, 119 n 35
Shamgar, Meir, Chief Justice, Supreme Court
— justiciability, 59, 173
Shamir, Ronen
— Court as a 'council of sages', 3
— Israel's multiculturalism, 183
Shamir, Yitzhak, Prime Minister, 109 n 16
Shapira, Abraham, MK, 135
Shapira, Anita
— Israel's multiculturalism, 183
Shas (party/movement), 123–5, 137–8, 181 n 1
— criticism of Court, 154–8, 160–1, 172
Sheleg, Yair
— religious-Zionism in hegemonic and post-hegemonic eras, 116, 118
Shilo, Shmuel
— Jewish law and Arab citizens, 43 n 28
Shine, Chaim, 125

Shinui (party), 149, 171
Silberg, Moshe, Supreme Court Justice
— Jewish law and Arab citizens, 43
Smilansky, Yizhar
— anxiety in Zionism, 128 n 52
Smoire, Moshe, Chief Justice, Supreme Court
— status of Jewish law in Israeli law, 40
Sommer, Hillel
— lack of criticism of Court, 154 n 134
Standing, 3, 57, 144–6
— criticism of Court's doctrine, 171–2
'State of all its citizens', 193, 195, 212
Stern, Yedidia
— establishment of halakhic arbitration tribunals, 190 n 34
Sternhell, Zeev
— changes in education in post-hegemonic era, 135
Supreme Court
— activism of, 1, 56–74, 144–7
— affiliation with liberal former hegemons, 1–2, 7–8, 101–3, 110, 143–53, 188
— changes in perception of role in 1980s and 1990s, 96–8, 147–8
— contribution to entrenchment of liberalism in Israel, 9, 38–41, 80, 160
— criticism by religious groups, 154–8, 160–1, 172, 188
— decline in trust among liberal former hegemons, 8, 160–1, 162–9, 225–6
— decline in trust among religious group, 160
— European culture approach in Zionism, 40
— explanations for changes in jurisprudence in 1980s and 1990s, 99–103
— formalism, 78–86
— formalism and Israeli literature in 1950s, 89–90
— gap between legal culture and general culture in 1950s, 87–9
— involvement in appointments of judges, 8, 160
— judicial review, 73–4, 147
— jurisdiction, 56–7
— justiciability, 3–4, 58–68, 144–6, 172–4
— lack of criticism of in 1980s, 154–8
— negative and positive rights, 151–2
— new self-perception in 1980s, 1, 96–8
— non-enforcement of rulings, 168
— non-formalism in 1950s jurisprudence, 85–6
— petitions of Knesset members, 148–50
— precarious situation in early twenty-first century, 8–9
— proportionality, 71–2, 146
— protection of freedom of occupation and competition, 153
— protection of property, 152–3
— reasonableness, 60–1, 68–71, 146, 172, 175
— standing, 3, 57, 144–6, 171–2
— value-laden jurisprudence in 1980s and 1990s, 1, 90–5, 147
Susser, Bernard
— 'crisis politics', 126–7
— war of cultures, 184

Tammuz, Benjamin, *Jeremiah's Inn*, 137, 142
Taylor, Charles
— constitutional patriotism, 188 n 29
Traditionalists, 208
Tsipper, Benny
— Benjamin Tammuz's, *Jeremiah's Inn*, 137

Ultra-Orthodox, Ashkenazi
— criticism of Court, 154–8, 160–1, 172, 188
— Jewish Enlightenment, 121–2
— opposition to liberalism, 204–5
— opposition to Zionism, 17, 122
— post-hegemonic era, 121–3
Ultra-Orthodox, Sephardic, *see* Shas

Walzer, Michael
— strangers and enemies, 129 n 56
— types of liberal states, 213
War of cultures, *see also* Civil war
— following rise of Jewish Enlightenment Movement, 13
— Israel, 1, 7–9, 29, 114–16, 138, 184–90, 215
— Jewish people in modernity, 2, 9, 184
Warhaftig, Zerah, MK
— Anglicization of Israeli law, 37–8
Williams, Raymond
— elements in culture, 112–14

Yakobson, Alexander
— inclusion of Arab citizens in definition of state, 214
Yatziv, Gadi
— Israel's multiculturalism, 182
Yehoshua, A. B.
— 1977 political turnabout, 128
— Zionism as 'backward-looking revolution', 23
Yemini, Ben-Dror
— decline in trust of Court, 163 n 6
Yogev, Esther
— 1977 political turnabout as cultural turnabout, 129
Yosef, Ovadia, 125, 154, 155, *see also* Shas

Zamir Yitzhak, Supreme Court Justice
— explanation for rise of judicial activism in Court's jurisprudence, 100
Zimuki, Tovah
— lack of criticism of Court, 154 n 134

Zionism and culture, *see also* Culture, Israel
— controversies in early Zionism, 14–15
— cultural revival approach, 15–16, 35, 51
— cultural thinness, 27–30
— European culture approach, 17–20
— halakhic approach, 16–17, 35
— Hebrew culture approach, 21
— Hebrewness, 23–6
— Hebrewness v. Jewishness, 22–30, 48, 113–14
— Zionism as movement of cultural change, 14
— Zionist culture in Eretz Israel, 22–9